LINCOLN'S BOLD LION

LINCOLN'S BOLD LION

THE LIFE AND TIMES OF
UNION BRIGADIER GENERAL
MARTIN DAVIS HARDIN
1837–1923

JAMES T. HUFFSTODT

CASEMATE
Philadelphia & Oxford

Published in the United States of America and Great Britain in 2015 by
CASEMATE PUBLISHERS
908 Darby Road, Havertown, PA 19083
and
10 Hythe Bridge Street, Oxford, OX1 2EW

ISBN 978-1-61200-339-9
Digital Edition: ISBN 978-1-61200-340-5

Cataloging-in-publication data is available from the Library of Congress and
the British Library.

10 9 8 7 6 5 4 3 2 1

Printed and bound in the United States of America.

For a complete list of Casemate titles please contact:

CASEMATE PUBLISHERS (US)
Telephone (610) 853-9131, Fax (610) 853-9146
E-mail: casemate@casematepublishing.com

CASEMATE PUBLISHERS (UK)
Telephone (01865) 241249, Fax (01865) 794449
E-mail: casemate-uk@casematepublishing.co.uk

CONTENTS

"The wicked flee when no one pursueth. But the righteous are bold as a lion."

—Proverbs 28: King James Bible, Cambridge Edition[1]

DEDICATION

Lincoln's Bold Lion is dedicated to Eugene E. Huffstodt of Peru, Illinois, my older brother and loyal friend; and my beloved sister, Sharon (Huffstodt) Badenoch of Amelia Island, Florida.

"The passing of General Martin D. Hardin removes from the rolls of the army a distinguished and altogether unique figure, . . . He came of fighting ancestry. His great grandfather, {"Indian Killer"} John Hardin, commanded a company in Daniel Morgan's celebrated regiment of Virginia riflemen at the battle of Saratoga. . . . General Hardin's grandfather, after whom he was named, was a co-laborer with Henry Clay in the effort to make Kentucky a free state, and they lost by a narrow margin. The grandfather served under General Harrison in the War of 1812. General Hardin's father . . . was killed while serving with General Zachary Taylor in the fiercely contested battle of Buena Vista. . . . General Hardin's father and Abraham Lincoln were close friends and served together in the war with Black Hawk's Indian warriors. . . . When General Hardin's father was killed in battle in Mexico, Mr. Lincoln took a fatherly interest in the son which continued until the day of his own assassination."

— MAJOR GENERAL (RETIRED) WILLIAM HARDING CARTER,
JUNE 11, 1924, in *The Annual Report by the United States Association of West Point Graduates*

AN EPIC LIFE

Hardin embarked upon a combat career in the Civil War which has few parallels in the annals of the army for gallantry, wounds sustained, and the obscurity into which he had lapsed a generation before his death.[1]—EZRA WARNER, *Generals In Blue: Lives of the Union Commanders*

When first reading those haunting words by historian Ezra Warner forty years ago, I was puzzled and saddened that such an extraordinary soldier and patriot as General Martin Davis Hardin should have been so quickly forgotten. He died on December 13, 1923 in St. Augustine, Florida at the age of 86—one of the last living Civil War generals and the last survivor of the West Point Class of 1859. Few outside St. Augustine, where he was a prominent and popular winter resident for a quarter-century, appeared to notice. Perhaps Warner was right when he speculated that Civil War heroes were hopelessly out of fashion by the time of the self-indulgent Roaring Twenties.[2]

General Hardin was born during the first years of the staid Victorian age into a prominent Jacksonville, Illinois family with strong Kentucky roots. The Hardins had been frontiersmen, soldiers, lawyers and politicians of note since before the American Revolution. His father, John J. Hardin (1810–1847), was Abraham Lincoln's friend and a Mexican War martyr. His grandfather, Martin D. Hardin (1780–1823), had been a noted legal scholar, political ally of Henry Clay, War of 1812 veteran, and a U.S. Senator from Kentucky.[3] His great-grandfather, the first John Hardin (1753–1847), had marched under Benedict Arnold to Quebec, foraged for the starving troops at Valley Forge, fought with Daniel Morgan's riflemen at the Battle of

11

Saratoga, helped settle Kentucky, and was murdered while on a mission to the Shawnee Indians bearing a peace overture from President George Washington.[4] On the maternal side, young Martin Hardin was descended from General Ben Logan (1742–1802), a contemporary of Daniel Boone and an equally legendary figure on the frontier described as the "dark and bloody ground."[5, 6]

Martin Davis Hardin, the grandson of Senator Martin D. Hardin and the subject of this biography, carved out his own memorable career as a soldier, attorney and military historian. This remarkable man, who knew Lincoln, Lee, Washington Irving and other giants of his youth, lived to see the advent of silent movies, Rudolph Valentino and the Jazz Age. In the late winter of life, the many-times wounded, one-armed officer, must have felt like some modern Rip Van Winkle, wandering largely unrecognized in an exotic new world of automobiles, Victrola phonographs, telephones, aircraft, machine-gun wielding gangsters, golf tournaments and moving pictures. This was a free-wheeling society vastly removed from the chaste frontier world of his youth; now young Flappers in short skirts danced the Charleston, puffed cigarettes in public, and guzzled bath-tub gin in Speakeasies.

Warner noted with regret in *Generals In Blue* that Hardin's death rated only a few lines in the Chicago newspapers, even though the late General had lived and worked there as an attorney since 1870, and had survived the Great Chicago Fire of 1873. There, in the great city by the lake, General Hardin and his first wife, Estella (Graham) Hardin, helped Mary Todd Lincoln nurse her dying son Tad, the beloved teenager whose death devastated his increasingly unstable mother.[7] Hardin's Chicago friends also included General Philip Sheridan, Mrs. Potter Palmer, General Nelson A. Miles, Robert Todd Lincoln, the Great Emancipator's only child to reach full maturity, and Fred Grant, the son of the famous Civil War leader and American President.

Most biographies of General Hardin briefly note a special relationship with Abraham and Mary Todd Lincoln, most often calling the younger man a protégé of the President. In seven years of research, the author discovered a series of letters and other sources that document and, to some degree, illustrate the nature of that special relationship between the young Hardin and his commander-in-chief. This is not surprising considering that Hardin's parents, Colonel John J. and Sarah (Smith) Hardin, of Jacksonville, Illinois, were among Lincoln's closest friends during his early years in Illinois. Lincoln and John Hardin were friends and political allies, although their mutual ambition tested the friendship on several notable occasions.[8]

John Hardin met Lincoln when they both served in the Illinois Militia during the 1831 Black Hawk War. Later the two men were young lawyers, riding the circuit together, serving in the state legislature, and becoming prominent members of the Illinois Whig Party. When Lincoln went to Congress to fill the seat formerly held by his friend Hardin, the latter volunteered for the Mexican War. He was killed leading the First Illinois Infantry Regiment at the battle of Buena Vista in 1847, when his son Martin was only 10 years old. The father is chiefly remembered today as the man who interceded at the last minute to prevent a tragic duel between Lincoln and their fiery Democratic friend, Irishman James Shields. Equally interesting is the fact that Abraham Lincoln first met Mary Todd, his future bride, at the Hardin home in Jacksonville.[9]

Fresh out of the West Point, Class of 1859, Martin D. Hardin was a brand new lieutenant of artillery when he was appointed aide-de-camp to Colonel Robert E. Lee in the immediate aftermath of abolitionist John Brown's capture at Harpers Ferry. Not long afterwards, Lt. Hardin volunteered to serve with a pioneering U.S. Army expedition to the far Northwest. The future Union General hunted buffalo on the Great Plains, crossed the wide Missouri, and rode across the high country among the still freeroaming Sioux, Blackfeet, Cheyenne and Nez Perce. He nearly lost his life in the Pacific Ocean when the sailing ship taking him to an obscure Army fort in Washington Territory was swept by a giant rogue wave.[10]

There is ample evidence to indicate that President Lincoln kept an avuncular eye on his old friend John Hardin's son during the Civil War, when the young man fought with distinction on many bloody fields including Malvern Hill, Second Bull Run, Bristoe Station, Rappahannock Station, Mine Run, Spotsylvania, the North Anna, and Bethesda Church. On July 3, 1863, young Hardin, from atop Round Top, witnessed Pickett's Charge at Gettysburg.[11]

He rose from lieutenant to brigadier general, suffering at least four major wounds during the war, two of which nearly took his life. One bullet wound cost him his left arm. General Hardin defended the Washington,

D.C. forts against General Jubal Early's Rebel raiders in the summer of 1864, when for two perilous days the capital was virtually undefended. And on that grim Good Friday of April 14, 1865, Hardin helped lead the hunt for Lincoln's assassin, John Wilkes Booth.[12]

Hardin's life was an incredible adventure peopled with heroic, even near-mythical, characters: Abraham Lincoln, Mary Todd, General John Reynolds, General George Meade, John Brown, Washington Irving, Lewis Thornton Powell (alias Lewis Paine), and John Wilkes Booth. They were all part and parcel of Hardin's young life. His personal drama was played out upon a background of great and momentous events that shaped modern America. This bold and brave soldier was also a man of sincere faith and an ardent convert to Roman Catholicism. He was particularly close to his brother-in-law, Father Clarence Walworth, one of the founders of the Paulist Order. In 1925, his second wife and widow, Chicago coffee heiress Amelia McLaughlin, restored the Lady of La Leche Chapel in old St. Augustine and dedicated it to the memory of her late husband.[13]

Perhaps Ezra Warner, that brilliant biographer of America's heroic Civil War generals (Blue and Gray), was too pessimistic in suggesting that General Hardin's name and fame had been largely lost to history. I think he would be pleased to know that, after a six-year search among a dozen libraries and archives, I discovered many of the missing pieces necessary to construct a worthy biography of this forgotten soldier. Of course, I owe it all to the trail-breaking biographical sketch of Hardin in Warner's *Generals in Blue,* which first sparked my interest in describing General Hardin's life. I only wish that Mr. Warner could read *Lincoln's Bold Lion* and discover the rest of the story of this distinguished American: a formidable soldier, intellect, public citizen, and devout son of the Roman Catholic faith.

LINCOLN REMEMBERED, 1909

Throughout the American nation on February 12, 1909, the people gathered. They came together in great cities and quiet hamlets in every part of a united country to remember and honor the Great Emancipator's memory on the Centenary of President Abraham Lincoln's birth.[1]

The people listened to speeches, studied Lincoln's immortal words in schools and churches, paraded in his honor, attended patriotic concerts, witnessed memorial ceremonies, honored the now aging boys in Blue who had answered Father Abraham's call, and joined in prayer for this great and good man—who had saved the Union and freed the slaves after the bloodiest war in American history.

On that day of remembrance, cannons in the forts surrounding New York Harbor thundered a salute to honor the fallen Lincoln, echoed by gunfire from the steel battleships in the anchorage and by National Guard field batteries at points around the great metropolis. Across the United States, a thousand orators vied with each other on the Centenary to capture in words the man and his vision. President Theodore Roosevelt spoke in Hodgenville, Kentucky, at the site where Lincoln was born in a primitive one-room log cabin. In New York's posh Waldorf-Astoria, former slave Booker T. Washington spoke to The Republican Club of the man who had liberated his race, even if they remained shackled by the invisible chains of prejudice.[2,3]

Forty-four years had passed since actor and rebel sympathizer John Wilkes Booth entered the Presidential box at Washington's Ford Theater and fired a Derringer bullet into the head of President Lincoln. The great man died the next morning without ever regaining consciousness, and the nation wept. By 1909, his widow, Mary Todd Lincoln, was long dead. So too were most of his peers: Secretary of War Edwin Stanton, Secretary of State William Seward, Secretary of the Navy Gideon Welles, and Senator Charles Sumner of Massachusetts. Lincoln's immortal paladins, Generals Grant, Sherman and Sheridan, had also departed the earthly stage. Soon, Lincoln would vanish from living memory, remembered only in photos and books.

But in 1909, there were still a few elderly survivors of that heroic time, who personally remembered the man and his genius. Among that dwindling number of men and women was a rather obscure, one-armed, 72-year-old retired Union Brigadier General named Martin Davis Hardin. He had looked into Lincoln's face, heard his voice, and remembered his wit and wisdom. Although largely forgotten on the national stage since the war, despite his family's connections with the Lincolns and his own remarkable battlefield exploits, General Hardin, a successful Chicago attorney in the postwar period, was also a respected winter resident in America's oldest city, St. Augustine, Florida.[4]

On the night of Lincoln's Centenary, more than 1,000 elegantly dressed spectators assembled in the splendor of Henry Flagler's Alcazar Hotel in St. Augustine to hear the old soldier share his personal recollections of Lincoln. General Hardin was well known by many of those present. Some in the audience undoubtedly knew the story that, after his father, Colonel John J. Hardin, died a hero's death in the Mexican War, his friend Abraham Lincoln kept a fatherly eye on the orphan son's fortunes during the Civil War.

"A vast assemblage" gathered at the imposing Spanish Renaissance-style hotel to witness the patriotic program.[5] As the crowd strolled onto the forecourt, they probably admired the electric sign glaring against the darkening sky: Alcazar Hotel. The massive building, designed to evoke the ancient Spanish reign, rose up in ornate splendor, flanked by two imposing towers reminiscent of Seville or Barcelona. This sprawling edifice, despite its foreign accent, spoke of a new America whose wealth, power and sophistication was far removed from the Kentucky frontier where Lincoln had been born 100 years before.

Many of those present that night, including General Hardin, probably read the prominent Associated Press story the next morning by James A. Edgerton in the *St. Augustine Evening Record*, headlined: "The World When

Lincoln Was Born." The wire-service reporter chronicled the tremendous changes that had swept the nation since his birth, when "steam was in its infancy" and electricity only a "scientific curiosity."[6] Lincoln's frontier world was indeed far distant from the modern America of 1909:

> In 1809 water and horseflesh were the chief motor powers . . . boats, wagons and stagecoaches were almost the exclusive methods of travel; candles and tallow dips were used as illuminants. There were but few newspapers, and poorly printed, and letters were infrequent . . . only a small percentage of the population was educated, dueling was in vogue, slavery was in existence on both sides of the ocean, there was little democracy or liberty anywhere except in America. . . . Yet that was only a hundred years ago, barely a lifetime for some people. Truly, the world moves. It took a long time to get into the habit, but it is "going some" now.[7]

General Hardin knew that vanished world. He had been born on the Illinois frontier, remembered his father leaving for the Mexican War, recalled visiting his Uncle's Mississippi plantation where he listened to ghost stories in the slave quarters. He had traveled in stage coaches and canal boats, and went up the Missouri River by steamboat to the Far West in 1860 when the native American tribes still roamed the Plains in the glowing twilight of their culture. And, tonight, the young and the old had come to hear the General speak of Lincoln and days gone by.[8]

The Alcazar's Lincoln Centenary program opened with the singing of the Star Spangled Banner and remarks by Master of Ceremonies Mr. G.S. Meserve, followed by the invocation by Reverend Fitzjames Hindry of Trinity Episcopal Church. The Alcazar Hotel Orchestra then entertained with the overture of Orpheus. Despite additional seating provided for the event, nearly 300 spectators remained standing throughout the two-hour program.[9]

Despite his years and iron-gray mustache, Martin Davis Hardin was a striking presence that evening, dressed in his perfectly tailored brigadier general's blue coat, the left sleeve folded and pinned, mute testimony to his sacrifice and heroism in what the old veterans of the Grand Army of the Republic recalled as The War of the Rebellion.

Hardin was a handsome, dignified old man of genteel manner and warm disposition. An audience of more than one thousand people was curious to hear this four-time wounded Union hero speak personally of his recollections of Lincoln and those tragic times when the nation nearly self-destructed over the issue of slavery and secession. The only surviving record of Hardin's speech was featured in the next day's edition of the *St. Augustine Evening Record:*

> General M. D. Hardin, U.S.A., retired, was announced for an address and the old warrior stepped to the front of the platform and gave a sketch of the life of the illustrious Lincoln, much of which he gathered from his personal acquaintance with the great leader . . . . General Hardin interspersed well-known historical facts with his own personal recollections of President Lincoln, who was a friend of the General's family. The gentle nature, strong personality and intense patriotism of the man were brought out vividly in the great struggles of the sixties and General Hardin had abundant opportunity of witnessing them, being a personal friend of the President and a frequent visitor to the White House. His tribute to the martyred President made a very deep impression on the audience and was listened to with breathless attention.[10]

Sadly, General Hardin's exact words spoken that long-ago night at The Alcazar are lost in time. Upon conclusion of the General's address, a choir sang: "God of Our Fathers." This was followed by Clarence M. Revan, who read The Gettysburg Address and Lincoln's Second Inaugural Address. At various points throughout the two-hour program, the crowd was entertained with appropriate musical selections, including "The Soldier's Farewell."[11]

In the event's aftermath, General Hardin mingled with well-wishers and likely elaborated upon his recollections. Many present must have asked further questions about his relationship with Lincoln in that last year of the war. Who knows what other valuable insights into Lincoln and his own brilliant career in the Army of Potomac, as well as 19th-century America he may have shared that long ago night?

CHAPTER 1

LITTLE BOY AFRAID OF GHOSTS

L ooking back on his childhood in Jacksonville, Illinois as a middle-aged man in 1882, Martin Davis Hardin recalled that his earliest memory was of sitting outside the gate to his father's home and watching the approach of a large crowd waving banners, playing musical instruments, and singing the wildly popular political campaign song of 1840, "Tippecanoe and Tyler, Too."[1]

Little Martin's father, John J. Hardin, was a prominent attorney and leader of the Illinois Whig Party, and marched in that parade. The 30-year-old Kentucky native had brought his family to Jacksonville a decade earlier, and already boasted an impressive resume. In a few brief years, he had volunteered as a soldier in the Black Hawk War, built a lucrative legal practice, and served in the Illinois State Legislature with his friend and fellow Whig, Abraham Lincoln.[2]

At age three, young Martin probably didn't connect the parade with the ongoing political campaign, which ended in the election of General William Henry Harrison, the victor of the Battle of Tippecanoe as the nation's chief executive, and Virginian John Tyler as vice-president. But as he grew a few years older, Martin learned that politics was his father's business, and indeed, had been the family occupation for several generations. The boy's grandfather and namesake, Martin D. Hardin, had been a colleague of the great Henry Clay of Kentucky, and served as a U.S. Senator from that state. Martin's father, John J. Hardin, would soon represent Illinois as a Whig congressman.[3]

Young Martin, whom his family called Dee, was Illinois-born, but his family's roots lay deep in Kentucky. His father had immigrated to Illinois in 1831, seeking to make a name and a fortune in the Prairie State. John J. Hardin brought with him a law degree from Transylvania University and the pride and confidence of a wealthy planter descended from military heroes. Early on, his son learned that much was expected of a man who wore the Hardin name.[4]

Dee's grandfather, the future Kentucky senator, had served with distinction in the War of 1812 as a staff officer with future American president General Harrison. His father, John "Indian Killer" Hardin, had been a legendary sharpshooter in the American Revolution and, later, as a bold Indian fighter on the Ohio-Kentucky border. Dee was also descended on his father's maternal side from General Ben Logan of Kentucky, another incredibly brave frontiersman, whose exploits were legend and on a par with his contemporary—and sometime friend—Daniel Boone. The Hardin and Logan families were Kentucky pioneers and proud Southerners.[5]

Life for a boy in frontier Jacksonville was a long outdoor adventure. Dee grew up hunting, fishing and riding. He was at home on the prairie and in the woods from a very early age; there he learned self-reliance and independence befitting his heroic lineage. However, there was a chink in his armor, a character flaw no Hardin could ever admit to. The boy was a coward in the dark.[6]

Dee was deathly afraid of ghosts. He was gripped with terror in the middle of the night when skeletal tree branches clawed at his bedroom windows. In his imagination, the boy envisioned ghostly apparitions sprung from the graveyard, and instead of the howling wind, he heard the tortured cries of the damned. Ironically, the boy who as a young man was to become one of the Union army's most celebrated combat commanders was afraid to walk by a graveyard at night.

Dolly Smith, a former slave belonging to his mother's family in Kentucky, and now a trusted family servant, was handmaiden to the little boy's fears. Like many whites and Negroes of that time and place, Dolly staunchly believed in the spirit world. The teenage servant girl delighted in telling ghostly tales to the Hardin children. Dolly's stories of the supernatural were both entrancing and terrifying.[7]

An imaginative and sensitive child like Dee was especially vulnerable and was often unnerved by Dolly's stories. The boy, who was a fearless horseman and who swam in creeks swarming with deadly cottonmouth snakes, trembled in fear when the night wind or the hoot of an owl suggested the presence of what Dolly called "haints."

On visits to his Uncle Abram Smith's (his mother's brother's) plantation near Philadelphia, Mississippi, Martin and his younger brother Lemuel, three years his junior, often visited the slave quarters where the boys listened to narratives of the supernatural, shivering in a mix of delight and terror. Afterwards, the frightened boys scrambled back to their uncle's mansion in mad flight, starting at every rustle in the underbrush or every shadowy form.

Sometimes, they were so frightened the boys lingered late in the slave quarters, only daring to return to their uncle's home when escorted by one of the older Negroes.

Forty years later, in 1882, the retired Brigadier General Martin D. Hardin, a Chicago attorney by then, penned an incomplete autobiography, in which he described one memorable encounter with ghosts during a picnic in Jacksonville during his childhood:

> Some children and I . . . were having a picnic in the beautiful grove east of our house, which was near the graveyard . . . Dolly {Smith} had charge of us and probably had (been told) that a ghost had been seen in the graveyard. At any rate, all the children and servants were sufficiently afraid of ghosts and graveyards. While we were in the midst of the pleasure of the picnic, some of the children came runnin' and screaming, "Ghost! Ghost!" There was, of course, a general stampede, and I suppose I ran with the crowd, but being small was outrun and left behind. Sure enough, there was apparently a Ghost . . . a hideous old woman. . . . chasing the party. As I have learned since, it was a crazy woman who was possibly hysteric.[8]

This fear of the supernatural continued through early adolescence. But one day young Dee resolved to confront his cowardice head-on. He asked Dr. Smith at Illinois State College in Jacksonville to take him through the dissecting room where young medical students studied human anatomy. The boy slowly conquered his fears of the dead, visiting the morgue on several occasions until his fear abated. This deliberate and successful campaign to overcome his superstition and terror speaks eloquently to Dee's character and fortitude, later displayed so conspicuously on many Civil War battlefields.[9]

Courage and character was certainly evident in the make-up of Dee's father, John J. Hardin. This educated, wealthy Kentucky gentleman had a profound distaste for slavery, and an overwhelming ambition to make a mark in the free state of Illinois. He rode into Jacksonville in 1830 at age 23, and according to an account penned by his eldest daughter, Ellen Hardin, "sprang from his horse in front of the courthouse" with his saddlebags stuffed with little more than his degrees in the classics and law from Transylvania University and a change of clothes. He immediately embarked on a whirlwind career as a lawyer, landowner, volunteer soldier and politician. Hardin built a law office on the square, and returned the next year with his new bride, Sarah Smith of Frankfort, Kentucky, an elegant lady with a taste for art and literature. Not long after, they built Jacksonville's first brick home, on State Street.[10]

The former Sarah Ellen Smith, a strong-willed, well-bred and educated plantation belle, had grown up in a Kentucky mansion surrounded by slaves and high culture. During her ten-year sojourn in Jacksonville she was viewed as an outsider. In fact, she was often absent, visiting relatives in Kentucky and Mississippi, apparently finding herself more comfortable back home than in the raw frontier settlement of Jacksonville.

If Hardin's bride found Jacksonville underwhelming we need not be surprised. One visitor to the Illinois village in 1830 described the place as, "a huddle of log cabins . . . clustered around . . . a rude courthouse in a rectangle of mud and dirt." Two years later, poet William Cullen Bryant dismissed the Illinois settlement as "a horridly ugly village composed of little shops and dwellings stuck close together around a dingy square, in the middle of which stands the ugliest of possible courthouses, with a spire and weathercock on its top."[11]

Jacksonville was in those early days a microcosm of the nation, its residents identifying themselves strongly as either Yankees or Southerners. The Hardin family remained proud Southerners, but stood strong against slavery. Like Senator Hardin's friend, Henry Clay, they hoped for a gradual elimination of "the peculiar institution." But they certainly weren't associates of the radical Abolitionists who had a significant presence in Jacksonville, especially at the new Illinois College, which many despised as an "engine of abolition."[12]

Years later, Martin's older sister Ellen "Nelly" Hardin looked back on Jacksonville with great fondness. In her memory, the little prairie town was a progressive community with a college, a woman's seminary, and various civic groups celebrating the arts and sciences. She was not alone in this regard. Thanks to forward-thinking community leaders like her own father, Jacksonville was indeed a city with a future. Interestingly enough, the citizens living there were either from the nearby southern border states of Kentucky or Tennessee, or were New Englanders attracted by Illinois College. In 1905, Ellen Hardin contended that the two groups complimented one another and worked together with little rancor or animosity.[13]

"The educational influences of the two were entirely of the New England type, but not so the social life, in which the Kentucky and Virginia elements prevailed and ruled as completely as Massachusetts and Connecticut in the schools," Ellen remembered sixty years later. "By mutual consent and written law, the utmost harmony and good feeling prevailed. . . . The utmost freedom of intercourse did not degenerate into vulgar familiarity nor rude intrusion. It was indeed an ideal society, intelligent, simple and refined. . . ."[14]

Ellen's recollections can't be entirely dismissed as the rose-colored nostalgia of a middle-aged woman describing a bygone place in time that had, through the passage of years, lost its sharp edges. Antebellum Jacksonville, small as it was, was recognized in the 1840s by many in the sophisticated East as a community of culture and learning. Some called it "The New Haven of the West" or "The New Athens." The Hardins were educated and refined, and indisputably bright ornaments in this golden age.

"In our little town we had brilliant pianists, gifted singers and some original composers," Martin's older sister recalled with pride. "There were concerts by the Hutchinson family. . . . the Swiss bell ringers; many fine lectures and works of art . . . brought west for exhibition, notably the pictures of Benjamin West. All of the intelligent people of the town attended these entertainments. Some of us young girls were taken now and then to St. Louis to hear Jenny Lind, see Charlotte Cushman in "Meg Merrilles" and "Much Ado About Nothing," and Forest or Booth the Elder in the tragedies of Shakespeare."[15]

Traveler Truman Marcellus Post also came to frontier Jacksonville but saw a raw prairie settlement filled with "trading, horse-racing, carousing, gambling, and fighting of all kinds." Post met Ellen's parents, describing John as a "rather crude and roughly dressed young Kentucky lawyer" and Sarah Hardin as a "brilliant young wife, a dashing Kentucky belle."[16]

Perhaps Easterners like the poet Bryant saw only a primitive backwater, but John J. Hardin saw potential. After all, his native Kentucky was only a few generations removed from the frontier. Illinois was a rich land and soon would sprout cities and industry. John Hardin planned to be a part of that new empire. And, in the space of a few short years, he made his mark on the little town and, increasingly, on the rest of the state where he became known and respected as a man of ability, eloquence and ideals.

Early on, the young attorney became a co-editor of the *Illinois Patriot,* a newspaper owned by Governor Joseph Duncan, won election to the state legislature in Vandalia, served as state's attorney for Morgan County, and gained a reputation as a powerful and persuasive speaker, despite a pronounced stammer.[17] Over the years the Hardin and Duncan families forged strong bonds of affection. Martin's sister Ellen and her best friend, Mary Duncan, would correspond faithfully for life.

Young John J. Hardin was tall, dark and forthright. His charismatic personality, innate honesty, and lack of guile won him many friends and admirers, who recognized the newcomer from the South as a progressive man of integrity, vision and Christian virtue. His prominence in law and government was matched with military ambition, eventually resulting in his promotion to general of the Illinois Militia.[18]

In those early years, John and Sarah Hardin were also busy growing their young family, which included Ellen "Nelly," born in 1832; Martin D., born in 1837; and Lemuel, who was born in 1840. The youngest child, Elizabeth, died tragically before her fifth birthday in 1848.[19]

Jacksonville was growing apace just as Hardin had foreseen. In 1839, when his elder son Martin was two years old, the railroad—that herald of progress and prosperity—came to town, in part due to the elder Hardin's politicking. The rails ran right through the center of the growing community as one contemporary observed:

The public square was filled with teams [horses] and whenever the engine steamed into the square making all the noise possible, there was such a stampede. . . . Many of the people were as much scared as the horses at the steaming monster as it came rushing into the square.[20]

Young Dee was surrounded by strong, independent spirits. One of those was his father's mother, Elizabeth (Logan) Hardin, a daughter of the illustrious General Ben Logan and widow of Senator Martin D. Hardin, who had died young at 43 in 1823, cutting short a promising career.

The widow later married Porter Clay, a younger half-brother of the famous Henry Clay. Porter had been a Kentucky state official and at one time built steamboats at Louisville. In 1834, they moved to Jacksonville and built an imposing home surrounded by a garden and grove encompassing an entire city block. Over the years they entertained such notables as Daniel Webster and Henry Clay, the Great Compromiser, leader of the Whigs, and Abraham Lincoln's beau ideal of a politician.[21]

Dee and his siblings spent many happy hours at Grandmother Clay's home. The fruit trees in her orchard were always a particular temptation for Dee and his friends. Unfortunately, Martin Hardin left behind no detailed description or reminiscences of his Grandmother. However, his older sister Ellen filled the gap with her recollections of a truly accomplished lady of culture and refinement.

Ellen described her grandmother as "dignified, beautiful, frail in looks, strong in character."[22] Many years later, Ellen, by then distinguished for her key role in creating the Daughters of the American Revolution (DAR), evoked the memory of Elizabeth Hardin Clay in a brief memoir, titled: *Earliest Recollections*:

> She had a disappointment in her face, yet was tender toward me and [was] evidently gratified always to see my father. He was her first-born, her strongest reliance, her brightest hope. In fact although she had married a second-time, she had followed my father to Illinois, had sold her grand old farm and handsome house, broken up her large establishment at Frankfort, Ky. [and] came to this new country to be near this well beloved son.[23]

The Clay home was an impressive residence built in the colonial style fronted with a long piazza with a broad double front door. Within was a large drawing room equipped with mahogany furniture and tastefully decorated with framed copies of the Old Masters. The landscaped grounds boasted various ornamental gardens and an orchard of fruit trees.[24]

The soul of the house was a large library that Ellen always associated with Grandma Logan. The trove of books spoke of gentility and intelligent conversation, strong reminders that the Hardin and Logan families were among the intellectual elite of that rough and ready era. Ellen remembered:

> It is here that I oftenest remember my beautiful and stately grand-mother, pale as a lily and very fair with brilliant black eyes and raven hair, soft and fine as floss, wonderful hair, that had not a gray line in it when she died at seventy-five years-of-age. . . . Here [in the library], among . . . books brought from the Kentucky home, she was in her element. . . . Bobby Burns and [Sir Walter] Scott. . . . and the "Spectator" and her Bible were here, ever present companions.[25]

The granddaughter recalled Elizabeth as a kindly woman given to nursing sick neighbors, and a talented cook whose kitchen was always aromatic with the tantalizing smells of simmering broths and other delectables. Yet one had to be careful with your language in Mrs. Clay's stately presence as Ellen noted: she was "a Calvinist of the rigid kind."[26]

Although Ellen's recollections of youth certainly were affected by the passage of time and the sentimentality that most of us indulge when remembering our childhood, the reader is left with the undeniable impression that this was a happy time for all the Hardin clan. Ellen wrote:

> O, the happiness of those hours around the old Franklin stove—ample as an ancient fireplace with its huge logs and brass andirons. . . . My grandmother would read to me stories from the "Lady of the Lake" and then hammer into my young memory the long sentences of the Westminster Catechism. And, there were dishes of nuts and bright red apples always at hand. . . . And later my father would come in and talk politics. . . . I listened with eager curiosity,

trying to understand, pleased to hear the names of Stuart, Lincoln, Logan, Baker, Shield and Douglas—all of whom I knew even at that early time.[27]

Later in life, Ellen's younger brother, General Martin Hardin, looked back fondly on his youth in Jacksonville as a boy's world—rough and tumble and lived mainly outdoors. There were bird hunts when his father returned from the prairie with a buggy filled to overflowing with prairie chickens. And, there was his beloved black Indian pony, on whose back the boy roamed with joyful abandon and a remarkable degree of freedom from an early age.[28]

Guns were a major part of the boy's existence. Martin never forgot the day his father allowed him—probably no more than five years old at the time—to fire a shotgun off the back porch. The recoil knocked the little boy sprawling to the ground, but he gradually grew to be comfortable and proficient with a wide array of firearms: rifles, shotguns and handguns. Later, the boy relished long chats with the local gunsmith discussing various firearms and their characteristics.[29]

Fishing expeditions to nearby streams were almost a daily occurrence when the weather allowed. Dee also swam in those same creeks and hunted prairie chickens in the surrounding fields with the single-barreled shotgun given him by his father. Although he claimed to be a good boy by and large, Dee later confessed to stealing apples from the Illinois College campus despite the watchful eye of the college president.

Of those sunshine days, the mature Hardin recalled: "I preferred my pony and my fishing line to books."[30] This simple declarative sentence best sums up his early years growing up outdoors in a world that must have seemed tailor-made for an active, curious young boy. They were days of adventure, discovery, and more than a whiff of danger.

"My most exciting hunt I was ever on as a small boy was a coon hunt at night with young [illegible] and our colored boys. We had a very fine bitch setter or pointer who was a desperate fighter. She had a set-to with a coon on a log in the swamp."[31]

This pugnacious canine was "Old Red Head," born on the same day as Dee in 1837. "Old Red Head" was probably the same dog that figured prominently in another story of Martin's youth. In his memoirs, the grown man recalled raising and training a dog to hunt rabbits. The boy and the dog were inseparable, spending long days together roaming the surrounding woodland and prairie. But that ended when Dee boarded a steamboat for his first trip to far-off St. Louis.[32]

"When I went away to St. Louis, the dog followed to the river and swam after the boat as long as he could. That was the last I saw of him. I was told afterward . . . by Dolly, that this dog committed suicide, that he returned home and wandered around the house but would eat nothing. And that [he] died of starvation."[33]

That journey to St. Louis, the "Gateway to the West," was one of Martin's first great adventures. The small, quiet boy wandered alone in that immense noise-filled, exotic, urban world, so strange, so fascinating. St. Louis was a huge city of more than 100,000 people in 1844—compared to Jacksonville's 1,800 souls. At any one time, hundreds of steamboats tied up at the river docks, loading and discharging cargo of every description. Its streets teemed with people of every hue and culture: Native Americans in their regalia, buckskin-clad mountain men returned from the Far West, black slaves, French-speaking merchants, and many German immigrants. A Babel of languages was spoken in the crowded streets. Years later, Hardin remembered the trip vividly even though it had occurred around 1844:

> We stopped at Scott Hotel. . . . I was seven years old at this time. It was the time I was lost. In those days, when children were lost, a man went through the streets ringing a bell, crying: "Lost Child!" I had wandered off on this occasion and got into the German part of the city. I was gone so long the town crier was sent ringing his bell for me. I recollect that I inquired my way back of many people, but they did not know, or did not tell me. . . . I know I began to get frightened . . . I met a drayman. I think probably an Irishman. He could not understand my description. I did not know the name of the Hotel where we stopped. But when I told him the sign over a drinking place . . . opposite our hotel. He knew at once and took me back on his dray.[34]

When Martin returned to Jacksonville, the youngster resumed his free and bold life. As always, he reveled in riding his pony wherever impulse led. On one occasion, unaccompanied by an adult, the boy rode his pony halfway to Merodosia, a little community on the Illinois River, nearly 20 miles from home where he enjoyed a barbeque among other diversions. Although punished by his father for this indiscretion, the reader is tempted to believe that perhaps John J. Hardin was a little impressed with his little boy's audacity.[35]

Those boyhood days were sometimes punctuated with events far more deadly than a spanking from a stern father. Dee vividly recalled a large rattlesnake concealed among the weeds by a path near his home that "gave him a good fright" when it lunged and nearly sank his fangs into his leg. On another occasion, while wading in a nearby creek near a bridge, Dee was surrounded by "a whole school of flat head moccasin snakes." Again, he escaped without injury.[36]

He swam everyday "when it was warm enough" and developed into a strong swimmer with a great love of the water. His younger brother Lemuel was a frequent companion in these outdoor adventures. Dee laughingly recalled teaching Lem how to swim in a nearby stream in 1847 or 1848, probably when they were around ten and seven years old, respectively. "He [Lemuel] was very short but active and strong. . . . I put him in [illegible] creek and he struck out bravely but went straight to the bottom. He learned to swim across the creek under the water before he could swim at all on the top of it."[37]

Dee's boyhood memories were not all pleasant, however, especially when the trees grew bare and the harsh wind swept in from the vast prairie. Illinois winters could be hard, even life-threatening. Dee experienced a "great storm when all the trees were blown down" and suffered a bad case of frost-bite. Once home, the little boy was promptly immersed in a tub of cold water as a brutal therapy. On another occasion, he recalled riding back in a buggy from Springfield in a blizzard, huddling from the wind as best he could at his father's feet.

Winter cold was often the subject of Martin's childhood memories. Out on the open prairie the icy wind was cruel and unrelenting. On one occasion, Dee was riding in the buggy with Dolly and other family members on one extremely frigid day: "She . . . tried to go to sleep but everyone kept pushing and shaking her to keep her awake." The fear, of course, was that if the beloved servant and friend slept in that life-threatening cold, she

would never awaken. Frontier life was often an unrelenting test of hardi-
hood and endurance, good training for a boy destined for the hard life of a
soldier.[38]

Martin's father certainly was the model of soldierly virtue. Dee's older
sister remembered John J. Hardin as a paragon: "My father was the prime
mover, the leading spirit of every occasion."[39] She was witness to the aftermath of a hunting mishap that tested her father's resolve and cost him an
eye. Martin may have also been present when John Hardin's hunting companions brought the wounded man back to a log cabin near the family
home, but we can't be sure. Later, Ellen wrote of the incident:

> . . . the operation on his eye for removing the bullet was performed
> in the large sitting-room of the log house. I stood in the room, qui-
> etly in the corner, perhaps without the knowledge of those present,
> as no one noticed me. It seems to me that I held my breath while
> the physicians were at work. I thought my father was so brave to
> utter not a sound, that I must not cry, although I seemed to realize
> his suffering, for even then I had an unbounded devotion to him.[40]

Dee's boyhood was a stern school spent largely outdoors. The youngster developed independence, endurance and toughness while riding for
hours on horseback, walking miles through prairie and woods in pursuit
of wild game, and swimming in the icy streams near Jacksonville. He had
his share of fights with the town boys, won most, and suffered one humil-
iating defeat: "the quickest licking I ever got."[41] That incident taught young
Hardin that strength alone didn't necessarily guarantee a victory against a
skilled boxer. By the time he reached his teens, he was proficient in boxing,
stick-fighting, casting the Bowie knife, and shooting a variety of firearms.
As a cadet at West Point, he employed private tutors to instruct him in the
finer points of swordplay. Although never quarrelsome, Dee was always
ready to defend his honor or life if challenged or threatened.[42]

This was the Hardin way. They were hardy spirits who had persevered
for more than a century on the Virginia and Kentucky frontier, battling
against the wild creatures—bear, cougars, wolves, venomous snakes—and
always serving in the front ranks during the ongoing wars against the
British and their Native American allies. Ellen, Martin and Lemuel inher-

ited a family tradition stressing grit, self-reliance, and stoic courage.

They would all have use of those stern virtues in the tumultuous years that followed.

CHAPTER 2

THE LINCOLN CONNECTION

O nly long years after his father's death in the Mexican War
would Martin D. Hardin come to appreciate the influence the
dead hero had on his life. His character was formed to a great degree not
only by the example of a noble father tragically slain in battle, but by his father's friend and political ally, fellow Whig Abraham Lincoln. In the years
to come, the Hardin family's Lincoln connection played a key role in
Hardin's eventual rise to be a 27-year-old brigadier general in the Civil War.

In 1864–1865, when General Martin Hardin commanded the northern
defenses of Washington, a friendship grew between President Lincoln and
his young protégé. The many times wounded son of his old friend visited
the older man in the White House on several occasions. It also seems clear
from surviving correspondence between President Lincoln and his dead
friend's widow, Sarah (Hardin) Walworth, that Lincoln felt a certain responsibility for Martin. Perhaps Lincoln felt a pang of remorse knowing that
his political outmaneuvering of John J. Hardin set the stage for the latter's
decision to fight in the Mexican War where he met tragic death at age 36.[1]

To understand the life of Union General Hardin it is necessary to
examine the close ties of affection between his father, John J. Hardin, and
young Abraham Lincoln. The two first met while serving as volunteers in
the Black Hawk War of 1831. Major Hardin swore in the gangly Lincoln
as captain of a militia company. The ambitious young men were certainly
opposites not only in appearance but in background.[2]

Although both Hardin and Lincoln had been born in Kentucky, the
former came from privilege and wealth, while the latter knew only poverty
and hard times. Hardin, the son of a Kentucky senator and a graduate of

Transylvania University, was well educated with social connections and considerable wealth. Lincoln lived in ramshackle frontier cabins and was largely self-educated.[3]

At one point in the 1830s, John Hardin's estate on the edge of Jacksonville, Illinois comprised a thousand plus acres. He and his siblings owned a total of around 2,500 acres in the surrounding area. Lincoln had only just escaped the village of New Salem where he'd been postmaster and a failed storekeeper. Hardin built the first brick home in Jacksonville; in stark contrast, Lincoln's first three years in Springfield were spent sharing a bed with store owner Joshua Speed. Despite the yawning gap in their backgrounds, Hardin and Lincoln grew close and developed a mutual respect.[4]

What apparently brought the men together was a shared belief in Henry Clay, the Whig party, and the sanctity of the Republic as reflected in the Constitution and the Bill of Rights. They were both dazzled by the brilliance of Clay. On another level Lincoln and Hardin shared a consuming ambition to succeed, to stand out and to make a mark in the book of history. Lincoln capsulized their relationship succinctly when he said: John J. Hardin was "more than his father to him."[5]

We don't know if Martin "Dee" Hardin in later life even recalled Lincoln visiting the Hardin home in Jacksonville. His sister Ellen, older by five years, did retain a distinct memory of the gangly young attorney and Illinois state legislator who towered over the other men in the room. Lincoln was among many rising young men who often gathered at her father's home.

At age nine, Martin probably only had a vague conception that his father was an important man to whom many deferred. And of course his father was often absent from the home in pursuing his ambitious goals. As an adult, Martin barely recalled his deceased father, and yet his own life was surely influenced by his exemplary career. John had inherited from his own father, Senator Martin D. Hardin, a revulsion for the institution of human slavery, although both father and son owned black slaves. The father, along with Henry Clay, had tried to bring about its eventual abolition without success. The son, John, deliberately left Kentucky and its slave-holding society behind at age 29 to settle in the free north.[6]

He soon became a close political ally of Illinois Governor Joseph Duncan. The two co-edited *The Illinois Patriot*, a newspaper owned by Duncan and a powerful tool for the Whig Party. After being admitted to the Illinois

Bar in 1831, John J. Hardin rose like a meteor streaking through the political sky. In today's parlance, the young man would be described as a straight talker who stated unequivocally: ". . . frankness and honesty are always the best policy."[7]

John J. Hardin's biographer, Karen L. Cox of Miami University of Ohio, sketched a vibrant word portrait of the 26-year-old Illinois state legislator in her 1964 master's thesis: "He was tall, handsome and well-dressed. One of a minority of college graduates or lawyers in the Legislature, Hardin had an adroit and well trained mind and a combative and courageous spirit. He led men by honesty rather than political maneuvers."[8]

This moralist and idealist distrusted the typical politician, adept at "stirring the billows of political strife."[9] Hardin prophesized that such slippery pragmatists would eventually see their honor and reputations swallowed by "some unseen quicksand and leave but a bubble to mark the graves of their hopes."[10] In contrast, he strove to be a man of character, honor and integrity, and—for the most part—succeeded. Indiana Senator Albert J. Beveridge, in his biography of Lincoln, noted that for all Hardin's virtues he lacked Lincoln's natural instinct for and adroitness in playing the political game.

Despite a pronounced stammer, Hardin was known as a persuasive speaker. One observer recalled the young lawyer's eloquence in pleading for his client's acquittal before a frontier jury, writing: "It was very interesting indeed. He had the audience both laughing and crying in spite of themselves. The Jury brought in a verdict of acquittal in seven minutes."[11] He was a man of marked political opinions who once called President Van Buren "a bundle of inconsistencies" and contemptuously dismissed President James K. Polk as "the pigmy Polk."[12] Illinois Governor Joseph Duncan's wife remembered John Hardin as, "a plain blunt man when his indignation was aroused. Woe to the man who . . . felt the heavy strokes of his meat-axe oratory."[13]

During the Black Hawk War of 1832, Hardin volunteered to help expel the Sauk and Fox Indians from northern Illinois, ultimately serving as a militia major general by appointment of Governor Duncan. During that rather sordid frontier campaign, Hardin swore in Captain Abe Lincoln as a militia volunteer. Neither man won significant laurels in the brief war. Lincoln recalled shedding copious blood to marauding mosquitoes; in contrast Hardin emulated his grandfather, "Indian Killer" Hardin, by burning an Indian village to the ground.[14] Through the rest of the decade the two disparate men established a political and personal friendship that was, for the most part, mutually beneficial.

After running successfully for the Illinois Legislature in 1836, 1838, and 1840, Hardin became firmly established in his adopted state. A contemporary described the former Kentuckian as "Popular in manners, an able lawyer, {and} a speaker of rare power."[15] Hardin, Lincoln, and their mutual friend, English-born Edward Baker, constituted the future of the Illinois Whig party. That future beckoned with infinite possibilities for the talented trio. Tragically all three men were to meet violent deaths: Hardin killed at Buena Vista; Baker killed leading Union troops at Ball's Bluff; and Lincoln slain by assassin John Wilkes Booth.

In the meantime, John Hardin and Abraham Lincoln fought many political battles together in the state legislature and rode the Illinois circuit together, defending clients and wooing voters. Hardin figured as an actor in one of the most popular Lincoln anecdotes, related by mutual friend Joshua Fry Speed (1814–1882), who recalled the incident as proof that Lincoln "had the tenderest {sic} heart for anyone in distress, whether man, beats, or bird."[14] The Springfield, Illinois storekeeper was riding one day with a small party including Hardin and Lincoln, who had lagged behind the rest. Speed later wrote:

A violent wind storm had just occurred. Lincoln and Hardin were behind. There were two young birds by the roadside too young to fly. They had been blown from the nest by the storm. The old bird was fluttering about and wailing as a mother ever does for her babes. Lincoln stopped, hitched his horse, caught the birds, hunted the nest and placed them in it. The rest of us rode on to a creek, and while our horses were drinking Hardin rode up. When asked "Where is Lincoln?" Hardin replied: "Oh, when I saw last he had two little birds in his hand hunting for their nest." In perhaps an hour he {Lincoln} came. They laughed at him. He said with much emphasis, "Gentlemen, you may laugh, but I could not have slept well tonight, if I had not saved those birds. Their cries would have rung in my ears."[15]

Martin Hardin's parents introduced young Lincoln to his father's third cousin, Mary Todd, of Kentucky. She had recently come to Springfield in June 1837 to live as a guest in the grand mansion home of her sister, Mrs. Elizabeth Edwards, wife of the wealthy and influential Ninian Edwards. This prideful man, the son of a former Illinois governor, was fond of entertaining the social elite, which included John and Sarah Hardin. Mary Todd was 21, outspoken and searching for a suitable husband: a man with promise and high ambition to match her own.

Almost immediately, Miss Todd became a member of the same crowd as John J. and Sarah, fellow Kentucky aristocrats on the move up the social and political ladder. Hardin's law partner, John Todd Stuart, was Mary Todd's first cousin, a family tie deemed important in the South of that day. Socially inept Abraham Lincoln was also a frequent guest at the Edwards' home where he was accepted despite his rustic mannerisms.[16]

Years later, Mary Todd Lincoln remembered those times with nostalgic fondness, describing John Hardin, Stephen Douglas, James Shields and her future husband, Abraham Lincoln, as among a "coterie of choice spirits."[17] The Kentucky belle may have had a mercurial temperament and was certainly prone to emotional outbursts, but she was an educated lady of breeding who spoke French fluently and was equally familiar with the language of politics. Despite Lincoln's rough edges, Mary Todd saw great gifts lying within.

Abraham and Mary Todd both loved the poetry of Robert Burns and worshipped Henry Clay, a friend of Mary's family in Kentucky. As a little girl, the precocious Mary had sat in Clay's lap proclaiming her life ambition to marry the President of the United States.[18] Mary Todd probably first met Lincoln at the Hardin residence in nearby Jacksonville. If Martin Davis Hardin remembered either Mary Todd or Lincoln at this point in his childhood, he left no record of it. Little boys his age usually don't take any interest in the conversation of adults, but that certainly wasn't the case with his Aunt Martinette Hardin.

This spirited young woman, like Mary Todd, was in full pursuit of a suitable husband. Martinette lived with her brother, John J. Hardin, in Jacksonville, where she attended an academy for young women. She came to know Mary Todd and Abraham Lincoln very well during these early years and, providentially, left us with an indelible portrait of the man who was to occupy the White House during the nation's greatest crisis:

He was so tall the first time I stood beside him I noticed that I only came above his elbow, and so awkward I was always sorry for him. He did not seem to know what to say in the company of women. He always prefaced his remarks with: 'I read a little thing the other day," or "someone told me," and then he would relate some anecdote or quote some saying that was appropriate.[19]

Martinette Hardin was less fond of Mary Todd. She claimed that most of Mary's acquaintances found the outspoken and strong-willed belle unlikable due to a volatile "bad temper." She also stated that Mary Todd was "the most ambitious woman I ever saw."[20] She was one of many who disliked Lincoln's future bride. Mrs. John A. Logan, wife of a Civil War general and Illinois senator, described Mary's tantrums as "a species of madness."[21] Another acquaintance described her "meanness as beyond belief."[22]

When Abraham Lincoln abruptly broke off his formal engagement with Mary Todd on New Year's Day 1841, he told John Hardin: ". . . he did not love her as he should and that he would do her a great wrong if he married her."[23] Lincoln immediately slid into a major depression. His friend, Joshua Speed, feared Lincoln might end his life and made sure that razors, knives and other sharp objects were kept hidden from his good friend.

Upon learning of Lincoln's eventual recovery from his depression, Martinette Hardin wrote her brother: "We have been very much distressed on Mr. Lincoln's account, hearing that he had two Cat fits and a Duck fit since we left."[24] She further noted it was "a very unsatisfactory way of terminating his romance." Others thought Lincoln had been temporarily insane during the 18-month estrangement from Mary Todd.

While his friend John Hardin assumed his place in the Illinois State Legislature, Lincoln slowly recovered his mental equilibrium and ultimately resumed his legal career and political life. In time, he also renewed his friendship with Mary Todd. Together with a third party they conspired to write a series of satiric letters making fun of their mutual friend, Democrat James Shields.[25]

The fiery, impetuous if diminutive Irishman was not amused; he demanded satisfaction from the author of the so-called "Rebecca letters." The pugnacious and prideful Shields was determined to preserve his honor against these slanders and ridicule. In a spirit of chivalry, Lincoln—who had authored only one of the offending letters—took full responsibility to protect Mary Todd and her friend from embarrassment. This public admission on the part of Lincoln triggered a challenge to a duel from the combative little Irishman.[26]

As the challenged party, Lincoln chose the weapons: heavy cavalry broadswords nearly 3.5 feet long, providing the six-foot, three-inch Lincoln with a tremendous reach advantage over the diminutive Shields. Apparently undaunted by the obvious disadvantage, Shields thought it ludicrous that anyone might think a true Irishman "would run at the sight of a broad sword." He insisted they settle their difference on the field of honor located on a small Mississippi River island located across from Alton, Illinois.[27]

Before the duelists could cross swords, however, John J. Hardin appeared on the scene in company with Dr. Revel W. English, both determined to halt the impending mayhem. In the years since, there have been a number of versions of what transpired that day. In *The Springfield Illinois State Journal* on April 27, 1860, an article stated unequivocally that John J. Hardin had prevented the senseless bloodshed on that occasion, calling both Shields and Lincoln a pair of damned fools, appealing to their common sense, and ridiculing the preposterous sight of "two well grown, bearded men" threatening one another with "a frog sticker in his hand."[28]

To Lincoln's great relief the incident ended amicably. Shields would go on to become a Union general—the only one to ever defeat Stonewall Jackson in battle (at Kernstown)—while Lincoln of course became his commander in chief.

Five days after the duel was averted, Lincoln accepted Hardin's invitation to attend the wedding at his Jacksonville home of his sister Martinette to Alexander McKee. Knowing that Mary Todd would also be present, the invitation was a deliberate attempt to provide the couple with an opportunity to reconcile. And, as later events proved, the Hardin wedding marked the resumption of their engagement and marriage.[29]

At this stage in time John Hardin was probably the most popular and influential Whig in Illinois politics, with a reputation for integrity, courage and ability. His rise to the top culminated in his election to the U.S. Congress in 1843. His friends and political allies, Abraham Lincoln and Edward Baker, also coveted the Seventh Congressional seat, but stood aside for the Kentuckian. However, Lincoln, in particular, believed they had agreed to an understanding that they would take turns in representing the only "safe" Whig District in the state. This would, in time, lead to a crisis in Lincoln's relationship with Hardin, when the latter violated the so-called Pekin, Illinois Agreement.[30]

Hardin's single Congressional term gave promise of his great potential. The tall, dark Kentuckian was a conservative Whig, especially in fiscal matters, but he supported aging former President John Quincy Adams, now a Massachusetts Congressman, in his fight against the Gag Rule forbidding discussion of the slave question on the floor.[31]

Not surprisingly, John J. Hardin, a man who left his native Kentucky to raise his family in a Free State, was solidly opposed to the annexation of Texas. He described President James K. Polk's initiative as "unwise, reckless, selfish, sectional and {a} slavery-extending policy."[32] Hardin was never an Abolitionist, but he stated unequivocally that slavery was "the greatest curse" staining the American Republic.[33] However, he was adamantly in support of annexing Oregon and believed in the principle of Manifest Destiny.

Hardin displayed a rather contradictory attitude toward the reality of politics. He apparently enjoyed the exercise of power but remained contemptuous of the often sordid give-and-take of political horse trading. "As yet we have no politics to animate us in Congress," he wrote his Illinois friend Orville Browning on December 26, 1843. "It is the most stupid place generally I was ever in, as two-thirds of the time of the House is occupied in discussing questions of order." On another occasion, he again expressed to a friend his disgust with Congress: "I would prefer speaking in a pig pen with 500 hogs squealing . . . or talk to a mob when a fight is going on."[34]

Whether these lofty sentiments and disdain for the gritty world of politics were genuine or simply an affectation remains a question mark. Perhaps the patrician Kentuckian considered himself morally above the typical political operative, ignoring his own driving ambition and occasional acts of political expedience.

His time in Washington could have easily ended in tragedy. Instead, a national disaster afforded young Hardin an opportunity to demonstrate his innate grace under pressure. The Whig Congressman Hardin and his wife, Sarah, were sailing aboard the new state-of-the art steam frigate U.S.S. *Princeton* on an afternoon gala cruise up the Potomac River. Passengers included President John Tyler, various members of the Senate and Congress, several

Cabinet members, and 76-year-old Dolly Madison, the revered widow of President James Madison.[35]

The cruise was a public relations effort by the U.S. Navy, an event derided by John Quincy Adams as a stunt to fire up the public to welcome another naval war. Captain Stockton, commander of the powerful vessel, was eager to demonstrate its formidable battery of heavy guns, which included the "Peacemaker," the largest piece of naval ordinance in the world. Hardin was one of many who marveled when the huge cannon was fired on several occasions that day, shells splintering the ice flows drifting down stream.

Hardin's wife, Sarah was below decks along with the elderly Dolly Madison and President Tyler when Captain Stockton ordered another volley from the huge cannon topside. Congressman Hardin was observing from perhaps 50 feet away at about 4 p.m. when the massive gun misfired with catastrophic result. The gun shattered at the breech; the explosion hurtling huge shards of iron into the cluster of spectators, killing eight outright. Among them were the Secretary of War and the Secretary of the Navy. Seventeen others were wounded including Missouri Senator Thomas Hart Benton.[36]

Congressman Hardin scrambled on deck to confront a smoking charnel house of bleeding bodies and severed limbs. In the aftermath, Hardin distinguished himself for his cool composure and competence in dealing with the wounded and stunned survivors of the disaster. A week later, he wrote a friend in Illinois describing the tragic event:

> The horrors of that scene are still before me. The ghastly countenances of the dead, the shattered limbs, the gashes in the wounded and their mournful moanings, can neither be described or imagined. Yet sadder and more piercing to the breast than this were the wailings and shrieks of agony of the wives of those who were killed.[37]

Upon returning to Illinois, this very capable man added additional laurels to his considerable reputation. He led the Illinois militia during the Mormon troubles of 1845–1846. The Mormon (Church of Jesus Christ of Latter-Day Saints) settlement of Nauvoo on the Mississippi River, 50 miles north of Quincy, had prospered, making it the largest city in Illinois; at the same time the Latter Day Saints maintained their own armed body rivaling in size and firepower the state militia. People became fearful, and fear fed hatred and suspicion of the strange sect.

The Mormon presence soon triggered a series of violent incidents culminating in the murder by Gentiles of church leader Joseph Smith in the Carthage, Illinois jail. This atrocity was followed by a spate of vigilante actions on the part of Mormon and Gentile night-riders; barns and homes were burned, and murders were committed with rope and gun. An editorial in the Warsaw, *Illinois Signal* newspaper spoke for many non-Mormons, calling for eradication or immediate removal of the sect. The headline read: "LET IT BE WITH POWDER & BALL."[38]

Historian Bernard DeVoto aptly summed up the precarious situation when he wrote: "On the frontier polygamy was dynamite with the fuse burning."[39] An outright war with the Mormons was narrowly averted, in part, due to Governor Thomas Ford's policy of negotiation, ably applied by Illinois Militia Major-General Hardin and his close friend, Militia Major Stephen Douglas, a close Hardin friend despite his Democratic Party affiliation.

The crisis came when Governor Ford dispatched Hardin with a force of 300 militia to march to Carthage in Hancock County where they confronted a large force of armed Mormons bent on revenge. Hardin ordered the Mormons to immediately disperse and he established order, forbidding the gathering of more than three or four citizens at any one time. In an October 30, 1845 letter to a Mormon leader, Governor Ford approved Hardin's strong actions and claimed that if he hadn't interceded, Nauvoo would have soon faced an attack by 5,000 armed men. "Nothing has saved an attack on your city, by that number, but the march of General Hardin by my order," Ford wrote.[40]

Mormon leader Brigham Young ultimately agreed to abandon the sect's Illinois stronghold and seek a safer haven farther west by the great Salt Lake Sea in Utah. ". . . if their {Hardin, Douglas, Ford} terms were harsh, they were also realistic," DeVoto later wrote.[41] The expulsion of the Mormons from Illinois was undoubtedly a bitter chapter in American history, but it could have ended in outright civil war if not for General John J. Hardin's measured blend of force balanced with restraint and diplomacy.[42]

Historian Robert Bruce Flanders eloquently described the aftermath to the Mormons' forced Exodus: "By autumn what had been the most populous city in Illinois was virtually deserted. Its founder was left buried in a secret, unmarked grave to prevent desecration of the body."[43]

At this point in time Hardin was much better known to Illinois voters than his friend Lincoln. But the Kentucky aristocrat seemed indifferent to politics. Then, in 1845, he suddenly decided to run once again for Congress, a body he professed to despise. He apparently forgot or ignored the Pekin agreement to take turns holding the office with other key Whig leaders. Perhaps he thought the office was his for the asking based on his education and pedigree.

Hardin's action certainly stunned Lincoln. Ambition had trumped friendship, as is so often the case in human relations. But Lincoln was more than up to the challenge. For many months, he had been busy developing grassroots support for his own candidacy, working the voters hard during his long rides on the circuit, and making a special effort to win the support of party leaders and newspaper editors along the way. By the time Hardin began his own campaign, the battle was lost. Much to his chagrin, aristocratic Major-General Hardin had been soundly outmaneuvered by the plebian Lincoln. Embarrassed, Hardin withdrew from the race to save face.[44]

At this point, the Lincoln-Hardin friendship was badly frayed, perhaps even broken. Historian Amy Greensburg states flatly that the two were no longer speaking. On the other hand, Lincoln wrote on several occasions of his respect for Hardin's abilities and cautioned his supporters to moderate their criticism of a fellow Whig.

Always the consummate politician, Lincoln was reluctant to burn bridges. And, then too, it seems likely that, despite their political clashes, Lincoln always retained affection for the man who had rescued him from the near-tragic duel with Shields. Even during the height of their battle for the Whig nomination for the Seventh District, Lincoln went out of his way to praise Hardin, calling him, "talented, energetic, usually generous and magnanimous."[45]

Some historians contend that the Hardin-Lincoln-Baker relationship was terminally damaged following Lincoln's triumph for the Whig Congressional nomination. Judge Gillespie, a political ally and friend of all three, claimed otherwise, stating: "Hardin was one of the most unflinching and unfaltering Whigs that ever drew the breath of life. He was a mirror of chivalry, and so was {Edward} Baker. Lincoln had boundless respect for, and confidence in, them both. . . . These men, Lincoln, Hardin and Baker, were bosom friends to my certain knowledge . . ."[46]

In short, Lincoln went to Congress where he became a staunch opponent of Polk's war in Mexico; Hardin went to the Mexican War as colonel of the First Regiment of Illinois Volunteers, where he became a hero. Like many men, Hardin thought it his duty to serve in his nation's wars despite any personal disagreement with its causes and purpose. On a more pragmatic level, John J. Hardin, was certainly well aware that a distinguished military record would boost his post-war political career. And, like many, he saw in the annexation of Mexican California and New Mexico an opportunity to win land and fortune.

Little Martin Hardin later recalled the excitement when his father volunteered for the impending war, writing in his *Reminiscences*:

I carried mail to my father who was commanding at Alton in 1846. . . . I have quite a clear recollection of the soldiers, the encampment and the excitement at Alton when the Illinois volunteers were collected before starting for the Mexican War. I also remember the excitement in our house.[47]

Colonel Hardin and his men sailed aboard the steamboat *Missouri*. Being the older by five years, the teenage Ellen Hardin retained a more vivid recollection of that dramatic event. In 1879, she wrote:

Though but a child, I remember well that bright summer day, made brilliant by the continuous strains of martial music, the dress parades of the regiments, the enthusiastic cheers of the thousands of people who had come to witness their departure. The tears of parting were suppressed, the forebodings of danger were silenced by the brightness, the glitter of the scene, and the hopefulness of the soldiers who soon crowded the broad decks of the great white steamer. It seemed to my young eyes to be bearing them away to some unreal world.[48]

After his father's departure for the Mexican War, young Martin Hardin resumed the all-consuming business of being a boy. It's doubtful that he gave much thought to his absent father seeking glory south of the Rio Grande. The nine-year-old, most often in company with his younger brother, six-year-old Lemuel, roamed the Prairie outside Jacksonville, fishing, swimming, hunting, exploring and riding horses.

Forty years later the adult Martin, then a successful Chicago attorney, sketched out those carefree days of his youth in the handwritten pages of his *Reminiscences*. A modern reader perusing these recollections comes away amazed at the incredible freedom and independence enjoyed by the young brothers. Their dawn to dusk adventures were apparently rarely monitored by adults and, in retrospect are evocative of Mark Twain's Huck Finn and Tom Sawyer.

The Hardin boys' youthful adventures weren't restricted to Illinois. On numerous occasions, they accompanied their mother on visits to family in Kentucky and also enjoyed extended stays at their maternal Uncle Abram Smith's large plantation in Mississippi. Their mother's brother was rather remarkable in many ways. He was a successful attorney, a member of the Mississippi state legislature, a plantation owner, and a Shakespearean scholar who had committed many of the Bard's sonnets and plays to memory, salting his conversation with favorite passages.[49]

If the Hardin boys were largely unconcerned with their father's faraway adventures, not so their older sister. Ellen, age 15, was mature beyond her years, and always her father's confidante and favorite.[50] She faithfully corresponded with her absent father who responded without patronizing the young lady. Colonel Hardin and his oldest daughter were bound not just by blood but a shared spiritual kinship—a truly special relationship. Her beloved father's subsequent death in distant Mexico was a terrible blow for Ellen, apparently more so than for her younger brothers who did not know him so intimately.

At the bloody two-day battle of Buena Vista on February 22 and 23, 1847, Hardin led the First Illinois Volunteer Regiment with grit and gallantry, calling on his boys to "Remember Illinois and give them Blizzard! They fall at every crack!"[51] One of Hardin's men later remarked that his commanding officer had ". . . only one fault in battle . . . he was too forward and too conspicuous a mark for the enemy."[52]

In the final impetuous charge on the second day of that bitterly contested fight, Hardin and his men were surrounded in a ravine by an overwhelming force of Mexican Lancers. Colonel Hardin was unhorsed and wounded in one leg. He killed one Mexican soldier with a pistol shot, and was drawing his sword as the enemy closed around him. He died as Lancers stabbed him a half-dozen times. Witness William Osman related, "Not a man got out of the ravine but made a hundred hairbreadth escapes."[53]

In the end, Zachary Taylor, notably assisted by Colonel Jefferson Davis of the Mississippi Rifles, artillery Captain Braxton Bragg, and other future luminaries, was able to win a narrow victory over Santa Anna's army. Afterward, Lt. Lew Wallace, future Union general and author of the novel *Ben Hur*, rode through the battlefield, which he described as horrible beyond belief: "The dead lay . . . body on body, a blending and interlacing of parts of men as defiant of the imagination as of the pen."[54] Ironically, along with Hardin among the dead was the son of his political idol, Henry Clay, Jr., who had gone to the war despite his father's intense opposition to it.

Colonel Hardin's wife and daughter, Ellen, were enjoying the sights of New Orleans when they learned the terrible news. Husband and father was finally coming home from the Mexican War, not atop a prancing charger but encased in a lead-lined casket. Lincoln said quite simply: "We have lost our best Whig."[55]

Widow Hardin was bereft: "My heart dies within me," she wrote a sister. "How can I live, how dark and lonely will be the journey of my life."[56]

During a memorial service held in Springfield, Hardin's old friend, Abe Lincoln, expressed his deepest grief upon John's death in battle. At about this time, Lincoln may have made some promise to Sarah Hardin to look after the Hardin children.[57] Lincoln's subsequent actions during his Presidency seem to support this claim. He appointed Martinette (Hardin) McKee's husband to a diplomatic post in Panama and took a personal interest in Martin Davis Hardin's career with the Army of the Potomac, eventually appointing him to brigadier general.

Had John J. Hardin survived the Mexican War and returned to Illinois with military laurels, he would have undoubtedly played a major role in the state's political debates in the 15 years preceding the Civil War. That remains one of the more interesting "what-ifs" of American history, especially in regard to the career of Lincoln. Judge David Davis, a close intimate of Lincoln, remarked at the time of Hardin's death: "Had Col. Hardin, who fell at Buena Vista, lived he would have controlled the politics & the offices of the State."[58]

CHAPTER 3

HOMECOMING FOR A DEAD HERO

N ew England journalist J.H. Buckingham (his father published the *Boston Courier*) was a guest at a Jacksonville inn on July 14, 1847, when the noise of a crowd awoke him from his slumbers. Looking out his window overlooking the square, the roving reporter was startled at the presence of an immense crowd, which, in his eyes, had the aspects of a festive holiday.[1]

The people were congregating for the grand funeral of the late Colonel John J. Hardin, commander of the First Illinois Volunteer Regiment, slain that spring at the Battle of Buena Vista and brought home for burial in a lead-lined coffin. Before the day ended, perhaps as many as 15,000 people came to pay their respects to the fallen officer.

"The numbers increase rather than diminish," Buckingham wrote, "and the people are coming from every direction and in all sorts of conveyances. Stage coaches are scarce, but large wagons are plenty. Women ride on horses and on mules. Whole families come in on large wagons, the travelers being seated on straw-bottomed country chairs. The females are dressed in all the colors of the rainbow; but white, or what was white when the dresses were clean, predominates. Parasols are as plenty as blackberries, and are only outnumbered by cotton umbrellas. . . . {The} day is devoted to the solemn duty of depositing in the grave the remains of Colonel Hardin, which have been brought from Mexico for that purpose . . ."[2]

Buckingham's narrative dripped with sarcasm; he was deeply against the Mexican War and felt a visceral contempt for the antics of what he considered a bunch of boorish Western primitives. In his account, Buckingham took special notice of the many drunken mourners, "abundant" and "noisy" despite the town's prohibition on the consumption of alcohol.[3] The New Englander was appalled at the spectacle of the funeral procession led by the Chief Marshall wearing white pantaloons, mounted atop a prancing horse, and gleefully lifting his hat in salute to the crowd. The reporter wrote:

> The infantry company followed, the band play Pleyel's Hymn in quick time. After the Masons and others came, the black hearse bearing the corpse, and then the horse of Col. Hardin, dressed in mourning. But what was all this to what followed? Next came the family coach containing the bereaved widow and orphans! I would not cast a word of censure upon anyone who really sorrowed. And, it is not for any of us to say who sorrows in this world, where the countenance and the actions so often belie the real sentiments; but a mockery does this seem to be of grief, to parade it before thousands of Strangers, to follow in a gorgeous pageant the decorated hearse in a march of some miles, through dust and noise, and surrounded with mounted marshals and racing cavalcade![4]

Buckingham condemned the proceedings of July 14, 1847 as nothing more than a reflection of "military mania," and more festival than solemn funeral. The journalist dismissed the motives of the young recruits for the Mexican War as being motivated by some "ambition to be something" rather than patriotism.[5] The reporter reserved special scorn for the widow Hardin: "Those of the returned volunteers who served under the deceased, and who belonged to the town, were treated to a collation at the house, by invitation of the widow!"[6]

Richard Yates, Hardin's former law clerk and a future Illinois governor, gave the eulogy, speaking movingly of "the mournful pageant which consigned to its repose the mangled form of the noble and lamented Hardin."[7] He described the occasion as an event that "stands in lone and melancholy preeminence, a center of strange and tender reminiscences."[8]

Yates' remarks touched on Colonel Hardin's many services to Illinois during the Black Hawk War, the Mormon crisis, and also alluded to his three terms in the state legislature and his term in the U.S. Congress, a seat now held by his friend Abraham Lincoln.[9] The speaker also drew the audience's attention to the presence of Colonel Hardin's family: his wife, Sarah, his daughters, Ellen and Lizzie, and his sons, Martin and Lemuel, saying:

> How shall I refer to the bereaved widow and orphan children? Ah!
> Who shall supply the place of the most devoted husband, the kind-
> est father? May they find some consolation in the fact that the tears
> of thousands now present, and of the State and Nation, mingle with
> theirs. While this earth cannot supply the place of the departed one,
> yet they shall not be alone. All over this land shall his children find
> brothers and fathers? The name of the father shall be the talisman
> for their protection. They are the children of the commonwealth.[10]

Martin Davis Hardin was 10 years old when his father died at age 36.
It's highly doubtful if, as a grown man, he even recalled Yates' fine words
spoken in tribute to his slain father. In the 1880s, the middle-aged man,
now a wounded and crippled veteran of the Civil War, jotted down what
little he did recall in a hand-written autobiography that was never completed:

> I remember his body was laid out in the parlor, but I don't think I
> saw the remains. His funeral must have been one of the principal
> events in the history of Jacksonville, but I remember scarcely any-
> thing about it. I remember Ben, who was father's body servant,
> brought back his horse & some of his uniforms. I think I felt the
> loss of my father so keenly that the Servants seldom spoke of him
> before me. Mother & sister simply mentioned him, but did not
> talk of him to us. I sincerely regret that I remember so little about
> him. I have not even a distinct recollection of his features aside
> from pictures.[11]

One of those pictures was a Currier and Ives print widely distributed
across the nation memorializing the death of Colonel Hardin at the Battle
of Buena Vista. The imaginary scene portrays a heroic Hardin waving a
sword from atop his magnificent steed, a romantic vision of noble death in
combat, tastefully absent the blood, the filth or the horror. In his son's eyes,
the father never grew old, never showed human shortcomings, and remained a model of manhood.

Colonel John J. Hardin's will is interesting in what he bequeathed to his children. Ellen, the oldest at 15, was given the piano; Martin received the watch once carried by his paternal grandfather, Senator Martin D. Hardin; Lemuel, seven, inherited "my swords and pistols."[12] The father also set-aside funds to educate both boys in the legal profession, appending the admonition that they be "inculcated in their minds that their first duty is to serve their God and next that they should learn to depend upon their own exertions to support themselves and their Mother."[13]

A few years afterward, an older Martin wrote how his brother Lemuel was the bravest of the Hardin clan and always had martial ambitions, symbolized by his father's deathbed gift of weaponry. On the other hand, Martin's earliest ambitions involved the law and life of the mind, as perhaps his grandfather's watch represented, since he'd been a noted legal scholar in Kentucky and graduate of Transylvania University.

Following John J. Hardin's death, the family remained in Jacksonville (except for frequent and often lengthy sojourns to visit relatives in Kentucky and Mississippi) where young Martin's education proceeded in makeshift fashion. The boy spent most of his days roaming the woods and prairies, fishing and hunting, and galloping about on his beloved black Indian pony. During his mother's frequent absences, Dee and his siblings were under the care and supervision of the former slave, now indentured servant, teenaged Dolly Smith. "After father's death our household was not kept very regularly," Martin remembered years later. "Dolly had the arrangement of the meals & I think Lem & I ate when we were hungry & mostly in the kitchen."[14]

Dolly, who Martin described as "my great friend," was the chief cook for the family.[15] She recalled Martin fondly as a boy with "a good appetite especially for bread & Milk, cakes & molasses, claiming that he survived solely upon those staples until he was eight years old. Again and again, Dolly emerges in Martin's recollections as a trusted, warm and loving member of the family. Sadly, no photograph survives of this young woman who held a special place in the hearts of the entire family.

In the absence of his father, Martin naturally looked to others as male mentors. In those first few years after his father's death, he apparently found a partial replacement in Harrison Allen, a hired man who farmed the Hardin acres. The boy often accompanied Allen to the fields, and recalled with pride how he once drove his wagon pulled by three horses.[16] "Allen was a famous hunter," Martin wrote, "& was a wonderful shot with a rifle, hitting a squirrel in the eye every time. He once, near our house, killed a hawk on the wing with his rifle. He had a most excellent temper—rather liked children & let us go hunting with him very often. He would go out very early in the morning & kill enough squirrels for breakfast . . ."[17]

Nature, in its wisdom, gives the young remarkable resilience in times of pain and loss. And in time Martin thought of his father less often, and became absorbed in the daily adventures in the woods and prairies surrounding their Jacksonville home: "Our amusements were riding, gathering berries, hazel {nuts}, hickory & walnuts, paw-paws, hunting, fishing & town ball {an early version of baseball}, marbles, etc.," he wrote later. "I think I went to school as a sort of a pastime after father's death."[18]

Sometimes Martin and his youthful companions would play along the old Strap Railroad. The iron rails ran from Springfield to Meredosia on the Illinois River, on which a few railroad cars were slowly pulled by teams of mules. Martin recalled playing along the route as "always a source of wonder and delight to us boys."[19] But even so, this paled in comparison to the joy of galloping madly about on a horse.

"In my boyhood, horseback riding was the favorite way of getting around," Martin wrote. "No one walked anywhere if he or she had a horse to ride. I spent nearly close to an hour chasing my pony about the lot to catch him to ride, probably not one tenth of the distance I had run chasing him."[20] Martin especially admired his older sister, Ellen, who he described as "a good & fearless rider."[21]

Horses on the Hardin place were often beloved and remembered for many years, almost with the same affection reserved for family and old friends. Of course Martin's favorite was his "little black Indian pony." But all the siblings were especially fond of Old Charley, "a sorrel mother had ridden from Kentucky years before." Martin later described the aging animal as "a lazy, good natured, old swayback who often carried 3 or 4 children on his back" and a stand-by mount for the entire family. Entirely the opposite from Old Charley was a retired race horse now being employed as a buggy horse. "Old Bet" was unreliable, Martin recalled, and prone to suddenly breaking out on a wild run without the slightest provocation.[22]

In 1850, Martin's mother apparently decided that the boy needed a regular, formal education to prepare him for adult life. She chose to board the 12-year-old at Jubilee College, founded a decade earlier by the first Protestant Episcopal Bishop of Illinois, Philander Chase, who had earlier founded Kenyon College in Ohio. Jubilee College was located near Jubilee Creek, a tributary to Kickapoo Creek in a beautiful area 20 miles north of Peoria.[23]

By the time of Martin Hardin's arrival, the institution was, if not thriving, certainly a going concern with a college as well as a secondary school. The facilities included a substantial chapel, a two-story building containing classrooms, plus a library and offices.[24]

Martin seemingly made the transition without much difficulty, arriving there in the early spring. The young boys were a hardy lot and often swam in the nearby ponds, barely thawed from the long winter. "We went swimming in ice water," Martin recalled. "One of the boys got the cramp & we had to dive for him. He came near being drowned."[25]

Hardin's recollections of life at Jubilee College's secondary school are almost devoid of any mention of classwork or serious studies. However, he did seem to have an enjoyable time with the other boys pursing various amusements. One popular recreation in the warmer months was to kill the numerous rattlesnakes found all about the nearby woods.[26] "At that time, one of our amusements that, I have the most distinct recollections of was hunting rattlesnakes; the country abounded in them," Hardin wrote. "We hunted them with dogs; it was customary for someone to suck the wounds of a dog that was bitten. We carried no weapons, only a small stick; the best weapon in the world to fight a snake with is a short hickory cane."[27]

Snake hunting wasn't Martin's only new interest at Jubilee College. Although still shy and laconic, the boy was discovering the charms of the opposite sex, and entertaining new desires and emotions rarely alluded to among polite society. Martin and his fellow male students were particularly fascinated with an English family residing nearby with "a bevy of attractive daughters."[28] "All the boys were sweet on the young girls of this English family," he wrote. "I amongst the number, but I'm sure I never said a dozen words to any member of it, but girls were scarce in this part of Illinois at this time."[29]

While a student at Jubilee, Martin endured a tremendous shock. He was soon to learn that his mother was marrying a stranger, a man from New York State she had only met once, during a recent trip to Louisville, Kentucky.

This stranger was Chancellor Reuben Hyde Walworth of Saratoga Springs, New York, who was then in his sixties, a generation older than the widow Hardin. This old-school gentleman was to have an incalculable impact on the lives of both Sarah Hardin and her family. Born the son of a Revolutionary War officer in Bozrah, Connecticut in 1788, Chancellor Walworth was a distinguished expert on equity law, and was wealthy, religious and a force in New York State Democratic politics.[30]

Early on, at age 16, Walworth taught school briefly in Troy, New York around 1805, where he soon entered the study of law in the offices of John Russell, State's Attorney for the Northern District, and reputedly a lawyer of talent. During the War of 1812, Walworth served as a Major at the Battle of Plattsburgh, New York, and acted as aide to General Benjamin Mooers of the New York State Militia.[31]

Young Walworth witnessed the great American naval victory won by Commander Thomas McDonough over the British Royal Navy on Lake Champlain, a triumph that defeated the final British attempt to invade the northern United States. Walworth ended the war as division judge advocate with the rank of colonel.[32]

In 1821, he served one term in the U.S. Congress, and then was appointed judge where he established a sterling reputation for probity and fairness. In 1828, Governor DeWitt Clinton appointed Walworth Chancellor of the Court of Chancery, an office he held for the next twenty years before the post was abolished. Walworth also served as an ex-officio officer of the Court of Errors and helped review the disputed decisions of the New York Supreme Court.[33]

Chancellor Walworth held court in his own Saratoga Springs home, Pine Grove, and won the admiration of Harvard University Professor Dane, who wrote: "No court was ever under the guidance of a judge purer in character or more gifted in talent than Reuben Hyde Walworth, the last chancellor of New York."

In 1844, a group of influential New York legislators put forth Walworth as a candidate for the U.S. Supreme Court, but President John Tyler never approved the appointment. During his lifetime, Walworth's numerous friends included a number of former Presidents of the United States: Andrew Jackson, Millard Fillmore, Franklin Pierce and James Buchannan. Other visitors to Walworth's Saratoga Springs mansion were writers Washington Irving and James Fennimore Cooper; future Lincoln Cabinet members Secretary of State William Seward and Secretary of War Edwin Stanton; abolitionist and millionaire Gerrit Smith; Henry Clay of Kentucky, "The Great Compromiser"; and General Winfield Scott, hero of the War of 1812 and the Mexican War.[34]

Walworth's first wife, the pious Maria Ketchum Avery, died on April 24, 1847, only a few months before the death of Col. John Hardin at Buena Vista. In the fall of 1850, widower Walworth was traveling on business in Louisville when he met the widow Hardin in company with her 19-year-old Ellen. Details of this encounter are lost in time, but based on correspondence between the two that followed, the admittedly staid, religious and—some said—stuffy older man was quite besotted with the young widow.[35] On November 26, 1850, Chancellor Walworth posted his first missive to Mrs. Hardin, posted at Frankfort, Kentucky. He wrote:

> The slight acquaintance formed with you on our recent casual meeting at Louisville had deeply impressed me with the belief that you are better qualified to render me happy as a companion than any other lady I have met with since the demise of my beloved & newly sainted wife. . . . Allow me therefore to ask your permission to correspond further with you on this interesting subject . . . & to visit you personally as soon as I can so consistently with other duties. Whatever you may say in answer to this will of course be considered by me as strictly confidential as I know this hasty note will be considered by you.
>
> I am with respect & esteem, yours,
R. H. Walworth of Saratoga Springs"[36]

The widow Hardin was quite candid in her response:

> I read with pleasure, and some surprise, your kind letter expressive of the regard and esteem you have for me. I feel highly flattered, and much gratified that one who I respect and esteem so highly to choose me from the world, to be a friend and companion. On my way from Louisville to this place, I found my thoughts frequently

reverting to the pleasant moments I had spent in your society, and, if the impression received on so transient an acquaintance be as lasting as they were bright and beautiful, I know of no good reason why matters should not terminate . . . as you desire . . .[37]

Walworth wrote the Widow Hardin again on December 23, 1850 from his Pine Grove Mansion in Saratoga Springs, stating quite simply what he required in a wife. The letter is oddly reminiscent of a Help Wanted advertisement: "The requisites I desire in her who is to be the partner of my bosom are gentleness, amiability of temper, benevolence, culture and a decided Christian character as distinguished from mere formalism in religion."[38]

After an apparent break in correspondence, Mrs. Hardin wrote back to Chancellor Walworth, postmarked Harrodsburg, Kentucky, on February 10, 1851, in which she acceded to his wish that she leave the Episcopalian Church and convert to the Presbyterianism. In the same letter, she noted her appreciation of the older man's character, claiming it was similar to that of her deceased husband, Colonel John J. Hardin. "They are those I most appreciated in my husband," she wrote. "They were an honest & manly expression of opinion, firmness, independence and sterling integrity, truth and piety were the fountain of his character."[39]

In regard to her own character, Mrs. Hardin remained rather elusive, saying only:

I hope you will not ask me to say anymore of myself. I may not do myself justice. I have some good common sense. If I were by your side with my hand clasped in yours, and the feeling I had an indulgent listener, I could confide to you all the faults and errors [illegible] in my past life. . . . The words are spoken, forgiven, & forgotten, and friends are drawn nearer to each other . . . but when the words are written, and only the cold, white paper reflects them, there is nothing but the dark characters to show. They are recorded against us, not even the tear of penitence can wipe them off.[40]

She also mentions her children and admits she has yet to tell them of her intent to re-marry. What is particularly concerning is her frank admission that she is unsure of her oldest son's present location, although she thinks Martin was taken by his sister, Ellen, and enrolled in a school "somewhere in Illinois, probably near Peoria, in charge of Bishop Chase." The startling fact that Sarah was not quite certain of her oldest son's whereabouts certainly raises questions about her long-distance parenting.[41]

In closing, she states bluntly that their marriage would not require "any sacrifice" on his part toward her children. "You cannot feel with me altogether on that subject, as your children have almost, all of them, formed ties of affection independent of you. Mine are so much younger and more dependent on the affection of a mother. Believing our heavenly Father will order all things for our good, I remain yours affectionately, Sarah E. Hardin."[42]

In reading Chancellor Walworth's correspondence with Mrs. Hardin, most modern readers would assume that he was indeed a strait-laced gentleman of the old school who took his religion and the care of his soul equally seriously. In a March 22, 1851 letter to his intended bride, Walworth writes:

> So far as respects my personal habits I am able to say, and I knew that must be gratifying to a lady of refinement, I never smoked a pipe or a segar [sic] in my life, & never had a quid of tobacco in my mouth. I can also add that I have not drunk a glass of any kind of ardent spirits since I was a boy, more than 45 years [ago]. These habits, or either the want of these bad habits, I admit are evidence of wisdom, but not of goodness. To this extent therefore I will admit that your intended husband is a wise man; though he has no pretensions to goodness.[43]

Interestingly, the widow Hardin makes a rather amazing admission in a March 9, 1851 letter to Walworth, acknowledging that they were still virtual strangers about to marry. She wrote:

> . . . tell me something of yourself. I am not satisfied with only a newspaper account of you; just think how little we have seen of each other. Would you know me, if you were to meet me on the street unexpectedly? I do not believe you would. I would send you

a likeness or a daguerreotype if you were not coming so soon. Yours ever, Sarah E. Hardin.[44]

There is certainly a rather cold-blooded aspect in Sarah's decision to marry a much older man, albeit wealthy and influential, on the basis of a single day together and a few letters. But then again, she was a widow with three children and limited by Victorian convention in pursuing alternatives open to succeeding generations. Her decision would eventually have a significant, and partly calamitous, impact on her own life and the lives of her children. But, for now, those gathering clouds were yet to appear.

CHAPTER 4

_____

SARATOGA SPRINGS:
ENTER SAINT AND SINNER

Following the marriage of the widow Hardin and Chancellor
Walworth, the Hardin family spent several days in Peoria
where they visited Martin Hardin at Jubilee College about 30 miles north
of the Illinois River town.

Martin's sister, Ellen, wrote her best friend, Mary ("Molly") Duncan
back in Jacksonville on April 30, 1851, confessing her growing pride in her
younger brothers, Lemuel, 11, and Martin, 14, on the eve of departure for
her new life at Chancellor Walworth's Pine Grove Mansion in far-off Saratoga Springs:

> We have been out to Jubilee today and back, a distance of 30 miles
> over rough roads; but we brought D. (Martin) back here to spend
> tomorrow with us, and have been compensated for our fatiguing
> ride by a most glorious "family meeting" this evening.
>
> Oh, Molly! I am the happiest, proudest creature in the world.
> I felt like a Queen this evening, when I walked out from the supper
> table between my two noble, dear brothers! Just think of having
> two great big, sure enough brothers to protect me. Who would
> want a husband under such circumstances? I have contempt for
> the very thought. Molly, don't you almost envy me my good for-
> tune? I don't see how you can help it.
>
> . . . We will not have time to go to Chicago before Sunday, and
> we cannot stay here too long, for we want to hurry on to Niagara
> and have some time to spend there. We all feel distressed at the

fought of leaving D., but think it best to let him stay. He is perfectly well-satisfied and wishes to remain. Bless his dear heart, he is a noble boy. The Chancellor is much pleased with him. He thinks that D. has a fine open face. All at Jubilee speak well of him.[1]

In the spring of 1851 Martin completed the term at Jubilee College. In company with Dolly Smith, the family servant and beloved friend, he boarded a steamboat at Peoria and began the first stage in a long journey to re-unite with the rest of the family already living in Saratoga Springs.[2]

Sixty miles upriver, they disembarked at the Steamboat Basin at La-Salle-Peru on the Illinois River about 100 miles south of Chicago. Beyond this point, the river rapids and shallow water made further travel by steamboat impossible. Passengers and freight bound for Chicago had to transfer at LaSalle to board a mule-drawn canal boat to take them the rest of the way via the Illinois-Michigan Canal.[3]

They took passage on the "Mail Packet" bound for Chicago. Martin recalled years later that the boat was "very crowded, having many passengers & much baggage. The cry of 'low bridge' was the source of much amusement. We were about 18 hours on board, spending our night, I slept on deck. We arrived in Chicago in the daytime . . ."[4]

At the canal boat landing, the travelers boarded a horse-drawn omnibus for the trip to the Fremont Hotel where they remained for several weeks. During this layover, Martin spent many pleasant hours with a friend from Jubilee, John Kinzie and his family. They hunted ducks together on a slough on the west side, and ate at Bull's Head Tavern. (Kinzie was later killed serving with the Union Army in the Civil War, one of many friends Martin lost during the war.)[5]

Martin and Dolly left Chicago on an old Great Lakes Steamer, which took two leisurely weeks to make the journey to Buffalo, stopping frequently at various ports to load and unload passengers and freight. Major ports along the way included Milwaukee and Detroit. During the War of 1812, Martin's grandfather, Major M.D. Hardin, had served with the American army outside British-held Detroit. Perhaps the young man recalled that event as well as the nearby American defeat on the Raisin River, which claimed his grandfather's brother-in-law, Colonel John Allen, among the slain.[6]

"We had rough weather part of the trip," Hardin recalled. "Dolly was very seasick. I was not & I feared that I laughed at her."[7]

Once they disembarked at Buffalo, it is likely that Dolly and Martin continued by stage on to Saratoga Springs, a venerable town located near the scenic Adirondack Mountains and near the Revolutionary War battlefield of Saratoga, where, ironically, Martin's revered great-grandfather, John Hardin, had won fame as a member of Daniel Morgan's rifle corps in 1777.

Saratoga Springs was a world away from the Prairie State. Thousands of visitors were drawn each year to the resort town due to the presence of the heated mineral springs deemed beneficial to health. Around the springs grew a constellation of exclusive hotels, casinos, restaurants, and concert halls patronized by the Eastern elite, but also by a contingent of wealthy Southern planters seeking refuge from the sweltering heat of a Dixie summer.

Martin's stepfather, Chancellor Reuben Hyde Walworth, was the most distinguished citizen of Saratoga Springs, and was a familiar sight on the streets as he rode about on one of his spirited stallions. He made it a daily routine to visit each of the popular hotels, checking the register for important visitors, many of whom he numbered among his friends and acquaintances, or for other prominent people he wished to meet. Here in this upper New York State community, Walworth was among the same elite class who visited the resort on a regular basis: senators, congressmen, judges, authors, scholars, entrepreneurs, former presidents of the United States— men of power and influence.[9]

At the core of Saratoga Springs in the 1850s were the Grand Union Hotel, the United States Hotel, and the Congress Hall along busy Broadway. In the season, the distinguished and not so distinguished rode in fine carriages pulled by well-groomed steeds through the streets in a daily procession of wealth. "Fashionably attired ladies, carrying gay parasols . . . tucked in beside gentleman whose dun-colored hats better displayed the bright sheen of their mustaches. Coachmen in long brass-buttoned coats, top boots and skin-tight breeches knuckled the curled brims of their own tall hats"[10]

We can reasonably assume that early on Chancellor Walworth introduced his Hardin stepchildren to the resort's many attractions. Young Martin, who later in his life confessed a fondness for elegant dining and surroundings, may well have sharpened those tastes in Saratoga Springs, perhaps at the

Grand Union Hotel where gentlemen and ladies—"the very best people of the land"—donned full evening dress at dinner, where they might sip fine wines and dine on Flandreau of veal, roast wild duck, rice croquettes flavored with wine, venison with currant jelly or Macaroni Italian.[11]

Martin spent those early days in Saratoga getting to know his prominent stepfather and his new step-siblings. That first summer in New York, he had the opportunity of spending a great deal of time in company with his stepbrother, Mansfield Tracy Walworth, the Chancellor's youngest son who still remained at home. The Hardin family would not meet the older brother, Catholic Father Clarence Walworth, until later. Both Walworth stepbrothers would have enormous influence on the entire Hardin family in decades ahead.[12]

Eighteen-year-old Mansfield and his much older brother, 32-year-old Clarence, were polar opposites: literally saint and sinner. Over the years, Martin came to see this dichotomy of character quite clearly. However, in those early years at Pine Grove, Martin probably didn't fathom the darkness of Mansfield's soul, although subsequent events ultimately revealed the monster behind the mask.[13]

In reality Mansfield Tracy became an only child following the early death of a sister, Fanny, at age five. The gap of 14 years between he and his older brother made Clarence more like an uncle than a sibling.

Perhaps Chancellor Walworth over-indulged the boy, or perhaps he was too Puritanical and distant. Whatever the case, Mansfield couldn't be mistaken for his saintly brother. Granted, the boy had gifts, was fit and handsome, and could be charming if so inclined, and demonstrated some talent as a writer. Early on, however, Mansfield displayed a self-absorbed, narcissist personality and a violent streak. How soon his stepbrother Martin discovered the true nature of Mansfield's character is not known. But others saw it early on.

In 1843, L.B. Proctor came to Chancellor Walworth's Pine Grove mansion to be sworn in as a solicitor in chancery. At the front gate, he encountered the 12-year-old Mansfield Walworth and left us with this vivid portrait:

> His form, set off by a fashionable dress, was exceedingly graceful
> and attractive; but it was not his form and dress that chiefly attracted
> attention; it was the bold, buoyant, intelligent expression that

presided over his handsome face. There was something in the rest-
less though penetrating and semi-impudent glance of his eye that
indicated a haughty, arrogant nature, and an ill-regulated mind.[14]

Mansfield's subsequent behavior that day confirmed Proctor's negative
impression. When Proctor proceeded to introduce himself to the child, the
boy replied in a tone of disdain: "Perhaps I have no desire to make your
acquaintance. You should have thought before you proposed to honor me
with an introduction."[15]

Proctor ignored the yet unidentified boy's rudeness and engaged in a
brief conversation while awaiting Chancellor Walworth to finish an ongoing legal proceeding in his court. Upon learning that Proctor was from
Cayuga County, Mansfield inquired of the older man if he was familiar
with a certain young boy he knew from school in Auburn. Proctor admitted
he was acquainted with the boy, prompting the 12-year-old to ask: "When
you see him again, tell him you met an old schoolmate of his at Saratoga."

"What name shall I give him?" Proctor asked.[16]

"Mansfield Walworth. I think he'll remember me, for I gave him a
thrashing just before we left school."[17]

Years later, Proctor recalled the unpleasant meeting with the youngest
son of Chancellor Walworth, writing: "His remarks and manner had something in them approaching the bizarre, blended with a kind of repulsive
sarcasm which he intended for dignity."[18]

After Mansfield reached maturity, a reporter from the Utica *Herald* later
compared the adult Mansfield to the monster from Mary Shelly's *Frankenstein*: "He was not only ready for the spasm of profanity, but for bloody
fight when the occasion required, at least with a weaker party, for like all
tyrants, he combined cowardice with arrogance."[19] His tenure as a student
at Union College, New York was noted more for his wild and rebellious
nature rather than scholastic accomplishments. Young Walworth stabbed a
fellow student in one instance, an incident that appears to have been swept
under the rug due to Chancellor Walworth's reputation and influence

Tragically, Martin's sister, Ellen, was blind to Mansfield's character
flaws, or perhaps overlooked them due to her stepbrother's smile, intelligence, smart clothes and physical beauty. She described Mansfield as "a
strange a boy that ever lived" in a letter to her best friend Mary Duncan in

Jacksonville. In the coming months, she and Mansfield grew very close. Perhaps in emulation of his older brother, Mansfield was considering conversion to the Roman Catholic Church, and he soon persuaded his stepsister of the wisdom of doing the same.[20]

At one point, Mansfield even convinced himself that he would soon take holy orders and become a priest in emulation of his older brother. The impulsive young man was fond of entertaining such wild enthusiasms, then ultimately abandoning them for some other unlikely scheme. On occasion, he expressed a desire to be a soldier or a poet, as well as a saintly priest like his older brother, savoring future triumphs, but ultimately never taking concrete steps towards making these wild dreams of priestly celibacy a reality.[21]

Mansfield was hardly an ascetic like Clarence; he was instead a man of large and unrestrained fleshly appetites with absolutely no concern for their impact on others. He did retain his fascination for the Roman Church for some time, and in 1853—probably with Father Clarence's help—he published an historical novel titled *The Mission of Death: A Tale of the New York Penal Laws*. The story was set in colonial New York City with a missionary priest as its central character.[22]

To the modern reader, *The Mission of Death* is a swamp of verbiage where the rare declarative sentence is festooned with innumerable adjectives. Yet this was the style of the era, and, the book sold, giving Mansfield the conviction that he was a talented novelist. Appropriately, his favorite reading was the work of Edgar Allan Poe, the tormented master of Gothic macabre literature.

Despite his Bohemian inclinations, Mansfield ultimately graduated from Harvard College and obtained a license to practice law.[23] But the narrow confines of the lawyer's life—in his distorted imagination—could not contain such a poetic sprit as that of Mansfield Tracy Walworth. No, the legal drudgery of drawing up contracts, wills, and the other routine of the lawyer's life held no charms for him. In the years to come, Mansfield saw himself as a great novelist, even a genius, stifled by the narrow confines of traditional society. This strange evil man was to wreak havoc in the coming decades bringing tragedy and sorrow to both the Hardin and Walworth family.

If Mansfield was the Sinner, then his older brother, Clarence, was the Saint.

During the Saratoga years, Martin Hardin grew to like and admire Father Clarence Walworth as a man of magnetic personality and high ideals. Almost from the beginning, this eloquent and sincere man of faith—by his example and his persuasive logic—began the process of converting all the Hardin family, one by one, to the teachings of the Universal Church of Rome.[24]

As a boy, Clarence showed precocious intelligence, a religious bent apparently inherited from his devout mother, and a studious nature. At the same time, he had a spirited, even rebellious nature best illustrated when he smashed the windows of the church, an act of vandalism that his father, the Chancellor, punished with a memorable whipping. He was no mollycoddle, and enjoyed dancing and singing, and was a proficient horseman.[25]

Clarence also demonstrated an admirable independence from the conventional wisdom of his place and time. This was best illustrated by his early empathy for the plight of the Native Americans. In his youth, Native Americans still came to Saratoga Springs to camp on the commons where they sold trinkets, baskets, and other handicrafts, or demonstrated their impressive archery skills.

At the age of six, Clarence's heart was touched when he encountered a scantily clad Indian emerging from the forest near their Pine Grove home.[26] The boy gestured for the Indian to wait while he ran to the family home and retrieved a shirt, which he gave as a gift. The impassive Red Man only grunted a response before moving on. Clarence's mother approved the charity, but noted the probability that the Indian would only trade the shirt for liquor.

Little Clarence was convinced otherwise. He had seen something in the Indian's eyes that told him different, despite the man's appearance and ignorance of white etiquette.

Saratoga Springs historian Evelyn Barrett Britten wrote how the same silent Indian appeared months later seeking young Clarence Walworth: "In his hands, he held a beautiful bow of well-seasoned wood and a good supply of arrows just the proper size for the lad to handle. No boy of his age in Saratoga had so choice an equipment! He himself had believed in the gratitude of the Indian and here was unmistakable proof."[27]

Britten wrote that the adult Clarence often defended the humanity of the Native Americans, especially when someone dared repeat the common admonition that the only good Indian was a dead one.[28] Clarence met author James Fennimore Cooper when the writer visited Chancellor Walworth. The youth read and treasured Cooper's books, and always insisted that his portraits of noble Indians were true depictions of a much-maligned race.

Chancellor Walworth was proud of his eldest son as he progressed in school, showing remarkable ability as he mastered Greek, Latin, and, much later, Hebrew. He graduated from his father's alma mater, Union College in Schenectady in 1838. That same year, however, Clarence attended a revival by a freelance preacher named Jacob Knapp, whose words stirred his soul, and—despite his many disagreements with Knapp's primitive theology—pointed him on a path toward salvation.[29]

Whatever ambitions Chancellor Walworth entertained for his brilliant elder son, they were far different from the life path Clarence ultimately chose. That choice severely strained, but never quite broke the chain of affection that bound father and son.[30] For a time, the Chancellor probably thought that this extraordinary young man would follow in his own footsteps.

And for several years Clarence did practice the law, but soon became disenchanted, not only with the life of the lawyer, but the worldly life itself. He was a moral purist and not given to making the small accommodations most humans make to win advancement in life. In point of fact, worldly achievement was not Clarence's purpose; his was a life increasingly drawn to the saving of his eternal soul and the souls of others.

In 1842, to his father's disbelief, Clarence gave up the law to study for orders in the Episcopal Church, enrolling in New York City's General Theological Seminary. He sought salvation for his soul, and would not settle for a grubby retainer, which required a moral expedience Clarence found repugnant.[31]

The Episcopalian Church, however, soon proved wanting. Clarence left the Seminary, searching for a purer religious experience. He finally found what he was searching for on a visit to Notre Dame Cathedral in Montreal. He was enchanted with the grand rites of Holy Mass, and irrevocably drawn to the discipline, ritual and ancient traditions of the Roman Catholic Church.[32]

This was a turning point. He joined the Catholic Redemptorist Order in New York City, and sailed on August 1, 1845 to Europe to begin his novitiate at St. Trond in Belgium. No arguments or bribes from his Presbyterian father, or tears from his beloved mother, Maria Ketchum Walworth, could turn him from his destiny: "The voice of God calls me elsewhere," Clarence told his family.[33]

Upon his return from the missions in 1851, Clarence met his new Hardin step-siblings and quickly exercised a powerful influence upon their religious thinking. But his younger brother, Mansfield Tracy, employed his own considerable charisma and charm to beguile his new stepsister, Ellen. Father Clarence was interested in claiming Ellen's soul for the Catholic Church; Mansfield's desires focused on the earthly pleasures of the flesh.

It seems likely that Chancellor Walworth was too absorbed in his own pursuit of love to pay much attention to these domestic intrigues. He enjoyed the company of his young bride and enjoyed their May-December affair to the full. If he was aware of the growing passion between his son and his new stepdaughter, the old Chancellor apparently made no moves to prevent it from continuing.

Years later a friend of Ellen recalled: "At the time Ellen Hardin was said to be engaged to a young Southerner, but her ambitious mother influenced her to break her engagement and marry a son of Chancellor Walworth by a former marriage. . . . She was brilliant, witty, gifted with a keen mind and charming personality, as well as beauty."[34]

Ellen Hardin and Mansfield Tracy Walworth made a striking couple to be sure. They were young, passionate and romantic. Left in each other's company for extended periods, perhaps their coupling was inevitable, an intoxicating mix of biology and Victorian sentimentality.

Interestingly enough, Ellen's 14-year-old brother, Martin D., was already aware of Mansfield's impetuous and impulsive nature. But he put things in the best possible light when he wrote Ellen of her impending marriage: "I think he will make a smart and honorable man if he once gets settled."[35]

That significant "if" suggests Martin had reservations about his new brother-in-law's maturity and character. But it seems unlikely that Ellen's younger brother had any real inkling of Mansfield's true nature. Only in time would the Hardin family discover that Ellen's charming husband was a violent wife-beater, a delusional egotist, and a depraved sensualist without morality. Ahead lurked tragedy, tears and murder.

CHAPTER 5

SHADOWS IN THE FOREST

During the first years of their May-December marriage, the Chancellor and Sara Hardin Walworth appeared primarily concerned with their personal happiness, using wealth and leisure to embark on a second springtime. Sara's prominent husband generously opened the doors to a whole new world of privilege and status for his Kentucky plantation belle. The 63-year-old Chancellor and his bride, younger by 23 years, were frequently absent from Pine Grove, as they explored their new relationship. In 1851, they sailed across the Atlantic to London in 1851 to attend the Exhibition of the Industry of All Nations, often referred to as the first World's Fair.[1]

The newlyweds were among a million visitors per month to walk through the enormous wood, iron and glass-plate Crystal Palace, which housed displays of fine art, machinery and other treasures from 38 nations. The structure itself was a wonder of the new industrial age, a great glass birdcage measuring 1,800 feet long, 400 feet wide, and 128 feet tall.[2]

Chancellor and Mrs. Walworth, like fellow visitor Queen Victoria, must have been astounded at the gorgeous riches of the interior courts featuring fountains, flower gardens, reflecting ponds, statuary from ancient Egypt and Rome, and performance spaces where musicians and orchestras entertained the crowd. Visitors seemed to agree that the most fascinating feature was the recreation of a prehistoric swamp inhabited by life-size statues of extinct dinosaurs. These creatures' fossilized remains had only been discovered thirty years previously.[3]

Sara's indulgent husband purchased for his bride an expensive American-made piano on display at the Fair and shipped it back at considerable cost to Pine Grove. In 1860 the Walworths entertained famed pianist Louis Moreau Gottschalk at their Saratoga Springs home, where he entertained with private nightly concerts. Legend claims that the musician used the piano at Pine Grove to compose two of his more popular pieces.[4]

Upon their return from London, Martin's mother continued to make the most of her prestigious position as Mrs. Chancellor Walworth, to the apparent initial approval of her infatuated older husband. He must have been pleased when he read an August 1855 newspaper account of the recent grand dress ball at Saratoga's Union Hall, which described the young wife of Chancellor Walworth as shining above "the three or four hundred of the most beautiful women who have ever graced any festal hall."[5]

Fellow Saratogan William L. Stone knew Chancellor Walworth and his wife Sarah, and he recalled that their family life was indeed a happy one, writing years later: "The new wife brought with her to Pine Grove not only a sweet and loving temper, but a certain Southern style of hospitality, which consorted admirably with her husband's own disposition. A cheerful circle of friends soon gathered around her. She loved to keep open house, and many more familiar faces passed in & out than ever thought to right the bell, or wait in the parlours."[6]

Stone also knew Martin and Lemuel Hardin, the Chancellor's step-sons, and recalled them as "two manly boys." He has also left us with a very positive portrait of their stepfather, who seems to have been a sincere Christian, and who took great pleasure in the company of others, young and old. Walworth's later declaration that he loved Martin like a son and his inclusion of all the Hardin children in his will is a strong indicator of his warm, generous nature.

Chancellor Walworth's personality, described in Stone's recollection, is characterized by "the kindness and affectionateness of his heart, the delicacy of his attention to others, the liveliness of his conversation, his exuberant and sometimes boisterous merriment. His fondness for the society of the young, with whom even in his extreme old age, he loved to romp without the slightest thought of his own dignity."[7]

All considered, Chancellor Walworth appears to have been a good role model for the fatherless Hardin children. He had firmly established over a long lifetime a reputation as a fair and honest man of strong morals. For years the Chancellor had served as President of the American Temperance

Society and was always quick to advocate cold well water over imbibing any alcohol-tainted concoction. He also abstained from tobacco and profanity. Stone asserted that the Chancellor was a man of old-fashioned probity: "He held in abomination that greedy and reckless traffic in the rise and fall of land, stock, securities, etc., which is commonly called 'speculation,' but which he denoted gambling."[8]

This is not to say that the Chancellor didn't, in at least one case, suffer from moral blindness.

New York diarist George Templeton Strong strongly implied that Walworth's legal involvement with the notorious Spike patent lawsuit was nothing more than legalized robbery. The Supreme Court had named Walworth as "special master" to determine damages, a never-ending process that provided participants with a rich, stable income for many years.[9]

One of many who benefited from the Spike Suit was Walworth's close friend, William Seward, future Secretary of State in the Lincoln administration. He argued for one of the clients involved in this Byzantine proceeding that so richly benefited the Chancellor, and ultimately won his case despite interminable delays. When the Chancellor's wife, Sarah, told Seward she had no understanding of the legal intricacies of the Spike Suit, Seward responded: "{that I} should be very much ashamed if you did. I have been engaged in it for several years, and I don't understand it yet."[10]

In his personal life, Walworth suffered a severe disappoint when, in his mind, God robbed him of another late-life chance to be a father. In April 1852 the Chancellor's young bride gave birth to Reuben Hyde Walworth, Jr. The Chancellor was delighted with the baby boy, and apparently held hope that he would grow up into a son cast in his own image. Those dreams and hopes were soon shattered when the child died at age six months.[11]

Sarah wrote to her mother in Jacksonville, Illinois, noting: "The Chancellor made an idol of the little fellow and is almost heart-broken at his loss."[12] No more children were to follow. This event cast a dark shadow over the Chancellor for a very long time.

Nevertheless, Walworth seems to have transferred his paternalistic nature to raise his Hardin stepchildren and grandchildren, upon whom he dotted fondly. His daughter-in-law, Ellen Hardin, expressed her deep affection for her stepfather, who with the passing years, increasingly took her side against Mansfield's repeated infidelities and failure to support Ellen and the children. Ellen would later recall the incredible beauty of the Chancellor's blue eyes reflecting kindness, understanding and love.

As the decade of the 1850s marched on, Mrs. Chancellor Walworth (Sarah) increasingly found herself attracted to Washington, D.C. society. The intelligent, cultured and politically aware woman felt at home with the nation's elite. She loved their society and was present at many of the Capital's soirees, often on the arm of the Chancellor in the early days. Later, when her older husband tired of balls, receptions and formal society functions, she continued to attend unescorted or in the company of friends.

But it would be a gross error to dismiss Sarah simply as a socialite with a charming Southern drawl. Behind the façade of manners dwelt a sophisticated, calculating, politically astute woman, who knew that friendships with the rich and the politically powerful could translate into material advancement for her family. Sarah Hardin Walworth knew the game of politics and, as future developments proved, played it exceedingly well.

Although Sarah operated within the rigid social constraints placed upon women in the America of the mid-19th century, she carved out a significant place for herself, especially in the area of historic preservation. Most notably, in 1856, she was elected vice-president of the Ladies Mount Vernon Association, dedicated to saving George Washington's deteriorating Virginia mansion. Her passion for preserving the national history was shared by her daughter, Ellen, who ultimately became one of the four founders of the Daughters of the American Revolution (DAR), and played a key role in preserving the Revolutionary War battlefield near Saratoga Springs.[13]

Oddly enough, Martin Hardin, who seriously contemplated running away to the Far West when he first learned of his mother's remarriage and their projected move to Yankee-infested New York State, apparently made the transition to the East with few difficulties. Martin wrote of that first summer in the Adirondacks with pleasure, recalling how the days were "occupied principally in hunting, fishing and learning the Eastern mode of expression."[14]

In the fall, his mother and stepfather enrolled him as a boarder in nearby Ballston Spa Academy, although he would return home frequently to Saratoga Springs during academic recesses. At Ballston Spa, the young man quickly learned that his haphazard education put him at a severe disadvantage in competing with his classmates in a decidedly rigorous academic environment. "My education was very backward," he later recalled. "I could read and declaim very well & I knew some Latin. I had scarcely any other book knowledge. Ballston Spa really commenced my education."[15]

The students of Martin's age at Ballston may have been his masters in academic subjects, but not his equal in maturity. "I had travelled so much and being the oldest boy had responsibilities thrown upon me for so long, I was as capable of taking care of myself as many boys of eighteen or twenty years of age . . ." he wrote. "I was an enigma to the eastern boys of Saratoga & Ballston Spa."[16]

Sport was an entirely different matter. Martin's athleticism quickly won admiration and friends among his peers. He was "very large for my age," weighing around 150 pounds and standing at nearly 5-feet, seven-inches tall.[17] A youth spent on horseback or hunting the prairie had given him an admirable physique and endurance. His physical prowess coupled with a warm, outgoing personality soon made young Hardin many friends among fellow students and professors.

Not surprisingly, Martin and his brother Lemuel later joined Saratoga Springs' first baseball team, where the participants often stopped play to pull out Spaulding's *Rules of Baseball* to determine what to do next. And, of course, winter brought with it sleigh rides through the snowy woods, downhill tobogganing, and skating over the ice-covered ponds.

Martin was young, eager and open to life. Even so, school remained a challenge. His many gaps in education forced Dr. Babcock, the school rector, to place him in the first term among a class of younger and smaller boys. "My pride was aroused and I studied very hard," he wrote.[18]

Soon, Hardin mastered Caesar's *Commentaries* and was making "rapid progress" in Greek; although math proved then, and later, to be a more formidable obstacle. Balancing that out, Martin could point with satisfaction when he was recognized as first in declamation (rhetoric) in his class.

His social life advanced in tandem with his improvement in school. Throughout his life, Hardin proved a likable individual and was adept in making friends. In fact, Martin recalled that Dr. Babcock regarded him as one of his favorite students. This is documented by the grade reports from that period. Dr. Babcock, in all cases, described Martin's deportment as "Excellent." Not long after his arrival at Ballston Spa, the Rector wrote:

"Martin so far proves an excellent scholar, and in all respects, gives us entire satisfaction."[19] By June 31, 1854, in Martin's final year at the school, the Rector simply noted: "All—as usual—entirely satisfactory."[20]

Hardin in turn gives us a graphic portrait of Dr. Babcock, who was not only the Rector of Ballston Spa but an Episcopalian minister: "Old Dr. Babcock was a very large man with enormous feet, and he generally wore slippers which must have been eighteen inches long & six broad. . . . He was very fond of good living, especially of buckwheat cakes."[21]

Although Hardin bloomed at Ballston Spa School and enjoyed his days there, he resented what he described as "an encouragement of deceit"[22] at the institution. "There was too much dependence placed on eavesdropping & catching the boys on the sly & no dependence upon their honor & trust," Hardin wrote. "I think he {Dr. Babcock} was always very kind to the well behaved boys, but watched the others too much. Altogether it was a good and very pleasant school for me, and the old Dr. always regarded me one of the flowers of his flock, and was exceedingly proud of my [illegible] career. I liked the old gentleman exceedingly & made it a point to call on him every time in Ballston Spa until his death."[23]

The Saratoga Springs years were largely happy except for a puzzling episode of random violence that almost took young Hardin's life. When not at school, it was his custom to take to the surrounding woods on long solitary hunting expeditions, often spending the night slumbering under the stars by a small fire with a rifle at his side. "I was in the habit of wandering off hunting with a crust of bread in my pocket & sometimes of remaining out overnight," he recalled without mentioning a specific date or year. "On one of these occasions I had been along the upper west ridge of Saratoga Lake having a small squirrel rifle and a knife, which I used for cutting up {musket ball} patches, preparing my kill, etc. Night caught me about five miles from home. I built a fire, cooked something to eat & then lay down in the top of a fallen tree."[24]

Sometime in the night the teenager was roused from sleep by the approach of three strange adult men with shotguns cradled in their arms as they suddenly emerged from the shadows of the forest. He wrote: "One asked to see my rifle & fired it into the air," Martin recalled. "I thought this very strange but nothing [illegible] remarkable."[25]

One man curtly ordered Hardin to come with him. The boy protested and insisted they let him return to his own home, but the intruders forced him to accompany them through the woods. In his account, Hardin never mentions whether the armed men considered him a trespasser, a poacher, or threat. Perhaps they never told him.

As they proceeded through the dark woods with Hardin in the lead, the boy's skinning knife slipped from his belt and fell on the ground. Martin stooped over to retrieve the knife, triggering a savage assault: ". . . one of the brutes hit me over the head with my rifle, breaking the stock & very nearly killing me!"[26]

Oddly enough, when Hardin regained consciousness and asked to be taken to Chancellor Walworth's home, his attackers acquiesced and loaded him into a wagon without argument. "I was very badly hurt but fortunately recovered entirely in a few months," Hardin wrote. "I was very indignant at the affair but, of course, could do nothing until I got well."[27]

Disappointingly, Hardin's account of the strange incident is incomplete and never explains the motive for the assault. The modern reader is also puzzled why these attackers were never taken to court after attacking the stepson of Chancellor Walworth, a real power in New York State. Even more puzzling is that Hardin's recollection of the incident also mentions that, months later, the men stole one of Hardin's shotguns that he had loaned to a friend. Was this a vendetta? Who were these men? One suspects that the young man from the Illinois frontier was somewhat unprepared for the more established property rights, and the inclination to guard them, that then existed in the East. Whatever the truth, the details and motives for this violent act are lost in time and will probably never be answered.

Those Saratoga years were full of adventure and discovery for the young man, and may even have included, if not direct involvement, knowledge of the Underground Railroad, that network of safe-houses in the north, which served as waystations on the road to freedom for thousands of escaped slaves.

Legend has it that Martin's dear friend, Dolly Smith, was one of the conductors on the Underground Railroad, and sheltered escaped slaves in the empty wine cellar at Chancellor Walworth's Pine Grove mansion. If this is true, Martin and the rest of the family would at least have tacitly approved of Dolly's blatant law-breaking.

The main source for this fascinating tale is Saratoga Springs historian

Ellen Barrett Britten, apparently relying on family stories she had heard from Martin Hardin's great-niece, Clara Hardin Bramlette, who died at Pine Grove in 1952. Britten contended that Chancellor Walworth, whom she described as friend of freedom for all, actively supported Dolly's Underground Railroad involvement.[28] Ms. Britten tells the story in a chapter titled, "The Underground Railroad and Dolly, The Slave Girl" contained in her 1959 history, *Chronicles of Saratoga*, claiming: "The slaves who were sheltered in the wine cellar of Pine Grove were most comfortable. Dolly saw to that! She fed them well, with the same food she served the chancellor's family. Behind the crates of empty wine bottles, Dolly provided good bedding."[29, 30]

Unfortunately, there is no surviving documentation establishing the truth of the story. Dolly's close friend, Martin Hardin, never mentions this fascinating fact about Dolly's life in his unpublished autobiography, an unlikely omission considering its drama. He does write about Dolly in several passages, but never claims that she'd been a conductor on the Underground Railroad.

Beyond that, Chancellor Walworth seems unlikely to have allowed his home to be put to such use. True, he thought slavery was an evil, and entertained various plans for its eventual demise, but these always included active support of reimbursement for the owners and the shipment of the freed slaves to Africa. In the end, Walworth proved a Union man, but he was never a warm friend of the Negro race.

Britten points to Walworth's friendships with noted Abolitionists to support the claim that the Chancellor would have been willing to help smuggle slaves to the North, but that doesn't seem to coincide with his numerous public statements on the issue. He never supported full civil rights for free Negros, and regarded the thought of inter-racial equality and especially the specter of racial intermarriage as abhorrent.

It is true that Chancellor Walworth did entertain in his home prominent Abolitionists, including Lloyd Garrison, Wendell Philips, and even Gerritt Smith, one of the secret financial backers behind John Brown's Harper's Ferry Raid in 1859. But Walworth never supported the radical views of these individuals who he dismissed at best as visionary incendiaries.[31]

At the same time, Walworth cultivated many warm, close personal relationships with Southern planters and politicians who visited Saratoga

Springs each summer. He sympathized with the South, although he always remained a strong Union man.[32] In most ways the New Yorker reflected the views of his Kentucky wife and step-family. The Hardins had for three generations condemned slavery, but were never Abolitionists. Unfortunately, Walworth's stepson Martin never put his views of this incendiary subject on paper. We can only assume that his beliefs were not far removed from those of his family, or for that matter, from his mother's old friend, Abraham Lincoln, another opponent of slavery who advocated moderation, compromise and conciliation with the South until the Civil War radicalized his views.

Like most young people of every generation, Martin Hardin in his teen years was quite likely far more absorbed in his studies, his pursuit of outdoor sports, and his growing interest in the opposite sex than in politics and current affairs. In his recollections of those youthful days, Martin never mentions such momentous developments as the Dred Scott decision, the Fugitive Slave Law, the incredible popularity of Harriet Beecher's Stowe's 1852 novel, *Uncle Tom's Cabin*, or the Kansas-Nebraska Bill, which soon gave birth to Bleeding Kansas. His concerns were apparently more personal and far more parochial.

Martin's recollections of his youth in Saratoga Springs do describe his continued frustrations with the abstractions of algebra. Midnight sleigh rides through the snowy woods, and dances which sometimes only concluded in the wee hours. Thirty years later, the adult Hardin recalled these as happy years filled with "jolly occasions," self-discovery, and the unadulterated joy of being young.[33]

This is not to say that Martin Davis Hardin did not possess a serious side. Indeed, he was proving to be a natural scholar, and more and more saw the life of an attorney as attractive. In 1854, during his last year of school at Ballston Spa, Martin wrote his mother, reflecting on the passage of the years: "One more month has rolled its time away, leaving me, but little advanced in learning although much in the short space allowed to man upon this earth. However, every little helps; one small mile added to many of its predecessors soon make man worthy of a high station in life."[34]

The road to that "high station in life" was soon to take the 17-year-old Martin Davis Hardin to the U.S. Military Academy. There he would become a reluctant if dutiful Cadet, learn the stern, unforgiving code of the soldier, and become a student of the bloody science of modern war.[35]

Destiny awaited the young man there at that fabled and forbidding military monastery on the Hudson. Young Hardin would meet many of the men who would write their names large during the coming trial of the Civil War, including Robert E. Lee, Oliver O. Howard, George Armstrong Custer, Joseph Wheeler, Fitzhugh Lee, Wesley Merritt, Stephen D. Ramseur, and John Schofield.

None of them knew it then, but they were all marching toward a national catastrophe of unimaginable proportions. In a few short years, most of them, including Hardin, would face former friends—even brothers—as enemies on a hundred battlefields.

A great storm was about to burst and Cadet Martin D. Hardin would be among the multitude to endure its terrifying wrath.

CHAPTER 6

WEST POINT: NO PLACE
FOR WEAKLINGS (1854–1859)

Despite Martin Hardin's family military heritage going back more than a century, this descendant of five generations of soldiers didn't want a military career; in fact, he dreaded going to West Point. Early on, he sought a career in the law, and by 1854 his ambition was to enroll as an undergraduate at Williams College in Williamstown, Massachusetts, one of the prestigious "Little Three" colleges of New England.[1]

But his strong-willed mother and Chancellor Walworth had other plans for the 17-year-old. Indeed, for several years, Sarah Hardin Walworth had been actively seeking an appointment to the West Point Military Academy for her oldest son. Her efforts led President John Tyler to offer an appointment, but the boy's age made him ineligible at the time. However, with Chancellor Walworth's influence, President Franklin Pierce approved an at-large appointment for young Hardin in 1854.[2]

"I had no special taste for the military service and I had great doubts about my ability to graduate at the Military Academy . . . I was a poor mathematical scholar," Hardin wrote many years later. "Having very unwillingly accepted the appointment to West Point, I studied with a [illegible] for the preliminary examination."[3]

The examination results were deemed sufficient, and young Hardin arrived at West Point on May 30, 1854 in company with his mother. He was now a Plebe and had to endure the hell of the summer encampment where he and his fellow newcomers were addressed by upperclassmen as "things" or "animals" among other demeaning adjectives. His grim premonitions of the military life soon took the form of reality.[4]

"I am very certain the first summer was the most miserable three months of my life," Hardin later wrote. Although he learned to adapt to the harsh environment, Hardin never romanticized life at West Point; in later life he frankly avowed that he would not repeat the experience even if they made him "commander-in-chief of all Uncle Sam's armies."[5]

Cadet George Crockett Strong of Stockbridge, Vermont, Class of 1857, was an upperclassmen when Hardin arrived at the Academy. His recollections, published in 1862, provide us a window into the institution's culture during that period. (Strong became a Union general during the Civil War where he was mortally wounded during the assault on Battery Wagner, Morris Island, Charleston, July 10, 1863.)

Strong didn't pull any punches in his 1862 book titled *Cadet Life at West Point*. The military college was a rigorous test of a young man's physical endurance, mental toughness, patience and maturity. The author estimated that three-fifths of the incoming Plebes would not see graduation. Each day began at 5 a.m. with the report of the signal gun and a rattle of drums announcing Reveille. Cadets had to dress, make themselves presentable, and be standing at attention in ranks less than ten minutes later.[6]

Incoming Plebe Martin D. Hardin quickly learned that the slightest violation of a regulation, no matter how seemingly insignificant, meant a demerit. Accumulate enough demerits and your expulsion was guaranteed. Hardin and the others also learned that the cadets had a slang term for each offense: Hair Too Long (Pil-Garlic), Profanity (Pyret), Inattention At Drill (Bender), Loud Talking After Taps (Bedlam), Shoes Not Properly Blackened (Beaute), Out of Uniform (Dickie), Out of Step (Hopper), Dropping Musket At Drill (Tombey), and Talking In Ranks (Parley). And, that is only a partial list.[7]

Cadet Stephen Dodson Ramseur, one of Hardin's West Point friends and a future opponent in the Civil War, wrote home describing one instance of the almost continual petty harassment that was daily occurrence at West Point: "Taps is at ten o'clock," he wrote. "I was pulling off my coat & was just about 1/2 minute too late, but I was late, & must be punished. This is West Point on a small scale."[8]

We don't know what Hardin thought of the military minutia that plagued a cadet's life, but we can assume that he, like most cadets, often wondered what this game of shiny buttons and creased trousers had to do with the study and practice of war. The story went around at the time that an unnamed President of the United States once wondered why a spot on white trousers should be assumed to affect the battlefield performance of a soldier, whether in constructing a fortification or charging the enemy line. Surely many cadets wondered the same.

Infantry drill, marching to class, guard duty and other military duties added to the burdens of a tough curriculum, which included: Infantry tactics and military policy, mathematics, French (Spanish was introduced in 1854), natural philosophy, drawing, chemistry, mineralogy, artillery tactics, engineering, the science of war, geography, history, ethics, swordsmanship, horsemanship, and cavalry exercise and tactics.[9]

It's probably safe to assume that an incoming cadet with deep reservations about attending West Pont, like young Hardin, was stunned when he learned that he was among those chosen to be among the first five-year class in the institution's history. Based on age, half of Hardin's incoming class was assigned to a four-year curriculum and the remainder to the five-year curriculum. Hardin found himself with the extra year.[10]

The decision was made by Secretary of War Jefferson Davis and Army Chief Engineer Joseph Gilbert Totten. They believed the additional year was necessary to provide the cadets with a generally higher level of instruction and more class hours in law, history, geography, and English. This unpopular decision led many members of the affected Class of 1859 to submit letters of protest to Congress, which went absolutely nowhere and only provoked many in the officer corps, who felt young cadets should never question authority. Whether Hardin lent his name to the protest is not known. The five-year track was abandoned within a few years. Only three five-year classes were graduated: 1859, 1860 and May 1861.[11]

When Hardin entered the Point, the Superintendent was Colonel Robert E. Lee, a hero of the Mexican War and number one in the West Point Class of 1829. Second-in-Command was Major Richard Garnett. Both were strict disciplinarians and would ultimately serve with great distinction in the Confederate Army. (Garnett was killed during Pickett's Charge at Gettysburg.) The faculty also included John Pegram, who taught cavalry tactics and became a Confederate brigadier general before dying in combat. Another celebrated Confederate leader who taught during Hardin's tenure at West Point was William J. Hardee, the author of a book on infantry tactics that became the bible for both Blue and Gray.[12]

Many of Hardin's West Point instructors would wear the uniform of the Union including future general officers: Oliver O. Howard, William Hazen, George L. Hartsuff, Fitz John Porter, Alexander McD. McCook and John M. Schofield. Hardin's classmates included future Confederate generals Joseph Wheeler, Stephen Dodson Ramseur and Fitzhugh Lee, the Superintendent's fun-loving, rule-busting nephew. Other cadets in the classes of 1860 and 1861, well known to Hardin, included George Armstrong Custer and Wesley Merritt; both men later shone as cavalry generals under General Philip Sheridan, first in the Civil War and then on the Great Plains fighting Indians (Custer's famous demise notwithstanding).

Early on, Hardin learned that there was a huge social chasm between cadets and instructors. Relations between teacher and student were strict and tolerated no familiarity and rarely even a hint of humor or amusement. Cadet Strong, two classes ahead of Hardin, explained that cadets must display "the most respectful deference" while instructors were expected to behave with "dignified reserve."[13]

"Remember never to expect any demonstrative approval from your instructors," Strong wrote. "Should your genius excite their imagination, or should you by close application to study, and a frank avowal of ignorance in the section room, upon any point you do not fully comprehend, thus merit their approval, you will find it out, if ever, in after-years, on the frontier . . ."[14]

Cadet Morris Schaff, Class of 1862, remembered that the young men of West Point were held to impossibly high standards of character and conduct, almost unobtainable except by prodigies such as Robert E. Lee, whose perfection as a cadet was not repeated until the arrival of Douglas MacArthur many decades later. Most cadets were far more human. Schaff described the majority as "no better and no worse than the young men of like age at any college." He saw "no pretense of holiness" or psalm-singing Saints, or discerned the absence of profanity among these men who marched about like so many marionettes.[15]

Indeed these very human cadets sometimes broke under the pressure. During Hardin's first summer, he witnessed an incident far more serious than profanity or missing roll call. One Plebe, provoked into a rage by the continual goading and baiting of an upperclassman—Hardin described it as being "deviled"—angrily bayoneted his persecutor. The victim survived with only a minor wound, and according to Hardin: "The matter was kept quiet in a military point of view but the Plebe was a marked man during his entire time at the Academy."[16]

Hardin probably meant that the bayonet-wielding cadet was "cut" by his classmates; in short, shunned, a cruel punishment for any young person who needed the friendship of companions as surely as sleep, food and water. Young Hardin found the tradition of "cutting" cruel and "something inherently wrong."[17] This reluctant soldier seemed ill-suited for a soldier's life. His presence at West Point seemed more motivated by a sense of duty and obligation to family wishes than any intrinsic love of the military world.

Interestingly enough, Hardin's strong-willed mother accompanied him when he reported to the Military Academy and later visited the post frequently overr the next five years, cultivating the various instructors and their families with her vivacity and charm. As she would do on a bigger stage during the Civil War, Mrs. Sarah Hardin Walworth played a crucial role in making her son's case to the influential and the powerful.

Whatever his reservations, Hardin dutifully plugged along that first year. "I studied very hard but could not make much headway in algebra," he wrote later.[18] The young man definitely wanted to succeed and certainly dreaded failure, especially in light of the example set by his illustrious forebears, who had for more than a century excelled in war, politics, and the law on the Virginia, Pennsylvania, Ohio, and Kentucky frontier.

"I was completely discouraged & thought I would go down a section," he wrote. "So that on the Saturday when the transfers were to be announced, I ran to a saloon back of Buttermilk Falls, had a big dinner and took about as much strong drink as I ever remember to have taken in one day, but was perfectly able to attend the Retreat Call. I remember it was called on the porch and, to my utter astonishment, I was transferred to the first section . . . the goal of all Plebes' ambition, it being a sure sign that he was competent to graduate if he desires. After this, I studied faithfully and never lost my position in the First Section . . ."[19]

Martin's mother and stepfather chose a completely different career path for his younger brother, Lemuel, despite the fact that the latter had always expressed an enthusiasm for army service. Repeatedly, Martin wrote that his younger brother was the true warrior in the family, not he. In an undated

letter posted at West Point to his brother, Martin encouraged Lemuel's martial ambitions:

> I hear you have taken somewhat of a fancy for {the} military, that
> is, you are forming militia Companies of boys at Saratoga. You
> know I always said, you were altogether the most courageous &
> military one in the family of us children. I wish you had come to
> West Point instead of myself. The only trouble you would have
> would be getting demerits & walking Extras; but that only lasts
> during the first Encampment & after that everything goes on
> smoothly. However, it is too late now to talk about your coming
> here. But I believe it would both please you & do you a great deal
> of good to go to a Military School for a short time.[20]
>
> I know very well how negligent you are about almost the only
> thing that they are particular about at such a school, those are, neat-
> ness of person & dress, and punctuality to "Roll-calls" & "Call to
> Quarters." When you first started to such a school, you wouldn't
> like it, even so much as you did Babcock's; but after a few weeks
> you would get so that as to almost love it. And then how much
> better does a Straight, cleanly young man appear than a dirty, neg-
> ligent one.[21]

Older brother Martin was obviously disappointed in Lemuel's failures
as a student. Perhaps he thought the discipline of a military education might
be the answer. In this letter he also reminded his younger sibling that
achievement in school and life was expected of a Hardin, writing:

> You will soon be a man, as you are now fourteen years old. And to
> see a Son of Col Hardin's, a young man almost entirely unedu-
> cated, it would appear ridiculous in the extreme. I don't think Mr.
> Durkee {one of Lemuel's teachers at Ballston Spa} can learn you
> as much in a month as you could learn anywhere else in a week.
> He is altogether too easy. I am going to try to get a "Permit" to
> come home Christmas & see you all. Should I get one, I will see if
> I can't bring you complete equipment in the way of dress & accou-
> trements.[22]

In closing, Martin took a more relaxed and teasing tone, asking his brother to give his regards to all the Saratoga belles and "dance with all the pretty girls for me." He also asked about mutual friends, how Lem liked the new boarding school on the hills, and the local gossip about the town's "Belles and Beaux," ending the letter: "Don't Spare my love to the Fair of Saratoga. Give my love to all. Your affectionate Brother, M.D. Hardin."[23]

Like many Cadets, Hardin was bestowed a nickname and was afterwards rarely addressed by his Christian name. The boys called him "Ben (Hardin), in reference to the famous first cousin of his grandfather, Senator Martin D Hardin of Kentucky. Most of the cadets were familiar with Kentucky Congressman Ben Hardin's reputation as a frontier lawyer and humorist; once, his intellect had been described as sharp as a knife, thereupon gaining him the appellation of "Butter Knife" Hardin. So to many of his West Point classmates, Martin was always their friend "Ben" even many years after graduation.[24]

Years later underclassman Morris Schaff recalled "Ben" Hardin as an outstanding cadet with "resolute face, voice, and manner." Of all the young men at the Point at that time, Schaff believed that "Ben Hardin from Illinois, a son of the Colonel Hardin who fell at Buena Vista," was destined for greatness.[25]

Hardin's closest friend at West Point was Francis J. Crilly of Philadelphia, the son of Henry and Jane Killion Crilly, Irish-born Catholics who had immigrated in their youth. Crilly's father had served as a soldier in the War of 1812, and had risen in society to become manager of the Beneficial 6aving Fund Society of Philadelphia.[26]

Cadet Hardin liked Crilly for his "courtly manners and sunny disposition," and admired his courage in openly following his Roman Catholic faith at West Point during a time when many Americans despised the followers of Rome. The example of Crilly undoubtedly influenced Hardin's own conversion later during the Civil War.[27] In 1908, when his life-long friend passed away in Philadelphia at 71, Hardin looked back on their West Point days:

> How well I recall the sight of Crilly, the lone student starting off
> Sunday morning to march himself to Buttermilk Falls to attend
> Mass—certainly then a Catholic hero. Little did the writer then

think that within a very few years, he would be wandering off alone
. . . oh, how lonely! To the conscience-sought field of Christian
safety, the Roman Catholic Church. It is impossible for the
Catholic millions of this generation, in which the church holds
such a high, honorable and weighty position, to appreciate the lone
position of its scattered thousands in the early "fifties" of the last
century.[28]

Political differences about the slavery question were another issue that
increasingly divided cadets. Oddly enough, Hardin later claimed that West
Point at that period was largely free of any deep sectional animosity or bitterness: " . . . there was a southern party & a northern party, but the feelings
between them never became so great that some cadets—myself amongst
the number—could not belong to both sets. Massachusetts men led the
northern {faction} & South Carolina the southern."[29]

Most often, according to Hardin, the cadets talked about horses during
their free time, complained about the quality of the food (bad) and exchanged tales of various scrapes involving fellow cadets, usually involving
forbidden visits to the nearby public house Benny Haven's for a round of
drinks and a good meal. One truly wonders if any cadet would have stuck
it out if it wasn't for the existence of the legendary Benny Haven's.

Hardin certainly had fond memories of the drinking hole, describing
himself as being "fond of good living." Nearly every Saturday, he traipsed
with chums to the famous rendezvous. "We never drank much on these
occasions and therefore never got into trouble," he claimed. Later, he stated:
"I had a strong head & was always perfectly able to take care of myself &
frequently had to assist others to get safely back into Barracks."[30]

One suspects that young Martin kept his drinking a secret from his
mother and stepfather. Chancellor Walworth was a life-long teetotaler, as
was Martin's biological father, the late Colonel John J. Hardin. Martin,
however, took a different path, and though never dissolute in his habits,
enjoyed a nip on occasion the rest of his long life. Like all young men at
West Point, Hardin simply needed an occasional outlet for his energy,
which stealthy visits to Benny Havens provided. Sometimes the cadets'
carousing at their sanctuary came very close to a riot, although Hardin apparently never participated in such, or at least admitted to it. Sometimes

personal feuds between cadets led to impromptu boxing matches held at nearby Kosciusko Springs.[31]

Other cadets tested the limits of discipline frequently, especially Hardin's friends like Custer—who Hardin described as prone to "all sorts of frolic"[32]—and Merritt, who both spent a great many hours walking off their demerits on the parade grounds. They exulted in defiance of authority, pushing limits to the edge, but not quite enough to merit dismissal. Even saintly Robert E. Lee's nephew, Fitzhugh Lee, was another scamp, described as a "wild, careless and inexperienced youth."[33]

Not long before Hardin came to the Point, another cadet wrote his father, reporting on a wild New Year's celebration at Benny Haven's when, "knives were used, and several first classmen were stabbed . . . another will be dismissed because he knocked down the Officer of the Day—one man stripped off his coat and shirt and fought desperately with a big carving knife in his hand."[34]

If a popular cadet was forced to resign, a pall fell over the Academy. And on several occasions, the cadets mourned the loss of beloved companions taken by death and injury. During Hardin's West Point tenure, one cadet drowned while swimming in the Hudson River; another was crippled—at first they thought he would not recover—when his horse fell backwards on him during an equestrian exercise. "We felt their loss more than boys usually do," Hardin wrote. "In fact, classmates at the Point have [illegible] trials and tribulations—together they become very much attached to each other."[35]

In many ways West Point was a band of brothers, but sometimes their names were Cain and Abel. Hardin witnessed a dramatic confrontation between avowed enemies that could have easily resulted in homicide or serious injury. Hard words on the parade ground led to threats between cadets Jessup and Paine once they returned to the barracks. Jessup attacked the other with a sword; soon they were slashing at each other in a full-blown duel.

"Both were good swordsmen," Hardin wrote. "Paine defended himself & being the cooler & stronger of the two would probably have hurt or disarmed Jessup when Stoughton {Hardin's classmate} got a sword and went to Jessup's assistance. Several persons at once interfered, but not before Col. Hardee appeared."[36]

Cadets Jessup and Stoughton both came perilously close to dismissal,

Hardin recalled, but incredibly the administration allowed both men a second chance. They also went on to graduate, despite their gross violation of regulation. "I think they {Stoughton & Jessup} and Custer spent more time in the guardhouse than any other cadets," Hardin recalled.[37]

If Hardin had any enemies at the Point, he never mentioned them. He stayed out of trouble and was popular with both cadets and instructors. He excelled at swordsmanship and boxing, and described himself as a competent horseman. His deficiency at math was overcome through diligence and effort to the point where, upon graduation, Hardin was selected for the artillery branch—a feather in his cap.

Cadet Hardin also had some strong opinions about the faculty. "R.E. Lee was not liked but his family was popular," he wrote. Superintendent Richard Delafield, Lee's successor, "was very smart but his word had always to be taken with a grain of salt."[38]

Of all his instructors, Hardin especially disliked Cadmus Marcellus Wilcox—a future major general in the Confederate Army—calling him "the most unpopular officer" at West Point. He told how Wilcox was, "sent away, so it was said, for carrying an umbrella in the rain."[39] This might sound strange, yet even in the 1960s, officers disdained carrying umbrellas, apparently believing a real soldier would never resort to such a feminine creature comfort—instead opting for a poncho or, even more admirable, simply ignoring the elements. In 1857 Mexican War veteran Wilcox was given a 12-month furlough from West Point due to health reasons. He spent the year in Europe and used the time to study European armies. Later, he published a technical manual on rifles and rifle firing and a book about Austrian army evolutions and tactics. When he died at 66, his pall-bearers included four Confederate generals and four Union generals.[40]

"Hardee was a good-hearted man but not very bright," Hardin judged, despite the fact that the future Confederate general had authored a book on infantry tactics regarded at the Point as a classic. In his recollections of his cadet days, Hardin revealed a taste for gossip, repeating a rumor about a certain Dr. J.: "He {the Spanish instructor} had married the widow of a man who was killed in a duel on her account," Hardin wrote. "She was never received by the families at the Point."[41]

Yet Hardin's deepest censure was marshalled in his description of an officer he refers to in his reminiscences as "Old P.": "The grossest single piece of injustice that I remember was the order for a class to fence in the snow because 'Old P' could not find out who made a noise in his fencing room," Hardin wrote. "The result of this piece of barbarism was almost total blindness of {name illegible} & sickness of other cadets."[42]

"Old P." also taught Spanish, prompting Hardin to describe his short-comings in that foreign language as "a gross outrage upon the Institution." Hardin charged that what Spanish grammar he and fellow students learned came almost exclusively through their own efforts. "He {'Old P.'} was utterly incompetent. He was the Butt & laughing stock of my class & the next class."[43]

Like most of his contemporaries, Hardin retained his youthful admiration for General Winfield Scott, the hero of the War of 1812 and the guiding genius behind the march from Vera Cruz to Mexico City during the Mexican War. Scott took "great interest" in the cadets and visited every summer, winning admiration "on account of his size and military reputation."[44]

Hardin graduated with the Class of 1859, an event recalled by underclassman Morris Schaff, who joined in the loud roar of cheering when Hardin's name was called, his popularity "plainly manifest."[45] "Had I been called on to select from all his class the man likely to reach the highest honors as a soldier, I should certainly have chosen Hardin," Schaff recalled.[46]

More than two decades after leaving West Point, Schaff met Hardin once again, in 1882 when the latter visited the Academy and Schaff was serving on the Board of Visitors: "He {Hardin} came to West Point, and together we walked to Fort Putnam, and to that beautiful spot where so many of the friends of our youth were lying, the West Point Cemetery. I discovered then, what I had not fully perceived as a cadet, the simplicity, the modesty, and the natural sweetness of his nature."[47]

One of the most revealing letters Martin ever wrote, in part a sincere expression of his deep patriotism, was composed on February 21, 1859, as he approached the end of his West Point ordeal. The soon to be commissioned officer wrote the letter to his dearest friend, the former slave and current Walworth family servant, Dolly Smith, in Saratoga Springs. The letter is remarkable in that it documents the deep ties of affection between the young man and this African-American woman, only a few years older, in a time when racial discrimination was the norm in both the North and the South:

Dear Dolly,

It is on the eve of Washington's Birthday, one that should arouse the dormant blood of every true lover of his country, every appreciator of true worth, manliness, talent & patriotism. Moreover he was the embodiment of warrior talents: If there is ought to make a young man love the army, it is that such noble and talented men as our country has seen have shed their blood in its armies.

But it would appear more dignified and truly devoted to our Country to employ his life in cultivating the arts of peace thinking only of war and its accompaniments when his Country is insulted, its honor, rights, or Soil invaded. A few months finish my school days and my school education, all the advantages wealth or position could give have been lavished upon it. It is to be hoped I will obtain a diploma next June from the Academy, second to none in the world. Even Englishmen acknowledge the thoroughness and advantages of it.

But it must be remembered life is only begun at twenty-one. Whether an army life is the one I should pursue is the question. Doubtless the full time, eight years from my entrance here will have to be served in it. {Two words illegible} three years' Service for the advantage of an education. However, we will drop this subject here which can be discussed next Sumner after I get home.

The whole of the Winter has passed along quietly, smoothly without any unexpected event arising either to raise or depress the Spirits. To be sure, all our young ladies have married or in some less natural mode conveyed themselves away, leaving us disconsolate in this respect, but as I am not much taken with ladies whilst my studies are to learn, good books to be read, or exciting riding to be performed. My heart is not quite desolate but in the intervals between going to bed and getting asleep my manly fancy will at times take the train of pleasing imagination instead of the dates of the Roman or Napoleonic battles upon which I am endeavoring to fix my thoughts. So [illegible] progress in learning, we feel how little we really know of the endless quantity of each kind in which the world abounds.

Read the history of America. Think you know everything that

could be said about it, but . . . the next book you meet is larger and contains more events in the life of one Revolutionary hero than were found in the entire volume you just read: Thus you perceive the common saying, "The more we learn, the less we feel we have accomplished," is verified.

Not being sufficient leisure last evening to finish this effusion I take the present as the first to do so. Our band gave us a serenade this morning early but I was too sleepy to listen very attentively. My time is too invariably disposed to admit of any interesting occurrence which would fall pleasantly upon your ear. Suffice it to say, we sleep between prescribed hours, take our meals at fixed times of determined duration, but not without marching in military style to & from the dining hall, recite or ride from 8 until 4, dinner {illegible}, gymnastics, parade, Study & bed . . ."[48]

Hardin then expounded upon his upcoming summer leave and rhapsodized how he would at last have time to pursue his interests, ride his horse Pete, and reacquaint himself with his Saratoga friends. Then he turned introspective again, writing:

It is to be hoped I will be more of a man, have more important thoughts. You know Saratoga is but little to my fancy, but there will be my sister's boys whom I have to teach Soldiering, horse riding and Frank {Frank Walworth, 8, his nephew} to swim, fish and all other Western accomplishments.[49]

In this long letter, Hardin also discussed at length his feelings toward beguiling females. The cadet cavalierly insisted to Dolly that he is a man more interested in study and good books than courting. These protests seem a little forced, especially when he expounded at length upon his current bachelorhood:

As to the young ladies, my thoughts about them are more under control, in short I am more of a bachelor than ever. You know my old Sweetheart is married. Of course I could not think of liking anybody for years yet. Most of my female friends are acting the above mentioned manner, very good one for three, but my earnest wishes for the happiness of their husbands. They say it is a very bad sign for a young person to declare they will never marry. I hope not. . . . It has come to me through some chance that Lemmy is quite taken with one of the ladies beyond the railroad; it strikes me he is the kind of man to know, vulgarly speaking, "Which side of his bread is buttered."[50]

In closing, Hardin complained about how family and friends are remiss in writing. He never says directly, but the impression is that, despite his air of maturity, he still misses home and family. Hardin mentions Grandma Clay in Jacksonville, an uncle, and others back in Illinois who only write on rare occasions.

Western people are so taken up with the business at hand they hate to write—as much to have a tooth pulled. It would be very pleasant to have Sister [Ellen] come down again before I leave and have you come along. It is a pleasant trip and not too far. We will see what can be done about it before May or June. . . . Give my love to Sister & kiss the babies. Yours truly, M. D. Hardin.[51]

Upon graduating West Point that summer of 1859, Hardin embarked on an extensive tour of Illinois and Kentucky, and even journeyed as far west as Kansas, although sadly he left no detailed account of his activities or impressions. Upon returning to the East, the young officer was enrolled in the School of Artillery at Fort Monroe, Virginia, located on the James Peninsula overlooking Chesapeake Bay.

This massive fortress oddly enough was the near neighbor of Port Comfort, a cluster of hotels and resorts that attracted many of the elites of the South. The atmosphere was certainly far removed from the monastic world of West Point. Historians Richard P. Weinert, Jr. and Colonel Robert Arthur, painted a vivid picture off the place and the time in their book, *Defender of the Chesapeake—the story of Fort Monroe*:

. . . Old Point Comfort was the most fashionable resort for the planters and statesmen from the southern states. Many of the wives and daughters of the members of Congress and of government officials spent the season at Fort Monroe . . . To the south, Old Point Comfort was the watering place of fashion and wealth that Saratoga was to the North.[52]

Hardin was delighted at his good fortune: "It was about the pleasantest station I ever had," he later wrote.[53] The young lieutenant hired a Negro boy as a personal servant and, with another officer, bought a small sailboat they christened "Ricochet," in which they cruised Chesapeake Bay in their idle hours.

Even though he was only a lieutenant, Hardin had finally gained admittance to the American officer corps, becoming a junior member of that select fraternity and quickly discovering that he enjoyed the company and the camaraderie of his brother officers. Even the commander of Fort Monroe, the Mexican War veteran Major Joseph Abel Haskins (later promoted to brigadier general in the Civil War), joined Hardin and the other junior officers in the recreation room.[54]

"One of our principal sources of amusement was billiards," Hardin recalled fondly. "I remember that Major Haskins . . . who had only one arm {lost in the assault at Chapultepec Castle outside Mexico City}, was the best player. He was certain to pocket anything which could be pocketed. . . . All of us were fond of a dark brandy which we bought at Hampton. I have never seen or tasted [its] like since."[55]

The young men often took advantage of the post's courtesy buggy and team, making frequent forays to nearby Norfolk, a major naval base and home to several of the nation's most powerful warships. There they caroused late into the night and learned to love the delectable flavor of "the deep water oysters of Norfolk."[56]

One foray almost ended in tragedy. "There was some considerable drinking," Hardin later admitted. "On one of our sprees, Sinclair and I had a desperate struggle where my skill with the sword & strength stood me in good stead."[57]

Of course, life at Fort Monroe was not all sailboat excursions and drinking sprees. Hardin had to buckle-down as he learned the arcane skills of the artillery officer. He found the School of Artillery challenging and interesting, and became familiar with the latest and most powerful rifled cannon capable of firing an explosive shell to a distance of 4,000 yards. War was rapidly becoming a contest of technology and industry, as would be grimly documented by the enormous casualties incurred during the coming conflict.

Garrison routine at Fort Monroe was shattered in October of 1859 when news arrived that a force of twenty heavily armed men had attacked the Federal Arsenal at Harper's Ferry in western Virginia. Notorious Abolitionist John Brown of "Bloody Kansas" fame led the terrorists bent on igniting a slave revolt against their white masters. A slave insurrection, long feared by the white South, seemed imminent.

Artillery Lieutenant Hardin was ordered to proceed immediately to the scene of what was later viewed as the match that ultimately ignited the fire of the Civil War. Harper's Ferry was in chaos. Several thousand armed whites had flooded into the riverside community after hearing the wildest rumors of what the Abolitionists might next attempt.[58] In Hardin's personal papers at the Chicago Historical Society is a brief postwar note in which he described his involvement in this dramatic episode:

> About the first of December 1859 the John Brown Raid on Harper's Ferry occurred; an artillery major & I think three companies of artillery were sent from Fortress Monroe to Harper's Ferry to retake the arsenal, which John Brown had taken. When we arrived there, we found Lieut. Col. R.E. Lee . . . in command. A company of Marines had arrived just before we did, and had been ordered to take the Water Tank {fire house}—a brick building one story high & about 12 feet around. Taking a ladder the Marines rammed the door & took John Brown & his followers (five or six) prisoners . . .
>
> There were reports that Brown had thousands of followers in the neighborhood. The troops were ordered to remain. L. Col. R.E. Lee put me on his staff & ordered me to ride around the country and report on the [methods?] of defending the Arsenal & {I} found the Heights commanding the place. . . . I reported to Col. Lee that they should be held. Subsequently, Genl. R. E. Lee's {Confederate} command took these heights three times, the Union commanders never seeming to have recognized their value. M.D.H.[59]

Sadly, Hardin's bare-bones recap of that momentous day in American history leaves us with far more tantalizing questions than answers. Did Hardin meet the wounded John Brown who was then Lee's prisoner? Did he speak with the Marines who had assaulted the Fire House, or the young Lt. Jeb Stuart, who was serving as an aide during the action to Robert E. Lee? Did he recognize at the time the historical significance of the raid? Did he view Brown as a liberator or as a terrorist? All the answers are left to our imagination.

If young Hardin failed to see the importance of the John Brown Raid—and his subsequent execution—at the time, many of his contemporaries were equally blind. Fellow West Pointer and Hardin admirer, Morris Schaff, put the "upheaving event"[60] in proper context decades later, writing: "How little we cadets at West Point foresaw what the death of that tall, gaunt, grey-bearded and coldly gray-eyed man meant . . . that the trap of the gallows creaking beneath him was the dying wail of an age."[61]

Indeed, in a few short years thousands of Union soldiers would be marching to a rousing tune called "John Brown's Body," until its lyrics were changed to gain a more respectable veneer and it become "The Battle Hymn of the Republic."

CHAPTER 7

ADVENTURES FAR WEST

S oon after Lieutenant Hardin reported back to Fort Monroe
following the Harper's Ferry episode, a new entirely different
opportunity for adventure appeared in the form of a letter addressed to him
from a fellow officer stationed in Washington.

Hardin's acquaintance reported that a major army expedition was then
being organized to transport 300 new recruits 2,700 miles up the Missouri
River to Fort Benton, Montana. From there, at the headwaters of the river,
they would continue to travel by ox-drawn wagon across a new road—not
yet complete—winding 500 miles across the Continental Divide and terminating in Walla Walla on the Columbia River, Washington Territory. The
Western adventure Hardin had long dreamed about now seemed within
grasp, and he wasted no time in applying to join the expedition.[1]

Washington issued the necessary orders sometime in late April 1860.
Soon Brevet 2nd Lieutenant Martin D. Hardin arrived in St. Louis, the great
Gateway to the Far West, where the expedition was being formed at Jefferson Barracks under the command of Major George A.H. Blake, a weathered
old dragoon who had served in the Seminole Wars, the Mexican Wars and
various Indian campaigns. They would embark on three steamboats with 300
badly needed recruits assigned to the isolated outposts of the Northwest.[2]

On his arrival in St. Louis, the 23-year-old Hardin was surprised to
learn that Jefferson Barracks was under the command of 64-year-old Colonel Bonneville, the hero of his youth, whose adventures "have been so delightfully sketched by Washington Irving."[3] Twenty-two years later, Hardin
wrote about his encounter with the Western explorer in *The United Service
Magazine:* "With age {64 when Hardin met Bonneville} his eccentricities

had increased so that by that time he was a living curiosity. . . . His favorite and oft-repeated advice to each and all of us was to learn to do without salt; he had not forgotten his sufferings for want of it when in his youth he was lost among the Indians."[4]

Just before the Blake Expedition departed for their voyage up the Missouri River, the Acting Inspector General of the Army, Colonel Joseph E. Johnston, personally inspected the contingent.[5] Hardin failed to note whether Johnston made an impression at the time, but he and the entire nation were soon to recognize the name of the officer who became one of the most respected Confederate generals in the Civil War.

Before leaving St. Louis, the expedition's officers were given three months advanced pay. Hardin recalled: "Unfortunately for me I had invested most of my advance pay . . . in saddles, fishing tackle, ammunition, etc, and with a rascally 'tooth carpenter' to whose industry rather than skill I am indebted for the only bad teeth in my head."[6]

On May 3, the men of the expedition boarded the 350-ton *Spread Eagle*, a side-wheeler, and the *Chippewa* and *Key West*, much smaller "mountain boats" equipped with stern paddles. Lt. Hardin and his men were quartered on the *Spread Eagle* commanded by Captain LaBarge. Hardin was among the ten officers assigned to the expedition. Several of the junior officers were former classmates, including Brevet Lt. Edwin H. Stoughton, the former sword brawler (who would later be famously captured by John Mosby a Fairfax Court House, Virginia).[7]

On the cargo deck the men secured the wagons, saddles, mule packs, and assorted gear for the anticipated journey on the new road across the Continental Divide linking Fort Benton with Walla Walla. That formidable project, dubbed the Mullan Road, was underway under the direction of its architect, Captain John Mullan of the 4th U.S. Artillery. The previous year, the nimble steamboat *Chippewa* had gone upriver winding through nests of boat-killing snags to within 17 miles of Fort Benton. This was a record, making her the crack boat on the river. Now Blake's Expedition hoped to best that mark by actually reaching Fort Benton, where they would then embark on the new road.[8]

The expedition was deemed significant enough to merit coverage in the *New York Times*, whose correspondent on the scene reported on the "Mountain Fleet's" May 3, 1860 departure from St. Louis:

Our departure was the signal for a slight demonstration on the part of the good people of St. Louis, who, as we passed along the river, signified their good wishes by cheers, to which we replied in a similar manner, and also by the discharge of the small mountain battery with which these steamers are provided . . . the whole number of souls on board the three steamers amounted to six hundred and thirty-eight—made up of United States troops, officers of the Indian Department, officers and crews of the steamers. {The steamboats} were freighted, in addition to the baggage of the troops and their five months' supply of rations, with the Indian annuities of the Sioux, Crow, Blackfeet and Flathead tribes besides the trading goods of the {American} Fur Company . . .[9]

In the journey up river the officers and men came to admire Pierre Chouteau, Jr., president of the American Fur Company, who had been contracted by the army to insure the safe passage of the troops and supplies. In the weeks ahead, many of the officers and men aboard the little fleet would come to like and admire this descendant of French fur trappers. Hardin described him as a "man of great force of character and fertility of resource, and he was a decided acquisition in every way."[10]

Moving upriver in those first days was slow and laborious. In part this was due to the dangerous shifting sandbars and underwater snags of the Missouri River; these obstacles could not only delay a steamboat, on numerous occasions they spelled their death. In addition, the steamboats had left St. Louis before melting snows in the distant mountains had flowed downstream to deepen the channel.

The *Spread Eagle* was an impediment to making good time. The much larger side-wheeler, which drew six feet of water under her keel, frequently ran aground on a sandbar or had to be moored on the bank to repair or clean its engines. From the beginning of the voyage her captain, LaBarge, knew that the larger boat would never make the trip all the way to the head of navigation. At some point around halfway to the goal, the plan was to unload the soldiers and what cargo remained aboard the *Spread Eagle* and transfer it to the two smaller mountain boats. They would continue to Fort Benton.

Hardin recalled one major incident involving the *Chippewa*, writing:

Our steamboats were all high-pressure, and on account of mud in the water, the boilers had to be cleaned frequently, which, as well as wood-cutting, required us to lay by. The boiler of the *Chippewa* gave out and had to be patched. The engineers worked at this three days and nights continuously. The chief engineer of the *Spread Eagle*, who had charge of all repairs, was a very skillful and experienced workman. But for him we would have been compelled to leave on the way one or more of our boats.[11]

During the early going, the passing scenery was rather dull. But the tedium was offset for Hardin after he became acquainted with First Lieutenant August Valentine Kautz. This remarkable officer was a German-born intellectual, fluent in both English and German, and well-prepared for the river voyage with the purchase of a store of good books in both languages, ranging from Shakespeare to abstruse scientific works. The cultured Kautz had just returned from Europe and certainly ranked as one of the more interesting officers assigned to the expedition. He and Hardin would spend many hours in each other's company during the coming months.[12]

Kautz was progressive in his views on the Native Americans; he was, in fact, married to an Indian woman, which in Western slang made him a "squaw man." But, unlike a number of frontier officers, Kautz advocated a policy of respect and compassion for the native tribes, despite having been wounded twice in combat against the tribes of the Northwest. This viewpoint was not shared by many contemporaries, either military or civilian. His tolerance and moderation were reflected in a letter he wrote a friend describing a mutual acquaintance in very positive terms: "I saw Mr. Gosnell, who also has volunteered to look after my Indian friends. I like his views about Indians. He is down on Indian killing."[13]

We can only speculate what Hardin thought of his fellow officer's views on race. The author suspects he was sympathetic based on his close friendship with African-American Dolly Smith and his respect for his stepbrother, Father Clarence Walworth, an outspoken friend of the Indian all his life. Perhaps Kautz spoke to Hardin about his wife, "Kitty" (Tenas Puss) and their bi-racial children. Their plan to educate their Indian offspring the same as "Boston children" only elicited incredulous laughter from one of Kautz' acquaintances, Dr. Berrien, who "ridicules the idea of their turning out like others."[14]

While Lieutenant Kautz pondered his tomes, the non-readers aboard pursued more plebian pleasures such as whiskey drinking. The men were well-supplied in that regard; the best of the rye went for a $1 a gallon. Later on, Hardin recorded how the men were reduced to consuming the "17-cent commissary whiskey."[15] Despite his tee totaling late father, Colonel Hardin, and his equally abstemious stepfather, Chancellor Walworth, Lieutenant Hardin imbibed with the others, claiming he enjoyed the cheap rot-gut the most. When not drunk, the expedition members indulged in other pursuits, according to the young officer's recollections:

> The sources of amusement were cards for those who like a "quiet game of draw" or whist, hunting, and studying the channel . . . the study of the current is a great means of occupation; the eye soon becomes accustomed to select the true channel. The pilots of these Missouri River boats (veritable tyrants) are most expert in selecting the best channel . . . and most skillful in avoiding the snags and sawyers, which obstruct the channel in every bend.[16]

Another fascinating personality among the expedition's officers was Assistant Surgeon, Captain James Graham Cooper, a thirty-year-old New York doctor, who was, by avocation, a serious and respected naturalist, ornithologist, zoologist and etymologist. Young Hardin and the other officers jokingly referred to him as the "bug doctor."[17] The inquisitive Cooper would spend much of his time searching for unusual fauna and flora. Cooper proved a favorite among the young officers who enjoyed seeking out unusual specimens for the "bug doctor" to identify. Hardin and several of his fellow officers were also not above playing a prank on the learned Surgeon Cooper:

> Whenever an officer went hunting or fishing he made it a point to find something for our "bug doctor" to name. Naturally the wags among us amused themselves at the doctor's expense . . . when one of our officers presented the doctor with a large black bug without legs, he studied it for several days, and was about giving it a new

fine-sounding name, when he was informed it was a common "tumble bug" with legs pulled off.[18]

James Graham Cooper is remembered today as a pioneer naturalist who gathered significant collections of flora and fauna during his days as an Army surgeon on the frontier. Prior to the Blake Expedition, Cooper accompanied several railroad surveying parties collecting specimens for the Smithsonian Institute. Cooper eventually became Director of the California Academy of Sciences.[19]

Cooper was only one of several expedition members to make a mark later in life. Civilian passenger William Jacob Hays was a 30-year-old New York artist possessing a talent for vivid and accurate wildlife paintings. His portrait of a wounded buffalo, composed during the Blake Expedition, may still be seen at the American Museum of Natural History in New York City. By 1875, the year of his untimely death at age 45, experts rated Hays as "one of the most able painters in the country."[20]

Captain Cooper, acting as a correspondent for *Century Magazine*, noted to his readers that Hays and another artist aboard were sure to bring back "treasures of art" from the voyage. "They have furnished the fleet with a banner, the design being a *buffalo courant, unsauvage rouge chassant,* on a field tert, or a red Indian chasing a buffalo, with the motto *Americain,* 'Fort Benton or Burst.'"[21]

Young Hays certainly didn't fit the profile of an effete Eastern artist, but rather expressed a bellicose nature in a letter to his father just before the expedition left St. Louis, writing: "There is some chance of trouble with the Sioux as they are dissatisfied with last year's pay, but as our party numbers 600 men {in actuality no more than 350 soldiers}, I think they will find it dangerous to molest it; however, I hope they will try it."[22]

The expedition reached Sioux City, Iowa, where the water began steadily rising. Beyond this point was the last substantial white settlement on the Missouri. Their next stop was the isolated frontier outpost Fort Randall, which they reached on May 27. Surgeon Cooper noted the event in a letter East:

There the full band of the Fourth Artillery greeted our arrival with harmonious strains, and cheered us, as we again started towards the wilderness, with the echoes of "Home, Sweet Home" and "The Girl I Left Behind Me." A short distance above, we passed an Indian camp, there the savage costumes, wild whoops, and cramped skin lodges gave us a foretaste of that wilderness we were soon to enjoy.[23]

Game soon became plentiful. Buffalo in small herds or singly were often seen on the riverbank or crossing the wide Missouri. These huge animals afforded targets for all the amateur sportsmen on the nearest boat. "In spite of the terribly bad marksmanship, a tough old bull occasionally succumbed," Hardin recalled.[24] Few at that time realized that the buffalo would nearly be exterminated in less than 20 years.

Hardin was one of the most avid and effective hunters among the expedition. He left the steamboat for frequent forays in the surrounding wilderness, stalking deer, elk and buffalo as a means to supplement their basic ration of canned beans, pickles and desiccated vegetables. His hunting companions were often the expedition's two professional hunters: a half-breed named Joe and a full-blooded Native American called Cadott. They schooled young Hardin in the best tactics to down the formidable buffalo or slay the aggressive and unpredictable grizzly, which they would soon encounter upriver.[25]

The young Brevet 2nd Lieutenant was an apt pupil, having already learned the basics of hunting and woodcraft as a young boy roaming the Illinois prairies, and later the game-rich Adirondacks in upper New York State. Throughout his life, Hardin proved a skilled and enthusiastic hunter, and those early adventures in the Far West were pure joy:

Early each morning the hunters landed and moved up the river, and, taking all the short cuts possible, killed such game as came in their way, and packed it on their shoulders to the river-bank, where they left it for the small boats sent out from the passing steamboats to pick it up. . . . On one occasion I was out with Joe, when we sighted in open timber a large herd of elk about a half-mile distant. I asked Joe how we could get near enough for a sure shot. He told me, to follow him and do as he did. Joe stood perfectly still watching the elk. One by one the members of the herd began to graze. Finally the last old buck raised his head into a small tree to browse. Instantly Joe begin a noiseless but rapid advance. The moment he noticed any member of the herd cease eating, he stopped and remained as still as one of the . . . shrubs. The disturbed elk beginning to eat again, Joe advanced as before, and thus he was not thirty yards from a full-grown buck when he fired. He got this one, and running into the herd, he turned several towards me so that I disabled one.[26]

Grizzlies were the unchallenged lords of all they surveyed in the vast western wilderness of the upper Missouri River. In the evening, the professional hunters undoubtedly regaled the tenderfoots with hair-curling tales of the fearsome animals that could weigh 1,400 pounds and run fast enough to overtake an elk in full flight.

Hardin recalled in detail the story of when expedition members first met the great and fearsome animal. One day, Hardin recalled, how one of the expedition's officers and a chief engineer from the *Spread Eagle* returned from the hunt harried and exhausted. They told their harrowing story, which began as they rested under a tree near the riverbank. In Hardin's words, they then glimpsed in the distance what appeared to be two large buffalos moving rapidly towards them:

> Both prepared for a shot. But when the animals came close enough to distinguish them the hunters recognized them to be two full-grown grizzles. . . . An animated discussion arose. . . . The engineer was for "lighting out" at double-quick, but the officer, being armed with a Sharp's breech-loading rifle, was for a stand. As he prevailed, the engineer slipped off his boots and made ready to climb the tree. When the bears came within range, he, forgetting his gun, made haste to mount the tree. The officer prepared to shoot, but being undoable to determine which bear to kill, or possibly attacked with the "bear fever," he . . . dropped his gun and made good time up the tree . . . the two monsters came on at a lope, and without so much as casting a glance up the tree, went into the brush beyond.[27]

Buffalo was the most prized prey for food, as well as sport, and Hardin found its meat especially savory. Revealingly, however, Lieutenant Kautz refrained from joining the buffalo killing frenzy. He saw no sport or pleasure in shooting helpless buffalo fording the river. He confided to his diary: "Wolves afford me pleasure, as also bears, but buffalo seem so helpless, and die so hard."[28]

While moored near the mouth of the Milk River on June 22, expedition members witnessed their first huge herd: "A herd of buffalo was crossing the Missouri, just below the mouth of this river," Hardin wrote. "It continued to cross night and day whilst we were there, and was still crossing when we left {three days later}. The herd was at least a half-mile wide where it entered the river. One can readily believe that this herd contained a million or more."[29]

Sometime around then the decision was made to send the 350-ton *Spread Eagle* back to St. Louis. The large side-wheeler drew way too much water to proceed further upstream. In short order, Lt. Hardin and his company transferred to the smaller and nimbler *Key West* for the remainder of the voyage.

Further upriver at Fort Pierre, Hardin saw his first free-roaming Indians, proud members of the Sioux who had come to receive their annuities and supplies for the year. Hardin recalled his impressions many years later, expressing his contempt when he saw how the Indian braves treated their women as beasts of burden:

> The Sioux we saw at Fort Pierre were fair specimens of the wild Indian. They were not very friendly, our numbers being our best safeguard. Here for the first time I noticed the subordinate position of the Indian women. The Indian supplies were unloaded from the boats to the shore near the river by our boats' crews. It is nearly two hundred feet up a steep bank from where these supplies were unloaded to the level plateau where are {found} Indian storehouses and village. Up this steep bank the women carried much of their supplies. I remarked one old woman carrying what I estimated to be two hundred pounds. She had a strap passed around her pack (which rested on her back) and around her forehead. She was about four feet six inches high, very squarely built with very small feet and very pigeon-toed.[30]

Government annuities to the Western tribes was denounced as a sham in a dispatch to *Century Magazine* by Hardin's fellow officer, Asst. Surgeon Cooper. He was cynical, believing that the tribes came to receive the tribute primarily to eat free and laze about in the shadow of the soldiers' fort.

"Indeed, the annuities to the great Dakota nation are so small when divided among their thousands, that many bands disdain to receive them, and were at the time of the distribution off on a war party against the Crows, which they considered more likely 'to pay'."[31]

One wonders if Cooper had discussed the issue with one of the passengers, Indian Agent Colonel Alfred J. Vaughan, who was in transit to the Blackfoot Agency. According to Lieutenant Kautz, Hardin's friend, the Indian Agent was "a jovial old fellow, who had a very fine paunch for brandy, and when he could not get brandy would take almost anything, which would make drunk (sic) come . . . He had a pretty young squaw for a wife."[32]

At one point during the journey Hardin and the other expedition members learned that an obscure Sioux chief named Sitting Bull was on the warpath with a large party of warriors planning to ambush an army surveying party. Sitting Bull ultimately failed in his attempt to locate and destroy the surveyors that year; he would be infinitely more successful 16 years later on the Little Big Horn, when he and Crazy Horse eradicated George Armstrong Custer's command.[33]

Soldier bullets killed far fewer Indians than European diseases, for which the Native Americans had no immunity. Hardin saw the impact near Fort Berthold, which the expedition reached on June 11. Here lived the Arickarees (Arikaras), a once great tribe, now decimated by smallpox and other diseases brought by white men, and the ceaseless depredations of other warlike tribes who preyed upon the survivors. "We were told that the smallpox was brought to this tribe by some blankets which had been purchased 'at a bargain' in New York and shipped as Indian supplies," Hardin wrote.[34]

The ravages of disease had literally driven some of the Arickarees to madness and suicide. Hardin was taken to the summit of a hundred-foot precipice overlooking the Missouri River near their camp, where he was told: "Many Indians attacked with the dread disease had leaped . . . into the roaring flood below."[35] At the time Hardin visited the Arickarees they had been reduced to a shadow of their former numbers and strength, numbering at most a dozen young warriors and three hundred women, old men and children. "The women were completely demoralized having lost about all the sense of chastity they ever possessed," Hardin wrote. "A tribe once one of the strongest in the far northwest was now one of the weakest."[36]

Fifty miles upstream, the expedition encountered another formerly great tribe, the Mandan, who had also been devastated by European diseases. Hardin estimated that the Mandan numbered only a few hundred, a pathetic fraction of their former population. The survivors, however, impressed Hardin by their bearing and grace, even though they could only muster around 50 warriors. He wrote:

> . . . these retained the bold bearing and magnificent physique of a
> dominant tribe. I have never seen handsomer specimens of the
> human form than were common to these warriors. They wore
> their hair in long plaits, which reached to the ground. They gave
> us a scalp-dance, having one fresh scalp for the occasion. Though
> so perfectly formed, and as active as cats and slippery as an eel (they
> were all well-greased, as well as gorgeously painted), these warriors
> were not so strong as the white laborer. We got up a wrestling
> match between one of these warriors and one of our stevedores.
> Our man would, by sheer strength, throw the Indian, but he could
> neither keep the Indian down nor keep on top.[37]

Above the Milk River, the Mountain Fleet encountered a series of rapids, which required the soldiers to go ashore and employ tow-ropes to drag the boats over the shallows. Sometimes a hundred men strained on the hawser, stumbling along the muddy bank or in the shallows of the river. The process, Hardin explained, was not much different from when the early fur traders had "cordelled" their keel boats up the same river before the advent of steam. The work was brutal and back-breaking.[38]

If Hardin had any illusions about the Wild West, they were surely dispelled following a showdown between one of the imperious steamboat pilots and a fellow army officer, Lt. George Carr. The latter Hardin described respectfully as "a large, fine-looking man with a mind and will for a soldier."[39]

Carr was drilling his company ashore while the wood-cutting parties gathered fuel. When the task was complete, the pilot of the *Key West* blew the boat's whistle in preparation for departure. The steamboat pilot was determined to cast-off immediately even though many of the soldiers would be left stranded ashore. "Lieutenant Carr was standing on the front part of the hurricane deck, with a carbine in his hand," Hardin remembered. "After the second whistle the pilot said he was going to leave, and rang the engine bell accordingly. When he said he was going to start, Lieutenant Carr told him to stop, but the pilot paid no attention to him. Lieutenant Carr turned to the pilot and threatened to shoot him if he did not wait for the men on shore; whereupon the pilot drew a pistol and fired, the bullet striking the lieutenant in the neck. The wound was painful but not dangerous. Lieutenant Carr took charge of the boat and had the pilot locked-up."[40]

Danger was a constant companion. Hardin's most harrowing experience came during one of his numerous hunting excursions ashore to secure meat for the expedition. He took a squad of soldiers with him aboard one of the yawls and landed his party on an island covered with hazel and brush. They made their way down to the far end, hoping to ambush buffalo that had been observed using the island as a way-station as they crossed the Missouri River. Hardin recalled:

> . . . we went cautiously through the brush, following the buffalo trails. I led. As I came out into a small opening near the lower end of the island I met a buffalo bull, face to face, certainly not ten paces away; the ground being wet and soft, we had not heard each other. It is difficult to say which was the most astonished. I and my whole squad fired, but, being victims of the "buffalo fever," we missed him clear though he certainly looked bigger than a barn door. The bull and those following . . . then wheeled and ran back into that portion of the river nearest us and swam for the shore, which was about one hundred yards distant. We fired at them as they climbed the bank; one which was mortally wounded ran more than a hundred yards, where we found him; three musket-balls had passed through both his side and heart.[41]

On the last day of the journey, only a day's steam from Fort Benton, located 50 miles upriver, the *Key West* was pushed to its limits. The craft churned up the narrow river, the paddle wheel churning a white plume in its wake: "We fed her fires with cracker-boxes, pork-barrels, and everything combustible on board," Hardin recalled years later. "This made the old boat shake and palpitate like a wind-broken horse. Many of us who had experienced steamboat races on the Ohio and Mississippi enjoyed a taste of the old excitement."[42]

At this point, the Missouri River was only a hundred yards wide and the current ran hard and strong. Then, in the midst of this final dash to Fort Benton, a soldier fell overboard. Immediately, two others dove into the tumult to rescue him. The first drowned as he, in a panic, tried swimming upstream against the current. Only one of the would-be rescuers emerged from the current nearly a mile below where he had entered the water. The tragedy undoubtedly tempered the men's elation at finally completing the long journey.[43]

On July 3, the *Key West* and the *Chippewa* hove into view of Fort Benton, Dakota Territory. They were greeted with cheers and a scattering of shots fired in the air. No steamboat had ever made it this far up the Missouri River. The first phase of the Blake Expedition had been successfully completed. Now they waited for Lt. Mullan's much anticipated arrival from across the mountains. To date the expedition had lost only two soldiers, both to the recent drowning. Plus Lt. Carr had been wounded in his altercation with the pilot, and several soldiers had deserted—probably hearing the call of the nearby gold fields.[44]

The Blake Expedition now had to wait at Fort Benton for Lt. Mullan's much-anticipated arrival from across the mountains, marking the opening of his 642-mile road to the headwaters of the Columbia River, Fort Walla Walla and points west. That winding track would take the expedition through some of the most spectacularly beautiful and rugged terrain in North America.

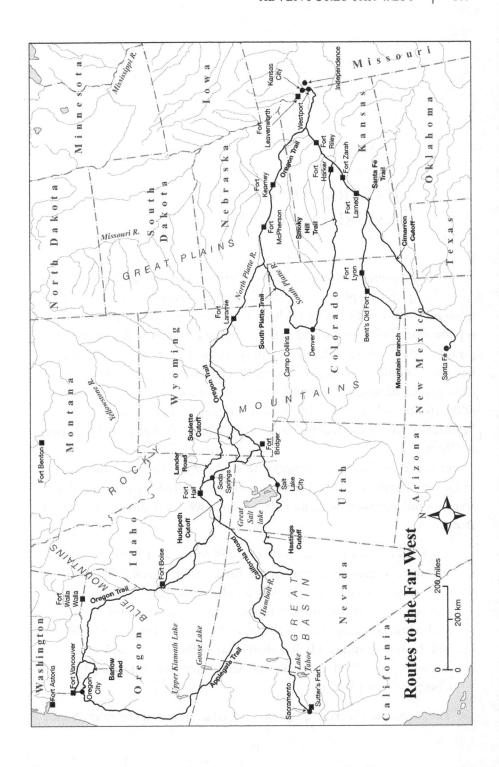

Routes to the Far West

CHAPTER 8

INTERLUDE IN THE AMERICAN EDEN

During his sojourn at Fort Benton, Dakota Territory, Hardin lived a pleasant life full of rich experiences forever stamped upon his memory. We can be fairly certain that young Hardin had no conception that this colorful world of free-ranging Native American tribes, the great buffalo herds, and the great empty landscape was to vanish within a few short decades. (Ironically, Martin D. Hardin would be among the audience when historian Frederick Jackson Turner announced the official end of the frontier while presenting his seminal paper, "The Significance of the Frontier in American History," at the 1893 World's Columbian Exposition in Chicago.)[1]

However, in the late summer of 1860, the Wild West was still a reality in Dakota Territory. There Hardin enjoyed an incredibly romantic landscape yet unblemished by roads, railroads and towns. Hardin described Fort Benton as:

> . . . a mud or adobe fort, similar in design to those built by our ancestors to protect themselves against Indian attacks. The fort walls were from twelve to twenty feet high, forming four sides of a square, about three hundred feet to a side; sheds along the inside of the low portions of the walls furnishing cover for the animals and the Indian stores. Higher sheds against the higher portions of the wall were divided up for residences for the American Fur Company's employees.[2]

The men of the Blake Expedition pitched a camp near the river about a mile above the fort near a high bluff providing a panoramic view of the surrounding country. In the weeks ahead the nearby Blackfeet, hearing of the arrival of their annuities, came by the thousands and established a city of tepees around the white Sibley tents of the soldiers. Hardin estimated that as many as eight thousand Indians gathered, including their large herds of calico ponies. Hardin often rode to the bluff at sunset to gaze upon the camp:

> Our camp with its white tents glistening in the clear atmosphere; the brown tepees a dark shade of the color of the prairie; the hundreds of horsemen herding their many-colored ponies; the bright river with its green fringe; the old adobe fort; civilized and uncivilized men encamped together—the combination formed a rare and peculiar picture.[3]

Hardin and the others lived an idyllic life while waiting for Mullan's arrival. They spent their days interacting with the Blackfeet, learning their customs, fishing the river, hunting and horse-racing. One day, they enjoyed the spectacle of thousands of Indians arriving in a great mass and crossing the Missouri River in small boats made of hide. "The women, children and other valuables were put into 'bull-boats' and towed across by the swimming horses and 'Bucks.' Lariats were used for attaching the horses to the boats; the men swam alongside of the horses to guide them," Hardin wrote.[4]

Hardin was impressed by the Blackfeet and their riding skills. He and other soldiers were treated to a "mounted drill" as the feathered and decorated braves galloped by atop their ponies. Their riding skill compared to the best-trained white cavalryman in Hardin's eyes.

Many of the soldiers and the Blackfeet enjoyed racing horses, both sides betting with great enthusiasm, and enjoying the excitement equally. Hardin, many years later, recorded on paper his impressions of the encounter: "They were at all times quite friendly, although they did not like the object of our expedition; were disposed to be amused; very curious, and most willing to exchange anything they owned, prizing their horses a little higher than their women. The worst trait that I remember was the abandonment of their helpless old."[5]

At the end of July, young Hardin was witness to the rather elaborate ceremony by which the grand chief of the Blackfeet, Little Dog, distributed the Indian supplies, which had been carried on the decks of the *Key West* and the *Chippewa*. The Chief insisted on personally presenting his people with the "gaily colored" blankets, calicos, sugar and flour. No Indian Department employee was allowed to partake in the ceremony. In Hardin's words:

> He arranged his people on the prairie in concentric circles, the oldest and principal chiefs forming the inner one; the next circle, separated about ten paces from the first, was occupied by lesser chiefs and warriors, noted for eloquence or war deeds . . . ; the third circle . . . was occupied by old warriors of little renown and very young ones—those who had passed their prime or had not yet distinguished themselves. About ten paces outside of this third circle was the first circle occupied by the females, wives of the principal chiefs and warriors. Some few of the favorite wives of the most noted chiefs were a little in advance of this line; each having a little space about here. All the other Indians, with the children, formed the next and outermost circle. After a speech such as one of our mayors or governors might make on such an occasion, Little Dog proceeded to distribute the supplies. He commenced with the inner circle, where he piled up everything in great profusion; then he selected special articles for each individual of the second circle, and did not neglect the young warriors of the third circle. He gave most bountifully to the favorite wives of noted chiefs, especially of gaily-colored blankets and calicoes. The "Hoi Polloi" he gave mostly sugar and flour.[6]

But of all the western tribes, the Nez Perce won Hardin's deepest admiration. A party of this tribe arrived at Fort Benton after having finished their annual hunt further east among the game-rich Yellowstone country. Lewis and Clark sixty years before had been equally impressed with these honest and courageous people. Hardin left us this impression of his memorable encounter with these princes of the west:

> They were the most intelligent Indians I saw on this trip; each warrior carried a rifle, while a number of bows and arrows were found with each party. Cadott, our Indian hunter, was the only other

Indian I saw carrying a rifle. We were told that these Nez Perce fortified their camps every night, and that twenty of their warriors (about the number in each party) were a match for all the Indians on this side of the mountains. . . . They certainly looked and acted as though they, rather than the Blackfeet, were masters of this country.[7]

One particularly interesting episode while awaiting Mullan's party from across the mountains involved a trip to the Great Falls, about 50 miles distant. The only negative was that Hardin and his small party were plagued by mosquitoes while camping at the landmark. Hardin later claimed that he had never been so pestered and plagued even in the great swamps of the South. Perhaps the magnificent scene that surrounded them there helped Hardin and his companions forget the suffering inflicted by the omnipresent "skeeters." Hardin recalled:

Here it {the river} first falls seventy feet, then flows quietly for a hundred yards, when it drops about twelve feet. Near these Falls, a few small trees and green shrubs cling to the crevices in the perpendicular sides of the canyon; the distance between the walls of the canyon at the point of fall is about three hundred yards. Standing at the bottom of the canyon . . . one witnesses a scene, which though not to be compared with that of Niagara . . . is one to be thoroughly appreciated by the eye, which has for months rested upon nothing more attractive than a muddy river flowing between banks lined with cottonwood, or a rolling prairie covered with sagebrush.[8]

On a subsequent foray into the encircling wilderness, Hardin and several other soldiers went out in pursuit of white-tail deer. The others, unused to navigating such a big country with few landmarks, soon admitted they were disoriented and lost, not even knowing the direction back to the fort. Apparently Hardin's youth on the Illinois prairie equipped him well to traverse these vast open spaces of the West; he took the lead, confident of their location and the route back to the fort. During their return, the small party of soldiers encountered a large band of armed Indian warriors.

Unfortunately in his account of the incident, he fails to identify the tribe, but wrote:

> When we arrived almost in sight of Fort Benton we met a large party of Indian warriors, fully armed. Their arms were single-barreled shotguns, the barrels cut to two feet in length, {and} bows and arrows. These Indians made signs for us to halt. We halted. They came all around us. Although we did not know their disposition, we knew it was best to appear as if it were friendly. They asked to see our guns. We at once handed them to them. They took the guns, cocked them, and aimed them at us. We, of course, treated this as a joke, but I cannot say we liked it. Finding we took things pleasantly they returned our guns and rode off, well-satisfied with their grim joke.[9]

Lt. John Mullan and his wagon train of road builders finally arrived at Fort Benton a month later than expected, and the Blake Expedition began last-minute preparations to embark on the final leg of the long journey.

On August 4, a straggling caravan of 150 pack mules, horses and 25 ox-drawn carts departed Fort Benton. They climbed ever higher into the great mountain fastness, where they followed Mullan's fabled road (really an improved track) to the Pacific Slope. Hardin noted that the nights grew ever colder and the wind blew steadily; on one occasion a terrific gust carried away their Sibley tents and strewed their belongings along the face of the mountain.[10]

Mules, being their cantankerous selves, provided both misery and amusement as the soldiers learned their many idiosyncrasies. "When you, for the first time, watch a packer, who, having blind-folded the mule, presses his knee against the side of the animal and draws the cinch until you think his {the mule's} ribs will certainly break, you heartily sympathized with the mule . . . but when you see the packer take off the blinder, nimbly spring aside to avoid the vicious kick he knows is coming, and you see the mule rush for the nearest tree, striking it with such force as to knock himself clear off his feet, fall over on his side, roll over his pack and kick himself free, you lost all sympathy with a pack-mule then and forever."[11]

That first day's march measured 26 miles, a terrible ordeal for the soldiers who had done very little marching for the past three months. The days were hot and the pace grueling. To encourage the men, Hardin and the other officers dismounted their horses and marched with their companies. Major Blake rode ahead to locate a likely camp for the night. When his straggling, exhausted command finally reached that point, they fell as if dead from the boot-blistering march. Hardin noted that it took another day of rest before the men were able to continue. Major Blake learned a lesson, and the long march was never repeated; the average day's march thereafter measured about 13 miles a day.[12]

Major Blake would normally stake out the camp by noon. His command would arrive on site about 2 to 4 p.m., a steady but realistic pace that still allowed the men plenty of time to rest, bath, fish or hunt in the late afternoon. "Only one grizzly was seen," Hardin recalled. "He was stampeded by a drummer-boy who happened to be some distance in advance of the command."[13]

Every day was challenging, requiring endurance and innovation. Hardin noted: "The hills were often steep, so that teams had to be doubled . . . at times the company on detail with the wagons applied the skill they had acquired ascending the mountains {probably meant river} to 'cordelling' the wagons up the steep ascents or checking their too rapid descent."[14]

On one day, the expedition made camp along the Prickly Pear River, where Hardin said they found "good wood, water and grass." Here they were visited by a Jesuit father from the nearby Indian mission located to serve the surrounding Flathead and Blackfeet tribes. He brought the officers a gift of fresh vegetables, a decided improvement on their typical diet of salt pork, hard crackers and beans.[15]

There in the clear mountain air distances were deceiving. Hardin remembered how they soon sighted a well-known landmark, Bird Tail Rock, which appeared less than a day's march away. Instead they didn't reach the foot of Bird Tail Rock for another week. The 300-foot-tall rock could be climbed by crawling up a series of narrow crevices. Hardin and a fellow officer were game to make the ascent:

> We met a herd of mountain sheep descending on the same ledge.
> As they met us, the leaders hesitated a moment as if to turn, when
> instinct, I suppose, telling them that to turn would be to precipitate

the whole band into the deep chasm to our left, they made a rush and scramble along the perpendicular rock on our right, and went racing over our heads. It was a wonderful sight, and one to take one's breath away. A misstep of a single goal would have been fatal to us. As soon as we got our nerves restrung, which seemed but a moment, the herd came into view on the open ground at the foot of the rock, yet they were several hundred yards away. We fired but missed; they were out of range before we could reload.[16]

After reaching the summit, Hardin and his companion were presented with a huge and stunning vista of mountains and plains. Looking back east, they could still glimpse the distant Missouri River. It was an incredible spectacle of natural beauty, which left them wordless. "It was one of the most extensive and grandest views in North America," Hardin later declared.[17]

In a few days the expedition was descending a gentle decline into the gorgeous depths of the Bitterroot Valley, where they paused for three days resting their stock and girding for the journey up the slopes of the Bitterroot Mountains. They followed a track made by Mullan along the twisting St. Regis Borgia, "a mountain torrent so tortuous in its course that we crossed it every few hundred yards."[18]

They reached the top and then began another easy descent to the Catholic Mission at Coeur d' Alene. Hardin was assigned to the wagon train at one point. This was arduous duty. The heavy prairie schooners were frequently mired in the ruts of the primitive road Mullan and his men had scratched out of the wilderness. The soldiers and their animals were physically tested to their limits by the ordeal.

But there were consolations. During his earlier crossing, Mullan had left several caches along the route for use during the return trip. These caches were rich in foodstuffs, but to the eventual detriment of the command they also included a good supply of whiskey. The men were constantly on the lookout for the caches as they trudged into the mountains.

Hardin had almost from the first known that his recruits, by and large, were a rather scruffy lot and quite disposed to drunkenness at every opportunity. Since the caches contained a supply of potent spirits, he and the other officers kept the boys under close watch. However, one company of soldiers managed to tap a cache without their officers' knowledge. The result was predictable. When Hardin's party came upon (Capt.) Landrum's wagon train it was stalled along the trail; most of the enlisted men sprawled about in various stages of drunken stupor:

> A few teamsters and one or two non-commissioned officers were up and trying to get things going, but most of the men could not be awakened at all. A whisky cache had been found the day before, and it had proved too much for all hands. It was my first and last experience of the total defeat of a command by "John Barleycorn." That Major Blake was mad, and that he expressed himself in vigorous English, can readily be imagined. We rolled the whole detachment into the ice-cold stream which flowed by, and very soon had the men on their feet again.[19]

This was beautiful country. At times during the march the caravan plodded along under the shade of giant redwoods; some of the trees measured five foot at the base and towered several hundred feet high. The expedition soon found a warm welcome when they visited the good Jesuit fathers at the Mission of the Sacred Heart, established at this location in 1846. The priests served the spiritual and educational needs of the Coeur d' Alene Tribe in what is now the state of Idaho. Hardin recalled their welcome: "We were also most noisily welcomed by the hundreds of 'coyote' dogs, half-cur and half-wolf, who seemed to make up their numbers for the lack of other domestic animals. These dogs were reputed to be able to steal a ham from under a cook's head without awakening him. Our experience confirmed this thieving reputation."[20]

At nearby Coeur d' Alene Lake, the expedition split into two commands: more than 150 men headed toward Walla Walla, while a smaller contingent, including Hardin, Lt. Kautz, and Dr. Cooper, headed for Fort Colville, Washington Territory. Their pack train managed to make nearly 18 miles a day despite the poor condition of most of the mules. At other times their progress was appreciably less due to the incredibly rugged terrain. Hardin recalled one particularly challenging obstacle, writing: "The ledge was so narrow, and the precipice to the right so deep, several of us got off our ponies to walk. We found we could neither walk nor crawl over. We crawled back to the place where we had dismounted and got on our ponies again. We learned then that a mule or Indian pony is as sure-footed as a man."[21]

The column made a pleasant camp near the Spokane Falls, where they encountered members of the Spokane tribe come to gather salmon above the falls. Hardin met a chief who had been educated at Union College, Schenectady, New York. This was the same institution attended by Hardin's stepfather Chancellor Walworth and his sons. The Spokane chief was "polite and attentive" to the white visitors until he learned they hadn't brought gifts. "This seemed to put him in a bad humor," Hardin said.[22]

All during the journey, Lt. Kautz liberally shared a jug of prune brandy with his companions. The liquor was a gift from the Jesuits at the Mission of the Sacred Heart. Each evening, they all looked forward to sampling the "Tuscannuggy," Hardin recalled. "I am sure I never enjoyed the contents of bottle, jug or barrel as I did my share of that little two-gallon keg," he wrote twenty years later.[23]

Upon reaching Fort Colville, they were greeted by its commander who had the unlikely name of Captain Pinckney Lugenbeel. During the next three days, Hardin and the others enjoyed the hospitality of the post. "We had a delightful visit; were most agreeably entertained by the officers and their families. There was a billiard table at the sutler's."[24] Hardin found it extremely interesting that every piece of furniture—including the billiard table—had been brought in piece by piece on the backs of pack animals and then reassembled at the post.

After a brief interlude, presumably spent largely at the said billiard table, Lt. Kautz led his party to Fort Walla Walla. They were now mounted on fresh horses, half-American and half-Indian ponies. On the evening of the first day of the trek to Walla Walla, the party encountered a large party of Indians, described by Hardin as "inclined to make trouble."[25] Unfortunately, as he was wont to do, Hardin failed to identify the tribe in his *Reminiscences*. He did leave a fairly detailed account of what transpired:

> Kautz, who led off, seeing at once our danger from the ugly disposition of the Indians, addressed them politely and drew out of the trail to let the Indians pass. We followed his example until it came to Dr. Cooper, who rode straight on. The Indians rushed their horses against him and threw him from his horse. Kautz insisted

upon our moving on without resenting the insult. We did so and thus probably saved ourselves from further injury . . .[26]

After this unpleasant encounter, the party rode on at a steady pace and passed through the Columbia desert without further incident. "Wood and water are very scarce on these plains," Hardin wrote. "For that reason I suppose every rock and ridge in the distance resembles a clump of trees or a glassy lake. Nature makes up here in delusions what she lacks in reality."[27]

When they arrived at Fort Walla Walla, a contingent of troops and a pack train commanded by one of Hardin's friends from West Point, Captain Marcus Reno, was preparing to leave the post. They were bound for the Snake Indian country where a party of emigrants had reportedly been attacked by a war party near old Fort Hall. The talk was that the "treacherous Snakes" had killed many whites, including women and children.

The relief column did not exactly gallop to the rescue with bugles blowing in the Hollywood tradition. Before they could hit the trail, Reno's men struggled mightily, loading the uncooperative mules with packs of provisions, water and ammunition. Nearly every man on the post was engaged in this tedious business. Their labor and their profanity was all in vain.

On the first night out from Walla Walla, Reno's mules stampeded and returned to the fort the next morning. Most of the mules shed their packs on trees and bushes, scattering the contents across the landscape. Hardin recalled how Reno's exhausted men had to round up the mules, retrieve the packs, and repeat the whole process. The battle between soldier and mules seemed eternal.[28]

Fort Walla Walla was a large post garrisoned by both infantry and cavalry. Here Hardin met many of his acquaintances from West Point, including Reno, Fitz Lee and Sol Williams. The officers at the outpost lived very Spartan lives. Their furniture consisted of trunks and packing boxes doubling as chairs, and a common pine table.

In September, Hardin traveled down the Columbia River by a small steamboat equipped with an extremely large paddle wheel to help power the boat as it rushed along the powerful current at nearly 30 miles an hour, a harrowing rate of speed in 1860. "The water of this river is very clear," Hardin wrote. "We could see great rocks apparently a few feet beneath the surface, but over which we rushed at railroad speed."[29]

They disembarked at Fort Dalles and the remaining men of the expedition set out for Fort Vancouver, passing through "the grand scenery of the Cascades of the Columbia." Hardin found Fort Vancouver to be "the handsomest and pleasantest post after Fortress Monroe that it has been my good fortune to visit."[30]

At this point, Hardin took the opportunity to visit nearby Puget Sound, Port Townsend and Fort Steilacoom. He then returned to Fort Vancouver and received his orders to join Company L, Third U.S. Artillery, stationed at Fort Umpqua on the Oregon coast. The most efficient route was to journey by coastal boat to San Francisco and then return by sailing coaster up the coast to tiny, isolated Fort Umpqua.

Post-gold rush San Francisco was to prove an adventure and a revelation for the young Hardin. He and several other officers had several days to kill before their coaster, the *Columbia,* left for Fort Umpqua. This gave the young men ample time to enjoy the delights—and perhaps the temptations—of this fabulous city on the bay, which seemingly burned down every few years, only to rise like the Phoenix in another, more sumptuous reincarnation. As Hardin remembered:

> I never enjoyed a visit to a city as I did this one, everything was so
> different from anything I had seen in the States. The restaurants
> were excellent. I had rooms at the Teham House . . . Open gam-
> bling had been stopped, but the only exchanges for business men,
> or clubs, where you could meet your friends and acquaintances,
> were the gorgeous drinking establishments. The most noted were
> the "Bank Exchange" and Barry & Patten's. . . . Many times I saw
> a "slug" (twenty-dollar gold piece) thrown on the counter, the
> whole of which was soon spent in treating the crowd . . . ; one
> would not be long in the "Bank Exchange" before he was intro-
> duced to about every one present. Drinks were a quarter apiece;
> this was the smallest coin in circulation . . .[31]

On the day the steamer *Columbia* departed San Francisco Bay, the weather had turned dark and menacing. Several of Hardin's newfound friends advised him to wait for another sailing, as the white caps were rolling across the South Spit at the Golden Gate. But, fearing to be left behind, he boarded the small steamer, commanded by Captain Bill Dall, said to be a reckless but skilled navigator. Whether young Hardin questioned whether Dall's skill might be cancelled by his recklessness is subject only to conjecture:

> We reached the mouth of the Golden Gate just as the sun was setting over the sand-hills; the breakers were still running literally mountains high, with muddy crests carried nearly to the north shore . . . As we approached this furious sea, we hoped the captain would wait till morning to cross, when it would have subsided somewhat. He was too impatient to wait a whole tide; he therefore ordered a full head of steam on, and we dashed in the . . . raging sea.[32]

On deck, Hardin sat on a bench with several other officers and ladies, one of whom was carrying a small baby in her arms. About 50 soldiers were located up toward the bow. The sea worsened and all the ladies went below except for the mother with the baby, who inexplicably remained topside despite the crashing waves and spray. Almost immediately afterwards, the *Columbia* headed straight into massive waves that broke over the little steamboat in a great flood. Hardin recalled:

> She stopped as though she had struck a rock, quivered, then rose like a sea-monster, her nose coming out, but her decks completely cleared by the great sea, which swept everything before it, tearing off hatchways, and carrying the sailors and soldiers from the forward to the after part of the ship, rushed down the hatchways and staircases, putting out some of the fires, and filling the cabin more than three feet deep with water.[33]

The powerful surge of water across the deck tore the baby from its mother's arms and carried it into the sea. Incredibly, moments later, the waves came back up over from the stern and carried the infant back onto the deck, where it floated toward the port rail in a two-foot stream of water; the steamer descended once more into a giant trough, and Hardin and another officer scrambled to snatch the child before it drifted once more into the tumultuous waters. They stumbled through the surging waters and, miraculously, rescued the baby just it was about to drift overboard once more.

"Having shipped so much water, even Captain Dall was alarmed," Hardin wrote. "He ordered the vessel put about, but the first turn towards the south brought another sea on board, fortunately not so heavy as the first. With true seaman's instinct the Captain ordered her ahead again, when we soon passed those dangerous, round rollers. Fortunately, no one was killed or lost overboard, though a number of the soldiers and sailors were badly injured."[34]

The *Columbia* proceeded north along the coast, making one stop at Humboldt Bay, where Hardin learned that a Lt. George Crook was leading troops in pursuit of some "bad Indians" who had escaped their Reservation. The locals also described how, "a harmless tribe of coast Indians had been massacred by whites on an island in this bay. One is not surprised that those on an adjoining reservation sought safety in flight."[35]

Hardin's final destination was Fort Umpqua—remote, isolated and lonely. It consisted of a two-story log blockhouse and barracks built in 1856 as the Rogue River War ended. This dismal little outpost was located on the north bank of the Umpqua River, two miles from where it emptied into the vast Pacific Ocean. The purpose was to guard the Siletz Indian Reservation, which stretched along 125 miles of Oregon coast, and prevent any hostiles from breaking out on a raid.[36, 37]

Not long after arriving at Fort Umpqua, the young lieutenant would discover that his main mission was not so much to protect innocent white settlers from the rapacious savages, but rather to shield the suffering, starving remnants of the various native tribes from ruthless white miners and settlers bent on their extermination.

CHAPTER 9

ARMAGEDDON BECKONS

Young Hardin's first command could hardly have been more insignificant, dismal or dreary than Fort Umpqua, Oregon Territory. Built in 1856, this frontier fort had only purpose: to guard the Siletz Indian Reservation where the Federal government had corralled the surviving Indians from the Rogue River War of a few years prior.[1] While the natives scraped out a pitiful existence, weeks would pass at the fort without a word from the outside world. This was the wettest military post in the west; nearly 70 inches of rain fell every year.[2] Often the days were cold, foggy and damp.

Boredom was as omnipresent as the rain. Only when a supply schooner made its appearance would Hardin and the small garrison have access to months-old letters and equally old newspapers from the States. Hardin described his situation in a letter to his mother dated January 4, 1861: "The news is very meager. We have no idea what is going on in the east until such a long time after it has happened, we had about as well not hear it at all. We are not much excited consequently are not so anxious about what is going to happen as those who are in the midst of it."[3]

Hardin also described in some detail for his mother the local Digger Indians, who speak "a jargon called 'Chinook'" and eat roots and fish. In the long months ahead, Lt. Hardin fought boredom and tried to keep his men busy while great events rumbled on the opposite side of the continent. Here in this rainy little outpost, they could only hear occasional echoes of the growing national crisis over Lincoln's election to the presidency.[4]

As young Lieutenant Hardin drilled his company of soldiers along the sandy, rain-swept Oregon coast, his mother and stepfather were deeply involved with the divisive aftermath of Lincoln's election in November of 1860. The South had threatened to secede from the Union if the "Black Republican" was elected, and now were carrying out that threat.

On the morning of March 4, 1861, Hardin's mother and stepfather, personally invited by President Lincoln and the First Lady, stood among the crowd of 25,000 to witness Sarah's old friend from Springfield be sworn-in as the nation's Chief Executive. Although the nation teetered over Armageddon, no blood had yet been spilled, no cannon fired. The United States flag still flew over Fort Sumter in Charleston harbor. Frail hope still flickered for a peaceful resolution to the looming confrontation.

The feisty and fashionable Mrs. Chancellor Walworth and her husband were at the very epicenter of the developing storm. Chancellor Walworth was horrified at the prospect of a civil war, and was a leader among the peace party urging compromise. Although not a supporter of slavery, he abhorred the Abolitionists, viewing them as rabid radicals determined to plunge the nation into a disastrous bloodbath over the slavery issue. But he remained staunchly Unionist, imploring his many Southern friends to draw back from the brink.

"Civil war will not restore the Union but will defeat forever its reconstruction," Chancellor Walworth told more than 100 prominent politicians from North and South during the Peace Conference conducted over three weeks at a hall in Washington's Willard Hotel in February 1861. Presiding over the distinguished conclave was former President John Tyler.[5] Delegate William Warner Hopping wrote his recollections of the doomed peace conference 30 years later:

> So the days went by: brilliant repartee, caustic irony and some sound logic from the northern side, the latter calling forth from the conservative south remonstrance, and from the ultra-south counter attack. Then came the last day when the speeches grew short, the situation more strained, and heart-sick honest men and true patriots prepared to go home and there await the next move. . . . Few were there, if any, who did not feel that compromise was no longer a sovereign remedy. Submission or war was the alternative.[6]

The compromise was sent to the United States Senate where it was rejected by a vote of 28 to 7; in the House of Representatives the measure never even made it to the floor.[7] War between the States seemed unavoidable.

Chancellor Walworth desperately sought to resurrect the spirit of Henry Clay, the Great Compromiser. He appealed to all Americans to remember the way the nation, North and South, had fought together against the British. In the spring of 1861, he wrote a fellow veteran of the War of 1812, Nicholas Rainey of St. Louis, recalling the shared sacrifice of that former conflict. *The New York Times* published Walworth's plea for reconciliation on March 21, 1861:

> Dear Sir: I was present at the battle of Beekman Town, and commanded the detachment which received the first fire from the British Army, just before the battalion of regulars, under Major Wool, wheeled into the road near me . . . from your description of it I have no doubt that you belonged to that gallant band, as stated in your letter & also saw poor Lieut. Runk as he was led off immediately after he received his death wound; and I distinctly recollect the night sortie from Fort Bowen by your gallant band of volunteers for that enterprise under the command of the brave Capt. McGlashan. And, I am so happy to learn that one who fought gallantly for the defense of our country . . . is now anxious to avert the horrors of a civil war, whilst he is contending manfully for all the rights of his adopted State to keep the Union . . . by compromise and conciliation. Yours, with respect, R.M. Walworth.[8]

As the days wore by, it became increasingly obvious that the "irrepressible conflict," predicted by Walworth family friend New York Senator William H. Seward, was at hand. Walworth was a Democrat and a friend of the South, but he gradually leaned toward support of the lanky Republican from Illinois. This old friend of his wife was indeed a man of moderation, except in the eyes of Southern firebrands. Ultimately, Walworth stood for Lincoln and the Union.

Who could have predicted in early 1861 what the future held for the nation? Sadly, even the Chancellor's worst fears would be realized, and drive him to the brink of despair during the next four years of mass slaughter. In the end the war he so desperately sought to avoid would savagely wound all the people he loved. The Walworth/Hardin family was destined to suffer terrible physical and emotional pain during the nation's fiery trial. Their ordeals to come mirrored the national calamity.

On the rainy morning of March 4, Chancellor and Mrs. Walworth were among the crowd who witnessed the swearing-in of Abraham Lincoln, the 16th president of the United States.[9] Some in the crowd undoubtedly thought and even hoped he would be the last. The existing Union was being forced to bend like a sapling buffeted by a relentless storm.

It seems likely that the Chancellor, a man of deep patriotic feeling, was receptive to Lincoln's plea for calm and reconciliation, as expressed so eloquently in his address which ended with the emotional plea: "The mystic chords of memory, stretching from every battlefield and patriot grave to every living heart and hearthstone all over this broad land, will yet swell the chorus of the Union, when again touched, as surely they will be, by the better angels of our nature."[10]

That evening, Chancellor and Mrs. Walworth were among the 3,000 guests at the Inaugural Ball. Ominously, most Southern Senators and Congressmen were conspicuous by their absence. Nonetheless, the participants celebrated and socialized as befitted a grand occasion. The fashionable Mrs. Walworth was in her element, wearing a splendid "gold satin gown."[11]

The President and First Lady Mary Todd Lincoln made their appearance at around 10:45 p.m. and greeted many of the guests before making their way to the separate dining room. They left around midnight, but the music and the dancing continued on until 3 a.m.[12]

Some of the more thoughtful revelers may have recalled another grand ball held on the eve of a great event, the Waterloo Ball. Many soldiers who danced on that festive night almost a half-century earlier met death or were wounded on the battlefield. The same fate awaited many of the young men who danced and laughed at Lincoln's first Inaugural Ball, leaving behind them weeping wives and mothers.

Following the inauguration, the Walworths remained in the capital city, that epicenter of power and influence. However, after a few days the Chancellor returned to Pine Grove in Saratoga Springs while his wife, Sarah, remained for several months, apparently relishing the drama and the excitement of a capital at war. During the war years, she returned frequently for extended visits, while the older Chancellor remained at home. In his letters to his absent wife, he repeatedly asked when she might return.

These Washington sojourns were not frivolous; far from it. Mrs. Walworth was a shrewd realist determined to advance the fortunes of her family. She knew how the political game was played and proved herself a master at currying favor among the wealthy and powerful. Sarah was also aware that her ace-in-the hole was her old friendship with President Lincoln and Mary Todd. She intended to make the most of it.

Her first effort to influence President Lincoln was hardly subtle or, in the end, effective. On December 6, 1860, Sarah wrote a long letter to the President-elect noting that he had earlier encouraged her to correspond. After an effusive congratulatory note upon his recent election she immediately got to the point: namely who should be in his Cabinet.

"You said you would be glad to hear from me at any time," she wrote. "And, I take you at your word, which I know to be sincere. . . . I hope you will pardon me if I venture to gossip a little on a subject on which the heart of the nationl is throbbing with curiosity and wonder who shall be the chosen to assist in bearing the responsibilities of the incoming administration—now I do not presume to give advice, but I write to mention one or two names for your consideration . . ."[13]

In the course of the letter, she recommended two of Chancellor Walworth's friends for Secretary of War: Judge Harris of Albany and Senator William Seward, both of New York State. Although Lincoln did appoint Seward Secretary of State, there is no evidence to suggest that Mrs. Walworth's recommendation was a factor. As there is no surviving reply, the reader can't help but wonder what Lincoln thought about Mrs. Walworth's audacity. Interestingly enough, at one point in the letter, she notes: "I am something of a politician."[14]

This ambitious and intelligent woman was much more successful in subsequent efforts to influence President Lincoln. She became, in effect, a skilled lobbyist primarily representing her family's interests with her eldest son, Martin D. Hardin. However, the first recipient of Sarah's lobbying efforts was her former sister-in-law, Martinette Hardin McKee of Kentucky. This was Martin's paternal aunt who had once talked of Lincoln's duck fits when he broke off his engagement with Mary Todd in Springfield.

Not long after Sarah contacted him, President Lincoln wrote a cover letter in March 1861 to Secretary of State William H. Seward, stating: "I know nothing of the gentleman recommended within, but the lady (Mrs. Walworth) in whose hands I find the paper is an old friend and acquaintance and I would like for her to be obliged, in the way named, or some similar one."[15]

The gentleman was Alexander R. McKee, Martinette Hardin's husband and the brother-in-law of slain Colonel John J. Hardin. Perhaps Lincoln failed to remember the husband, but he certainly knew Martinette. Lincoln instructed to give the Kentuckian, an avowed Republican, "a place in one of our departments." Seward ultimately named McKee to a consular posting in Panama.[16]

Although Mrs. Walworth undoubtedly enjoyed exercising her new influence in Washington, there was also a scent of danger in the air. In those early months of 1861, the capital was decidedly vulnerable should the Secessionists attempt an armed coup. Rumors swirled in the streets, the taverns and the hotel lobbies, as people exchanged the latest stories of Rebel intrigue and plots, some imaginary, others all too real.

On April 22, 1861, Mrs. Walworth wrote to her daughter, Ellen, who had recently moved with her children to the family's estate, the Bird's Nest, located near Louisville, to escape her abusive, unstable husband, Mansfield Tracy Walworth. The letter is a remarkable document reflecting the precarious state of affairs in the nation's capital where the loyal Union population felt that, on any day, they might suddenly come under attack by the Rebels gathering just south of the Potomac River in Virginia:

> I can scarcely realize the strange situation I find myself placed in or think I am in the capital of a great and free nation. But there are stranger things in reality than we read of in fiction or even in history. Here are the President, and his Cabinet with the Great Chief of the Army, shut off from the rest of the world. All communication is cut off by mail, and the army checked in their march to protect the capital, and yet everything seems as quiet here as a Sabbath Day.
>
> The Cabinet has regular meetings. General {Winfield} Scott sits up in state. The President cracks his jokes. Mrs. Lincoln takes her regular ride every afternoon, delighted with her fine horse which was a present from some New York gentlemen. Truly, we are living history here now. I would not be anywhere else for the

world! I have not felt the first sensation of fear as yet. In after years, I shall be able to describe to my grandchildren these scenes. I can tell them the afternoon that Fort Sumter was taken I was riding out with Mrs. Lincoln and her little boy who gave me his picture. [Note: probably Tad Lincoln.]

But we did not believe the reports that they were fighting at Charleston. The Seventh Regiment (New York) has not arrived yet, and there may be trouble, but they are trying all that can be done to avoid a collision. The Secretary of War Stanton was with us on Sunday evening and pretended they were expected that night, but we all knew he was not in earnest. I suppose they have orders to stay at Annapolis until they can come without having trouble.

As for the city being attacked, they are prepared for it, but it will not be done yet. I am sure the south is not ready for it. They do say the Old Chief [General Scott] is somewhat embarrassed in his movements by so many of the best officers of the Army and Navy resigning. But no one knows what they are about. I have not time to write anymore; a steamer is just going out.[17]

Despite the alarms, Washington remained safe through early 1861, and was soon flooded with Union volunteers. The city was teeming not only with new soldiers but with thousands of civilians on the make: businessmen eager for juicy military contracts, missionaries hoping to save the souls of young soldiers facing temptation, and a legion of prostitutes, pimps, roughs, pick-pockets and con-artists. Saloons and hotels did a thriving business; the atmosphere was electric with greed and unbridled ambition.[18]

Julia Ward Howe, the woman who wrote the lyrics to what we know today as the "The Battle Hymn of the Republic," left us a brilliant portrait of Washington during that first year of the Civil War:

Politicians of every grade, adventurers of either sex, inventors of all sorts of military appliances, and simple citizens—good and bad, flocked thither in great numbers. . . . Within the city limits mounted officers and orderlies galloped to and fro. Ambulances drawn by four horses drove through the streets. . . . From my window (Willard's Hotel) I saw . . . the ghastly advertisement of an agency for embalming and forwarding the bodies of those who had fallen in the fight or who had perished of fever.[19]

Martin's mother was still in Washington in July 1861 when General Irvin McDowell led his superbly equipped and confident Union army west of the capital to drive the Rebel army from its position at Manassas Junction near a stream called Bull Run. Sarah Walworth wrote her daughter describing the momentous events that followed:

> Today is Sunday, the 21st of July. The sun rose hot and strong today. I talked with President Lincoln at church. Suddenly, it seemed the whole city was aroused. Our two great armies were standing face to face at Manassas, only 32 miles from our great capital. Couriers hurried to and from the White House. When I caught sight of the President later, there was deep anxiety on his face. The North and the South were in battle. The two great fighting forces were in deadly combat.
>
> First came the word of the victory of the Union forces, then word ceased. We all waited anxiously. Dispatches stopped. The prolonged silence was terrifying and we were all seized with a great fear.
>
> At 6 o'clock a statesman hurried to the White House. "The battle is lost," he exclaimed excitedly. "The Confederates are coming!" President Lincoln, it is said, quietly turned and without a word, went to the War Department. The telegraph instruments were ticking the story of the fearful disaster and the probable capture of Washington. Returning to the White House, he threw himself on a lounge.
>
> It was midnight when the routed army staggered across Long Bridge into the city, and by morning, the defeated soldiers were pouring into Washington. President Lincoln, who had not closed his eyes, arose and greeted the disheartened soldiers and in his face they read the fierce determination of a man grown strong in defeat.[20]

Soon her son, Lt. Hardin, would be joining the Army of the Potomac in what now promised to be a long and bitter struggle. In October 1861, he and his men at little Fort Umpqua received orders from Brigadier General Edwin Vose Sumner, head of the Department of the Pacific, to rendezvous with other regulars in San Francisco. The growing national crisis necessitated the recall of all available troops stationed in the far west for shipment back east.

Hardin was among approximately 500 soldiers from various western garrisons who boarded the steamer *Orizaba* on October 21, 1861 for the transit to Panama (then called New Granada, a province of Columbia). The expedition, under the command of General Sumner, would sail to the west coast of Panama, disembark and continue their journey by railroad across the Isthmus to the Caribbean shore. Then they would board another steamer in Aspinwall (present-day Colon, Panama) for the final voyage to New York City.[21]

Expedition commander General Sumner was an imposing, determined, presence: a man made of leather. Forty years older than Hardin, Sumner was living history, having joined the army as a Second Lieutenant in 1819 only a few years after the War of 1812. The 62-year-old was born in 1797, in a different century, really a different world; John Adams of Massachusetts had been President and Napoleon's career of conquest was in full sway.[22] His penetrating gaze, posture as straight as a musket barrel, and his iron-gray beard gave him the look one might expect of a grizzled veteran.

In the old army, Sumner was nicknamed "Bull Head" (or sometimes "Bull"). Legend stated that during the Mexican War battle of Cerro Gordo a spent musket ball bounded off his cranium without ill effect. The old soldier had also waged war against the fearsome Cheyenne Indians in 1857. Many years later, Hardin included Sumner among his personal list of fighting generals who had inspired his particular loyalty and admiration.[23]

Sumner and his detachment, dubbed by the press as Sumner's Panama Expedition, steamed away from San Francisco Harbor aboard the *Orzizaba* on October 21, and then briefly docked in San Diego where they boarded a number of civilians. Among the new passengers were former California Senators William Gwin and Joseph L. Brent (a future Confederate Brigadier General); and Calhoun Benham, one-time U.S. Attorney for California for President James Buchanan.[24] While at sea, General Sumner learned from an informant that the three Southerners were Confederate agents who had been fomenting treason among his officers and men.

Upon learning this intelligence, General Sumner met with the three, charged them with treason, ordered their arrest and confined them to quarters, apparently trusting their word as gentlemen to remain there for the rest of the voyage. Unfortunately, Sumner failed to search their cabins. This allowed the suspects to hastily pitch various secret documents and letters through a porthole. One letter from Gwinn to Benham was, however, retrieved. "The Cotton States are out forever. The Border States will follow; it is only a question of time," Gwin wrote.[25]

We can only imagine the excitement this development created among Hardin and the officers and men when they learned that these fellow passengers were spies. That excitement peaked again when the steamer anchored on the west coast of Panama. Sumner learned from American diplomats ashore that a group of Panamanian roughs had been allegedly recruited by other agents of the Confederacy. They planned, the report noted, to rescue the Rebel spies from the train which was to transport them and Sumner's men across the Isthmus to Aspinwall on the opposite coast.[26]

Sumner ordered his contingent to break out their rifles before boarding the train and repel any rescue attempt. The train proceeded trough the lush tropical landscape without incident, but the trip led to a strong protest from the New Grenadian government, which rightly regarded it as a violation of national sovereignty. Not concerned with diplomatic niceties, Bull Sumner simply ignored the protest.[27] Once the train arrived in Aspinwall, the armed Federal troops escorted their prisoners aboard the steamer *Champion* for the final leg of the voyage to New York City.

It seems likely that Hardin was eager to share these adventures with his mother, who awaited him at dockside in New York. At the same time, Mrs. Sarah Hardin Walworth had plenty to tell her son about her efforts to seek his advancement. During a war there would be opportunity for promotion and even fame. His mother was determined that her son be among those rewarded when that time came.

Indeed, not long after the *Champion* docked, Chancellor Walworth, Hardin's doting and influential stepfather, had, perhaps at his wife's urging, written newly elected President Lincoln on November 18, 1861, asking preferment for Lt. Martin D. Hardin. A personal letter from such a distinguished personage and power in the New York State Democratic Party could hardly be dismissed by the politically astute Lincoln:

My step son Liet. (*sic*) Martin D. Hardin of the 3rd Regiment of U.S. artillery, the oldest son of your deceased friend Col John J. Hardin, who fell at Buena Vista, has just returned from Oregon, where he has been stationed for some time, & is as I understand now at Washington, or in the vicinity with his company.

In June 1854 I got him in, as a cadet at large, at West Point; where he was an officer of the cadet corps nearly the whole time he was there. He graduated with much credit, & high up in his class, and I have no doubt he is one of the best and most reliable officers of his age in the army. Previously to the breaking out of the rebellion he had, with my concurrence & approbation, determined to leave the army, & to become a lawyer. But before he left California he wrote to his mother that he considered it his duty to serve his country in the army until the termination of the war; before he commenced the study of law.

I have not seen or communicated with him since his return; and his mother is now absent having gone down to New York to meet him the moment she heard that the steamer arrived. But I am very desirous that he should at once obtain a higher situation than that of a first lieut. In the Army; where he may not only be useful to his country, but may also acquire reputation, while he is receiving such pay as to be able to lay by the means of educating himself for the law when the war is at an end. I know he is brave, as his father was, and will not spare himself but court danger. And I fear that if he stays in his present situation as a lieutenant of artillery his life will be unnecessarily sacrificed; or if he survives will neither acquire reputation nor the means of future support.

I hope therefore, for his father's sake as swell as his own, you will be able to give him some higher or better situation, either in the staff of some of your generals, or elsewhere, that will enable him to distinguish himself & to receive an adequate remuneration for his services. I confess I feel great solicitude on his account, for his good conduct & gentlemanly bearing have always been such that he is as dear to me as my own sons.

I have written to him & enclosed a letter to be presented to the secretary of war, & have requested him to get leave of absence &

to call on yourself & on the secretary. But I fear he will be too unassuming to do so unless you should send for him. If his mother returns from New York without going to Washington, she will probably write to you on this subject.

I am with respect yours &c Reuben H. Walworth.[28]

What is perhaps most interesting about Walworth's letter is that he addressed it care of the First Lady, Mary Todd Lincoln, stating the she "must feel deep interest in the children of the lost Col. Hardin. . . . I fear if I send it to him {the President} directly he will never see it."[29]

CHAPTER 10

TRAITOR IN THEIR MIDST

Martin Davis Hardin's mother came to New York City to greet her son upon his arrival back in the East. After such a long absence they had much to discuss, and not just about Martin's adventures in the Wild West. His mother had plenty to tell her son about the crisis that had unfolded in his absence.

Their homecoming was brief, however. Hardin departed almost immediately to the Washington garrison where he joined Battery H, Third U.S. Artillery (Stewart's Battery), spending his days instructing his gun crews in the deadly ballet of artillery drill. Hardin's outfit was attached to the Pennsylvania Reserve Division, a unit composed of 13 regiments of nearly 10,000 volunteers from the Keystone State. It was a unique division, in that after Lincoln's original call to arms in 1861, the state of Pennsylvania provided far more men than the Federal government wished to accept.[1] Rather than turn away the volunteers, Pennsylvania Governor Andrew Curtin arranged for their training and equipment with his state's resources. Although described as "reserves," the division would fight in the Army of the Potomac's front lines in nearly every major battle over the next three years. Hardin did not know it at the time, but the Pennsylvania Reserve Division was to figure prominently in his future combat career.

Training, drilling and, no doubt, the inevitable grousing continued through the early spring. One brigade of the Pennsylvania Reserves under on General Ord won a minor victory at Dranesville, Virginia, Dec. 20, 1861, which received a great deal of press coverage in the North, though Hardin's battery did not see action.

"After the battle of Dranesville the camp {Fort Pennsylvania, later

133

named Fort Reno} was visited by many distinguished persons, and the Reserves were the heroes of the Winter," Hardin wrote. "Many congratulatory orders were issued . . . General Ord suggested the use of distinctive badges: the origin of corps badges. No order was given to build Winter quarters, but temporary huts, three to four logs high, with tents over them, were erected. Sheet iron stoves furnished heat. Drills were required whenever the weather permitted, and there was much picket duty. These duties filled in the time until Spring."[2]

In the spring, the Pennsylvania Reserve Division marched across the Potomac River and made camp about a mile outside of Alexandria, Virginia with the rest of General George McClellan's Army of the Potomac. When not on duty many of the men and officers sought solace in the bottle. "One man had a barrel up his chimney, another a barrel on top of his house from which he drew liquor by a gas jet . . . ," Hardin wrote. "The weather . . . here was cold, rainy and unpleasant, rendering the ground mostly unfit for drilling, but every favorable opportunity was taken advantage of for that purpose. We received full rations and a ration of whisky was served out every rainy night."[3]

During this tedious calm before the storm, Hardin came to know many of the officers and men of the Reserves and was impressed by the spirit of the volunteers. One of his close friends during the early days of the war was General Frank Bayard, USMA Class of 1856, a cavalry leader with the Reserve Corps. While serving in Colorado during the Kiowa-Comanche uprising of 1859, Bayard was badly scarred by an arrow striking him in the face. The Indian war may have, in fact, been triggered when Lt. Bayard allegedly killed the Kiowa Chief Big Pawnee.[4]

The quality of the Pennsylvania Reserves' top officers was unusually high for a volunteer outfit. Many were professional soldiers and West Point graduates; other had learned their sanguinary trade in the Mexican War. They were fine men destined to make a mark in the coming war, officers like George Gordon Meade, John Reynolds, and Edward O. Ord. Young Hardin saw them as models and mentors, striving to emulate them as a soldier and a man.

His family had great confidence in Hardin's potential. They believed in the young man, and that he would distinguish himself on the field of battle as had his father, grandfather and two great-grandfathers. All he needed was opportunity. His mother continued her lobbying efforts with her usual zeal. Not long after her son's return from the West she wrote to Abe Lincoln's closest friend from the Springfield years, Joshua F. Speed, who was also well known to the former Sarah Ellen Hardin. She shrewdly saw an opportunity to reach the President through his old friend.

In the spring of 1861, Speed was living in Louisville, Kentucky. In fact, he had visited Sarah's children, Lemuel and Ellen, who lived at the nearby Bird's Nest homestead. These associations were undoubtedly helpful in Mrs. Walworth's effort to enlist Speed in the informal campaign to win preferment for her son.

At some point, Hardin's mother learned of Speed's planned visit to Washington where he was expected to have a personal audience with their mutual friend, President Lincoln. Mrs. Hardin Walworth was determined that Speed mention her son's name during the course of that conversation. Thus she must have been delighted when Speed wrote to her on January 16, 1862 from Louisville, expressing his willingness to advocate for Martin in Lincoln's presence:

> Dear Madam,
> In reply to yours of the 7th, I expect to go to Washington next week when I will see Mr. Lincoln & endeavor to get your son Martin D assigned to duty in Ky. I understand that we are very much in want of artillery officers here. In [illegible word] of this it will afford me great pleasure to promote your wishes & advance your son.
> Your children have purchased a very comfortable place {the Bird's Nest}. We called to see them at Galt House soon after our return. They are I understand quite well.
> > With kind remembrances from Mrs. Speed I am,
> > Sincerely
> > Your friend,
> > J. F. Speed[5]

Hardin's mother didn't leave a stone unturned in her effort to promote her son's military career. She even solicited the help of her husband's old Mexican War commander, 79-year-old General John Wool, now command-ing at Fort Monroe, who sent her a polite if non-committal response. One wonders if Sarah was aware that her late husband had quarreled incessantly with General Wool prior to his death at Buena Vista, and could hardly be considered a friend. Then again, Colonel Hardin had been dead for going on 14 years, and perhaps his widow hoped that the bitterness had mellowed with passing time. Wool responded with a polite note but without committing himself to Martin's cause.[6]

Shockingly, all of Sarah's carefully orchestrated efforts on behalf of Martin D. were suddenly jeopardized following the calamitous news of an event occurring February 7, 1862.

The unpredictable Mansfield Tracy Walworth, Sarah's stepson and the husband of her daughter, Ellen, was arrested as a Confederate spy in Washington. The scapegrace son of the respected Chancellor Walworth of New York, and the stepbrother to a promising Union officer had been apprehended at 4 a.m. in the hotel room of a reputed Confederate agent, Mrs. Augusta Morris, a woman of dubious reputation.[7]

Mansfield was now imprisoned at the Old Capital along with other suspected Confederate agents and sympathizers. Worse yet, because of Mansfield's traitorous acts, the Hardin branch of the family was now suspect because of their strong Southern ties. Later, in fact, Martin's beloved younger brother Lemuel would fight for the Confederacy, causing a major rift in family relations. None of this boded well for Martin Hardin's future in the Union Army.

It's highly doubtful that the narcissistic Mansfield was motivated by anything more than opportunism. Months before, he had approached Union General John C. Fremont with an offer to act as a secret agent for the North, citing his Hardin family's Kentucky connections as possible avenues of military intelligence on the Confederate armies. The would-be spy was disappointed when Fremont declined his offer.[8]

Whatever his true feelings, Mansfield Walworth wasn't about to settle for a career as a clerk. His romantic nature and egomania demanded a far more glamorous and significant role. At work here, too, was his long infatuation with the rich planting class of Southern aristocrats, many of whom he had met in the pre-war years during their frequent visits to the Saratoga Springs resort. Mansfield liked their style, their manners, their disdain for grubby commerce, and their love of honor; they were proud men who would never suffer insult.

As a civilian clerk in the office of Adjutant General Lorenzo Thomas,[9] Hardin's brother-in-law was certainly in a position to access classified information useful to the Confederacy. Mansfield's fatal misstep occurred when he entertained his cousin, John Barbour, a lawyer serving on Secretary of State William Seward's staff, one evening. In the privacy of his Washington hotel room, Mansfield confided to his cousin that he held an officer's commission on the staff of Rebel General P.G.T. Beauregard. Then, he foolishly paraded about the room in a new Confederate officer's uniform, no doubt all the while casting admiring glances at himself in the mirror.[10]

Not long afterwards, Barbour reported the incident to his superior and close Walworth family friend, Secretary of State Seward. Mansfield's arrest occurred shortly afterwards. As would most fathers, Chancellor Walworth did his best to intercede on behalf of his imprisoned boy by contacting powerful friends. These efforts produced an alternative to a jail cell, which Reuben H. Walworth explained to his son during a visit to Capitol Prison. All the young man need do was sign a loyalty oath. Mansfield refused.[11]

For some headstrong, inexplicable reason, Mansfield rejected the offer of freedom, perhaps seeing himself as a brave innocent imprisoned in a tower by jealous enemies—in other words, as a character lifted from the pages of one of his lurid novels: " . . . the indefatigable man of will, the soul that aspires to the possession of the pure, the beautiful, the intellectual, the grand."[12]

Before returning to Saratoga Springs, Chancellor Walworth visited his stepson, Lt. Hardin, who was stationed near the capital with his artillery battery. It seems likely that they would have discussed Mansfield's action and its possible negative consequence for the family and, in particular, for Martin's military career.

One account of Lt. Hardin's meeting with his stepfather states that the discussion centered on the young man's conflicting emotions on the eve of armed hostilities. It seems Hardin wondered if he could bring himself to wage war against fellow Americans, his fellow Southerners. He was revolted at the thought of possibly slaying a friend or even family member on the battlefield. Despite those understandable reservations, Hardin remained loyal to the Union, as his subsequent combat career amply documented. But it's reasonable to assume that, on a certain emotional level, he was a reluctant warrior in this battle of brothers.[13]

The Hardin family had for several generations been uncomfortable with the institution of slavery. Martin's grandfather and namesake, one-time Kentucky senator Martin D. Hardin, had, along with his friend, Henry Clay, hoped for a gradual end to the institution. His father, John J. Hardin, immigrated to Illinois, rejoicing to finally live in a free state. The Hardins were never Abolitionists, but for a half-century they stood for moderation and revered the Union above all other considerations.[14] Thirty years later, Martin Hardin revealed his thoughts about the cause of the great Civil War:

> The Southern people had been for years grossly deceived by their political leaders as to the character of their fellow citizens of the North, and of their feelings toward them. The Northern people had been represented as all being violent Abolitionists, ready to destroy the Union in order to extinguish slavery: and, at the same time, as a set of cowardly traders, who under no circumstances could be induced to fight, while on the other hand, the people of the Northern States believed the Southern people would only bluster, make a great fuss and then, finally, accept some compromise which would prevent the extension of slavery, and gradually put an end to it. Probably some such compromise could have been effected had the extremists on both sides been willing to wait. *However, the war was possibly inevitable to punish our people for inaugurating African slavery in our country.*[15]

After visiting with Martin, Chancellor Walworth returned alone to Pine Grove. His disappointment in his youngest son, Mansfield, was a deep and searing wound. Walworth's grief and shame were aggravated as the whole degrading tale of Mansfield's imprisonment appeared in various newspapers. *The Troy Times* in New York State featured the scandal and described Chancellor Walworth's son as "a sort of nothing: a wild, reckless, impetuous, dare-devil fellow, without much principle or any reputation."[16] The anonymous reporter also stooped to sly innuendo, noting that, "the Chancellor married a Southern widow some years ago, and Mansfield's wife is her daughter."[17]

The implication was hardly subtle: if one of the Walworth-Hardin clan was a traitor and spy, perhaps all were.

Back at Pine Grove, Chancellor Walworth sank into depression. Despite his strongest efforts, the nation was engaged in a bloody Civil War; his youngest son was imprisoned on charges of spying for the South; his beloved stepson, Martin D, was preparing to join in the carnage. And his young wife was absent again playing her role as society matron in Washington. Lemuel Hardin, his sister, Ellen, and Ellen's children were gone as well, living in Louisville.

In his despondency, the lonely old man wrote to his absent wife: "I am broken down and desperate at news of my country and the troubles of my own family, and I fear that my mind will give way under it before long. But I shall endeavor to hold up my head before the world as long as I can although I cannot see any bright spot for the future this side of the grave."[18]

After three months in prison, during which time his cellmate, another suspected Rebel agent, was shot and killed by a guard for allegedly refusing an order, Mansfield finally tired of his role as a martyr, and signed the loyalty oath. Secretary of State Seward released him to the custody of his father with the understanding he would remain in a sort of house arrest until the war concluded. During this period, his estranged wife and children remained at the Bird's Nest near Louisville.[19]

Father and son lived alone for most of the war in the Pine Grove Mansion. Chancellor Walworth was increasingly engrossed in researching and writing an in-depth family genealogy,[20] and Mansfield was equally absorbed in penning a lurid novel inspired by an actual event, a hotel poisoning that had almost claimed President James Buchannan's life in 1857.[21] Father and son lived in the same house for the remainder of the war, but they might as well have been a continent apart.

The old Chancellor must have felt the isolation deeply. Almost everyone he loved was gone. Mansfield's wife, Ellen, remained in Louisville for the rest of the war, never once visiting her disgraced husband in Saratoga Springs. For much of the time, her mother, Sarah, remained away too, on long excursions to Washington, Louisville, New York City and Pittsburgh. The old Chancellor was abandoned to his misery, repeatedly pleading for Sarah's return, writing on one occasion: "You had better come as soon as you can; it is very lonely here above stairs and there is an Irish carnival in the kitchen every night."[22]

Of course, there was gossip generated by Mrs. Chancellor Walworth's rather Bohemian behavior. Some undoubtedly questioned the motives which led her to marry a much older man in the first place. One prominent personality in New York society, diarist George Templeton Strong, was among those who viewed Martin's mother as a rank opportunist and pitied her husband as a foolish old man infatuated with a younger woman:

> He {Walworth} left the bench with an exalted reputation for learning, ability and integrity, but his record since has been less than brilliant. He married a splurging Western widow (Mrs. J.J. Hardin) for his second wife. It's said that her fast, expensive ways demoralized the staid, strait-laced, rather puritanical old fogy; threw him off his bearings, and made him rapacious, if not corrupt. . . . Such is the story, whispered about and disbelieved at first . . .[23]

Despite the whispers, Mrs. Walworth continued to be at the center of Washington society throughout the war, never relenting in her effort to promote her son. Those efforts may have led, after his promotion that spring to First Lieutenant, to a promising new position—he was now aide-de-camp to Colonel Henry Hunt, the top artillery officer in the Army of the Potomac.[24]

In April of 1862, McClellan's huge army embarked on a fleet of transports voyaging to Hardin's first posting, Fort Monroe on the James Peninsula. From this base, they would march to Richmond, win a grand battle with the Confederate forces, occupy the Rebel capital, and squash the rebellion. This, at least, was the vision of General George B. McClellan, considered to be America's "young Napoleon." For 24-year-old First Lieutenant Hardin, the war was about to begin in earnest.

CHAPTER 11

THE HEAVENS RAIN
FIRE AND IRON

When Lieutenant Hardin returned to Fort Monroe in the spring of 1862, he was part of an immense host of superbly trained, well-equipped, and well-armed soldiers. In less than three weeks, 329 vessels of the Union Navy had transported to the York Peninsula 121,500 men, 14,592 horses and mules, 1,224 wagons and ambulances, and 44 artillery batteries. The Army of the Potomac was confident of its power and had implicit faith in its leader, General McClellan.[1]

Young Hardin, like so many others, must have been awed by this incredible show of Federal power. One Massachusetts volunteer described how in the evening the lights of the warships and transports at anchor near the old fort seemed as "thick as stars on a clear night."[2] On April 3, 1862, McClellan ordered the Army of the Potomac to advance up the peninsula to Richmond, the Confederate capital. Who could stand before this terrible juggernaut?

Seventeen miles from Fort Monroe, McClellan's gigantic host halted in its tracks on April 5 before Confederate entrenchments at Yorktown, the old Revolutionary War battlefield. The Rebs were dug in, manning a 14-mile stretch of entrenchments running across the waist of the peninsula from Yorktown on the York River to Mulberry Island on the James River to the south. Confederate General John Bankhead Magruder commanded with fewer than 10,000 troops to resist the Yankee horde—less than half the number needed to even adequately man the defense line.[3]

What followed became legend. In the old army, Magruder's nickname was "Prince John." He was remembered for his eccentric manner, taste for fine clothes, and a passion for amateur theatrics. In the coming days, this military impresario stage-managed an elaborate performance beyond his wildest dreams. He ordered his regiments to parade back and forth in view of the enemy presenting the illusion of numbers. Magruder prayed that this audacious deception would at least delay a Union assault until reinforcements arrived.[4]

Lieutenant Hardin, serving as an aide on the artillery staff of Colonel Hunt, was among the first to observe the Confederate position at Yorktown:

> The writer (Lt. Hardin) went in person amongst the Union pickets to a position where he thought a line of battle could be formed which could carry the Yorktown entrenchments; that is, when the Union army first arrived in front of them. The writer . . . with others urged that an attempt be made to carry the enemy's works. He was disappointed at hearing talk of a siege before anything was done to test the strength of the enemy's position.[5]

Unfortunately, this was more than just talk. McClellan, ever-careful, soon ordered his engineers to begin work for a formal siege of Yorktown. In retrospect, the decision was a major mistake, born of his essential timidity, blind faith in widely exaggerated estimates of enemy strength,[6] and perhaps a near-fatal lack of imagination. In this case, at least, young Lieutenant Hardin was absolutely correct in his view that the line could have been breached by an immediate and vigorous assault.

Looking back more than three decades later, Hardin noted: "McClellan, naturally cautious, became over-cautious. The writer thought, at the time the army reached Yorktown, it could, by a little hard fighting and by rapid movements, have forced the enemy's position there. Since he has learned how small a force Magruder had at the time, he is confirmed in his opinion."[7]

The Army of the Potomac halted in its tracks while siege works were dug and heavy artillery was placed in the line. Ironically, before McClellan was ready to launch his attack—after a needless delay of nearly a month—the outnumbered enemy abandoned the position in the night and withdrew up the peninsula.[8] Magruder's theatrics gave the Confederacy the precious gift of time to concentrate its forces and prepare to defend Richmond.

Right after the Yorktown siege fiasco, Lt. Hardin came down with a case of malaria. He subsequently spent three weeks in April and May recuperating at Fort Monroe, now commanded by his father's old division commander, General John Wool. When Hardin rejoined the Army of the Potomac, it was poised on the outskirts of Richmond, only five miles away.[9]

One Pennsylvania soldier remembered they could easily see the city's church spires at that point, prompting an officer to wager one hundred cigars he would be in the city within the week. His prediction held true, but the gambler entered the city not as a conqueror but as a prisoner along with hundreds of other Union soldiers.[10]

The opening act of an unfolding tragedy began May 31, 1862 when Confederate General Joseph E. Johnston, the victor of First Bull Run, attacked McClellan's Army of the Potomac, positioned awkwardly astride the Chickahominy River. Johnston's goal was to concentrate south of the river and destroy the isolated Union Fourth Corps at Fair Oaks, commanded by General Erasmus D. Keyes. Poor coordination and confusion prevented the attack from commencing at dawn as Johnston had planned. The main assault didn't even begin until 1 p.m.[11]

During the battle, Union Artillery Chief Colonel Hunt employed his aides as gallopers carrying orders to various batteries and unit commanders from one end of the battlefield to the other, often at great personal risk. Lieutenant Hardin was continuously in the saddle throughout the two-day battle. After much hard fighting, the struggle at Fair Oaks (also called Seven Pines) ended inconclusively with 5,071 Union casualties compared to 6,134 for the attacking Confederates.[12]

Nearly 11,000 soldiers, blue and gray, bled or died at Fair Oaks, but the most significant casualty on either side was Confederate General Johnston. (The same officer who had inspected Brevet Lt. Hardin's recruits at Jefferson Barracks in St. Louis in 1860.) Johnston suffered a severe wound on the second day that required a long convalescence and forced him to cede command of the army.[13] His replacement was General Robert E. Lee, well-known to Hardin from West Point days and the Harper's Ferry incident, but not yet nationally famous. His ascension to command of the Confederate Army outside Richmond marked a turning point in the Peninsula Campaign, and, ultimately a profound change in the character of the entire war in the East. In the days and years ahead, Lee wrote his name large in the history of military commanders.[14]

In a series of battles historians call the Seven Days, Lee revealed himself to be a brilliant and pugnacious warrior. Unlike his opponent McClellan, Lee was willing to take risks and suffer heavy casualties to impose his will on the battlefield. He was a ruthless and relentless enemy, possessing in spades what professional boxers call the killer instinct. Lee was similar in that respect to his future opponent U.S. Grant, whose military legacy was once summed up as: "Blood is the price of victory. One must accept the formula or not wage war."[15] In the North, they came to call Grant a butcher; but in the South, Lee was revered as "Ole Marse."

After a probe by McClellan in the center was repulsed on June 25, Lee attacked. First, he sought to annihilate Porter's Fifth Corps north of the Chickahominy River at the battle of Mechanicsville, June 26. His plans were well made but the sword that became the Army of Northern Virginia had not yet gained a sharp edge. At Mechanicville and in all of the Seven Days battles that followed, Lee was handicapped by poor staff work and lack of coordination. Unfortunately this initial lesson cost the Confederacy 1,484 casualties to only 361 casualties for the Union.[16]

Despite having held at Mechanicville, McClellan pulled the Fifth Corps back to higher ground closer to the Chickahominy at Gaines' Mill. Indeed, the Union commander would never again take the initiative on the Peninsula, except to stage withdrawals. On June 27, Lee attacked the Fifth Corps again, this time from two sides. In bitter fighting the Southern army suffered horrendous losses but finally cracked Porter's perimeter, capturing dozens of cannon and forcing a wholesale retreat across the river. Casualties were reported as 8,751 for the Confederates; the Federals lost 6,837.[17] At this point McClellan decided to abandon his supply line on the York River above the Peninsula and "change his base" to the James River to the south. The Army of the Potomac thus faced the dangerous task of turning its back on an aggressive enemy while it conducted its long retreat to the James.

In retrospect, Hardin was critical of a commander that he otherwise admired in many ways. But he was frustrated that McClellan was again absent from the Gaines' Mill battlefield at a critical moment. Writing in 1890, Hardin stated:

McClellan, as Commanding General, ought to have been at Gaines' Mill early in the day to have assisted by his presence the officers commanding in that battle, and . . . to have determined when reinforcements were necessary and whether they could be spared from the south bank. With modern weapons, the action moves faster than formerly; consequently, the commanding generals of brigades, divisions, corps and armies must be present in person if possible, at the key or hard-fighting points.[18]

On June 28 both sides regrouped: the Northerners destroying abandoned stores and beginning their withdrawal; the Southerners redeploying to pursue. At Savage's Station on June 29, the scenario was again repeated— Lee attacked and McClellan fell back. The Union soldiers fought well and their superior artillery mowed down hundreds of Confederates. But McClellan seemed to have no stomach for combat; he seemed more like a fugitive who pauses to throw a chair in the way of his pursuers only to resume his flight.[19]

On June 30, 1862, the various Union infantry corps were positioned in a defensive arc behind White Oak Swamp. Their mission was to protect the army's enormous supply train, logistical tail and reserve artillery slowly making its way to safety toward Harrison's Landing on the James River. The Pennsylvania Reserve Division and other units from General Porter's Fifth Corps stood astride the strategically important New Market Cross Roads. Meantime Lee attempted to orchestrate his army into a crushing three-pronged attack.[20]

Should Lee's attacking force pierce the Union lines here, they could chop off a large part of the Army of the Potomac and be in superb position to destroy the rest. In the center of McLellan's left flank was General George McCall's Pennsylvania Reserve Division, the Third Division of Porter's Fifth Corps. To the right of the Reserve Division was General Phil Kearny's Third Division, Third Corps; on the Reserve's left was General Joseph Hooker's Second Division, Third Corps. Hunt's Artillery Reserve, including several batteries manned by German-speaking troops, was with McCall's Division. But once again General McClellan was absent from the field.

Lieutenant Hardin was incredulous. The Army of the Potomac was momentarily expecting another Confederate attack; yet no one was in overall command. Just as disconcerting: there were gaps between McCall's division and the Union divisions on either flank. This failure to present a solid unbroken line put the Pennsylvania Reserve Division at serious risk of being flanked and routed.[21] Military historian Uzal W. Ent summed up the situation succinctly in his history of the Pennsylvania Reserve Corps: "McClellan was not anywhere near. The divisions would fight independently."[22]

Around 11 a.m., General James Longstreet's Confederate infantry fell on the Union position with terrible ferocity. James Kemper's brigade was the leading element of the Confederate assault, and he described how the enemy [Hunt's German batteries and McCall's infantry], "poured an incessant fire of shell, grape, canister and lead upon my lines, and did much execution. . . . When the command came upon the enemy's batteries there was no perceptible faltering in the advance of these brave men, who rushed across the open field, pouring a well-directed fire into the enemy, driving him from his breastworks and the battery to our front. The guns . . . were abandoned to us for the time being, and my command was in virtual possession of the chosen position of the enemy."[23]

Hardin remembered the chaos, especially when the Union batteries hesitated in firing upon the oncoming enemy for fear of striking Union infantry fleeing before the Rebel onslaught. The Union line broke, many threw up their arms in surrender; and two of the German artillery caissons (Captains Otto Diederich's and John Knieriem's batteries) racing away in panicked retreat apparently ran down a number of their own infantry.[24] This was the beginning of the worst day of the war for McCall's division, and Lieutenant Hardin was a witness to the debacle.

Badly crippled, the Pennsylvania Reserves nonetheless recovered their equilibrium as the afternoon progressed. Short on ammunition, the survivors ultimately launched a wild bayonet charge to recover several artillery pieces lost early in the fight. Hardin described the charge as "an instance of heroism not often repeated during the war."[25] The day was a series of attacks and counterattacks. Despite their determined efforts, the Confederates never reached the crossroads where they could have wreaked havoc on the Federal supply train.

McCall's Pennsylvania Reserve Division had been shattered that day. In addition to the 1,800 men lost at Mechanicsville and Gaines' Mill they had just lost 1,200 more, which included 400 captured.[26] Division commander Archibald McCall was a prisoner, and brigade commander George Meade was shot twice during the action. Also wounded was Union General Edwin V. Sumner, Hardin's commander during the Panama Expedition. The total butcher bill for White Oak Swamp—alternatively called the Battle of Frayser's Farm, Glendale, or New Market Crossroads—totaled 3,673 Confederate casualties against 3,797 Union.[27]

Only with the fall of darkness did the firing slowly ebb. The last shots were fired around 9:30 p.m. In the gloom of night, the Union army resumed its weary march to Malvern Hill.[28] Confederate division commander D.H. Hill summed up McClellan's performance with terse eloquence: "His movements have been characterized by great prudence, not to say great timidity."[29] That the Army of the Potomac still remained intact was due solely to the fact that Stonewall Jackson's wing of the Rebel army had remained idle throughout that day, for reasons that are still unclear. If his divisions had attacked the Federal right and rear—as Lee intended—at the same time Longstreet and A.P. Hill were hammering the flank, little could have prevented a disaster to the Union cause. Confederate General Benjamin Huger's division also failed to join the battle, reporting that its roads were obstructed.

Nevertheless, all Union thoughts of capturing Richmond and ending the rebellion had vanished in less than a week. Those dreams were swept away by a crescendo of Rebel yells and deadly volleys of rifle fire accompanied by the thunderous cacophony of artillery. Ahead lay three more years of bitter war before the National banner would once again fly over the Rebel capital. A vast array of young men, both in blue and gray, would never live to see that long desired dawn of peace. The long road to national reunion would be marked by endless white crosses.

The final fight of the Seven Days Battle took place on July 1, 1862 at Malvern Hill.[30] This rise was what the military called perfect high ground for the defense: an elevated plateau rising 130 feet above the James River providing a natural platform for artillery with a wide open field of fire below. Lt. Hardin and his fellow aides galloped back and forth across the hill carrying out Colonel Henry Hunt's instructions; in the end the master of the Union artillery placed 250 or more cannon on successive elevations up the slope, providing tremendous potential for concentrated fire.[31] They were supported by infantry from John Fitz Porter's Fifth Corps. Surely, only a fool would attack such a strong position studded with cannon.

General Lee was no fool, but on this day he was certainly less than wise. He began his attack at 1:30 p.m. with an artillery bombardment in support of the planned infantry attack. Within an hour, devastatingly accurate Union cannon fire virtually silenced the Rebel batteries. Once more, Hardin was to witness one of the great butcheries of the war. Thousands of Rebel infantry stormed the heights in the late afternoon and evening of July 1, 1862.[32]

The Confederates came, in the words of one Union soldier, "with all the frenzy of maniacs."[33] These incredibly brave attackers were soon enveloped by a hurricane of cannon fire, the intensity of which had never been equaled in the history of war. One witness called it, "Majestic Murder."[34] Confederate courage and elan foundered in a sea of blood inflicted by modern cannon and massed rifle fire. More than five thousand Rebel infantry were killed or maimed in this mechanized meat-grinder, a preview of the mass slaughters that were to come in the 20th century. Artillery officer Hardin described what he witnessed at Malvern Hill in vivid imagery:

> Brigade after brigade formed under cover of the woods {and} started at a run to cross the open space and charge our batteries. But the heavy fire of our guns, with the cool and steady volleys of our infantry, in every case sent them reeling back to shelter and covered the ground with their dead and wounded. . . . The enemy persisted in his efforts to take the position so tenaciously defended . . . his repeated desperate attacks were repulsed with fearful loss. . . . Darkness ended the battle at Malvern Hill, though it was not till after 9 p.m. that the artillery ceased its fire.[35]

Amazingly, despite the Union superiority in position and artillery, the Confederates somehow managed to inflict 3,214 Union casualties during the battle, though many of these consisted of stragglers scooped up after the Army of the Potomac once again vacated the field.[36]

After the day's victory, Fifth Corps commander Porter and Henry Hunt, Hardin's immediate superior, were among those who urged McClellan to hold his position and even consider resuming its advance on Richmond.[37] Young Hardin was particularly critical of McClellan, pointing out he had spent too much time in the rear and because of that suffered from a "demoralized condition."[38] Three decades later Hardin made it clear that he was in total agreement with those officers who advocated remaining in their strong position:

> After the battle of Malvern Hill, in which the Confederate Army had been severely punished . . . , the fighting generals of the Army of the Potomac were unanimous for remaining where they were, or for making an advance towards Richmond. The ground at Malvern Hill was high and dry, and could be easily entrenched so as to be perfectly safe for even a smaller force than the Army of the Potomac to hold.[39]

Instead McClellan chose to abandon the heights and resume his retreat to Harrison's Landing on the James. "How many brave men laid down their lives, and how many of us will go crippled to our graves by reason of this decision," Hardin wrote later. "At what a fearful cost of noble life was it that we got back here in 1864 on the James River, from which it was so easy to move us {in 1862}?"[40]

On July 8, 1862, Martin D. Hardin, newly promoted from Lietenant to Lieutenant Colonel, was transferred from Henry Hunt's staff and assigned command of the Twelfth Pennsylvania Volunteer Regiment, Pennsylvania Reserve Division. While at Harrison's Landing following the Seven Days, the men of his new regiment were discouraged, weary and clad in filthy rags. Motivating them would be a stern test for the young West Pointer who had never before led infantry in combat. In that sense, Hardin's war was only just beginning.[41]

Presumably because of his West Point training, Hardin immediately set about imprinting his personality upon the regiment and keeping them too busy to dwell on their horrific combat experiences. As he later wrote:

> Orders were issued for putting the camp into perfect sanitary condition. Good sinks, perfectly screened, were constructed. Deep wells were sunk by placing barrels on top of each other; a depth of at least three barrels was required. Drills were resumed and efforts

made to get the men to move about and rouse their spirits. All men of the regiment who had been found by the late campaign to be unfit for military duty by reason of physical disability were discharged. The serious cases of sickness were sent North, and everything possible done to get an effective force.[42]

Like any good commanding officer, Hardin placed the health and welfare of his men at the top of his priorities. He later admitted that during the first two weeks at Harrison's Landing "things looked very blue." However, morale gradually improved, especially when fresh vegetables became available and the men donned new, clean uniforms. "The majority of the members of the regiment plucked up their spirits and began to look hopefully to the future," he noted.[43]

After three weeks in command, Hardin could proudly point to a regimental hospital almost free of sick men, although many still suffered intermittently with diarrhea. The turning point came when the regiment began feeding on a supply of green corn, despite warnings from the medical officer. "The green corn . . . was devoured by the dozen ears to the man," Hardin wrote. "The doctors said this would kill us, but on the contrary this cured the diarrhea, set us up, and gave us great spirits. Ever since then we have known how the 'Johnnies' managed to fight so well. Corn and bacon are far superior to hard tack and coffee, even with 'salt horse' {preserved meat} thrown in, for soldier food."[44]

Hardin was certainly being judged in these early days, not only by his superior officers, but more importantly by the rank-and-file of the regiment. These men were tried veterans. Sergeant Thomas W. Dick, Co. H, 12th Pa. Reserve Regiment, undoubtedly spoke for many others when he mentioned the new regimental commander in a letter to his brother, August 1, 1862: "Liet. Col. Hardin is in command; he is since recommended by General McClellan for Col. I suppose it will be confirmed. He is a good officer in camp and sees to the welfare of the men. How he will lead us in the field of battle we have to find out."[45]

Hardin's men had endured a terrible ordeal in the Peninsula. At one point, they had fought three hard battles in a space of five days. They desperately needed this relatively calm interlude at Harrison's Landing, to regain their emotional bearings and cope with the memory of the bitter combat that had taken so many beloved comrades or rendered them crippled and maimed. Lieutenant Chill A. Hazzard, a former Pennsylvania newspaperman, serving with Company F of Hardin's regiment, spoke for many when he wrote his father of the nightmare of the Seven Days Battles: "Dear Father: I wish this letter was written! That all I have to tell was told. The horrors of war are far beyond description, and I have seen the horrible awful scenes of the past week, more than a lifetime can tell. Of the single fact that I am safe, among the thousands of others . . . , the rest is a wild, weary dream, like unrealized mass, crowded together, something that I cannot analyze."[46] Hazzard remained a close lifetime friend of Colonel Hardin, who had come to deeply admire.

Another of Hardin's men, Sergeant Major William Meyers, wrestled with his own private demons. He had seen a cannonball rip off the leg of his friend, Private Alexander Rankin, Company H, 12th Pennsylvania Volunteer Regiment. Meyers had taken the fatally injured soldier to the hospital where Rankin repeatedly begged his comrades to shoot him until he finally died. In a letter to the deceased man's brother, Williams wrote: "He dwells in the Land of the Spirits. He was a good soldier, respected by all who knew him, and fell as only a man can fall who fight for their country."[47]

Leading men in battle is the true test of any officer. Until Lt. Colonel Hardin passed that cruel exam at the head of the regiment, most of his combat tested soldiers, like the skeptical Sgt. Dick, would withhold final judgment.

The tedium of the camp at Harrison's Landing was relieved on July Fourth when the troops staged a grand review before General McClellan. Four days later, President Lincoln visited the men, but declined a formal review; he preferred visiting with the men in their camps where he received a warm welcome. Yet, for some strange reason, most men in the Army of the Potomac continued to believe in Little Mac, including Hardin who certainly was keenly aware of the commanding general's considerable shortcomings.[48]

Their Confederate enemies were quiet during the Harrison Landing interlude, except for one memorable exception, which most of the men remembered their entire lives. On August 1, 1862, Hardin and his men bolted awake in the dead of night to the roar of a surprise Confederate artillery attack.

Rebel artillery batteries, recently placed in secret on nearby high ground overlooking the Landing, rained shells on the Union encampment. The spectacularly brilliant display of pyro-technics made a deep impression on those present. Several decades after the war, a Union veteran wrote of the incident in a letter to *the National Tribune*, the official newspaper of the Grand Army of the Republic (GAR):

> The night was exceedingly dark. There had been rain, and the sky was yet cloudy and threatening. And, looking in the direction of the river, they beheld what seemed a myriad of shooting stars, a meteoric shower, rushing directly upon them . . . the heavens were raining veritable fire and iron. . . . The enemy's fire guided by lighted tents, was at first remarkably directed; and even after the lights had been extinguished there was no lack of precision.[49]

Within a half-hour, the Union batteries ashore, supported by Navy gunboats on the river, quickly silenced the Rebel batteries. Oddly enough, despite the grandiose nature of the bombardment, the Union Army suffered few casualties. Hardin's Regiment came through completely unscathed. But, until the end of their lives, the men never forgot the fierce beauty of the fiery Rebel bombardment at Harrison's Landing.[50]

A truly large morale boost for the Pennsylvania Reserve Division came in August when Division commander George A. McCall and Brigade commander John F. Reynolds, along with nearly 400 enlisted men taken prisoners during the Seven Days were exchanged. The returning prodigal sons were greeted joyously by their comrades at Harrison's Landing. Not long afterwards, General McCall, a Mexican War veteran who had served under General Zachary Taylor, resigned his commission due to poor health and returned to Pennsylvania. In his place John Reynolds, as senior brigadier in the Pennsylvania Reserves, assumed command of the division. In the tumultuous days ahead, young Hardin came to admire Reynolds greatly.[51]

Hardin's task as a regimental commander was especially challenging. His outfit, the Twelfth Pennsylvania Reserve Regiment, had been roughly handled during the Seven Days. They were battle-hardened veterans who knew the score; they had seen the "The Elephant." However, few of the men—if any—wanted another close-up look at the creature. There was only one way their youthful commanding officer could meet this formidable challenge and win his men's trust, confidence and respect: he must lead from the front by example and share the dangers and privations of war alongside his soldiers.

Perhaps the young regimental commander drew inspiration from his own family's illustrious military heritage, stretching back more than a century to the time of the French and Indian War. Hardin and Logan men had led fighting men on a dozen battlefields and their last names had become synonyms with courage, honor and duty. Now in the summer of 1862, it was Colonel Martin D. Hardin's turn to emulate those shadows from the past, not the least of which was his own father, Colonel John J. Hardin, the slain hero of Buena Vista.

On August 11, 1862, the men of the Pennsylvania Reserve Division boarded steamboats for a voyage to Acquia Creek, Virginia, a key army marshalling center south of Washington. After a pleasant two-day voyage, the men disembarked and continued their journey by rail to Falmouth, Virginia. There they joined General Irwin McDowell's Third Corps, part of the newly created Union Army of Virginia. The commanding general of this new entity was General John Pope of Illinois. This supremely confident—some said arrogant—soldier was a friend and favorite of President Lincoln, the victor of several battles in the Western Theater, and a relative by marriage to First Lady Mary Todd Lincoln.[52]

Hardin and his men remained at Falmouth waiting for the order to move. Their mood was foul. Hardin wrote: "Our baggage, knapsacks, etc., went on to Washington. We haven't got them yet. For the coming campaign we were to be in light marching order, sure enough."[53] Much later, they learned to their chagrin that that their personal belongings and bags were ultimately given away to runaway slaves. So went the fortunes of war. They would experience much worse before it was all over.

Hardin's regiment was part of the Division's Third Brigade (Ninth, Tenth, Eleventh and Twelfth Regiments) commanded by Colonel Conrad Ferger Jackson.[54] This tough old Mexican War veteran and former Quaker finally put the men on the road at 10 p.m., August 21, heading south to the Rappahannock River. The movement was made with dispatch; President Lincoln was anxious that these and other reinforcements from McClellan's Army quickly support Pope's Union Army of Virginia, which was now confronted by General Lee. That always aggressive soldier was moving fast, concentrating his forces, and planning to destroy Pope and his army in a battle of annihilation.

Their first destination was Kelly's Ford on the Rappahannock River. Despite all the need for speed, Hardin recalled that the early going was a confused undertaking marked by many pauses and changes of direction. The column blundered about aimlessly during a night Hardin described as, "dark as Erebus."[55] Daylight found the exhausted men back in sight of their old camp. They had literally marched all night in circles.[56]

With the sun now high in the sky, General Jackson finally found the right road and drove the tired men another six or seven miles before allowing a brief halt during which the soldiers lit fires and brewed coffee. After an hour's rest, they wearily resumed the march. Hardin wrote:

> The night had been hot and sultry; the morning began hotter still with a brilliant sunlight. . . . The march was continued with infrequent and very short halts till dark, when an enforced bivouac was made in a fine open wood. The men had by reason of the heat and rapid march, and previous nights' march, fallen out along the road till the brigade was less than a regiment and the regiments' only companies. The white, glistening turnpike, with very little water, had been a most trying route . . . one of the hardest we ever made.[57]

Many hours later Hardin and his men literally collapsed when they finally received the order to fall out. No one even had the energy to start a fire and brew coffee, the black fuel that powered the army from dawn to dusk. Instead, they slept like the dead right where they lie. "The men's misfortunes were not yet full," Hardin wrote. "Just as they began to get strength to move about, a Virginia Summer thunderstorm broke upon them . . . our beautiful woods was a swale, which . . . received all the water in the vicinity."[58]

Pelted with rain, the soaked, sore and miserable men endured the long night. Hardin attempted to sleep balanced atop a large log, dozing fitfully until he fell splashing into the water below. With thoughts of the old saying, "easy as rolling off a log," the soggy Hardin finally compromised by sitting up against the "angle of a worm fence." There he sat miserably awaiting the dawn.[59]

What was left of the brigade—many had straggled during the march—got an early start that morning and finally arrived at Kelly's Ford around 10 a.m., only to learn that General John Reynolds and the lead elements of the division had already departed for Rappahannock Station further downriver. Hardin remembered that when they finally made the rendezvous later that afternoon, they encountered a stirring sight indeed:

> . . . instead {of finding Union troops, the brigade}found the Confederate cavalry, followed by the Confederate infantry skirmishers taking possession of McDowell's earthworks near Rappahannock Station. Skirmishers were thrown out from the head of the division, at sight of whom and the Army of the Potomac flags, borne by the division, the Confederate cavalry and skirmishers evacuated the station and our division took possession.[60]

The Pennsylvanians learned that McDowell's corps was marching to Warrenton, Virginia, and quickly set out to join them there. The bedraggled men of the 12th Pa. Regiment tramped along with the rest of the division; they soon heard the ominous rumble of artillery in the distance. Hardin wrote: "Darkness and rain soon came, also a few of the enemy's shells . . . There was Confederate cavalry all around us; no one dared to straggle; we had neither ambulances nor wagons; it was necessary to keep up or go to Richmond {as prisoners}. Human endurance was put to a severe test that night. The march only terminated with daylight, when we came upon one of McDowell's divisions in camp."[61]

Disheveled, their wool uniforms seeping water, the tired Pennsylvanians, in Hardin's words, were "ragged shoeless, footsore, tired to death, with nothing but our guns and our battle-stained flags to show that we were soldiers. McDowell's men were fully equipped, completely uniformed, knapsacks and all, 'spick and span' new. They looked to us like a militia command out for a parade."[62]

One of McDowell's infantryman suddenly shouted: "Stop and grab a root!" That was Civil War army slang meaning stop and eat. The Pennsylvanians were more than pleased to accept the invitation and, in Hardin's words, "were soon enjoying a hearty breakfast."[63]

Many of the men in the Twelfth Reserve Regiment were surprised to learn that McDowell's well-equipped corps seemed in no danger whatsoever. No battle was raging, and the only sign of the Rebs in the vicinity were roaming Confederate cavalrymen. Hardin shared his men's anger that they had been driven so hard for apparently no reason. He later asked the question that soldiers have been asking since the siege of Troy:

> Why march men as we had been marched? We had lost by exhaustion nearly one-third of our command, and that for nothing. Our division started from Falmouth nearly 4,000 strong; we reported with little over 2,500. The distance by the route we marched was about fifty miles, passed over in the hottest of weather, with thunder-storms at night. We naturally asked: "If there were such urgent necessity for reinforcements to Pope's army, why did our division remain so long at Falmouth . . ."[64]

Pointless marches and counter-marches, hesitation and confusion, foul-ups with their baggage, over-confidence and arrogant assumptions, were rife in this new Army of Virginia. General Pope, famous for his victory at Island Number Ten in the Western Theater, had taken command eager to teach the Eastern armies how to fight, stating undiplomatically that in the west, they were accustomed to seeing the enemy's back, not the other way around. His hubris and contempt for the Eastern soldiers immediately alienated those now under his command.[65]

The men and officers of the Army of the Potomac resented his suggestion that they were a bunch of cowards. Not a few among them, remarked that this arrogant Illinois friend of Lincoln would soon think different once he met "Bobby Lee" and his formidable Army of Northern Virginia on the battlefield.

That moment was not far distant. General Lee was not about to wait until McClellan's entire army united with Pope's forces and marched south again in overwhelming numbers. He determined to strike swiftly and destroy the Federal Army of Virginia in a daring campaign of movement. The odds were high against him. Pope commanded 75,000 men to 55,000 of Lee's.[66] Incredibly, against all conventional military logic, Lee split his outnumbered forces into two separate wings and began a campaign of brilliant audacity unrivaled in the history of the war.

On August 25, 1862, General Stonewall Jackson led one detachment of 24,000 soldiers on a wide sweep around Pope's right flank using the Bull Run Mountains to screen his movement. The goal was to eventually turn east, push through the mountains via Thoroughfare Pass, and descend with a vengeance upon the Union rear. Jackson hoped to cut Pope's railroad supply line and threaten Washington.[67]

Lee, with around 30,000 troops, remained for the time being on the line of the Rappahannock in front of Pope's Army. Distracted by artillery demonstrations, Pope apparently believed that any movement to his right was headed toward the Shenandoah Valley and ignored that threat.[68]

Colonel Hardin and thousands of other Union soldiers camped at Warrenton saw the dust cloud to the west marking the initial progress of Jackson's column. Yet no orders came down from General Pope to counter the movement. The Union divisions remained in place. Hardin was puzzled at his commander's inactivity. Even this early in the campaign Colonel Hardin believed that Pope had, "lost the confidence, not only of his general officers, but of the rank and file as well, for the latter, as well as their commanders, saw this turning movement of the enemy, and saw nothing and heard nothing being done to meet it."[69]

Jackson soon reached the Union rear, and on the night of August 26, his fast-moving column put the torch to the railroad station and massive supply hub at Manassas Junction astride Pope's supply line. Finally, Pope moved north to concentrate his scattered forces and surround the Rebels before they could escape or be reinforced by Lee. "We shall bag the whole crowd," Pope announced.[70] Like many of his pronouncements these words came to haunt the proud man from Illinois.

Jackson's raiders abandoned the smoldering ruins of Manassas Junction late that night and withdrew northwest to a strong position along Stony Ridge near Groveton where they utilized an unfinished railroad cut to serve as a ready-made trench.[71] Their strongpoint was only a few thousand yards north of the old Bull Run Battlefield. There Jackson waited for the Union forces to find him, confident in his men's ability to fend off Pope's expected assaults long enough to allow Lee's force time to arrive and descend on the Union flank.

"This movement of Jackson's was not as risky as it has generally been considered," Hardin contended three decades later. "He could always fall back toward the Shenandoah Valley. Moreover, he had a preponderance of cavalry which enabled him to screen himself and to keep watch of the movements of the Union Army."[72]

The clock was running, however, and for the moment Jackson was vastly outnumbered should Pope concentrate against him. Soon General Lee with his 30,000-man wing of the army under Longstreet was marching north along the same route Jackson had taken earlier. Lee's intent was to arrive on Pope's flank while he faced Jackson, and strike his army a killing blow. If successful he hoped to cut off their retreat along the Warrenton Turnpike to the strongly fortified stronghold of Centreville, and destroy them in detail.

About 5:30 p.m. on August 28, Jackson revealed his location along the abandoned railroad line by attacking a Union division moving down the Warrenton Pike. Now Pope acted swiftly, ordering his army to concentrate on Groveton and converge on Stonewall Jackson's force. Then and later, General Pope seemed unconcerned or unaware of the location and intent of Lee's main body. It was almost as if his entire focus was fixated only on destroying Jackson's little army.

On the morning of August 28, the Pennsylvania Reserve Division, under the command of General John F. Reynolds, was moving about a mile past Gainesville. Initially, Hardin recalled, he and the men of his regiment were "highly elated and marched cheerfully,"[73] confident that they would soon find and destroy the Rebels in their rear. Their progress was halted for two hours early in the day when higher command ordered them to allow the passage of a supply train.

When the march resumed, their column was joined by corps commander General Irvin McDowell and his staff. The column crossed a small stream, Hardin recalled, when Confederate artillery on their left opened a sudden and accurate bombardment: "The enemy's artillery fire at the first discharge killed and wounded some men in the Eighth Reserves. General McDowell and staff rode hastily off to the right to some high ground," Hardin recalled. "We saw this hasty retreat of the corps headquarters, and would have thought no more of it except as a joke on McDowell and his staff to have to 'skedaddle' . . . , but it happened that our division did not see or hear from McDowell that day, nor so far as the writer is concerned until the morning of August 30." The sudden flight of their corps commander was just the first episode in what Hardin remembered later as "this unlucky day."[74]

Strange events soon seemed commonplace on this chaotic battlefield. After the Union and Rebel batteries exchanged a few shells, the Reserve Division moved off south of the Pike in the opposite direction of where the enemy artillery was located. "This caused remarks at the time," Hardin wrote. "An officer or two rode off in the direction of the firing, the only effort that was made to find out what the enemy was."[75]

An hour passed before the division formed in line of battle to the right of the Warrenton Pike and advanced across a stretch of rough ground through patches of woods, dry streambeds and fields. After two hours of uneventful marching in blazing heat the troops were exhausted and were soon without water: "After the entire command was about used up, the division was halted and waited for orders," Hardin wrote.[76]

Division commander Reynolds left his unit in search of the missing corps commander, but he never did find General McDowell. Finally, Reynolds located General Pope at Manassas Junction, who ordered him to move his division towards Centreville. Reynolds rejoined the Pennsylvania Reserves and moved them out, only to receive a countermanding order some time later, directing him to march towards Gainesville in a totally different direction.

"There was no enemy, and no other Union troops in sight or hearing, at any time after the division left the Warrenton Pike that morning," Hardin remembered." Towards nightfall, firing could be heard toward our front, in the direction of Gainesville. General Reynolds went off again to get orders, or at least to find some neighboring troops. When night overtook the division it was completely isolated and practically lost. The division . . . was bivouacked in an old field; no water could be found. Pickets were thrown out in all directions. Never before or afterwards did the division get into such a predicament."[77] Hardin joked that instead of bagging Stonewall Jackson that night, they faced the prospect of being bagged themselves if the division didn't soon reunite with the main body of the army. They endured a thirsty night in the field and "rested quietly, very quietly, until daylight," he recalled.[78]

During the long night the men must have been plagued by dread of what the rising sun might bring. They knew that some of them would die by bullet or shell; others crippled, maimed, blinded or captured. Many surely worried that, in their fear and weakness, they might let down their comrades and shame the folks at home. A reasonable assumption is that many during that long night found comfort and solace in God and his Holy Word; while not a few nursed a hidden flask of liquor to calm their trembling hands.

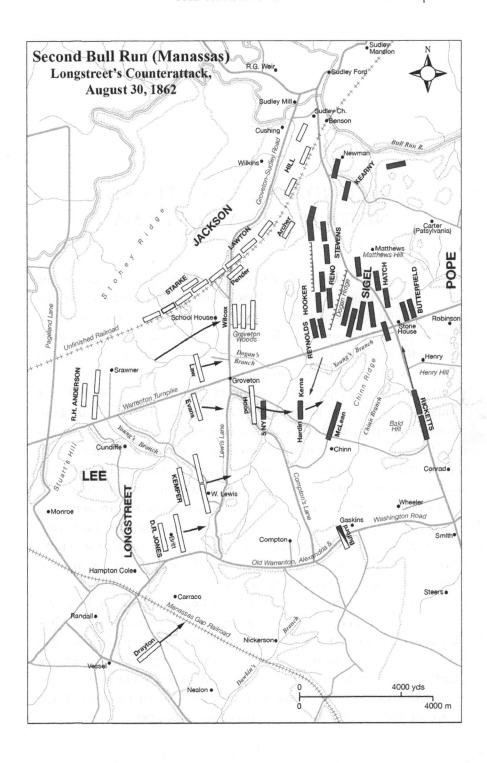

Second Bull Run (Manassas)
Longstreet's Counterattack,
August 30, 1862

CHAPTER 12

SECOND BULL RUN: "THE SUN NEVER SET ON A BRAVER MAN"

As the first rays of sunlight filtered through the clouds on the morning of August 29, 1862, artillery fire rumbled in the distance. General Reynolds had still not returned to camp, but his senior brigadier, General George Meade, assumed command and put the Pennsylvania Reserve Division on the march. They tramped toward the sound of the guns off toward their right front.[1]

Reynolds briefly rejoined the command about 7 a.m. during a halt near a small stream flowing between the Henry House Hill and Bald Hill. Shortly afterwards, the division commander galloped off again to investigate the source of heavy gunfire.[2] Soon General Pope issued orders directing the bulk of his army north of the Warrenton Turnpike to launch heavy infantry assaults against Stonewall Jackson's position near Groveton.

Incredibly, Pope either ignored or dismissed various reports indicating that Lee and Longstreet were now moving rapidly toward the battlefield. Should the other wing of the Army of Northern Virginia arrive before Jackson was destroyed, they would have the opportunity to strike the Army of the Potomac a massive blow on the left flank.

About mid-morning, the Pennsylvania Reserves moved towards the Rebel fire. Colonel Hardin's regiment was on the left of the division. Minutes later Hardin noted that the units on the brigade's opposite flank had become engaged in what he described as sharp fighting. For the time being Hardin's regiment had not yet been engaged. At this point in the battle, around 11 a.m., the Pennsylvania Reserves were advancing in line of battle about one mile south of Groveton. As Hardin remembered:

Just before halting the Twelfth Regiment crossed a fence, which was bordered by brush and trees. The regiment being closed in mass became somewhat disordered. . . . The regiment came out beyond the fence into an open field, where it was being re-organized, when a Confederate battery was run up to the crest of a hill to the left rear of the regiment, not more than one or two hundred yards distant and fired one round. Fortunately for the Twelfth Regiment the aim was high. The men instinctively dropped and the charge struck only the right front corner of the regiment, killing and wounding a small number.[3]

Hardin's regiment fell back with the rest of the division for about a half-mile while still under fire from the Rebel battery. Once out of range they reformed, and with the rest of the division resumed the march, moving doggedly hither and yon without apparent purpose. Confusion seemed to be a prominent actor on the Bull Run battlefield throughout the long day. The division remained essentially unengaged while Union assaults against Jackson were launched without success.

Finally, about a half-hour before sunset, the division finally moved against the enemy. The Second Brigade was on the left and the Third Brigade (containing Hardin's regiment) on the right of the line of battle. In their immediate rear, the First Brigade followed as a reserve. The division was advancing behind a thin line of skirmishers over some of the same ground they had traversed earlier that day.

Rebel and Union skirmishers sniped away at one another. "The Pennsylvanians pushed ahead and made their way up a gentle slope," Hardin remembered.[4] When they crested the rise the men were "face to face with the Confederate line of battle. In front of the Third Brigade's line were two batteries and three lines of infantry, one behind the other, all evidently waiting for our troops to endeavor to cross the grassy slope. . . . The division halted before the enemy fired. It was evident to everyone that there was no chance with a single line of battle of carrying this triple line."[5]

Hardin's men instinctively "dropped at once" to the ground at the intimidating sight of the massed Rebel infantry.[6] Seconds later, the Confederate artillery opened with a roar, firing at an angle into the ranks of the Twelfth Regiment. Hardin was leaning against a tree when an exploding

shell tore away the roots, sending both the tree and the regimental commander rolling down the slope. Embarrassed but unhurt, Hardin dusted
himself off and resumed his place at the head of his troops.[7]

The regiment recoiled from the heavy enemy fire and began falling
back despite the best efforts of Hardin and other officers who moved up
and down the line pleading for the men to stand and rally. That's when
Captain Lucas of C Company shouted to Hardin: "Duck, Colonel! Duck!"
Hardin turned his head slightly just as a Rebel bullet cut away half of his
cap brim and scorched his ear.[8] He spun away and tumbled in the grass.
He was only slightly wounded from the bullet graze and quickly regained
his feet and composure.

Retreat was sounded not long afterward. The men fell back, one regiment at a time, and in good formation. Hardin watched as the Sixth Pennsylvania Reserves moved out first in "beautiful order" until an enemy shell
plowed an "ugly lane" through its ranks. Soon after, Hardin's regiment
began its withdrawal. In Hardin's words, they were moving back through
the cornfield when enemy infantry and artillery joined "in letting us have
it."[9]

Many years later, Hardin made a point to emphasize that his regiment
never ran during this heavy fire, but he did candidly admit the boys walked
to the rear at a very fast pace.

Night found Hardin and his Twelfth Regiment encamped near a small
farmhouse: "Camp fires had scarcely been lighted when a Confederate battery opened on our camp," he reported. "Fires were at once extinguished,
but the enemy's battery having got the range continued to fire for an hour
or more. This artillery fire was very destructive."[10]

During the bombardment, Hardin left his regiment and walked in the
growing darkness to division headquarters near Bald Hill. He intended asking General Reynolds to either silence the enemy guns with counter-bat-
tery fire or permit him to move the regiment from its exposed position.
The division commander, however, was absent, once again seeking orders
from corps headquarters wherever it might be. Mercifully, the Confederate
artillery fire finally ceased of its own accord not long afterwards.

In the pitch black, Hardin began his cautious return to the regiment.
He knew the dangers of stumbling upon some trigger-happy rifleman. So-
called friendly fire was a constant danger in the aftermath of a fight. Pickets

tended to be jumpy and often shot before confirming whether the shadow or sound was friend or enemy.

Hardin carefully and quietly made his way among the shadows, and soon became aware that he had strayed into the Confederate picket line. Around him he could hear the whispered drawl of Rebel soldiers in conversation. Years later, Hardin made little of the incident, saying only that he escaped unnoticed with the aid of the "Egyptian darkness."[11] In truth, the young colonel came perilously close to being killed or captured. If the Rebel pickets didn't shoot him down, the equally nervous Union pickets might have done the job for them.

Looking back on the first day of the Second Battle of Bull Run, Hardin noted with chagrin: "All our movements this day seemed to be without design . . ."[12] Indeed, Hardin's division commander Reynolds seemed to be continually absent while searching for his Corps and Army commanders for want of orders. "No one who was not with us at this time can properly criticize the action of isolated commanders," Hardin wrote much later. "It is seldom in war that division commanders are so isolated as they were at this time."[13]

While Hardin and his men slept on the battlefield that night, they were wary that soon the other wing of the Army of Northern Virginia would be poised to strike the Union Army of Virginia like a thunderbolt. Much worse, the army's commander, John Pope, appeared to dismiss the threat of this enemy attack; instead, on the second day, he resumed his frontal attacks on Jackson's men. Apparently Pope was confident that he could overwhelm Jackson in time to face the threat from Lee and Longstreet on his open flank.

By this time Colonel Hardin had lost faith in both Pope and corps commander Irvin McDowell. To add to the general unease and misery, the men were completely without rations, the result of Jackson's destruction of their supply depot at Manassas Junction. During the long fitful night, one wonders if Hardin traced with his fingers the shallow blood-encrusted groove where the Rebel Minie ball had grazed his head earlier that day. Lady Luck had been at Hardin's side on that occasion, but would she smile again when the battle resumed?

The day of August 30, 1862 began as a frustrating repeat of the previous. All through the morning Colonel Hardin and his men, exhausted and hungry, marched back and forth along the Union army's left flank. Around noon, the Pennsylvania Reserves formed into column and boldly, perhaps foolishly, moved along the front of several enemy artillery batteries "strung along their edge of the woods near Groveton. These batteries had a perfectly open and enfilade fire on our division as it advanced," Hardin wrote. "We were certainly astonished at our movement. The enemy watched us, but evidently thinking it was a ruse on our part, did not fire. Reynolds' Division soon withdrew into a wooded area."[14]

Not long after the division's fortunate escape from the Confederate artillery, Union skirmishers on the left of the army reported to General Reynolds that Longstreet's force was forming behind the woods south of Groveton. The commander of the Pennsylvania Reserves rode forward and confirmed the intelligence, then galloped off to inform General Pope of the impending attack. Pope remained convinced that Jackson's line was about to break, in spite of the repeated and bloody Union failures. Proud, insolent and overbearing, Pope was still at this late stage apparently divorced from reality.

When Reynolds reported that an entirely fresh Rebel corps was about to descend on the army's weakened left flank south of the Turnpike, Pope, managed to ignore for the moment his obsession with destroying Jackson's detachment, and directed Reynolds to move his division across to the high ground along Chinn Ridge south of the Turnpike to meet any threat. Yet Pope soon ordered Fitz John Porter's Fifth Corps to launch yet another assault against Jackson. Somehow he had convinced himself that the enemy was in retreat.

Colonel Hardin had a clear view as Porter's blue infantry advanced across the corpse-littered field:

> From in front of Bald Hill we could see Porter's left brigade. It moved out of the strip of timber and formed a deep column fronting Groveton, and advanced rapidly toward that point. As soon as it was clear of the woods the Confederate batteries above the unfinished railroad . . . opened on it, taking it in front and flank. The destruction was terrible, but the brigade moved bravely on, even after all organization was destroyed by its losses. Nothing human could reach that timber . . .[15]

Porter's men fell back in disarray before a scythe of enemy rifle and cannon fire, leaving the field dotted with blue. The Rebels were snapping at their heels when they were suddenly in range of Union artillery and massed infantry fire from Sykes' Division. "At this moment the Union guns near the Pike opened, every shot making a lane through the Confederate columns," Hardin observed. "Still they came on, the rear in disarray. The front entered the strip of woods, where it met a sheet of flame. . . . In a moment the Confederate yell ceased and the column stopped, then swayed; then those not disabled started to the rear . . . this fine brigade, as had the Union on the same ground, left its bravest and best dead or dying."[16]

Not long afterwards the Third Corps commander, General McDowell, rode up to the Pennsylvanians in an extremely agitated state and ordered them to leave their position south of the Turnpike to support Porter. Hardin later recalled that McDowell was "the most excited officer" he had ever seen on a battlefield.[17] By now it was apparent to almost everyone that this would leave the door open to Longstreet's impending assault. One Civil War historian claimed that this was clear to even the privates in the ranks, quoting one enlisted man who worried that if "the Johnnies should reach the Warrenton Pike {they would cause} irreparable injury to the Union army."[18]

Hardin considered McDowell's decision that day to be inexplicable. He was hardly alone in this view; many officers even suspected McDowell might have been a Confederate sympathizer, deliberately providing Longstreet with the opportunity to destroy Pope's army. That seemed to be the only logical explanation since the decision ran counter to almost all military logic. "This blunder was seen by us and commented on at the time," Hardin wrote.[19]

While the Pennsylvania Reserve Division began moving across the Turnpike into place, an aide to the Third Brigade's commander, General Conrad Jackson, rode up to Hardin and delivered a startling message: General Jackson was seriously ill (he had suffered a burst blood clot), and Division commander Reynolds had ordered Hardin to assume command of the brigade.[20]

That announcement came at a critical turning point in the battle and must have hit young Hardin like a thunderclap. The 24-year-old had only commanded his regiment in battle for less than two days; now, during the crisis he was elevated to brigade command. At this juncture the Third Brigade, along with Mark Kerns' artillery battery, formed the tail of the Pennsylvania Reserve Division in its movement north of the Pike.

Sharp firing to the south of the Pike suddenly signaled the long-feared attack by Longstreet.[21] Colonel Hardin and battery commander Kerns immediately spurred their horses and rode back across the Pike. They galloped up a small knoll about 500 yards west of Chinn Ridge. From this vantage point, the two officers beheld the beginning of a Union route. A mob of colorfully uniformed Union Zouaves from Colonel Gouverneur K. Warren's New York State Brigade was running towards them in wild disarray. Behind them came Confederate General John Bell Hood's howling Texans. This thunderbolt of Confederate infantry came on in a rush, shrieking the dread-inspiring Rebel yell.

The Zouaves had been the only significant unit left to guard the flank, and now they were in shambles. In ten minutes one of these units, the Fifth New York Regiment, suffered 60 percent casualties.[22] Colonel Hardin and Captain Kerns witnessed their ordeal from the knoll. Survivors were streaming back at a full run, although some paused occasionally to fire and then resume their flight. Snapping at their heels came the ragged Confederates like so many rangy hunting dogs closing in on their prey. "The only alternative was to fly or surrender," one New Yorker who survived stated.[23]

There was no time for Hardin and Kerns to seek orders from division. They acted entirely on their own without second thoughts: Kerns announced he would plant his battery on that very spot; Hardin immediately agreed to support the rifled ten-pounders with his infantry brigade. Then he rode off to turn his brigade around and bring them back across the Pike to the small knoll. There, this relative handful of Union soldiers confronted the onrushing Confederates.

"Colonel Hardin galloped backward to the Third Brigade . . . gave the command, 'Left into line, wheel!' and moved the brigade up to the crest on the left of Kern's battery. Hardin gave the order to fire."[24] The first Yankee volley exploded into the faces of the charging Confederate infantry; dozens fell dead or wounded as the cruel rain of lead splintered their ranks. Now both sides exchanged fire at will, giving and taking death and wounds in the frenzy of a close-up infantry firefight. Hardin wrote:

The enemy advanced without firing until he reached the foot of the hill, where he was checked by Kerns' battery, when he {the Rebels} moved by his right flank to the strip of woods and commenced firing. The enemy's fire began slowly to move around towards the left of his {Hardin's} Third Brigade. He found he could not take the battery in front. His reinforcements could be seen moving to his right. The firing soon became so hot on the left that the left regiment of front line was partly moved to face it; then the second line was ordered to join the first. . . . The enemy's fire, now both on the front and left of the brigade, was terrific.[25]

Men from the Confederate Fifth Texas delivered a scathing fire from their flanking position in a nearby wooded area. In Hardin's front, he faced a determined advance from Hampton's Legion and the 18th Georgia Infantry. The Union brigade began to waver in the storm of bullets. But the enemy was bleeding, too, especially from the savage blasts of canister and grape from Kerns' artillery.[26]

Colonel Hardin was speaking (probably yelling over the din) with Lt. Col. Peter Baldy, who had only just taken his place at the head of the Twelfth Regiment; just when Hardin turned away he was struck down by a Rebel Minie ball.

The rifle ball burrowed into Hardin's torso and penetrated the "left side of the thorax two or three inches below the clavicle, perforated the pectoral muscle, and exited out through the scapula."[27] By some act of God or simply luck, the bullet didn't pierce his lungs or other vital organs. Hardin's left arm now dangled helplessly at his side.

Several infantrymen carried him to the rear. Bleeding profusely and sinking into shock, all Hardin would later remember of the incident was encountering Lieutenant Lamborne of General Reynolds' staff near the Pike, who paused to give him a swig from "a flask of brandy."[28] In Hardin's mind, this jolt of stimulant saved his life that day.

Somehow the unidentified infantrymen managed to convey their badly wounded commander through the confusion and chaos of the battlefield. Later, he would state that the entire episode remained a black gap in his mind. Behind him his beleaguered brigade broke before the Rebel assault and the remnants fell back to Chinn Ridge, which was now held by several

Ohio regiments. They, too, were defiant and stubborn, buying time for
Pope to try to adjust to the new emergency. They, too, eventually gave way
and fell back to Henry House Hill. Here, the Pennsylvania Reserve Division under General Reynolds stood strong with other Union defenders,
helping hold the door open while the army fled east down the Warrenton
Pike and across Bull Run bridge.[29]

The Union army finally found blessed sanctuary in the strong fortifications around Centreville where they licked their wounds. Once again,
Robert E. Lee had dealt the Union a severe defeat and had come very close
to achieving his desired battle of annihilation. But of these events the
wounded Hardin probably knew little at the time. He was busy waging his
own desperate battle of survival in one of the army's aid stations.

One of the Pennsylvania boys recorded his impressions of a surgical
station on that final day of Second Bull Run. It may have even been the
very station where Colonel Hardin was taken, or at least was similar in its
grisly horrors:

> The surgeons were cutting off arms, feet, hands and limbs of all
> kinds in what looked like a little country schoolhouse. And, as an
> arm or leg was cut off, it was thrown out an open window. The
> cut-off limbs had accumulated so that they blocked the window .
> . . a detail of a few men were hauling away the limbs with a wheel-
> barrow. . . . It had the appearance of a human slaughter house.[30]

What we do know for certain is that Hardin was soon taken to a Washington hospital, where his younger brother, Lemuel Smith Hardin, found
him a week later. In a few days Lemuel accompanied his badly wounded
brother back home to Pine Grove Mansion in Saratoga Springs. Colonel
Hardin could at least die there comforted by those who loved him.

In the excruciatingly painful days ahead, however, the young colonel
displayed an amazing resilience and slowly rallied. He won his fight against
the Death Angel and began a long, halting convalescence. Like any soldier
fresh from the trauma of combat he needed time, not only to heal the
wounds of his flesh, but to cope with the mental wounds that invariably
linger long after the physical body has recovered.

Second Bull Run had been an unmitigated disaster. Yet the wounded

Hardin must have felt proud of his behavior on the battlefield when his brigade faced Longstreet's powerful attack. Hardin, Warren, Reynolds and their soldiers had all made significant contributions toward delaying the inexorable Rebel advance. Hardin's friend, Captain Mark Kerns, gave his life that day on the small knoll where they made their desperate stand, manning his artillery pieces to the very end before being shot down. The artillery officer was among the first of many Hardin friends who gave their lives in the long war.

The private soldiers had no reason to be ashamed for the defeat at Second Bull Run. The Union rank-and-file fought with grit and determination. Their heroics, however, were again squandered by the Union high command's incompetence. Pope's poor leadership and decision-making, coupled with McClellan's deliberate, almost treasonous failure to promptly and adequately reinforce the beleaguered Army of Virginia during the crisis, were key factors leading to the defeat.[31] Once again Union valor had been betrayed by poor and self-serving commanders.

Most importantly for young Colonel Hardin, he had passed his test of valor on that bloody battlefield, winning the respect and admiration of his men. Sergeant David Shirk, Co. G, Twelfth Pa. Reserve Regiment, probably spoke for many others in the enlisted ranks when he wrote a letter home describing Second Bull Run:

> . . . during the 3 days fight, we had the misfortune to lose 2 men killed and 2 wounded {Company G's losses} . . . We also had the misfortune of having our Lt. Col. M.D. Hardin wounded in the breast, he having command of the Brigade when wounded. He is one of the bravest officers ever the sun shone upon, and the Regiment now being deprived of his presence for the present, and if it should be our misfortune to lose his services, our Regiment will deplore his loss very much, as he has gained the confidence of the entire Regiment, and the Regiment has gained laurels, but if he should not again return to take command the reputation of the Twelfth Regiment will again be blasted. Lt. Col. Hardin is a son of Col. Hardin who fell at Buena Vista, and the Public will see that his son is good pluck, as he has shown in the late engagements in Virginia.[32]

As for General John Pope, the Battle of Second Bull Run was total humiliation. Relieved of his command, Pope was banished to the Minnesota frontier where he enjoyed a rather sordid success against the Santee Sioux Indians. Years later the historian of the Union's Second Corps wrote a pitiless summation of Pope's performance on the field of battle at Second Bull Run, writing:

> The braggart who had begun his campaign with insolent reflections . . . had been kicked, cuffed, hustled about, knocked down, run over, and trodden upon as rarely happens in the history of war. His communications had been cut; his headquarters pillaged; a {Confederate} corps had marched into his rear and had encamped at its ease upon the railroad by which he received his supplies; he had been beaten or foiled in every attempt he had made to "bag" those defiant intruders; and, in the end, he was glad to find refuge in the entrenchments of Washington.[33]

CHAPTER 13

SLAUGHTERED FOR NOTHING

After suffering his near-fatal wound at Second Bull Run, Colonel Hardin spent nearly nine months recovering. Despite enduring at least one painful operation, he never recovered use of his left arm, which hung useless and limp at his side—sad testimony to the intense suffering he had undergone. Some soldiers would have considered applying for a medical discharge, but there is no indication that Hardin entertained that option.

A few weeks before Christmas of 1862 his mother, Mrs. Chancellor Walworth, wrote a letter to Martin's sister Ellen, then living with his brother Lemuel in their country estate, the Bird's Nest, outside Louisville. She updated the siblings on their brother's injury and recuperation:

> I had heard nothing from Martin D since he left home except that Ed Thompson told me he went to Washington the Friday after he left home. It seems he returned in a few days for the purpose of having an operation performed, by D. Parker of New York. He came in just as we got up from the supper table this evening—looking in very good health—he says Dr. Parker took out several large pieces of bone and lead pieces of the bullet from his shoulder and there was a large discharge of blood and matter, which had collected about the broken bones. I have no doubt he suffered more than he let us know, which was one reason for his extreme nervousness at times. The surgeons in Washington gave him leave

for the winter—he says Dr. Parker thinks he will soon be well now. He returns to New York in two or three days to see the Dr. and will go to Washington but I do not think he will try to do active service very soon.[1]

Army surgeons determined Colonel Hardin fit enough for light duty in late March 1863, and he was ordered shortly afterwards to supervise the Army draft depot in Pittsburgh, where he remained through early May. The draft marked a new chapter in the war. With volunteers no longer rushing to the colors after the bloodlettings of 1862, the ranks were now being filled with conscripts. The Draft was unpopular in many parts of the North, especially among New York City's Irish residents, many of whom were enthusiastic participants in the infamous Draft Riots which erupted later that summer. Hardin's brother-in-law, Father Clarence Walworth, was an eyewitness to those horrors when the mob burned and looted large sections of the city and lynched innocent Negroes. Only the intervention of Army troops quelled the massive riot.[2]

During those long months at the Pine Grove Mansion in Saratoga Springs, Hardin had the opportunity to review the tragedy of Second Bull Run in his mind, and assess the failures of leadership that led to the defeat. Hardin believed that the incompetence of General John Pope, the commander of the short-lived Army of Virginia, and General Irwin McDowell, his Third Corps Commander, were chiefly responsible for the fiasco. "{Artillery Captain Mark} Kerns and many noble men sacrificed their lives, and many more of us will go maimed to our graves, by reason of a military mistake, which ought not to have been made," Hardin wrote later.[3]

Like so many of his fellow officers, Hardin was embittered by Pope's failure to recognize the looming threat of Longstreet's powerful corps, despite repeated warnings from scouts, and he was outraged at Pope's scapegoating of General Fitz John Porter for his corps' failure to destroy Stonewall Jackson's men behind the railroad escarpment. "A gallant assault was made by the men under Porter's command upon a position that had been so frequently assaulted without success that it was a military error to assault it again," Hardin contended. "Then a most bloody and desperate resistance was successfully made to a thoroughly prepared assault by more than half of the Confederate Army under their ablest fighting corps commander {Longstreet}. This assault had been foreseen by Reynolds, whose careful preparations to meet it were destroyed by McDowell. Yet Porter was dismissed and his command abused . . ."[4]

Hardin was scathing in his evaluation of McDowell. The latter had ordered Reynolds to move his Pennsylvania Reserve Division from its defensive positions south of the Warrenton Turnpike to support Porter's corps following its failed attack on Jackson. Many of the men in the ranks were equally incredulous when the division was forced to leave the army's southern flank unguarded at that critical juncture. Everyone seemed aware that Longstreet was up on their left and poised to attack except Generals Pope and McDowell.

"No doubt General McDowell promised General Reynolds to replace his division, and did try to do so, but time is valuable in the face of the enemy and a general must keep his wits in battle," Hardin concluded.[5] Like many Union soldiers, Hardin seriously wondered if McDowell's actions that day weren't motivated by support for the Confederate cause rather than poor judgement. How else could one explain such a gross military error?

During Hardin's long absence from the front, the war continued to go badly for the Army of the Potomac. Hardin's regiment, now commanded by Captain Richard Gustin, and the Pennsylvania Reserve Division, now led by General George Meade, had been roughly handled at South Mountain, Antietam and Fredericksburg.[6] As so often, the Union army's heroic efforts were squandered by poor leadership at the very top.

Following up his victory at Second Bull Run, in early September 1862 Robert E. Lee had initiated his first invasion of the North. The Army of Northern Virginia crossed over the Potomac River into Maryland, hoping to win that border state to the Confederacy and divert the Union Army— now commanded again by George McClellan—from launching offensive operations against Richmond. Lee was also hopeful he could attract recruits to the Southern cause while re-supplying his army with food and fodder gathered from the rich Maryland countryside.[7]

As he had at Second Bull Run, Lee again split his outnumbered army into two wings, apparently confident that the ever-cautious McClellan would fail to act aggressively. Stonewall Jackson took two-thirds of the army to capture a large Federal garrison left behind at Harpers Ferry, while

Lee and Longstreet operated farther north in Maryland. However, fate handed McClellan the very keys to victory. A stray copy of Lee's plan for the campaign, Special Orders 191, was retrieved by Union soldiers at an abandoned Confederate campsite, providing McClellan with the enemy's dispositions. McClellan now had an incredible opportunity to attack and destroy Lee's army while it was divided.[8]

The Army of the Potomac began to surge west, aiming at gaps in the mountains through which it could then descend on Lee's isolated force. The Pennsylvania Reserve Division was engaged at the Battle of South Mountain on September 14th, an all-day struggle against Confederate General D.H. Hill's division.[9] The Union forces eventually seized the high ground controlling Turner's Gap and other passes, and this victory opened the door for an advance to the Potomac near Sharpsburg to which Lee had retreated.

General Joseph Hooker, commander of the First Corps, praised the Pennsylvania Reserves and their commander in his official report following the victory at South Mountain: "Meade moved forward with great vigor . . . driving everything before him; every step of the advance was resisted stubbornly by a numerous enemy. . . . He had great natural obstacles to overcome, which impeded his advance but did not check it. . . . This {the pass} was taken in fine style between sundown and dark. . . . On reaching the summit, Meade was ordered to hold it until further orders."[10]

Lee's timetable had been upset. While Jackson had yet to reduce Harpers Ferry, McClellan had moved with unexpected speed, and the Federals had now poured through South Mountain and were heading toward his isolated force. Lee's army north of the Potomac River totaled only about 19,000 effectives while McClellan had some 80,000 at hand.[11] Instead of quickly retiring across the river—the prudent move—Lee daringly chose to await McClellan's army behind Antietam Creek, near Sharpsburg.[12]

McClellan, in fact, soon returned to form, cautiously gathering and preparing his forces throughout the day of September 15 prior to resuming his advance. Meantime on that morning Harpers Ferry finally surrendered. Jackson immediately began marching his men north to join Lee, leaving behind only A.P. Hill's division to take care of the 12,500 prisoners and captured material. As McClellan renewed his approach toward Sharpsburg on the 16th, Lee's army gradually received Jackson's reinforcements and would eventually number as many as 40,000 men.

At dawn on September 17 McClellan launched a series of attacks on Lee's army, from right to left. The result was the bloodiest single day of the war. The combat was incredibly intense and protracted at little patches of Hell remembered as the Cornfield, the Dunker Church, Bloody Lane and Burnside's Bridge. Casualties for both armies tallied at least 25,000 men killed, wounded and missing. Several times during the day the issue hung in the balance, but McClellan's piecemeal attacks gave Lee time to meet each thrust in turn, partly as Jackson's men continued to arrive on the battlefield.

In the late afternoon it seemed that the Confederate struggle had been for naught as the Federal Ninth Corps finally streamed across Burnside's Bridge and began rolling up the Rebel right, threatening to cut the entire army off from the river. At that moment, however, A.P. Hill's division appeared on the battlefield, having force-marched all day from Harpers Ferry. Hill's men slammed into the flank of the Ninth Corps and sent it reeling back to the Antietam.[13]

In the end, Lee fought McClellan to a standstill, and even defiantly remained in position the next day, as if daring the Federal commander to attack his smaller force again. On the night of the 18th, though, he pulled his battered and bloodied legions out of line and withdraw unhindered across the Potomac back to Virginia.

Although a tactical draw, Lincoln and the North saw Antietam as a strategic victory. Lee's invasion of the north had been repelled and the Army of the Potomac was left in possession of the battlefield. Lincoln had been waiting for a Union victory to issue his momentous Emancipation Proclamation. After the document was made public in the wake of Antietam, the war to save the Union was transformed into a revolutionary struggle to end human slavery in the United States. Nothing was ever the same again.

Although not present at the Antietam fight, General Hardin commented on the famous battle three decades after the war. "It was the hardest and best fought battle by both sides of the war," Hardin wrote. "Lee . . . held a chosen position with ample time to prepare it; this advantage {coupled} with modern weapons, fully counterbalanced McClellan's superior numbers. Moreover, McClellan had to retain one-fourth of his command practically idle to hold the connection between his widely separated wings. McClellan's attack on his right was too much by piecemeal, and made without sufficient artillery. These were faults too common throughout the war. . . . The attack on the left was badly managed . . . especially too slow after it was begun."[14]

Despite McClellan's documented shortcomings as a commander, he proved a veritable Napoleon compared to his successor, the hapless General Ambrose Burnside.

On December 13, 1862, Burnside committed the Army of the Potomac to one of its greatest disasters of the war by attacking the Army of Northern Virginia head-on at Fredericksburg, Virginia. Under the cover of a huge array of artillery on their side of the Rappahannock, the Union army—some 106,000 strong—laid pontoon bridges and crossed the river on December 11. Waiting for them was Lee's Army of some 75,000, dug-in along heights less than a mile away. Stonewall Jackson's corps held the right, below the town, while Longstreet's corps was in position behind Fredericksburg itself.

Early in the morning of December 13, General Edwin Sumner's left Grand Division—including the Pennsylvania Reserve Division under George Meade—began its attack on Jackson. One of Hardin's veterans, Sgt. Thomas W. Dick, Co. H, Twelfth Pa. Reserves, remembered the bitter cold, the danger and the terror of that memorable fiasco in a January 3, 1863 letter to his parents in Pennsylvania:

> Our troops advanced steadily forward under the shot and shell of the enemy. We moved on for some distance and then halted for some time, but not long. For, as usual, the old reserve corpse {corps} had to kick up a fight. So we were ordered to charge on the enemy's works, which I think was done in gallant style. We had to advance over a piece of low marshy ground and the rebels were posted in the woods on a range of hills in front of us; thus have all advantage in position. But still we advanced over their rifle pits and had them drive away from their guns, but we had no support and consequently had to fall back. I think whoever is responsible for this grand movement across the Rappahannock managed it very badly. For any person of common sense with no military ability would know that it was impossible to take that position.[15]

During the height of the battle, the Third Brigade, commanded by

General Conrad Jackson (including Hardin's old regiment), attacked a strong Rebel force placed behind a railroad embankment. "Taking the railroad, members of the Third Brigade dashed across it, to be met by a veritable sheet of flame and musket balls," wrote Historian Uzal W. Ent. "Many of the surprised men fell dead or wounded, and the others sought the shelter of railroad ditches . . ."[16]

Mounted on a gray horse, General Jackson rode up and down the brigade line shouting for his men to rally. (Hardin had replaced Jackson briefly as commander of the third brigade during Second Bull Run.) "He rode to the center of his line and told the Fifth Reserves to move to the left," Ent wrote. "Just then, a shower of bullets killed his horse, throwing Jackson to the ground. He drew his sword and jumped onto the railroad . . . As the General turned to urge his men on to the woods, another volley felled half of his staff, and he was killed instantly by a bullet to the head."[17]

Even though elements of Meade's division penetrated the Confederate line, the spearhead numbered no more than around 1,000 disorganized men and were not properly supported. They soon fell back before a strong Confederate counterattack. Out of 4,500 men engaged that day, the Pennsylvania Reserve Division incurred 1,853 killed, wounded and missing for a casualty rate of 41 percent.[18]

Although the Federals had failed against Stonewall Jackson's wing, the real disaster of the day, and perhaps the most egregious folly of the war, came when Burnside ordered repeated attacks up the slope toward Marye's Heights behind Fredericksburg itself. From a sunken road Longstreet's corps laid down a withering blaze of rifle fire on the exposed attackers, while artillery above them raked the ground. Fourteen times various Union units charged fruitlessly up the hill; each effort was repelled with incredible loss of life.

"I felt sorry for those poor Yankee soldiers as they marched into the very jaws of Death," wrote one of the Confederate defenders.[19] On their left against Jackson, the Army of the Potomac had lost about 4,500 men compared to some 3,700 Confederates. In the one-sided fight on their right however, at least 8,000 fell, as opposed to barely 1,500 Rebels.[20]

When Hardin learned of the defeat, he must have been shocked at the losses. His Twelfth Regiment was badly hurt losing 13 killed, 70 wounded and 33 missing for a casualty rate of 50 percent. Company C of Hardin's regiment suffered 40 casualties out of 49 present for duty.[21] His former brigade commander, Brigadier General Conrad Jackson, was shot dead; and his good friend, Brigadier General George D. Bayard, was mortally wounded in an artillery barrage.[22]

Colonel Hardin briefly rejoined his regiment in late December 1862 at their camp near Belle Plain, Virginia, where he undoubtedly heard many accounts of the Antietam and Fredericksburg battles.[23] The Pennsylvania Reserve Division was now a shadow of its former self, numbering less than 2,500 men following the Fredericksburg ordeal.

"The losses in the Reserve Division had been so great in the battle of Fredericksburg, it was necessary to reorganize it and fill it up or to break it up," Hardin wrote years later. "Its conduct had been so brilliant in this battle even the Secretary of War {Stanton} could not but see it would be best to retain the organization."[24]

The Pennsylvania Reserves, the only division in the Union army consisting solely of men from a single state, continued to serve as a unit until their three-year enlistment term expired in late May of 1864. Luckily, the division was spared General Joe Hooker's catastrophic defeat during the Chancellorsville campaign May 1 through May 4th. This is considered by many students of the Civil War to have been Lee's most brilliant victory. Unfortunately for the Southern cause, Lee's strong right hand, General Stonewall Jackson, was mortally wounded by nervous Confederate pickets firing in the shadows late on the battle's second day, immediately after Jackson had caved in the Union flank for his most renowned exploit of the war.[25, 26]

Colonel Hardin's return to the regiment in December 1862 had been premature. He had not completely recovered from his Second Bull Run wound, and suffered severely during the wet and cold December days in camp. He soon went back north on convalescent leave and would not see duty again until March.[27]

By the time, Hardin returned again, the Pennsylvania Reserves had journeyed by steamboat to Alexandria across the Potomac from the Capital. They then bivouacked on Union Hill where the weary men were to rest and recuperate from their hard service.

"The Reserves had been transferred to the Department of Washington to give them rest, but the guerrilla, Mosby, was so active, the picket duty here became more arduous than it was with the Army of the Potomac," Hardin stated. " . . . altogether the duties were no lighter nor the quarters any better than they were in the active army. The command failed to obtain the rest it required, and consequently, the slightly wounded and sick absentees were in no hurry to rejoin their command."[28]

One of Hardin's veterans, Sgt. Thomas Dick of Co. H, seemed blasé about Mosby's fabled guerrillas. In a February 22, 1863 letter to his brother, the veteran of so many battles made only a casual mention of the guerrilla danger: "Have nothing to annoy us, but the guerrillas. They pop one over occasionally. Major Larimer of the Fifth (Pa. Reserve Regt.) was killed a short time ago while leading a skirmish party."

On April 20, 1863, Colonel Hardin once again re-joined the regiment although his health and stamina remained questionable. His regiment and the rest of the Third Brigade, now commanded by Colonel Joseph Fisher, were assigned to Washington where they would guard Confederate prisoners. Hardin was given command of the Twelfth and Ninth Reserve Regiments and assigned to Carrol Barracks on Capitol Hill.[29]

Like most battle-tried veterans, the Pennsylvania Reserves had long ago learned that frontal assaults against an entrenched enemy were suicidal. Most remained loyal to the cause of Union and would stand by their comrades under the heaviest fire. But it's reasonable to assume that most of the men were wary of charging across open ground. They would have agreed with Hardin's assessment: "Even a temporarily fortified position can only be taken under favorable circumstances for the offense such as dense woods near the enemy's position, fog, darkness and the like."[30]

Even good soldiers will waver if their lives are repeatedly squandered in senseless head-on attacks. Many of Hardin's men must have wondered whether the Union commanders knew what they were doing following the defeats of the Seven Days, Second Bull Run, Fredericksburg and Chancellorsville. They had proved themselves to be an army of young lions led by jackasses in gold braid.

One of Hardin's veterans, Sergeant Dick, spoke for many in the ranks, when he wrote his parents of his disappointment in the leadership shown by the Union's top commanders:

> No wonder our army is discouraged. We have been slaughtered for
> nothing. We have always been led to expect great things and nearly

always been disappointed. We are all willing to do or to suffer anything for our glorious cause, but we are not willing to see our comrades cut down beside us and still accomplish nothing. All we want
is good leaders—God fearing men who will do their duty. For
surely the army had done its duty, the people have done theirs, so
it must be with our leaders. I have never felt so lonely in my life as
I did after the battle, the last of my messmates gone.[31]

First Sergeant Frank D. Stevens, Co. I, Twelfth Pennsylvania Reserve
Regiment, was another of Hardin's veterans who had grown weary of the
interminable war. He was quite frank in a letter home to his father when
he admitted his willingness to remain safe in garrison for the duration of
the conflict:

The weather is wet—ground muddy. Col. M.D. Hardin is again
in command of the Regt. He is a regular, and the consequence is,
we have to keep ourselves clean—have to wash our faces every
day—comb our hair—brush our clothes & blacken our shoes twice
per day; so you see we are playing Sunday soldiers. Duty is put on
double quick—men have to go on guard or picket every other day,
it is middling thick, but they may put us on double duty & half
rations all the time, if they promise to not fight us any more . . .[32]

CHAPTER 14

WHITE, HOT, DUSTY ROAD
TO GETTYSBURG

If Hardin's men were increasingly reluctant to wage war following the Fredericksburg defeat, they underwent a dramatic change of heart following electrifying news in the summer of 1863: the Army of Northern Virginia had once again crossed the Potomac into Maryland, and seemed intent on invading the Reserves' own state of Pennsylvania.

Many soldiers in the Pennsylvania Reserves, formerly content to guard prisoners and government buildings in Washington, now clamored to rejoin the Army of the Potomac to defend family and fireside back in the Keystone State. They even petitioned the government for that privilege.[1] Colonel Hardin no longer worried about motivating his men; they were straining at the bit and eager to once again confront their old enemy:

When the Reserves heard that Lee again threatened to invade Maryland and possibly Pennsylvania, officers and men began to take on a military air, which had been somewhat put aside after Fredericksburg, and talk of applying to rejoin their comrades of the Army of the Potomac on their march northward became prevalent. This went so far, in one case at least, as to be put in the form of a written petition. Whatever the form, the feeling of the command, from drummer boy to chaplain, was to take another turn at the "Johnnies"—to go in for a fight . . .[2]

General Joseph Hooker, the over-confident soldier who had been humbled by Lee in the Battle of Chancellorsville, was still commanding the Army of the Potomac. But after a dispute over the disposition of the Federal garrison at Harpers Ferry, "Fighting Joe's" tenure as army commander was to end upon the order of President Lincoln.

Lincoln appointed General George Gordon Meade, head of the Fifth Corps, and former commander of the Pennsylvania Reserves, to lead the Army of the Potomac. This news was received with joy by Colonel Hardin and his men. The irascible Meade had some rough edges to be sure, but he was competent and battle-tested. Private A.D. Benedict of Hardin's regiment confided to his diary: "We have confidence in 'Old Google Eyes' as we call Gen. G. Meade."[3]

The Pennsylvania Reserve Division was also under a new commander: General Samuel Wylie Crawford. The 42-year-old Pennsylvania native was a medical doctor with a degree from the University of Pennsylvania who had served as an army surgeon in the Regulars for ten years before the war. In the summer of 1861 he was among Major Robert Anderson's Fort Sumter garrison in Charleston Harbor.[4]

When the Confederate bombardment began on 1861, the doctor quickly traded his scalpel for a sword. Assistant Surgeon Crawford treated the wounded initially, but then volunteered to command one of the fort's massive cannon, directing fire at the Rebel batteries ashore.[5] This man of healing showed a pugnacious and aggressive and, as events soon proved, a voracious appetite for military laurels.

After the surrender of Fort Sumter, Crawford was exchanged and sent north, where he soon left the medical corps to command an infantry regiment and then a brigade, proving himself a physically brave, if not a gifted, commander of troops. He distinguished himself at Cedar Mountain and was badly wounded at Antietam.[6] In his home state of Pennsylvania, Crawford was politically well connected, came from a wealthy and influential family and—primarily for those reasons—won command of the Pennsylvania Reserve Division.

Unfortunately, unlike previous commanders of the Reserves, Crawford would not prove to a be a stellar military performer. In fact, after the war, one of his brigade commanders, Colonel Joseph Fisher, described the former doctor as a prolific blunderer.[7] Even worse, he came to be viewed by his officer peers as a self-aggrandizing glory hunter, always quick to exaggerate his battlefield exploits. On several occasions, he unashamedly played the sycophant with superior officers.

Although lacking knowledge of military science, Crawford did at least have the bearing and presence of a combat general. Tall and imposing, his stern features were framed by giant bushy sideburns that brushed his shoulders.[8] One soldier styled Crawford as "a tall, chesty, glowering man, with heavy eyes, a big nose and bushy whiskers."[9] Although brave and patriotic, Crawford ultimately stained his reputation by unashamedly claiming more laurels than were his due. Modesty was not in his make-up.

The men in the ranks called him "Old Pills" among other less flattering appellations.[10] Perhaps they had heard that before joining the division, General Crawford had once berated an infantry unit by calling them "Pennsylvania cattle." Supposedly, one of the infantrymen remarked to his comrades the hope that Crawford might become a victim of "accidental" Union fire during the next battle.[11]

Now on the eve of a great battle, Hardin and the other veterans of the Pennsylvania Reserves, would be led by an incompetent commander with political connections and a deep thirst for personal glory. Crawford was a far cry from those professional soldiers who had previously held high command in the Keystone division: Generals John F. Reynolds, George G. Meade, Truman Seymour, and Edward O. Ord.

Hardin's surviving personal papers are without any reference to General Crawford. So we are completely in the dark as to his personal opinion of his much-maligned commanding general. It's difficult to believe that the West Point trained Hardin, an ardent admirer of Meade and Reynolds, would not have quickly spotted Crawford's professional shortcomings. Perhaps young Hardin, in his ambition to rise, prudently chose to keep his judgments to himself? We do know that Crawford respected and liked young Hardin, whose mother once wrote that the General treated D. like a son.[12]

On June 24, 1863, the men of the Pennsylvania Reserves cheered the announcement that their petition had been granted. They were ordered to join General George Sykes' Fifth Corps soon departing with the rest of the Army of the Potomac to meet Lee somewhere in Pennsylvania.

Unfortunately, the orders did not include the division's Second Brigade, which was ordered to remain on provost guard in Alexandria. Hardin and most of the Reserves were puzzled by the decision, which had been influenced by General John Potts Slough, Military Governor of Alexandria, another political general. As General Hooker still commanded the Army of the Potomac at that point, he tried to convince Slough to reconsider, but to no avail. Already understrength, the Pennsylvania Reserve Division was to enter battle without one of its three brigades.[13] Colonel Hardin expressed his outrage at this incredible stupidity:

> He {General Slough} thought a veteran brigade necessary to keep convalescents in camps! In violation of all military principles (and it might be said in violation of patriotic motives), he retained this splendid body of veterans against their will and in disobedience of General Hooker's orders. However, he was sustained by the actions of the military coterie, which surrounded our noble President. This coterie never forgave Hooker for his first dispatch upon assuming command of the Army of the Potomac, namely requesting that General Stone be made his chief of staff. Not only did this coterie refuse to entertain General Hooker's charges against General Slough . . . but it . . . ultimately forced him to throw up the command of the army.[14]

Hardin never identifies the members of this "military coterie," although he may have been referring to General Henry Halleck and his assorted military bureaucrats, who fought their battles with memos and telegrams rather than pistol, rifle or cannon. Whatever, the truth of the matter, Crawford's Pennsylvania Reserves moved north with only 3,400 infantry. Originally, the Reserves had mustered more than 10,000 when they first arrived in Washington only two years previously.[15]

The division was definitely understrength; efforts to recruit since becoming part of the Washington garrison had been disappointing. Several recruiters had returned from Pennsylvania without a single new volunteer. Hardin's Twelfth Reserve Regiment had been especially whittled down over time by combat and disease. Sergeant Thomas W. Dick, of Company H, Twelfth Pa. Reserves, wrote a candid appraisal of Hardin's Twelfth in a letter to his brother at home:

Our company presents quite a different appearance now to what it did when we were here before {Falls Church, Va.}. It is but a skeleton of its former self. We now draw rations for over 40 men. How does that compare with last winter when we drew rations for over 90 men; and the missing, where are they? The bones of some of them black in the blood-stained soil of the peninsula: Some of them repose on the disastrous plains of manses [Manassas]. While others who fell at south mountain (sic) and Antietam received a decent burial in the faithful old state of Maryland . . . others yet who perished at Fredericksburg to swell the number in the grave-yard of Virginia. There are others still who may be classed among the missing . . . some of them are languishing in the hospitals that have become so common in our land, and others I suppose you see almost daily: some with their arms hanging powerless by their sides; and others with their limbs bent in an uncomely shape . . . some with an empty coat sleeve that shows to (sic) plainly that they were members of the glorious old reserve.[16]

Just after daylight on June 28, 1863, Crawford's Division fell into line and began moving north. They crossed the Potomac River at Edward's Ferry on a pontoon bridge. At some point in the day, Hardin, who had re-mained behind in Washington for some unexplained reason, joined the division. It is quite possible that he was detained while trying to convince the army doctors that he was physically fit for field duty. The fact that his left arm hung useless and limp from his Second Bull Run wound was evi-dently overlooked. Every man was needed in the coming crisis.

Crawford's Division caught up with Sykes' Fifth Corps and camped on Ballinger's Creek, about two miles from Frederick, Maryland.[17] The weather was clear and the pause allowed Hardin to visit with fellow officers and participate in a discussion of the ongoing campaign against Lee and his army: "There was an assemblage of officers of the Reserve Division whilst it was camped near Frederick, looking over the maps of the country and guessing at the future movements of the Union and Confederate armies. Col. Warner of the Tenth Reg. and {Hardin}, agreed that the chances were in favor of a fight at or near Gettysburg, the next good crossing place in the mountains, north of our position."[18] On that same day, Hardin later joined some officers on the division staff camped nearby. They too agreed that the armies would probably meet at Gettysburg crossroads.

Crawford's Division lingered at Ballinger's Creek until around noon, then marched perhaps a few miles before being ordered to halt and allow the passage of other units and the massive Union artillery train. By then, Hardin had rejoined the command and took the opportunity of the delay to visit fellow West Pointer and friend, Lt. Charles "Cog" Hazlett, Class of 1861, now commanding Battery D, Fifth U.S. Artillery. Undoubtedly, they had been in frequent association during the Peninsula campaign when Hardin served as aide-de-camp to then artillery Colonel (now Brigadier General) Henry Hunt.[19]

"The weather was very warm and Lieutenant Hazlett wore a small soft white hat. As the writer {Hardin} left him to rejoin his command, he called back: 'Cog, we are going to have a fight soon. Don't wear that white hat into battle.'"[20]

Once Crawford's men were allowed to resume their march, they slogged in the army's rear far into the night, only coming to a halt well after 10 p.m. Hardin remembered this trek north as one of the great ordeals of the war because of the merciless heat and relentless pace:

> The long delay . . . caused our division to get far behind the other divisions of the corps. We had to rush along, well into the night, to reach the corps camp where the leading divisions had arrived early in the evening and in good order. Having arrived . . . late, and it being very dark, we made a bivouac whilst we saw the other divisions . . . in a regular camp. Most of us were so hot and tired, we dropped down and went to sleep without even making coffee. A bad beginning for a long march.[21]

On June 30, 1863, Hardin led his men on another brutal 20-mile march, a stop-and-go affair that severely taxed the command. Adding insult to fatigue, the Pennsylvania Reserves earned a rebuke from Fifth Corps commander Sykes for their alleged foot-dragging. Hardin wrote: "This march was the cause of great injustice done the division by our new corps commander, in that he reported to the army commander that our division could not march as fast as the other divisions."[22] Hardin was outraged that

Sykes failed to account in his critique the extenuating circumstances of repeated stops to yield to other units, crowded roads and a late start.

Sykes was an officer of ability, but without inspiration or personality. He lacked the dash of a Reynolds, Custer, Barlow or Chamberlain. He was a 41-year-old West Point graduate, a conventional, by the book martinet, who earned the nickname "Tardy George."[23] Lt. Frank Haskell, aide to Union Cavalry General John Buford at Gettysburg, gave us a rather detailed portrait of the Fifth Corps commander, who he depicted as, "A small rather thin man, well dressed and gentlemanly, brown hair and beard which he wears full, with a red, pinched, rough looking skin, feeble blue eyes, large nose, with the general air of one who is weary, and a little ill-natured."[24]

To his credit, Sykes was a professionally trained officer, liked by his peers, strong on discipline, and—if not particularly brilliant—not likely to blunder or bluster. Sykes would never be loved by the men in the ranks, but he was steady, prudent and competent.

Sykes could never be confused with General Crawford. When the Reserves reached the Pennsylvania state line, the new division commander made a blustering speech to the men urging them to drive the invaders from their home soil.[25] Apparently, the talk was well received, as was another speech by Third Brigade Commander Joseph Fisher, a veteran soldier but new at brigade command. Private Benedict, a soldier with Hardin's Company C, recorded the event in his diary:

> The Colonel halted us at the line and the boys gave three cheers for old Pa. and we vowed never to leave the State until we had driven the rebels out, we felt enthused and showed our determination by increasing our speed. There was no nonsense about us. . . . We have been in the service long enough to know that fighting is no child's play, but we want to be led against the enemy now because we are determined to drive him out of our state or perish in the attempt.[26]

Hardin's men were veterans, young men with old eyes and dark memories. They were proud of their record, to be sure. But like many others in the Army of the Potomac, they prayed for the "dawn of peace" and hoped that the next battle would end the war. Perhaps the coming battle in Pennsylvania would finally end the national agony. They would soon find out at the crossroads town of Gettysburg.

By all accounts the march on June 30, 1863 was an incredible ordeal. The division left Hanover, Pa., at 5 a.m. and pounded the road relentlessly for hours with only an occasional and momentary break. Despite the broiling heat, the exhausted men pushed the pace. When they passed hamlets, civilians lined the road dispensing water and food and shouting encouragement. Many of the jaded soldiers in the ranks were unimpressed, and called out to young men along the road to grab a musket and fall in. Few if any accepted the invitation. Darkness finally came and a bright moon lit their way as they continued trudging north.[27]

They threw themselves to the ground at Uniontown at about 3 a.m, but were up again at dawn and back on the road on July 1, 1863. At that very moment Union General Buford's cavalry was battling advancing Rebel infantry on the western outskirts of Gettysburg, where they were soon reinforced by infantry under their own beloved General John Reynolds, commanding the First Corps.

Later during their march they would learn of the Union defeat that took place that day. The battle resulted in the surrender of nearly 5,000 Union soldiers and General Reynolds' death. Their old division commander was shot from his horse by a Rebel rifleman, perhaps a sniper using one of the fine English Wentworth rifles equipped with a telescopic scope. But the Union army rallied by nightfall and had retreated to a strong line just outside the city. General Winfield Hancock steadied the shaken survivors and prepared for a Rebel attack the next morning, July 2, 1863.[28]

Crawford's Division toiled all that day in a desperate effort to reach the battlefield, moving and sometimes staggering down the road, which Hardin described as, "white, hot and dusty." Their salvation came in the form of rich and succulent cherries "which overloaded the trees along the roadside."[29] Hardin and his men ate the cherries while they marched, the red juice staining fingers and mouths like a bloody promise of what was to come.

CHAPTER 15

THE ROUND TOPS: EVERY MAN
A COWARD IN THE DARK

During this arduous march, Colonel Hardin displayed high character and leadership by setting an example for his men. As tired as the soldiers in the ranks were, they must have been impressed by their commander's example of perseverance and grit. After nearly a year of convalescent leave and light duty assignments, Hardin must have suffered intensely during this brutal march in the sun. But in the Hardin family tradition of duty, courage and sacrifice, the young Colonel resolutely led his regiment toward the sound of the guns. His father, the slain hero of Buena Vista, would have expected no less.

Crawford's Pennsylvania Reserve Division joined the rest of Sykes' Fifth Corps late in the morning on July 2, 1863. They were part of the Union reserves located between the Baltimore Pike and Taneytown Road behind the army's left flank near two conical hills we know today as Little Round Top and Round Top. The men were totally spent after their tortuous 70-mile march over three and a half days, much of it in blistering heat. Now they faced the imminent prospect of combat.[1]

The men were given a few hours to brew coffee, eat, chew on hardtack and rest behind the lines while the sounds of battle sounded ominously in their ears like a distant train growing ever closer. Some men wrote brief notes to their loved ones, some read the Bible, some threw away their cards and dice; no doubt a few drank from hidden whiskey bottles. They knew, in the language of the common riflemen, that a big killing was just ahead. Here, they learned of General Reynolds' death and some swore revenge for their old commander.

"As soon as we had feasted, many of the mounted officers of the division started out to see the line of battle," Hardin wrote. "We rode to the rear of the town of Gettysburg, then moved along the line-of-battle to General Meade's headquarters, where we had a conversation with members of his staff, then we started to ride down General Hancock's battle line when we heard the commencement of Sickles' fight."[2]

General Daniel Edgar Sickles was a rather disreputable political general, a member in good standing of New York City's Tammany Ring, and an admitted murderer. On this day, he commanded the Union Third Corps. Defying orders, he had advanced his lines toward the enemy, creating a salient or vulnerable bulge in the Union line about three-quarters of a mile toward the Rebel right fronting the Emmitsburg Road, near a peach orchard where soon men in blue and gray would kill and maim one another by the hundreds.[3]

Around 3:45 p.m., Sickles' Corps came under attack by General James Longstreet's Corps. The Confederate general was the same brilliant battlefield commander who had punished Hardin's Brigade so severely ten months earlier at Second Bull Run. Rebel soldiers attacked with great elan and skill. Fierce fighting erupted in the Peach Orchard, the Wheat Field, and Devil's Den.[4]

Isolated and soon flanked on his left, Sickles' Corps splintered apart before the Confederate advance. Sickles, a physically brave man if not a competent soldier, was seriously wounded by cannon fire and evacuated to the rear. Later, an Army surgeon amputated his wounded leg. Despite receiving reinforcements and fighting tenaciously, Sickles' Corps was crumbling now like a sand castle before an incoming tide. Historian Mark Adkin points out the incredible achievement of Longstreet's men who "inflicted more losses on their enemy than they themselves sustained—a difficult thing for any attacker to achieve."[5]

General Crawford's Pennsylvania Reserves were moved closer to the threatened front where a bitter and ultimately legendary fight was underway on the slopes of Little Round Top. The crucial piece of high ground had been practically devoid of Union troops earlier in the day until its importance had been recognized by Union General Gouvernor K. Warren. This future corps commander, along with Colonel Strong Vincent and Lieutenant Ranald McKenzie, played key roles in shifting troops in the nick of time to this threatened sector.[6]

Brigadier General
Martin Davis
Hardin in 1865.
—*Library of
Congress*

President Abraham
Lincoln, General
Hardin's mentor
and friend.
—*Library of
Congress*

Cadet Martin D. Hardin was a member of the Class of 1859 at the United States Military Academy, West Point, New York. He was the last surviving member of the class before his death in December 1923. —*West Point Library Photographic Collection*

An artist's rendering of an Indian village just a half-mile down river from Fort Umpqua, Oregon where Lieutenant Hardin commanded the small garrison in 1860–61.—*Library of Congress*

General Martin D. Hardin and General Wesley Merritt, friends from West Point, pose for their picture in 1865 Washington. Merritt stayed in the army after the war and won distinction in the Indian Wars and later during the early stages of the Philippine Insurrection in 1899.—*Library of Congress*

Catlett's Station, Virginia, circa Civil War. Near here Colonel Hardin was ambushed in December 1863 by Confederate marauders dressed in Union uniforms. A bullet wound suffered in the attack required amputation of Hardin's left arm. —*Library of Congress*

Above: General Hardin and staff under canvas near Fort Slocum, Washington defenses.
—*Library of Congress*

Major General Samuel Crawford, commander of the Pennsylvania Reserve Division. Hardin commanded a regiment and then a brigade under this unpopular officer.
—*Library of Congress*

Monitor *Saugus* at anchor in the Potomac River. General Hardin, in company with Fanny and Augustus Seward, boarded the warship on April 18, 1865 to identify their father's attacker, Lewis Thornton Powell (alias Paine).—*Library of Congress*

The monitor *Saugus*, where General Hardin escorted Fanny and Augustus Seward aboard to identify Powell as their father's attacker. Powell recognized Hardin as one of the Union officers he had ambushed at Catlett Station in December 1863.—*Library of Congress*

Above: Photo of General Hardin's family in post-war Chicago, circa 1870. *Rear:* Ellen (Hardin) Walworth, sister; General Hardin. *Front:* Lemuel's wife, Annie (Jacobs) Hardin, Lemuel Hardin, and General Hardin's first wife, Estelle (Graham) Hardin. Lemuel was wounded in the leg while fighting for Confederate General John Hunt Morgan. The war strained but never broke the ties of love between the brothers.—*Saratoga Springs History Museum*

Reubena Hyde Walworth, the daughter of General Hardin's sister Ellen, volunteered as an army nurse during the Spanish-American War. She contracted typhoid fever at Camp Wykoff, Long Island and died a celebrated heroine of that war.
—*Saratoga Springs History Museum*

Mansfield Tracy Walworth

Mansfield Tracy Walworth was both General Hardin's step-brother and brother-in-law after his marriage to Ellen Hardin. The violent, deranged and abusive pulp-novelist was imprisoned at the start of the Civil War as a Confederate spy.—*Saratoga Springs History Museum*

Frank Hardin Walworth, General Hardin's nephew, shot his father to death in a New York Hotel room in 1873 before turning himself over to police. The resulting trial was a national scandal and garnered coverage in all the major newspapers and magazines. Reporters called it: "The Walworth Parricide." —*Saratoga Springs History Museum*

Chancellor Reuben Hyde Walworth of Saratoga Springs, New York was Hardin's step-father and a well-respected judge and legal scholar, who wrote President Abraham Lincoln at the beginning of the Civil War on behalf of young Lieutenant Hardin, then serving in the artillery in Washington.—*Saratoga Springs History Museum*

Left: Robert Todd Lincoln, circa 1861–65, was a long-time friend of General Hardin. They were both practicing attorneys in Chicago following the war. —*Library of Congress*

Bottom left: General Hardin's first wife, Estelle Graham of Kentucky, was descended from a prominent Kentucky pioneer family. The photo was taken in London, circa 1866–1867, during their European vacation. *(Photo Courtesy of Laurie Parker Nesbitt, a descendant of Estelle's sister, Grace [Graham] Parker)*

Bottom right: Sarah Smith Hardin Walworth was General Hardin's mother and played an important role in lobbying for his promotion to general during the Civil War. She was a close friend of Abraham and Mary Todd Lincoln as was her first husband, Colonel John J. Hardin, who died at Buena Vista during the Mexican War in 1847. —*Saratoga Springs History Museum*

Above: General Hardin and his second wife, Amelia (McLaughlin) Hardin, a Chicago coffee heiress, were regular members of St. Augustine's reigning high society scene during the Gilded Age. This photo was taken at the Ponce de Leon Hotel at a ball sponsored by Mrs. Henry Flagler around 1910. —*St. Augustine Historical Society Research Library*

Right: Photograph of Brigadier General (Retired) Martin D. Hardin at about the time he spoke during a Lincoln Centennial event at the Alcazar Hotel in St. Augustine, Florida. Hardin was a regular winter resident at the resort city for forty years.—*St. Augustine Historical Society Research Library*

General Hardin dozes while being photographed at Fort Slocum, Washington, DC, 1865.—*Library of Congress*

The Brigadier General and his staff at Fort Slocum, part of the northern defensive perimeter surrounding Washington, 1865.—*Library of Congress*

Left: An artist's sketch of the Fort Reno signal tower atop which General Hardin observed the approach of the Confederate army on the morning of July 11, 1864. Hardin believed that Rebel General Jubal Early's failure to immediately attack the Washington defenses that morning cost him a golden opportunity to capture Washington.—*Library of Congress*

Below: This house was a nest for Confederate snipers during heavy skirmishing on July 11–12, 1864, when General Hardin led troops in defense of Washington, DC.—*Library of Congress*

General Hardin and staff at Fort Slocum. —*Library of Congress*

Brigadier General Hardin and Mrs. (Estelle) Hardin are shown in this rare April 1865 photograph of his downtown headquarters on West Nineteenth Street, Washington, DC. In the close-up, below, they are standing together between a tree on their left and a lamppost just to their right.—*Massachusetts Commandery, Military Order of the Loyal Legion and the U. S. Army Military Institute, Carlisle, Pa.*

Lewis Thornton Powell (alias Paine) shackled aboard the monitor *Saugus* after his attempt on the life of Secretary of State Seward. Sixteen months before, he had been one of the Confederate raiders who wounded Colonel Hardin near Catlett Station, Virginia resulting in the amputation of his left arm.—*Library of Congress*

Independent Civil War scholar John Elliott magnified several photographs taken during the execution of the Lincoln Conspirators in 1865. He is convinced that the one-armed mustached man in the straw hat is Brigadier General Martin D. Hardin. —*Library of Congress*

General Hardin's winter residence at 20 Valencia Street in St. Augustine is now known as the Union Generals House. Before Hardin leased the home it had been occupied by Union General John Schofield.—*Author photo*

The Hotel Alcazar in St. Augustine is where General Hardin spoke on the centenary of Abraham Lincoln's birth, February 12, 1909.—*Library of Congress*

General Hardin was among the notables attending the 1891 dedication of the General Grant Statue in Chicago's Lincoln Park. More than 200,000 people participated in the parade following the dedication ceremony keynoted by President Henry Harrison.—*Author photo*

Brigadier General Martin Hardin (1837–1923) and his second wife, Amelia (McLaughlin) Hardin (1863–1939) are buried in St. Augustine's National Cemetery under the tall cross. In the background are three pyramid tombs containing the remains of soldiers killed during Florida's Second Seminole War, 1836–1842.
—*Author photo*

General Hardin (second from right) is shown, circa 1920, with a group of his retired military friends at the ancient Spanish fortress, Castillo de San Marcos, in St. Augustine, Florida. The resort was a popular winter residence for many retired high-ranking navy and army officer in the post-war years. *From left:* Sergeant Brown, a caretaker at the fortress and a popular tourist guide; Admiral Henry Walton Grinnell, who sailed into Mobile Bay in 1864 with Farragut's fleet, fought in the Spanish-American War and became an admiral in the Japanese Navy; Admiral Cameron McRae Winslow, an 1874 Naval Academy graduate, who was wounded and cited for valor during a hazardous mission in the Spanish-American War; Medal of Honor winner General John Brooke, who was badly wounded at Gettysburg and Cold Harbor; Dr. Webb of St. Augustine, a close friend of General Hardin's, unidentified; General Martin D. Hardin; and unidentified.—*St. Augustine Historical Society Research Library*

When the Confederate attackers struck Little Round Top, they met Colonel Strong Vincent's Third Brigade, First Division, Fifth Corps; and General Stephen Hinsdale Weed's Third Brigade, Second Division, Fifth Corps. Confederate General John Bell Hood's division repeatedly attacked these two Union brigades in the late afternoon and came perilously close to turning the Union army's left flank. At the very far left flank of the entire army stood Colonel Joshua Chamberlain and the men of the Twentieth Maine Regiment, who defied repeated infantry assaults and launched a sudden counterattack that hurled back the startled Confederate infantry.[7]

Farther to the right, closer to the center of Cemetery Ridge, other Confederate brigades were plunging into Hancock's Union Second Corps. First, William Barksdale's Mississippians nearly broke through after a mile-long charge through the peach orchard and up the gentle slope; and then Ambrose Wright's Georgians crossed the Emmitsburg Road and reached the ridge, both brigades only to be hammered back by fresh Federal troops rushed to the scene.

While these dramatic events were unfolding, the Pennsylvania Reserve Division moved up in support of the hard-pressed Union left wing. "As we advanced, we began to meet wounded men returning," Hardin wrote later. "Soon the road was . . . encumbered with wounded walking to the rear and ambulances going the same way. We had to take to the woods along the side of the road. This caused some delay. We filed up on the north side of the ridge to the right of Little Round Top. The ground here was rocky and covered with thick brush; some time was taken getting into position; eventually we got into line by brigade front, the Third Brigade (Colonel Fisher) in front. We then advanced to the crest of the ridge."[8]

Looking down on the battlefield, Hardin beheld a terrible vision of a beaten army in full retreat. These frightened men were the remnants of Sickles' corps scrambling down into the valley and then splashing across a small stream (Plum Creek), before resuming their flight up the gentle slope toward the Union Fifth Corps. Hardin later wrote a vivid description of what he witnessed in those disturbing and disheartening moments:

> The whole valley between us and the ridge opposite, about a third of a mile off, was filled solid with our retreating soldiers and batteries, thousands of the soldiers wounded and all the batteries dis-

abled. Some of the men, especially toward the left-front, were retreating at a run. The enemy's line was only visible by the white puffs of smoke at the crest of the opposite ridge. Very few of our men were firing. A man, now and then, would stop and take a shot. This great mass of thousands in the valley was moving sullenly to the rear at a walk. There seemed no organizing force, a mere mass of men, officers and men, inextricably mixed—all seeking safety behind the ridge {Little Round Top} upon which we stood.[9]

There Crawford's division apparently paused while an artillery battery galloped up and deployed on their right. These guns soon began blasting away, joining the fire of other cannon already placed to the left along Little Round Top. At one point Colonel Hardin ran ahead of his regiment to more closely observe the enemy's position from the heights. He later wrote about what ensued in the third person: "When near the top, he met a party of officers and men carrying General Weed, who was mortally wounded. The writer, who knew the general personally, stopped to see if he could be of any service. Whilst conversing here, another party came along bringing back his old friend, Lieutenant Hazlett, who in the haste of going into action had forgotten that fatal white hat. He was shot through the head."[10]

A Rebel sharpshooter first shot Brigadier General Weed in the chest, and then, when Captain Hazlett bent over the wounded general, the Rebel rifleman took aim at Cog's conspicuous white hat and fired another fatal round. Both men were mortally wounded. In the space of a few minutes, Hardin had lost two friends; however, in the wild tumult of the ongoing battle, there was no time for mourning. Hardin quickly rejoined his regiment just as the Pennsylvania Reserve Division was ordered to advance on the enemy.[11]

General Crawford ordered the Third Brigade to move off to the left around Little Round Top and reinforce the battered brigades there. To his front at the bottom of the little valley, portions of three disorganized Confederate brigades were advancing towards the Pennsylvanians. Grabbing an American flag, the mounted Crawford led a spirited charge down into the valley with his Second Brigade (Colonel William McCandless) supported by the Third Brigade's Eleventh Pennsylvania Reserve Regiment.[12]

The Pennsylvanians swept down into the valley, waded across Plum

Creek, and drove the Confederates before them. The Union soldiers ultimately formed along a stone wall near a corpse-strewn wheatfield where they remained, although plagued by sniper fire on their left from the collection of huge boulders dubbed The Devil's Den.[13] The Union counterattack had been perfectly timed and spectacular, although it appears the Confederate advance may have already spent its force before the blow was struck. Still, this was a memorable moment and deeply stirred the emotions of Colonel Hardin, who with the others of the Third Brigade, cheered wildly from Little Round Top while the drama played out:

> We saw the First Brigade and Eleventh Regiment make their gallant advance through the retreating multitude as we clambered over the rocks on top of Little Round Top. We joined in their cheer and started at a double-quick . . . stumbling over rocks, and the numerous dead of Vincent's and Weed's gallant brigades. As we advanced, a few . . . shots came from the retiring enemy. . . . Thus our small division coming on the field in the nick of time and advancing boldly, turned the tide of success on the left, and the enemy's great efforts . . . were rendered entirely futile.[14]

Hardin's men took position near the saddle between Round Top on their left and Little Round Top on their right. In the early evening hours Confederate infantry at the summit of Round Top continually spattered the Pennsylvanians with sniper fire. By now, it was obvious to most everyone that the commanding height should be seized before the Rebels occupied it in force during the night.

Third Brigade Commander Joseph Fisher was ordered to accomplish the crucial mission, probably by General Crawford. What followed immediately afterwards was the subject of bitter debate for decades after Appomattox Court House. Colonel Fisher was reluctant to carry out the ascent and expressed his reservations to Colonel James Rice, who now commanded the slain Strong Vincent's Brigade, and to Colonel Joshua Chamberlain, commander of the Twentieth Maine, who had fought so valiantly on Little Round Top.[15] Chamberlain claimed that Fisher was adamant that the Maine soldiers lead the way: "He emphatically declined {making the advance} & I remember him saying his men were armed with some inefficient rifle 'smooth bores.' It seems to me he said, & especially that the ground was difficult & unknown to his men. He & his men were much agitated."[16]

Chamberlain ended up waking his sleeping men and asking for volunteers to form a skirmish line to lead the way up Round Top in front of Fisher's two regiments. To a man, these bloodied and exhausted men from Maine grabbed their rifles and formed up at the bottom of the hill. Many must have wondered why they had to lead the way for a brigade that had not suffered one casualty that day when they had suffered so grievously.

A few minutes later, at Chamberlain's command, they moved up the steep, rock-strewn hillside. "We heard squads of the enemy falling back before us, and, when near the crest, we met a scattering and uncertain fire," Chamberlain later wrote.[17] Thirty or more Texas Rebels were captured or killed in the advance. One of Chamberlain's officers was killed in the exchange and several enlisted men wounded.

The Maine men were now on the summit of Big Round Top and waiting for Colonel Fisher to follow with Hardin's Twelfth Regiment and Lieutenant Colonel George Dare's Fifth Regiment. There appears to have been a long delay before the Pennsylvanians finally formed a line of battle at the base and were ready to move. Hardin recalled Fisher giving the order to advance in "Stentorian tones";[18] It was pitch-black now as the regiments moved up the forested slopes:

"The line upon advancing in utter darkness was almost immediately broken and became confused by the rocky, precipitous and difficult ground," Hardin recalled. "Officers became separated from their men, but all pushed on up the mountain; when, about one-third way up, all order was lost. Officers and men of different companies and even of different regiments became intermingled. The commanding officers of the brigade and even of different regiments began calling to each other; the rocks and woods resounded with the cries."[19]

They were moving up the rugged slope when several Rebel riflemen, concealed in the wooded darkness, opened fire on the Union soldiers, precipitating a mad flight back down the hill. Colonel Chamberlain at the summit heard the shots and the stampede down the hill that followed. He compared Fisher's contingent to a herd of antelopes spooked by a few rifle shots.[20]

Years later Hardin lightheartedly remarked that whatever Confederate infantry remained on the summit must have bolted in the other direction when they heard the noise made by the fleeing Pennsylvanians, which sounded like an entire corps coming up the hill. One seriously doubts whether Colonel Chamberlain or his men would have appreciated the humor of the remark.[21]

The most succinct account of the aborted advance up Round Top was a diary entry by one of Hardin's riflemen, Private Benedict: "Colonel Hardin marched us up to the top . . . where striking the enemy in the dark and a gun being discharged we fell back off the hill & in doing so got lost for a while."[22] In fact, the Pennsylvanians took nearly two hours to make their way back in the darkness and assemble for another ascent. At one point Colonel Hardin with around 70 of his men were completely disoriented. At the edge of the trees, they glimpsed the flickering flames of campfires.

Wisely, Hardin sent two riflemen off to investigate. The Union scouts crept forward and then called out from concealment asking the identity of the men gathered around the campfire. Southern accented voices replied they were the 15th Alabama. Without replying, the Pennsylvanians melted back into the dark forest and reported in whispers back to Colonel Hardin. He then quietly led his contingent in the opposite direction from the fires and eventually they reached Union lines. Hardin and his men had narrowly averted a long stay in a Southern prison camp.[23]

While the Pennsylvania Reserves were wandering lost on the tree-shrouded hill, Colonel Chamberlain's small skirmish line was left unsupported at the summit. Feeling uneasy, the Maine colonel led his men back down the slope until he encountered the 83rd Pennsylvania Infantry. Together, they moved back up Big Round Top without encountering any Confederates and quickly secured the summit.[24] The Confederates had evidently been unaware that the hill had been temporarily abandoned and had made no move to retake the key piece of high ground. Instead, the Rebels dug in around the base of Round Top to wait the dawn.

At some point that night, Colonel Fisher's two-regiment contingent was finally ready to climb the hill once again. At Colonel Hardin's suggestion, they went up the hill by the flank and arrived at the summit in good order without any difficulty.[25]

Early the next morning of July 3, 1863, the Union troops on Round Top gathered rocks and tree branches to construct an improvised breastwork in preparation for the anticipated Confederate attack. The Union forces now had a continuous battle line from the top of Round Top, across the saddle between the two hills, and along Little Round Top. All through the day, they endured steady sniping from the Confederates located at the base of the hill. Blue and gray riflemen played their deadly game sending the deadly balls whistling through the air. Bullets ricocheted off rocks, thudded into trees, or burrowed into the soft earth. Occasionally, there was a groan or cry when a missile struck human flesh.

Private Benedict of Hardin's regiment described the events of the day in his diary: "We heard considerable firing . . . saw the enemy moving with their artillery towards our right—our artillery kept firing upon them by spells all day. . . . Our skirmishers in front kept up firing some through the day; one of the skirmishers out of Co. A of our Regt. was shot in the head & killed instantly."[26]

Later in the afternoon, Hardin and his men heard the enemy's hour-long bombardment of Hancock's men down along Cemetery Ridge on the right. This massed cannon fire was prelude to the grand Confederate assault of 13,000 men, known as Pickett's Charge. Many historians have described the bold attack across more than a mile of open ground to be the high tide of the Confederacy.

During this epic event, Colonel Hardin and his regiment were merely deeply interested spectators to the magnificent but doomed Confederate assault. "The grand scene was clearly in view to any member of the regiment who would chance his life against the deadly sharpshooter by raising his head above the stone breastworks," Hardin wrote.[27]

That night, Hardin's men remained on Round Top and shivered in a driving rain that continued through most of the 4th of July. On the next day they learned that Lee's Army of Northern Virginia had left the field on its long retreat south with trains of wagons and ambulances bumping along with their suffering wounded tortured by every jolt and bump along the way. The Rebels left behind a small army of dead.

One of Hardin's men described exploring the now vacant enemy positions in the silent aftermath of the great battle: "I have a vivid recollection of what we saw and how cautiously we approached the stone walls, the earthworks, and entered the woods. We found no enemy . . . except a Georgian, sleeping by a tree in the woods. He was somewhat surprised when he awoke and found himself surrounded by Yankees. Going a little further we met some Sisters of Charity [an order of Roman Catholic nuns] in an ambulance coming to the battlefield. They told us that the enemy were in full retreat and eight miles away."[28]

The Army of the Potomac had finally won a significant victory over Lee and his splendid Army of Northern Virginia, but at terrible cost. In three days of bitter fighting, the Union casualties totaled more than 23,000 killed, wounded and missing; the Confederates lost at least as many. Around 3,100 Yanks lost their lives, compared to around 3,900 Confederates. The stench of the dead pervaded the battlefield for many weeks, a distasteful reminder of the sordid reality of war.[29]

Hardin had led his regiment with competence and courage during the battle. But the Twelfth had played only a supporting role, suffering only one man killed and another wounded, both by sniper fire on July 3rd. Fisher's Third Brigade, of which it was part, incurred only three percent casualties, the lowest figure of any of the Fifth Corps brigades engaged on July 2nd. On the other hand, Hardin suffered grievous personal loss during the battle. Former Reserves commander John Reynolds was dead, and so too were his friends, Lt. Cog Hazlett and Brig. Gen. Stephen Weed. For Hardin, Lincoln's memorable phrase "the last full measure of devotion" was not an abstract concept.[30]

Returning to the fight after his nearly fatal wound at Second Bull Run and the long, painful convalescence that followed, had been a hard test for Colonel Hardin. At Gettysburg, he proved himself one of those iron soldiers who would return repeatedly to the killing ground motivated by pride, personal honor and devotion to his men. At Gettysburg, Hardin led with one arm hanging limp and useless at his side, winning the respect and admiration of many. Colonel Fisher of the Third Brigade made special note of Hardin's contribution in his after action report:

"I beg leave to call your attention to the conduct of Colonel Hardin of the Twelfth Regiment, who, still suffering from wounds received at Bull Run, went gallantly up the mountain, leading his regiment to where hot work was expected."[31]

CHAPTER 16

ATTACK, RETREAT, ENDURE

In the aftermath of the epic Battle of Gettysburg, General Meade's Army of the Potomac cautiously trailed the retreating Army of Northern Virginia south to the Potomac River. President Lincoln urged Meade to finish the job, hoping that one more blow against the weakened enemy would end the national agony.[1]

Yet Meade knew his army had been weakened also; it was weary and a quarter of its men had already become casualties. In the end, he followed Lee's retreating army at a respectful distance, too leery to risk his own battered army in an ill-considered frontal assault. Instinctively, he knew that a wounded tiger posed great risk to its hunters. A steady rain beginning July 4th also hindered the Union pursuit.

Lee entrenched at Williamsport on July 7th, waiting until his engineers could replace the pontoon bridge across the Potomac recently destroyed by Union cavalry. Meade made no attack and, on the night of July 13–14 the Army of Northern Virginia withdrew unmolested back into Virginia. There was a messy rear guard action at Falling Waters the next morning involving an impetuous Union cavalry charge that accomplished little except the loss of several dozen horsemen and the mortal wounding of Confederate Brig. General James J. Pettigrew. Eventually about 500 Rebels, mostly wounded or stragglers, were scooped up, along with two artillery pieces.[2] "If I had gone up there, I could have whipped them myself," Lincoln later said. "Our army held the war in the hollow of their hand and they would not close it."[3]

Lincoln may not have realized how much the Gettysburg victory had depended on Meade's holding the superior ground against Rebel attacks.

With Robert E. Lee holding a superior position, as at Williamsport, and with Meade forced to be the attacking party, the odds for another Union success were not as great as the President assumed.

After Gettysburg, Colonel Joseph Fisher went on extended leave and Hardin assumed command of the Third Brigade, Pennsylvania Reserve Division. At the same time, division commander Crawford, suffering the lingering effects of his Antietam wound, went on convalescent leave.[4] In his absence, Colonel Buck McCandless, a competent and respected officer, took over division command. During the late summer and fall of 1863, McCandless led the Reserves on many a hard march, punctuated occasionally by skirmishes and exchanges of artillery fire with the enemy.

On September 8, 1863, the Pennsylvania Reserve Division established a permanent camp near Rappahannock Station on the Rappahannock River, although even then the men were rarely idle.

"Dug wells, made screened sinks, placed brush over the shelter tents, built bough arbors and made ourselves as comfortable as possible," Colonel Hardin wrote. "Clothing and full rations were issued. Sutlers, with full supplies, joined their commands. Daily papers received, bathing in the Rappahannock; daily drills and camp amusements fill up the time."[5]

Only a week later, however, Hardin's men much to their regret were again on the march. Third Brigade commander Hardin spoke for many in the ranks regretful to leave behind the pleasant Rappahannock encampment, "the most agreeable we had during our term of service."[6] After two days pounding the dusty roads, the Reserves settled into another encampment about four miles outside Culpeper Courthouse where they would remain for the next several weeks.

This interlude was marked by brigade drill for the men, and saber drill and mounted exercises for the officers. Onlookers included General Gouverneur K. Warren, the officer whose decisive intervention on July 2nd led to the Union occupation of Little Round Top. Hardin recalled that Warren and the other high-ranking spectators observing the October mounted exercises were treated to a hilarious comic-opera performance: "At every exercise one rider at least suddenly and unexpectedly dismounted, to the amusement of the spectators," Hardin would write. "The cavalry officers were no more proficient either in riding or saber exercises than the other mounted officers."[7]

Early on the morning of October 10, the Pennsylvania Reserves along with the rest of Meade's army headed south once more, crossed the Rappahannock River, and then the very next day withdrew north again at Beverly Ford. Like boxers, the Army of the Potomac and the Army of Northern Virginia were bobbing, feinting and weaving while looking for an opening.

General Lee began a wide swing around Meade's right flank aimed at Warrenton, Virginia, hoping to cut the Yankee army off from Washington. The Rebel commander saw an opportunity to isolate and destroy a part of Meade's army as it withdrew back to the safety of its formidable defense lines at Centreville near the Bull Run battlefield. The always aggressive Lee saw an opportunity and, at the very least, hoped to isolate and destroy one of Meade's retreating corps.

Despite having recently dispatched General Joe Hooker with two army corps to the Western Theater to assist in the ongoing Chattanooga campaign, the Army of the Potomac still outnumbered their Confederate opponents by a ratio of eight to five. Even so, Meade was determined to avoid a battle. Old Goggle Eyes was intent on taking his army to safety in the tranches around Centreville. He had no desire to cross swords in open battle with Lee unless he had a huge advantage in position or numbers.[8]

But in its retreat north, Meade's various corps became strung out on the march and vulnerable. General A.P. Hill, one of Lee's most outstanding division commanders, was now leading a corps in hot pursuit of the fleeing Yankees. Hill was eager to make a mark and act as Lee's strong right arm in emulation of the late and lamented Stonewall Jackson.

Hardin's Third Brigade was bringing up the rear of the Pennsylvania Division, which formed the rear guard of Sykes' Fifth Corps. Early on October 14 they passed through Catlett Station and Bristoe Station and then marched north along the west side of the Broad River. They began crossing the river near Milford, only about thirty miles west of the Centreville fortifications. There, they rested near the ford around the noon hour. In the early afternoon, the Fifth Corps resumed its march. Crawford's Division was the last to begin moving, at around 2:30 p.m., with Hardin's Third Brigade bringing up the rear.[9]

At about the same time, General Warren's Second Corps was heading toward Bristoe Station, trying to make up time after a minor clash with Confederate pursuers near Catlett Station. They moved parallel to the

Orange and Alexandria Railroad tracks on their way to the Broad River. At this point neither General Warren of the Second Corps nor General Sykes of the Fifth Corps knew that A.P. Hill's advance elements were already approaching Milford. They arrived just as Hardin's Third Brigade was leaving its noon bivouac by the Broad River ford. The rest of the Pennsylvania Reserve Division was already pushing east along with the other two divisions of Sykes' Fifth Corps.

Confederate General Hill was now in a perfect position to concentrate on the rear elements of the fleeing Fifth Corps with good prospects of winning a victory. Excited at the prospect, Hill ordered an artillery battery to take the Yankee column across the river under fire. At the moment, the Confederate commander's focus was on the Pennsylvania Reserve Division; Hill was totally unaware that Warren's Second Corps off on his right flank was rapidly moving up parallel to the railroad moving toward Bristoe Station.[10]

Hardin's brigade suddenly came under accurate artillery fire. Several shells exploded among the marching column with devastating effect. "Several officers and men of the Third Brigade were struck by the first fire of the enemy's battery, which fired directly down the marching line of the brigade," Hardin remembered later.[11] From across the river, Confederates cheered at the sight of the blue-coated soldiers rushing frantically to avoid the exploding shells.

A.P. Hill was now bringing up his infantry, intending to cross the Broad River and crush the Pennsylvanians. Sykes and the rest of the corps, despite Meade's admonition to stay in contact with Warren's corps should they require support, was well down the road to Centreville and out of the tactical picture entirely. A significant victory seemed just within Hill's reach. Hardin's brigade and the rest of the Pennsylvania Reserves formed up to receive an attack from across the river, but then events took a completely different turn.

The rumble of Rebel artillery fire had alerted General Warren to Hill's presence north of Bristoe Station. The Union corps commander immediately dispatched two infantry regiments from his lead division to form a skirmish line and advance toward the sound of the firing. These Yanks soon engaged Confederate infantry from Hill's corps. A brisk firefight erupted and now General Hill's attention turned to the threat on his flank. The

Rebel corps commander ordered his infantry to push south against Warren's now retreating skirmishers. The Rebels came on blind without proper reconnaissance.[12]

If Hill's men had beaten the Yankee Second Corps in this race to the Bristoe Station railroad embankment, they would have cut the retreating Yankee army in two. Instead, Warren's Union corps won the sprint by a slim margin—perhaps only by a margin of ten minutes. But, that gave them time to form a strong line behind the embankment. The Union Second Corps was shielded by the embankment, which rose from five to ten feet to their front. From the cover of this veritable breastwork, Warren's men prepared to meet the Southern advance with a wall of fire.

On the north side of the Broad River, Colonel Buck McCandless, acting division commander in Crawford's absence, ordered the retiring Pennsylvania Reserves to form a line of battle and await developments. A rider had been sent down the road to request an artillery battery for support, but for the moment the outnumbered Union infantry braced for the expected assault from across the river.

Hardin and his men saw that the Rebel artillery had now shifted its fire south toward Warren's advancing corps. They remained drawn up in line of battle, distant spectators as Hill's men charged the Union Second Corps at Bristoe Station. One of the Pennsylvania batteries had finally come up to the ford and was firing at the attacking Rebel columns now moving towards Warren's men. Then they saw the attackers suddenly enveloped in smoke and flame.

Warren's massed infantry had risen from behind the railroad embankment and delivered a withering fire on their attackers, which some later compared to the eruption of a volcano. Looking back on this Union victory three decades later, General Hardin wrote: "They were repulsed with severe loss in guns, killed, wounded, and prisoners. The action of the Second Corps at this time was most brilliant . . ."[13]

Hundreds of Confederates died or were maimed in this brilliant and horrific bloodletting. As on so many occasions in the bitterly contested war, the valor and spirit of the attackers was crushed by weight of metal. Firepower trumped courage. As at Malvern Hill and Gettysburg, the Confederate sword once again shattered in a hopeless attack; and, in each instance, Colonel Martin D. Hardin was witness to the butchery.

"Little Powell" Hill knew he had failed miserably and never regained his former confidence. His impetuous drive to crush the isolated corps commanded by Union General G.K. Warren, was a grave blunder. Rebel casualties totaled 1,380 to only 540 for the Union.[14] In the dismal aftermath of the Confederate debacle, General Robert E. Lee appeared at the scene of the repulse and listened in silence to Hill's explanations. Finally, apparently weary of the disturbing details, Lee dismissed Hill with the words: "Well, well, general, bury these poor men and let us say no more about it."[15]

In sharp contrast, Colonel Hardin was elated. In his 1890 *History of the Twelfth Regiment, Pennsylvania Reserve Volunteer Corps*, Hardin expressed the view that his division had performed a crucial role in the victory by distracting Hill from an immediate advance south to Bristoe Station: "Neither the Reserve Division nor its commander {McCandless} ever received any credit for their action in this battle," Hardin wrote. "A study of the ground, the circumstances of the action and of the Confederate reports, proves conclusively that it was the presence of our division and the battery which joined it that delayed or rather prevented an overwhelming attack on the Second Corps."[16]

In Hardin's view, Confederate General Hill should have promptly attacked the Pennsylvanian rear guard when he encountered it at the Broad River ford. Of course, Hill was unaware that the main force of General Sykes' Fifth Corps was already marching rapidly away from the developing battle. Had he attacked the Pennsylvanians promptly he would, in Hardin's view, have won a quick victory before Sykes' main column could have intervened. Colonel Hardin believed that the Pennsylvania Reserve Division and Warren's Second Corps had been essentially deserted by the Union corps commander.

Late in the afternoon, Hardin's Brigade, along with the rest of the Pennsylvania Reserves, briefly recrossed the Broad River and advanced south without encountering the enemy. When darkness fell a few hours later, McCandless ordered them back across the ford, formed the men into columns and headed up the road to join the remainder of the Fifth Corps at Centreville. Warren's Corps also withdrew that night across the Broad River at Bristoe Station, unmolested by Hill's badly wounded Confederate force.[17]

That night Hardin and his men slept at Centreville among the dead of First Bull Run. The exhausted men slept in the shadows surrounded by skeletal remains which the rains had washed out from shallow graves. Eyeless skulls stared at former companions, a stark warning of the cost of war. Considering their fatigue, we can safely assume that Hardin and his men slept soundly, too exhausted to ponder long those grim white reminders of mortality.

By early November, the back and forth, see-saw nature of the struggle once again saw Meade's Army of the Potomac headed south. On November 7th, the army was poised on the north side of the Rappahannock River near Rappahannock Station. Although Lee had withdrawn his main force, he left behind a strongly fortified bridgehead on the north bank. Meade could not advance without first eliminating this strong outpost from which the Rebels could threaten his rear.

Meade moved with expedition and launched a three corps attack on Kelly's Ford further south of Rappahannock Station. This movement was successful and now Union General "Uncle John" Sedgwick moved against the Rebel redoubt at Rappahannock Station with elements of the Fifth and Sixth Corps.[18]

Hardin commanded several hundred skirmishers selected from three divisions of the Fifth Corps to move down on the south side of the railroad to the river. This line of about 900 men included about 200 men from Hardin's old Twelfth Pa. Reserve Regt. This long wave of skirmishers (including a line of Sixth Corps soldiers on the opposite side of the tracks), moved astride the line of the railroad under the overall command of Union General K. Garrard:

> The line was posted in front of the corps on the south side of the railroad, and about 3 p.m., I received orders to form my whole forces as skirmishers, to advance with my right on the railroad, and to establish the picket line on the Rappahannock River, driving in the enemy which was in front. At 3:30 p.m., the advance was made, and in an hour or less the line was on the river on my left . . . [19]

Colonel Hardin and his men now paused and awaited orders. As the sky darkened in the late fall afternoon, Rebel artillery opened a steady bombardment. Within the Rappahannock bridgehead were two thousand veteran

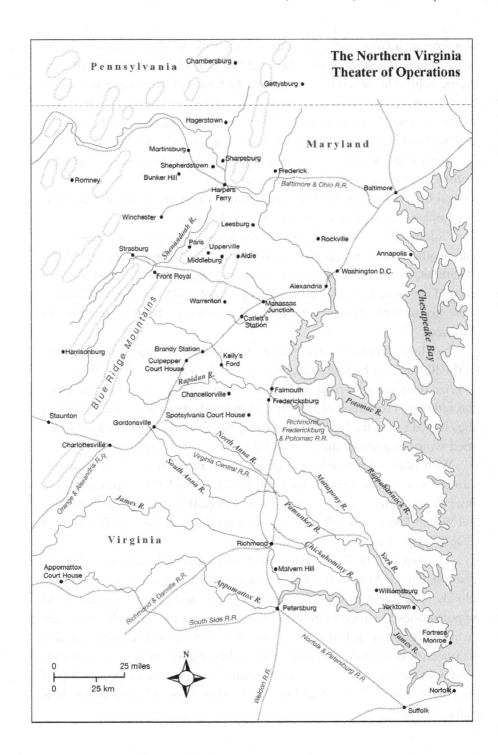

The Northern Virginia Theater of Operations

Pennsylvania

Chambersburg •

Gettysburg •

Hagerstown •

Maryland

Martinsburg •
Sharpsburg •
Shepherdstown •
Bunker Hill •
• Romney
Harpers Ferry

• Frederick

Baltimore & Ohio R.R.

Baltimore •

Winchester •

Leesburg •

Strasburg •
Paris •
Upperville •
Middleburg •
Aldie •
• Front Royal

• Rockville

Annapolis •

• Washington D.C.

Shenandoah R.

Alexandria •

Warrenton •
Manassas Junction •
Catlett's Station •

• Harrisonburg

Brandy Station •
Culpepper Court House •
Kelly's Ford •

Rapidan R.

Chancellorville •

Falmouth •
Fredericksburg •

Potomac R.

Staunton •

Gordonsville •

Spotsylvania Court House •

Richmond, Fredericksburg & Potomac R.R.

Charlottesville •

North Anna R.

Blue Ridge Mountains

Virginia Central R.R.

Orange & Alexandria R.R.

South Anna R.

James R.

Pamunkey R.

Mattaponey R.

Rappahannock R.

Virginia

Richmond •

Appomattox Court House •

• Malvern Hill

Chickahominy R.

York R.

• Williamsburg

Appomattox R.

Richmond & Danville R.R.

• Petersburg

Yorktown •

South Side R.R.

Norfolk & Petersburg R.R.

Fortress Monroe •

James R.

Norfolk •

Weldon R.R.

• Suffolk

0 ____ 25 miles
0 ____ 25 km

N

Chesapeake Bay

Confederate infantry and a four-gun artillery battery. These Louisiana Tigers were commanded by Brigadier General Harry T. Hays, who must have felt secure behind his revetments. If anyone had learned anything in the war to date, it was that good infantry, backed by artillery and protected by breastworks, was nearly impervious to direct assault. But events soon upended that battlefield equation with disastrous consequences for the Confederates.[20]

Hardin and his men served in a supporting role in the drama that unfolded before them. As dusk fell about 5 p.m., General Sedgwick ordered several brigades of the Sixth Corps to launch that most rare and perilous of gambles: a night attack against a fortified position.

Colonel Emory Upton, one of the Union Army's most innovative young officers, led the assault. He ordered his lead element, the Sixth Maine Regiment, to advance rapidly with bayonets only, relying on speed and surprise. The startled enemy managed only a single volley before the Yankees were among them. Bayonets flashed and men fought hand-to-hand in the darkness.[21]

Not long afterwards, the Fifth Wisconsin poured over another section of the Rebel redoubt. Upton alertly ordered the 121st New York Regiment to seize the pontoon bridge and slam the door on any Rebel retreat from the redoubt. Hundreds of Rebels surrendered; some were shot down as they bolted across the bridge under heavy fire from the New Yorkers; some tried swimming across the river and drowned. Many died.[22]

With both sides employing about 2,000 men on that November 7, Confederate General Hays lost 1,670 killed, wounded or captured in the brief struggle; the attackers suffered only 419 casualties. Confederate Colonel Walter Taylor on Lee's staff summed up the brief battle: "The saddest chapter in the history of this army."[23]

The Army of the Potomac now had three successes under its belt: Gettysburg, Bristoe Station and Rappahannock Station. Finally, after so many bloody reversals, incompetence in high places, and countless squandered opportunities, the men in blue were reaping victories. The soldiers of the Army of the Potomac had always been brave, determined fighters, but they had been wasted and scourged at places like the Peninsula, Second Bull Run, Chancellorsville and Fredericksburg. Now, under the leadership of irascible General George Gordon Meade, they were at last realizing their full potential.

Always conservative, General Meade would have preferred to retire to winter quarters at this point to rest and re-equip for the spring campaign. Lincoln and other powerful men in Washington wanted more; they pressured Meade to make one more attack south before the winter snows came. Above all, President Lincoln desperately wanted to end the slaughter; he knew only another smashing blow like Gettysburg would compel Confederate surrender.

We can assume that for the mass of the enlisted men in Meade's army, the prospect of yet one more battle with Lee's seasoned army was daunting. For most of the men, the euphoric days with bold talk of battlefield glory, heroic death and quick victory must have seemed like a dimly remembered dream. They were for the most part, to borrow a phrase from the moving song so often sung around the campfires, "tired of war on the old camp ground."[24] Much of their bitterness was directed to the home front where so many young men sat out the war in safety and comfort.

One of Hardin's boys in Company I, Twelfth Pa. Reserve Regt, First Sergeant Frank D. Stevens, penned a letter home to friends, eloquently expressing the bitterness of a veteran soldier towards stay-at-home civilians:

> . . . it seems to me if these patriotic men in the north, who cry war eternally, were to get a sly sight of the animal it would settle the hash in them. It is a big thing for men at home, who never had their ears smoked, to be patriotic, but we soldiers can't see it. It is nice for them to sit back in their arm chairs, their heels cocked up & cigars in their mouths & read the history of the traitors in their imagination; they say sustain the Government at all hazards— never yield an inch till every man falls; they think it a small matter as long as they are out of it; they know their lives are not at stake & think soldiers' lives are no more valuable than the dogs. . . . If they were put out in the front rank & made to bite the Secesh bayonets once or twice, they would come to the conclusion that this war has lasted long enough.[25]

Hardin's challenge as brigade commander was to motivate these veterans, to apply discipline where it was needed, and to exercise restraint when appropriate. His men knew the score, and were, in the main, resolved to see the thing out to the bitter end. But it was also increasingly apparent that they weren't ready to risk their lives in foolish dashes across open ground, or simply stand in ranks when raked by a killing flanking fire.

As the weather turned cold and drizzled a cruel rain, on November 26th the Army of the Potomac once again headed south and crossed the Rapidan River. Lee's Army of Northern Virginia was strung out in a series of winter camps nearly 40 miles in length on the south side of the river. Meade's plan was to drive through the enemy line and launch a great sweeping end run that would destroy the enemy piecemeal.[26]

The plan depended on speed, aggressive leadership and—above all— dry roads. The advance was led by the Union Third Corps, commanded by General William Henry French. He seems to have botched the assignment, blundered in confusion, and stalled in the mire while a steady rain pounded the dirt roads into muck. The proposed lightning strike across the river was instead cumbersome, ponderous and plodding.[27]

The Pennsylvania Reserves moved up on November 27th to support General David M. Gregg's Cavalry Division. The beleaguered horse soldiers were stalled in their attack against Confederate cavalry, infantry and artillery strongly placed behind an abandoned railroad cut near New Hope Church. Writing of himself in the third person thirty years later, Hardin described that short, bloody fight: "Colonel Hardin commanded the skirmishers on left of the road, where the enemy's skirmishers made the greatest resistance, they being supported here by a battery. A shell burst under Colonel Hardin's horse, upsetting horse and rider without doing either any serious damage. General Sykes, for once, was complimentary of the Reserve skirmishers."[28]

Unfortunately, there was not much to celebrate about the Union thrust. With his typical efficiency, General Lee had concentrated his scattered elements, struck hard with a spoiling attack, and now withdrew behind a strong line along the west bank of Mine Run, a stream flowing into the Rapidan. The Army of Northern Virginia was solidly entrenched, confident in its strength, and hoping for another Fredericksburg.

While Hardin and his men awaited orders they suffered severely from the weather during this rugged campaign. Many later remembered it as the worst ordeal they suffered during the war. Hardin wrote: "A cold rain had fallen, and the weather turned very cold, so that lying in line-of-battle without fires, officers and men suffered terribly. Some men were frozen to death."[29]

For four days, the Army of the Potomac hesitated. At one point, Hardin selected Lt. Rohm, C Company, Twelfth Pa. Reserve Regt., to take a picked party of men and conduct a reconnaissance, determine the enemy's exact location and strength, and find a suitable ford across Mine Run for the long anticipated advance.

The young officer accomplished his mission and returned without suffering casualties, to Hardin's great praise. But his report was anything but reassuring. Rohm had found Lee's troops well entrenched, supported by artillery, and shielded by the flooded Mine Run creek, which rose four feet deep in places.

Worst of all, the assaulting Yanks would have to advance across more than a mile of relatively open ground even before reaching the water barrier and then must continue the attack uphill. Hardin forwarded the grim intelligence up the chain of command, but it seems safe to assume he would have been surprised if the assault was cancelled.

Hardin was not alone in fearing any assault against the Rebels at Mine Run would be bloody and futile. But, as is often the case in war, the planned attack seemed to be moving forward on its own momentum. All the men could do was hope that the high command would see the looming disaster and cancel the projected attack. They shivered and huddled together in misery; some cursing and many undoubtedly praying.

General G.K. Warren was in direct command of the 18,000-man strike force. They would storm the enemy entrenchments on the early morning of November 30, 1863 following an hour-long artillery bombardment. In the pre-dawn, Hardin's men stacked their packs in preparation for the charge, pelted by rain and pondering the grim prospects of this poorly conceived attack. Soon the artillery began firing on schedule. One of Hardin's Pennsylvanians remembered shivering in dread as he awaited the order to advance: "The morning was bitter cold and I knew if I did escape the bullets I would freeze to death after going through the Run."[30]

In those final minutes, after a final personal inspection at the point of attack, General Warren did what many generals would never even have considered. Upon his own authority, without first informing his commander,

Meade, Warren cancelled the assault, knowing full well he would face the fury of his superior. The commander of the Army of the Potomac was under great pressure from the powers in Washington to strike; if he failed to comply, it could mean his dismissal.[31]

When Warren and Meade finally met after the former had cancelled the attack, the two high-strung officers engaged in an angry, shouted exchange. However, in the end, Meade accepted Warren's decision. Another senseless slaughter on the order of Fredericksburg had been avoided. At Gettysburg General Warren had demonstrated his ability and intelligence; at Mine Run, he proved himself a commander morally courageous enough to change his mind.

CHAPTER 17

BUSHWHACKED: LITTLE
HOPE OF RECOVERY

Even though the giant armies had settled into winter quarters, the skirmishes and ambushes went on as inevitably as the sun rising each morning. Death never took leave or slumbered; he was always still busy at his grisly work.

In December of 1863 Colonel Hardin took command of a battle group including the Fifth Pa. Reserve Regiment and his Twelfth Regiment, plus a detachment of cavalry. Based at Catlett Station, their mission was to guard the Orange and Alexandria Railroad from attack "from cavalry and guerrilla raids."[1]

This was no easy task because Colonel John Mosby's Rebel raiders boldly operated with relative impunity inside the Union lines. These irregulars had proven on countless occasions to be formidable opponents. Colonel Hardin held to the increasingly anachronistic concept of a gentlemen's war, and disdained Mosby's reliance on stealth, deceit and ambush. But few soldiers, no matter how genteel, questioned Mosby's effectiveness in harrying the Union Army. The impact of his lightning raids was vividly documented in James G. Ramage's *Gray Ghost: The Life of Col. John Singleton Mosby:*

> . . . Mosby threw away the rules and never fought fairly. Here was no gentlemanly thrust and parry, but revolver bullets, noise, and smoke; men falling to the ground wounded and dead; and riderless horses jumping out of control. The Union commander was

usually one of the first down, and in shock and confusion his men had the urge to drop their reins . . . and run away.[2]

On December 14, 1863, Colonel Hardin, in company with his executive officer, Lieutenant-Colonel Richard Gustin and a mounted orderly, rode along the railroad lines selecting sites for constructing blockhouses. The Union officers were a few miles from Catlett Station when Hardin observed the approach of five mounted soldiers. He told the story of what happened in his regimental history 30 years later, writing in the third person:

> . . . Colonel Hardin rode up to the officer who was riding in front (the entire party wore black slouch hats, Union overcoats and top boots), and {had} just asked: 'Where are you going?' when the . . . five raised their revolvers, which they had concealed behind their right legs, and fired. One shot struck Colonel Hardin in his crippled left arm . . . ,one struck Colonel Gustin in his right hand, two struck Colonel Hardin's horse, which sprang forward a few paces and fell dead. . . . The guerrillas, after firing, turned off into the brush and were seen no more.[3]

The bullet shattered Hardin's left arm. The badly bleeding and wounded officer was quickly taken to the nearest army doctor, who ordered immediate amputation. Once again, Hardin was struggling for life against desperate odds. Amputations were often fatal to the patient, who died of shock, uncontrolled bleeding, or suffered a lingering death when gangrene set in.

Colonel Hardin's mother, Sarah Hardin Walworth, was staying at the National Hotel in Pittsburgh when she learned of her son's most recent wound. Her husband, Chancellor Walworth in Saratoga Springs, wrote her with the shocking news on December 15, 1863: "I regret to inform you that the surgeon finds it necessary to perform an amputation. Your son is comfortable & will leave tomorrow."[4] Walworth didn't mention where the operation had taken place, but told his wife to be "on the look-out" for Martin in one of the many Washington Army hospitals.'

Two days later, Martin's mother found her son at the Ebbett House in Washington. She dashed off a brief note to her husband in Saratoga Springs and gave him a gloomy report: "I found Martin D. here yesterday; his arm was taken off just below the shoulder, the same side he was wounded before. His situation is critical, of course, and I have but little hope of his recovery. The Dr. says he is doing well, but he would not say anything else. . . . I will write again tomorrow. Yours aff. S. E. Walworth."[5]

Three days later, Martin's mother wrote a follow-up letter to Chancellor Walworth, which he must have read with a sigh of relief:

"Martin D. is still improving—all his symptoms are favorable at present. He thinks he will be able to leave here by the middle of next week." In this same letter, Sarah added more detail about the ambush, suggesting that Martin could have been easily taken prisoner by the raiders except for the nearby presence of Union pickets. "Regiments of men started after them, but they disappeared as effectively as if they had gone into the ground," she wrote. "His arm was so much shattered, both the bone and the flesh, that there was no other way, but to have it taken off."[6]

All through young Hardin's ordeal, his commander—the often maligned General Crawford—proved a loyal and compassionate friend. Martin's mother wrote her husband: "Gen. Crawford did everything for him he could have done if he had been his son. He went to Washington for a surgeon and had a consultation with the division surgeons and had him brought to the city as safely and comfortably as could be. I do not think he suffers as much as he did before but the crisis is not past yet."[7]

On January 7, 1864, less than a month after the Catlett Station ambush, Martin's mother wrote her old Springfield friend, President Abraham Lincoln at the White House. The letter, postmarked from New York City, is remarkable in its stark simplicity:

Mr. Lincoln,

I hope my dear friend you will not forget Martin D. when you are making your appointments this winter. He has had the misfortune to lose his left arm. But by the aid of a good constitution and a brave spirit, he has resisted all despondency and is rapidly recovering. I had a very kind letter from Gen. Crawford—before Martin was wounded—speaking in the highest terms of him as an active and efficient officer, saying he intended to recommend him to the Secretary of War for promotion.

Yours respectfully, S. E. H. Walworth[8]

Colonel Hardin underwent a long convalescence at Pine Grove, the Walworth mansion in Saratoga Springs, where he was surrounded by family and friends. His stepbrother, Mansfield, was still living at home under a loose form of house arrest. The Chancellor's youngest son had largely abandoned the law by this point and was writing what can only be described as a Gothic romantic novel. He now envisioned himself as a tormented artistic genius misunderstood by lesser men and women.[9]

By this time in their relationship, Martin was probably aware of Mansfield's deep character flaws and his mental and physical abuse of his wife, Ellen Hardin Walworth. She and her children lived during the war in the Bird's Nest estate in Louisville, safely removed from Mansfield's rages and delusions. We can only imagine what emotions Martin felt toward his strange stepbrother and brother-in-law, but one suspects their relationship must have been strained.[10]

Not so with his Martin's other stepbrother, Father Clarence Walworth. The priest visited the recuperating hero and they undoubtedly discussed the Catholic faith. Despite Martin's early prejudice toward the religion of Rome, he was deeply influenced by his charismatic stepbrother. He was either very close to converting at this stage or had already done so.

That was hardly surprising since Father Walworth was widely acknowledged as one of the most persuasive and eloquent evangelists for the American Catholic Church.[11] Before he was done Father Clarence Walworth had converted Ellen, Martin and their servant and close family friend, Dolly Smith, and eventually even Martin's mother, the strong-minded, formidable Mrs. Sarah Hardin Walworth.

Only Chancellor Reuben Walworth seemed impervious to his oldest son's religious arguments. However, the father had long before come to terms with his oldest son's conversion and the filial bonds remained strong despite their religious differences. This was in stark contrast to Chancellor Walworth's deteriorating relationship with Mansfield. Even a father's love could not blind the Chancellor to his youngest son's self-absorption, amoral nature and selfishness, much less Mansfield's cruel abuse of his wife, Ellen.

By now the old Chancellor regarded Ellen, Martin and Lemuel Hardin as dear to him as natural-born offspring, although his regard for Lemuel was severely tested when the boy joined Confederate General John Hunt

Morgan's Confederate cavalry in January of 1863. Embarrassed and angered by his stepson's actions, the Chancellor, a strong Union man, removed Lemuel Hardin's portrait from its place on the wall.[12]

Despite that crisis in the relationship, it seems Chancellor Walworth always retained respect for Lemuel's sincerity and personal character. The Chancellor certainly believed the boy had made a terrible error in donning Confederate gray, but recognized him as an honorable man whose character was infinitely superior to his stepbrother Mansfield's. His youngest son was the Chancellor's antithesis, a debauched, twisted and increasingly unstable voluptuary.[13]

The Civil War often divided families, North and South. This was precisely the case for the Hardin and Walworth clan. For them the phrase a war between brothers was literal reality. However, surviving letters are silent regarding the strong emotions that must have resulted with one brother in blue and the other in gray.

By New Year's 1863, Martin had recovered sufficiently from the amputation to report for light duty. The Army assigned him to court-martial duty in Boston and New York City from January 10 to March 26, 1864. His next assignment was in Pittsburgh, where he was in command of the Draft Rendezvous there until the middle of May. Increasingly, the public was tired of the never-ending sacrifice demanded by the endless war, and the draft was hardly popular in most circles. This assignment must have sorely tested the wounded soldier's tact and patience.[14]

Shortly after her son reported for duty in Pittsburgh, his mother was back in Washington, working her network of influential friends upon her oldest son's behalf. One can't help but think that she found wartime Washington far more exciting than life with her older husband, back in quiet Saratoga Springs. On March 6, 1864 she wrote her daughter Ellen at the Bird's Nest in Louisville:

> My Dear Nellie,
> You will think it strange that I am in this city, but so it is. . . . There has been a sister of Mrs. Lincoln here, Mrs. White, from Selma, Alabama. She came with her mother to bring Mrs. Helm, whose husband was killed in the Southern Army. Mrs. Lincoln refused to see her in any way and Cousin John Stewart {probably Stuart}

made her come over to me to get a pass to go south in the best way she could. We had a hard time to get at Mr. Lincoln, but he had promised her a pass, and she was determined to get it, and she wanted to take some supplies for her family. We had to get Governor {Lazarus W.} Powell to send a letter through the private secretary, which reached him {President Lincoln} at last. But he would not let her take anything but ordinary baggage.[15]

This episode involved Mary Lincoln's half-sister, Emilie Todd Helm, the young, attractive widow of Rebel General Benjamin Hardin Helm, who fell at the Battle of Chickamauga. Her residence at the White House fueled the ongoing rumors that Mrs. Lincoln was a secret Confederate sympathizer. Oddly enough, in Mrs. Walworth's letter to her daughter, she failed to mention that the slain Confederate general was a distant Hardin cousin. Then again, the family connection may have been known to Ellen and didn't need mentioning.[16]

In the same letter, Mrs. Walworth stated unconvincingly that this would be her last visit to Washington "unless some pressing necessity calls me." On this trip, she was escorted to the Bull Run battlefield where "Martin D received that fearful wound." Of course, Mrs. Walworth also spent a great deal of time socializing among the rich and the powerful, commenting, "The Society is better than it has been for the last two or three years."[17] On another occasion, Mrs. Walworth accepted an invitation to visit the encampment of the fabled Army of the Potomac, where she dined and danced with the political and military elite:

I went to the ball and saw a review of the Second Corp where Mrs. Gen. Curtain {she may have been the wife of Brevet Brigadier General John I. Curtin} reviewed the troops on horseback. We stayed three days in a very comfortable tent at General Caldwell's headquarters, were feasted and treated to everything that was nice. I danced in a set with Gen. {Alexander Stewart} Webb, a classmate of D's and in the set were General Meade, Mr. {Hannibal} Hamlin and daughter, Mrs. Gen. {John Wilson} Sprague and one or two other distinguished individuals.[18]

Later in the spring, Mrs. Walworth returned to Pittsburgh and visited Martin D., but her son was soon ordered to report to Washington. She expressed her concern about his possible return to a combat command after such a brief—five month—recuperation following the amputation of his arm. She expressed her feelings in a May 22, 1864 letter posted in Pittsburgh and addressed to her husband, Chancellor Walworth in Saratoga Springs:

> I saw Martin D there. He could not come home with me as he was ordered to Washington. I have not heard from him yet. Hope he has not gone to the front—I do not think he would volunteer to go as he is conscious his nervous system has not quite recovered from the loss of his arm and he has not been on horseback since. It would require strong nerves to command in such battles as have been fought between Grant and Lee. The Penn. Reserves were to have been mustered out the fifteenth of May but I see nothing of it in the papers.[19]

On the day Mrs. Walworth wrote that letter, her son had already been serving at the front for four days, commanding the First Brigade, Pennsylvania Reserve Division in the ongoing battle of Spotsylvania Court House. This was the scene of some of the heaviest fighting of the war. The young officer had, despite his major physical and mental wounds, volunteered for combat duty.[20]

Few if any of his peers would have judged Hardin harshly if he had chosen to leave the army at this juncture. His division commander, General Crawford, had already approved a medical discharge right after the Catlett Station ambush. It seems possible that Hardin seriously considered leaving the service at that point. Considering his combat record and his narrow escapes from death on so many occasions, the young colonel surely knew that no one could question his honor if he resigned from the army.

The author believes Hardin returned to the fight primarily because of his loyalty to his fellow officers and men of the Pennsylvania Reserves. While in Washington on special duties, he must have seen the long trains of ambulances entering the capital with the thousands of wounded from the Battle of the Wilderness. Colonel Hardin knew his boys were in the thick of it as General U.S. Grant drove the Army of the Potomac south against Lee. How could he, in good conscious, remain safe and secure behind Washington's cannon-studded forts, when his soldiers were fighting in the field?

Historian J.R. Sypher wrote a few years after the war that although the 26-year-old Hardin "had not yet fully recovered from the effects of the amputation, as soon as he learned that his regiment was to engage in Grant's campaign to Richmond, he procured permission to leave the special duties to which he had been assigned at Washington and immediately went to the front to join his command. He arrived at Spotsylvania and was assigned command of the First Brigade."[21]

CHAPTER 18

EVEN BRAVE MEN RUN: FIGHTING WITH GRANT'S ARMY IN 1864

The war had now entered a new phase under the overall leadership of Ulysses S. Grant, a stubborn and aggressive commander. Now there was rarely a day without combat for the men of the Army of the Potomac. This was continuous war, remorseless, relentless—a grinding campaign of attrition with no hope of respite until final victory. During Hardin's absence, his division had been engaged in the Battle of the Wilderness (May 5–6) where they suffered 573 casualties out of some 3,500 engaged.[1]

The Army of the Potomac overall suffered 17,666 out of some 100,000 who fought there; the Confederates lost about 8,000 out of 61,000.[2] The tangled terrain on which the battle was fought negated the Union's superiority in artillery and prevented decisive maneuver save for blind gropes through the second-growth forest. More familiar with the area, the Confederates were able to launch a surprise flank attack that nearly destroyed Hancock's Second Corps, until the accidental wounding of Longstreet caused the counterattack to pause in confusion.

By the end of the two-day battle the Union army had been punished severely, but its commander-in-chief ignored the losses and shifted his offensive to the west and south in an effort to seize the key crossroads at Spotsylvania Court House and flank Lee's Army of Northern Virginia. Grant did not retreat, but kept coming, leaving behind a bloody wake of dead and wounded numbering in the thousands. Mrs. Lincoln, and others, called him a butcher.[3]

Unfortunately the Confederates saw the movement and won the race for Spotsylvania, thus beginning another brutal head-on confrontation, this one lasting ten days. Hardin took command of the First Brigade, Pennsylvania Reserves on May 18 in the final phase of the still raging battle. The division was dug-in on a line fronting Laurel Hill (a patch of pine woods atop a slight rise) south of the strategic crossroads. The Army of the Potomac had again been stalled in its tracks, squatting in the mud, pelted by rain, and harassed by sporadic Rebel artillery fire and almost incessant sniping. But despite their misery, Hardin's Pennsylvanians were the lucky ones, at least this time around.

The fiercest fighting of perhaps the entire war took place on May 12 northeast of the Pennsylvania Reserve Division, Fifth Corps. On that grim and gruesome day, the Union Second Corps and supporting units, a total of 20,000 men, assaulted a salient in the center of the Confederate line called the Muleshoe. After an initial breakthrough by the attackers, they were met by strong Confederate counterattacks. A hellish fight ensued in which the two armies fought face-to-face in a driving rain for an incredible 22 hours. Grant's army suffered more than 10,000 casualties; Confederate losses were heavy but never documented. The Muleshoe salient went down in history as the Bloody Angle. Stalemate was the only result.[4]

Although they didn't suffer anywhere near the casualties of the Second Corps, the Pennsylvania Reserve Division and the remainder of General Warren's Fifth Corps met repeated reverses in several attempts to seize Laurel Hill. They were charging against an entrenched and determined enemy with predictable results. At one point, after being ordered to attack again despite an earlier reverse, General Crawford of the Reserves became distraught. One witness wrote: "He was gesticulating in an excited manner . . . and he exclaimed in a tone of extreme anguish, 'I tell you this is sheer madness, and can only end in wanton slaughter and certain repulse.'"[5]

By the time Hardin rejoined his unit, they had been through nearly two continuous weeks of brutal fighting. The Reserves had made numerous and costly attacks with little or no gain. Colonel Buck McCandless had been severely wounded in the hand; Lieutenant Colonel George Dare of the Fifth Pa. Reserves was among the killed, and division commander Crawford had been temporarily invalided when struck by a tree toppled over by Confederate artillery fire. Historian Uzal W. Ent believed that "morale was at rock bottom" among the men, who well knew the futility of attacking such a strong position.[6]

On the day of his return in the 4 a.m. pitch-dark, Hardin led the First Brigade in yet another desperate assault on the Laurel Hill front. During this back and forth fighting, Hardin employed picked men from the Bucktails to form an advanced skirmish line. These men of the Thirteenth Penn. Reserve Regt. posed a formidable threat on the attack or the defense thanks to their deadly seven-shot Spencer repeaters. They could lay down a withering fire equal to several regiments armed with conventional single-shot muskets. Hardin was to increasingly rely on them in the bloody days ahead.[7]

Late in the day Hardin's brigade did push the Confederates back and seize a slight crest of ground. "It was hoped that this good position could be held, from which an attack could be made the next morning,"[8] he later wrote. Just before dark, Hardin's men were relieved by another Union brigade commanded by Colonel Coulter. Hardin warned their commander "to expect the enemy to try and drive in this advanced picket line."[9] Hardin's warning was well-founded and the Rebels did indeed attack later in the night.

Coulter's two regiments quickly withdrew in the face of the Rebel attack and lost the crest. Hardin recalled that Colonel Coulter attempted to rally his men with "his usual boldness."[10] But Coulter was soon hit by enemy fire, and his men fell back in disorder. This was a familiar pattern seen repeatedly in the fight for Laurel Hill.

On the next day, May 19, Confederate General Ewell attacked Union General Robert Ogden Tyler's raw division (composed of heavy artillerymen converted to infantry) along the Fredericksburg Road, about two miles to the right of the Pennsylvania Reserves. Hardin's brigade and the other veteran units doubled-timed to their support. From the volume of fire, Hardin's men assumed a major battle was underway. Colonel Hardin penned his account of the affair 30 years later: "It {the Penn. Reserve Division} passed by the lines of knapsacks left by Tyler's men, and came up behind the left of his line of battle; his men were standing up in line of battle and, every few minutes, blazing away at nothing, unless a shot from a straggling Confederate could be called something. It seemed impossible to stop this firing."[11]

Hardin's First Brigade was ordered to advance in front of Tyler's trig-

ger-happy division and determine the actual strength of the opposing Rebel
force. However, Hardin was not about to send his men forward to where
they would be exposed to the wild firing of panicked troops. Instead, he
filed his brigade off to the left, halted them, and then formed a skirmish
line of Bucktails in a nearby patch of woods. "The enemy had already
retired," Hardin wrote.[12]

His Bucktails remained in their forward position the entire night,
where they were still wary of friendly fire by Tyler's unsteady troops. That
morning Colonel Hardin rode up to inspect the skirmish line and saw an
"extraordinary state of affairs."[13] His soldiers were hiding behind a breastwork of shelter tents and packs they had hastily constructed, not as protection from enemy fire, but facing Tyler's nervous Union riflemen to their
right and rear, who seemed ready to open fire at the slightest provocation.

"The pickets said they received a blizzard every little while from the
Union line, and only an occasional shot from the enemy's side," Hardin
wrote. "Yet these new troops {Tyler's} had shown good pluck in resisting
Ewell's reconnaissance. Lee's veterans were surely as two to one of such
troops, however courageous."[14]

Looking back at the Laurel Hill battles, Hardin placed much of the
blame on a lack of cavalry for proper reconnaissance during a crucial stage
in the campaign. General Phil Sheridan had embarked on a grand raid
against Richmond, leaving the army blind in his absence. Although Hardin
respected Sheridan as the "kind of leader to make successes,"[15] he believed
the pugnacious Irishman had erred badly by leaving the Army of the Potomac without cavalry: "The principal reason why the infantry was marched
hither and thither was to find out positions, which the cavalry would have
found for it," Hardin said. "The infantry was so much exhausted by marching, especially at night in rain, it had little stomach for a fight when the
attacks were ordered."[16]

In truth the Pennsylvania Reserves had not pressed their attacks with
the same elan and aggressiveness shown on previous battlefields. After
more than two years of war, they were tired and disillusioned and probably
sick of risking their lives in senseless attacks. In two weeks of ferocious
combat since the nightmare in The Wilderness, the Army of the Potomac
had suffered 36,000 killed, wounded, and captured for a 31 percent casualty
rate.[17]

But there was much more fighting ahead. Lee shored up his lines around Spotsylvania Court House, and once again Grant shifted his army off to the left, pushing his exhausted troops to quickly cross the North Anna River and slice into the rear of the Army of Northern Virginia. Hardin's First Brigade moved out at midnight on May 21, 1864, along with the rest of Warren's Fifth Corps. The Pennsylvania Reserve Division led the advance behind a strong screen of skirmishers.

In mid-afternoon the Pennsylvanians approached Guiney's Station where Hardin's Bucktails skirmished with a force of Confederate cavalry numbering several hundred or more, which they took under fire from behind trees in a nearby orchard. The outnumbered Bucktails pressed the action vigorously and began severely punishing the Confederate horse soldiers, who appeared at one point to be forming for a charge, which never materialized.[18]

An elated Colonel Hardin galloped back to division where he requested General Crawford to send one or two more regiments to support the Bucktails, "who are in the woods driving in cavalry and chickens."[19] The regiments were dispatched, but didn't arrive before the fall of darkness as the fighting gradually faded away.

Later that night, Colonel Hardin detected the "savory smell" of roasting chickens and followed the scent to an encampment of Bucktails.[20] The riflemen gathered around the fire hailed their brigade commander and cheerfully invited him to dine on their confiscated Confederate chickens. Hardin promptly accepted the invitation and shared in their feast. The incident was remembered fondly by the participants for many years after the war.

On May 23, 1864, Hardin's men crossed the North Anna River at Jericho with the rest of the Pennsylvania Reserves.[21] Colonel Charles Wainwright, who commanded the Fifth Corps artillery, looked down upon the scene from a nearby eminence: "Crawford's division crossed also at the same time. The deployment of the troops on the opposite bank was a beautiful sight as we watched it."[22]

Then the Confederate infantry struck hard, pressing the line where General Charles Griffin's left flank and Hardin's First Brigade merged. Colonel Hardin refused his right flank, ordering one of his regiments to form on a line perpendicular to the main battle line. He also requested support from General Lysander Cutler's brigade, who quickly dispatched two regiments to the threatened sector where "a hot infantry fight" ensued.[23] "They {Cutler's men} were of the right material," Hardin wrote, "and they went in with a will; they forced the enemy back, and this part of the line was fully restored."[24]

Hardin's men had not had time to entrench and were standing in battle line in open country, facing the enemy. Suddenly as many as 30 Rebel artillery pieces opened a devastating fire. " . . . the men were under about as warm artillery fire as they ever had in the open," Hardin noted.[25] Another participant wrote: "The air seemed filled with the shrieking shells and whizzing fragments. The men could scarcely do more than to lie down and let the storm rage."[26]

One enemy shell scored a direct hit on an icehouse serving as Hardin's brigade headquarters, blowing it to bits. Luckily, no one was inside when the shell exploded. During this rain of shells, Hardin rode about on horseback, trying to rally and encourage his men to stand firm. Suddenly horse and rider vanished in an exploding geyser of dirt and smoke.

Once again Hardin narrowly escaped death. A shard of shrapnel struck him with great velocity on his right side. What could have been a fatal wound, was averted only by the fact that Hardin had stuffed a thick order book in his jacket pocket, which absorbed the shell fragment. Hardin was heavily bruised, probably in mild shock, but otherwise unhurt. This was his fourth wound of the war.[27]

Not long afterwards Hardin ordered his Bucktails to advance under Major William Ross Hartshorne and seize a house located to the front of the division. From this captured vantage point, they turned their fast-firing breechloaders on the Rebels, who were forced to move their deadly artillery to another position.

Heavy fighting continued on the right flank for some time until a flanking attack by Lieutenant-Colonel McCoy's 83rd Pennsylvania drove the enemy back and took several hundred prisoners. On that bright note, the fighting finally sputtered to a conclusion. Darkness fell and the men, as good veterans always did, dug themselves in for what the morning might bring in the way of bullet and shell.

The Pennsylvania Reserves were ordered to move out that next morning to guard another ford downstream and hold the right bank, to allow

General Ambrose Burnside's Ninth Corps to cross. After a cautious advance, Hardin ordered his men to entrench again, "expecting every moment to be attacked."[28] When the advancing troops finally arrived, Hardin was appalled by the troops' incredible behavior:

> Burnside's troops now came down to the river and went to washing, bathing and swimming, at the same time hallooing and making all the noise they could as though there were no enemy within miles. The writer was never so indignant in his life. His troops were then in peril of their lives, and had been in the utmost danger of capture since early in the morning, holding an uncovered position of the right of the river within sight of the whole Confederate army.[29]

Six hours passed before Burnside's men finally crossed the river, allowing the enemy, according to Hardin, to heavily entrench in anticipation of an attack. " . . . when it {Burnside's force} attacked," Hardin wrote, "as it did about sundown, with considerable spirit, it struck entrenchments, lost heavily and gained nothing."[30] Once again poor Union leadership resulted in a waste of good men. "We all said then we would be better off without Burnside's army, as it was then commanded," Hardin wrote.[31]

Grant's army had crossed the North Anna, but now found itself in mortal danger. Lee's strategic defense at the river was, in effect, a clever trap. The Rebel army was protected in trenches which formed a V with the apex of the V at the river's edge where they controlled about a half-mile of the bank. Grant's army forded the river on either side of the V, which left them divided into two wings.[32]

Using a railroad line that connected the feet of the V, Lee could quickly shuttle troops to concentrate on one isolated wing of the Union Army and destroy it piecemeal before Grant could support them in time, since reinforcements from the unengaged half of the army would be forced to cross the river twice—a time consuming and tricky maneuver.[33] Grant's precarious position would become even more perilous should a heavy rainfall sweep away his pontoon bridges.

This was an opportunity, in Lee's words, "to strike them a blow."[34] Unfortunately for the Confederate cause, Lee fell ill and was unable to carry through with his designs. And the rain held off, enabling Grant to withdraw his army from the jaws of the trap. He recrossed the North Anna and once again moved by the left flank toward Richmond. The Army of the Potomac had narrowly escaped a telling defeat.[35]

Several days later the Pennsylvania Reserves crossed the Pamunkey River and were now within 20 miles of the Confederate capital. The men were understandably hoping they could avoid further combat. The Pennsylvania Reserve Division was only a day away from the end of its three-year term of enlistment. On May 30, they would be withdrawn from the line and return to Pennsylvania where they would be disbanded. Some of the men had re-enlisted and would be re-assigned to other Pennsylvania regiments, but the majority were going home. They didn't relish the prospect of dying on the last day of their enlistment.[36]

On Monday morning, May 30, 1864, General Crawford's Pennsylvania Reserve Division advanced on the far left of the Army of the Potomac and moved south across Shady Grove Road while other units moved west along the same route. Crawford ordered Hardin's brigade to advance further south to a point about a half-mile northwest of Bethesda Church. This was a ramshackle country house of worship, which was soon to give its name to one of campaign's most brutal slaughters.[37] Fifth Corps commander General Warren was irritated at the absence of Federal cavalry to reconnoiter west of his infantry to determine enemy strength and intentions.

Hardin's Pennsylvanians had encountered a determined group of enemy infantry supported by several artillery pieces positioned in a patch of woods near the chapel on the Old Church Road. He ordered the Fifth Pa. Reserve Regt. to take the woods, but they were driven back. The Tenth Pa. Reserve Regiment was then ordered to the attack and they also failed to drive the enemy from this strip of woods. Hardin believed this position was strongly held by Confederate infantry skirmishers. At around 5 p.m., division commander Crawford ordered Hardin's First Brigade to again attack the stubborn Rebel position. As Hardin later wrote:

> The Bucktails, led by Major {William Ross} Hartshorne, began to work across an old cornfield, which lay between the woods on one side and the strip of timber . . . , in a manner to excite the admiration of friend and foe. Being deployed at our edge of the timber, they

made a rush into the open, which drew the enemy's fire. The instant this fire began the Bucktails dropped. As soon as the enemy's fire slackened, the Bucktails rose and delivered a rapid fire of three to five shots apiece from their breechloaders, advancing at the same time. As soon as the enemy had loaded he began firing again; in an instant the Bucktails literally disappeared. The enemy's fire diminishing, the Bucktails again rose, delivered three to five shots in rapid succession, and ran for the enemy's strip of woods, which they carried, the enemy falling back to a house where he made a short stand, but was soon driven out and back to his main line.[38]

While the Bucktails continued their skirmishing to the west, Hardin ordered his other regiments to demolish the fences and construct a breastwork. Realizing that his brigade was now dangling at the extreme left of the entire army, Hardin sent a runner back to Division asking for immediate support or permission to withdraw north back to the Shady Grove Road. The First Brigade commander had accomplished the purpose of reconnoitering the enemy's position, although he would have much preferred if the job had been handled by cavalry.

The uneasy Hardin must have been disappointed when Division told him to hold and await reinforcements. As the men listlessly set about their work in constructing a breastwork, the skirmishing to the west intensified. Soon a messenger from Major Hartshorne with the Bucktails informed Hardin that as many as two Confederate divisions were advancing in battle line west on either side of the Old Church Road.[39]

Hardin's men were outnumbered, perhaps by as much as four-to-one. The enemy force straddled the pike and its wings extended far beyond Hardin's unanchored left and right flanks. The Rebels were going to squeeze Hardin's Brigade in a giant nutcracker. West Point textbooks described the maneuver as a double-envelopment. " There had been only time for the First Brigade of Reserves to pile up some fence rails and lay down behind them, when this column came rushing over them," Hardin later wrote. "The volley or two delivered by our feeble force made no impression on the enemy; he ran over and around the piles of rails, and his division headquarters arrived amidst the headquarters of the First Brigade before the latter could extricate itself."[40]

Witness to this unfolding spectacle was artilleryman Colonel Charles Wainwright. The diarist later penned his impression of the stampeding Pennsylvanians:

> Now the enemy came in from the south and along the pike, making their whole attack on Hardin's brigade, which had no line formed and was not in condition to receive it. I waited to see how much of an attack it was, which I soon found out, for in five minutes Hardin's brigades were running. . . . I pushed at once for headquarters, where my batteries were, things looking very squally for a complete turning of our left. When I went up the road, the reserves had much the appearance of the devil take the hindmost.[41]

Luckily for Hardin and his fleeing men, the enemy's charge continued south down the pike parallel to the main Union force to the north, essentially putting them temporarily out of the tactical picture. "The enemy was so confident of his ultimate success, he did not stop to secure the First Brigade prisoners, but continued on his charge down the pike," Hardin wrote.[42]

Had Confederate General Robert Rodes been able to quickly reorganize his victorious division and immediately change front and direct it northward, the great flanking movement would have had an excellent chance of success. But the momentum of the Rebel charge carried many of the attackers further east and away from the rest of Crawford's division located north along the Shady Grove Road. Men from different units had become intermixed and their officers were forced to invest valuable time in reorganizing their ranks.[43]

This allowed the remnants of Hardin's Brigade to retreat north where the Colonel rallied most of them in an open field. They fell back before aggressive Rebel skirmishers until they linked up with Colonel John Howard Kitching's brigade (the Sixth and Fifteenth New York Heavy Artillery Regiments), who had been on route to reinforce them just before the Confederate attack. The artillerymen had recently been converted to infantry and were commonly referred to as Heavies.[44] Enemy artillery now opened an accurate fire on the Union infantry. Hardin described the event later in his regimental history, writing in the third person:

Kitching's men were standing up on the crest firing as fast as possible; Colonel Hardin went up to this line and tried his best to get the men to lie down, as the skirmish line—the only fire of the enemy—was dealing destruction among them. No amount of persuasion nor orders could make the men lie down; Colonel Hardin finally ordered Colonel Kitching to move his brigade back to where a strong defensive position had suddenly and miraculously taken shape along the south edge of Shady Grove Road.[45]

Under the overall direction of Fifth Corps commander Warren, the Yankees had gone to work with spoons, shovels, bayonets and tin plates, digging in with all the speed and urgency of men who knew a great Rebel storm was brewing to their front. In less than an hour, they had built a sturdy revetment using fence rails, logs, stones and packed earth. One Pennsylvania boy wrote: "The men threw up a rifle pit of rails with marvelous rapidity. Aladdin could not have raised a house quicker."[46]

This new line was formidable indeed. Hardin's reformed First Brigade held the center; Colonel Joe Fisher's Third Brigade held the right wing, and Kitching's men manned the left wing. The Union line formed a crescent, angling inward at perhaps a 20-degree angle. This strong line of entrenchments stood atop a shallow ridge looking down upon the approaches from the Bethesda Church crossroads to the south.

General Warren and his staff were near the Armstrong farm on a rise to the northeast looking down at the Union line. Union artillery had been placed there to support batteries positioned on the Bowles Farm to Hardin's left rear and along his center. An enemy frontal attack moving straight up the rough trail leading north from Bethesda Church would encounter a terrible cannon crossfire. The Yankees had laid a deadly trap during that brief interlude while the enemy reorganized and hesitated.

At about this time Union General Charles Griffin, whose division was further west down the Shady Grove Road, appeared on the scene, apparently curious about the reason for the heavy firing of only an hour before. He approached Hardin and brusquely demanded to know why so many troops were concentrating there and digging in with such frantic haste. By this point, the firing had died out almost completely and the enemy was momentarily out of sight.

Rather than give a long explanation of the situation to Griffin—described by historian Mark Boatner, III as "bluff, bellicose, outspoken," and touchy, Colonel Hardin invited Griffin to ride south with him where he could see for himself.[47] The two officers rode a short distance and crossed the road where Hardin pointed out the Confederate division head-quarters flag and enemy infantry massed nearby. "I'm satisfied," General Griffin curtly replied, and promptly galloped off to the west to see to his own troops.[48]

In the enemy camp, General Jubal Early finally concluded an impromptu staff meeting and reluctantly consented to his subordinates' desire to send a single infantry brigade directly up the trail to the north to test and as-certain the strength of the Union line. "Twenty-three-year-old Colonel Edward Willis, at the head of John Pegram's old brigade, had the post of honor. Despite having suffered a wound at the recent Battle of the Wilder-ness, the young officer seemed eager to accept the challenge.[49]

A Rebel artillery battery near Bethesda Church began shelling the Union lines, shooting "remarkably well" in the words of Union artillery-man Wainwright.[50] Yankee gun batteries replied almost immediately when Willis' lone brigade began its advance. Right behind Hardin's lines, an enemy shell struck the Bowles farmhouse and ignited a ablaze. Shortly afterward, a woman with a baby in her arms and holding a small child by the hand emerged from the house and ran in confusion parallel to the Union line until soldiers guided her off in a safer direction.

In a scene that must have been reminiscent of the British attack on Gen-eral Andrew Jackson's ragged little army at New Orleans, the Confederates came on in the old style. They won the admiration of their opponents for their bold advance: a brave, grand spectacle of determined men marching into certain death. No Rebel yells pierced the air that afternoon. The men in gray came on at right shoulder arms as if on parade, steady and silent.

One of Hardin's riflemen remembered: "Orders were given not to fire one shot until the enemy reached the line of an old fence half-way across the open space between us."[51] Hardin ordered the Bucktails to hold their fire until they could clearly make out the faces of the oncoming enemy. They cocked their deadly Spencer repeaters and patiently waited until the enemy came to within 100 yards—point-blank range.

At about 6 p.m., the Union lines erupted with rifle and cannon fire.

Hardin's riflemen fired directly ahead, while the flanking brigades delivered a devastating crossfire.

Confederate Colonel Willis was struck in the abdomen by shrapnel and mortally wounded. Many other officers were soon either killed or wounded in the rain of bullets and shrapnel. The Confederates rallied three times and pressed the attack. One Rebel color bearer actually marched to within 20 feet of a cannon's mouth before being blown into pieces. One of the surviving Confederate officers claimed the Union barrage was, "the heaviest and most murderous fire I had ever seen."[52]

Infantryman George Darby, serving with Hardin's old Twelfth Reserve Regiment, vividly described the terrible impact of the combined artillery and massed rifle fire on the advancing Rebels: "In less time than it takes to tell it, the rebel brigade was almost annihilated, a very few only making their escape back to the woods. As I was firing across the top of the pit, a piece of a human jaw containing five teeth struck and stuck upright in a rail just in front of me. I suppose the rebel to whom it had belonged had been hit by a cannon shot and his head dashed to pieces . . ."[53]

Another Union soldier told of staring at the ghastly sights of "fragments of human flesh hanging to the lattice fence, thrown there by cannon shot."[54] The attackers died in their own blood and guts. Survivors flattened themselves on the ground, while Yankee bullets hissed overhead and cannon shells exploded above with terrible effect. "The slaughter was so sickening that Major Hartshorne {Hardin's Brigade} leaped to his feet and called upon his assailants to surrender," recalled a fellow soldier.[55] Several hundred stunned and dazed Rebel survivors, many bleeding from terrible wounds, rose up from the ground and stumbled towards the Yankee lines.

General Crawford ordered a counter-charge, but with dark falling nothing much came of it. Many of the Union boys laid their rifles down and walked the battlefield, offering the enemy wounded water and helping them make their way to medical assistance. As many as 400 Confederates had fallen in the suicidal attack.[56]

Stretcher bearers brought one badly wounded Confederate regimental officer to General Crawford, whereupon the Yankee division commander offered his enemy a slug of whiskey and his unabashed admiration for that brave, doomed charge. Crawford ordered the wounded officer taken to his headquarters and promised him good treatment.[57]

This final bloodletting at Bethesda Church (also called the Battle of Totpotomy Creek) marked the end of the war for the majority of the men in the famed Pennsylvania Reserves. Their three-year enlistments expired on the very day of the action, and the next day they would march to the rear and board trains to Harrisburg. It was fortunate timing for the Reserves, as they were able to miss a far larger battle three days later, in which the tables would be turned and thousands of Union attackers would be gunned down in droves: Cold Harbor.

Meantime, upon arriving in the Pennsylvania capital, the Reserves were paraded before cheering crowds and saluted in a speech by Governor Andrew G. Curtin. For them, the war was over.[58] Not so for First Brigade commander Colonel Martin D. Hardin.

The four-time wounded, one-armed officer was ordered to Washington, where he was given another convalescent leave to recover from the recently completed campaign and the lingering effects of the wound suffered at the North Anna. There, he awaited orders in the city he had grown to know well since first coming there in the first months of the war.

By now Colonel Hardin was much admired by his soldiers and his peers. General George Gordon Meade, the former commander of the Pennsylvania Reserves and the victor of Gettysburg, would later praise Hardin's patriotic services with which he was "personally acquainted" in a letter of recommendation, adding: "Gen. Hardin has rendered much faithful & distinguished service during the war being conspicuous for his gallantry, zeal & energy . . . {he is} an officer of education & a gentleman of high character."[59]

Perhaps Hardin's decision to remain in the service was simply obedience to the Hardin family code. Serving the nation in war had been the calling of five generations, famed for bold courage and perseverance demonstrated over more than a century. Hardin men had fought against the French, the British twice, the Native Americans on many battlefields, and, of course, against the Mexicans. A Hardin simply didn't quit; it wasn't in his make-up. Following that family tradition, Colonel Martin D. Hardin would see the Civil War to its bitter end no matter what the price.

CHAPTER 19

DESPERATE HOURS: REBEL
RAIDERS MENACE WASHINGTON

While Colonel Hardin was leading his brigade of Pennsylvanians south as part of General Grant's drive against Richmond in the spring of 1864, his mother, Mrs. Sarah Hardin Walworth, had once again returned to Washington, D.C., where she resumed her own campaign to win a general's star for her son.

This was a subtle campaign waged with smiles and clever conversation at tea parties, cotillions, and tête-à-têtes with the political and military king-makers of Washington City. Nonetheless, the success of Mrs. Walworth's social and political strategy was crucial to Martin's future as a soldier. Winning the star was usually much more than a question of battlefield bravery or brilliance. Political influence and social connections were trumps in Washington.

Luckily for Colonel Hardin, his mother was a formidable personage and wise in the ways of the powerful. She brought to the task a strong will, intelligence and the social credentials that opened doors in official Washington. Few would dare rebuff a request for an audience from the wife of the esteemed Chancellor Walworth, who also happened to be the widow of a slain Mexican War hero. Most importantly, Sarah was an old friend of Abraham and Mary Lincoln from Springfield, which brought with it access and influence.[1]

Unfortunately, the surviving record does not specify exactly who Mrs. Walworth contacted during her month-long visit to Washington that spring and summer of 1864. We can safely assume that she spoke with Mary Todd Lincoln, if not directly with the President. And, it would be logical that she used her second husband's name to gain access to Secretary of State William Seward and Secretary of War Stanton; both men had practiced law early in their careers before Chancellor Walworth's bench in Saratoga Springs. It also seems likely that Colonel Hardin's mother also contacted former Illinois Senator Orville Browning, then residing in the Capital. He was an old intimate of Lincoln and a close political associate.[2]

Sarah's various efforts to promote her son finally bore fruit on June 30, 1864. That day President Lincoln read a letter from Mr. V. Holt recommending Colonel Martin D. Hardin, late of the Pennsylvania Reserves, for services in the field. The President scribbled a short but revealing note on the back of the envelope: "Col. Martin D. Hardin named within is a son of a very Dear Friend of mine who fell at Buena Vista, has himself a West Point education, has fought in the War, losing an arm and been shot through the body, and if there is any vacancy, send in nomination for him as a Brigadier General at once."[3]

On July 2, 1864, Congress acted on the President's note and promoted Colonel Martin Davis Hardin to the rank of Brigadier General in the Regular Army for "meritorious services on the field of battle."[4] On July 4, 1864, on the eighty-ninth anniversary of the Declaration of Independence, Mrs. Sarah (Hardin) Walworth, informed her husband in Saratoga Springs of the glad tidings:

> I have succeeded in the object which has kept me here for the last month. Martin D. was nominated and confirmed on Saturday as Brigadier Gen., which will place him in his proper position and in some measure pay for his services and sacrifices in this unhappy war. I have had kind and influential friends—or I could not have accomplished what I had done. Nellie {Martin's sister Ellen} has telegraphed me to come to her or I should come home—for I need rest—but these are not the "{illegible} times of peace" and I must go where duty calls. I have kept my health—the climate here is hot and dry—there are forty thousand sick here and the sight of the wounded and dead is a heart sickening scene.[5]

Although Mrs. Walworth didn't mention the fact in surviving correspondence, we can be fairly certain she was also pleased that her son would command the forts guarding the Capital on the north bank of the Potomac River. For a four-time wounded soldier and veteran of 17 battles, this safe assignment must have seemed only just. Others could take the risks while General Hardin enjoyed the relative comfort and security of garrison life. For the past three years, the Washington defenses had never seen the approach of a Confederate Army.

Hardin's mother proved to be wrong on that count within only days of Martin's promotion. After years of false alarms, the Rebels were finally coming. Confederate General Jubal Early had led a small army—mainly consisting of the late Stonewall Jackson's corps—across the Potomac River on July 5, and was now threatening Washington. Young General Hardin would soon confront a crisis in which the final outcome of the desperate struggle hung in the balance.

After defeating or driving off several Union forces, Early's Army of the Valley was descending on the northern approaches to Washington with a force of nearly 15,000 lean and deadly infantry. Worse yet, the Washington defenses, regarded as immensely formidable, had been stripped of troops to reinforce Grant's army in his advance on Richmond. The under-manned garrison was short of veterans. Washington was ripe for the taking.[6]

In those perilous days ahead, Hardin played a major role in what became one of the most dramatic chapters of the war. To many it seemed incredible that the Capital could be in such peril. Washington was probably the most fortified city in the world, its 37-mile perimeter bristling with 68 enclosed forts and batteries and 20 miles of rifle pits. More than 807 cannon and 98 mortars provided the citadel with impressive firepower.[7] Surely even the most audacious Rebels would shrink from attacking such a fortress. Even more daunting, Hardin would soon find himself commanding the defenses around Fort Reno, where the Confederate blow was expected to fall.[8]

But there was a chink in the armor that summer of 1864. Like Hardin, himself, most of the men in the northern defenses—around 9,600 men— were convalescing from wounds, illness and/or hard service; or serving in various Veteran Reserve units, formerly called the Invalid Corps. Due to the Army of the Potomac's enormous casualties during its Overland Campaign, Grant had taken most of the able-bodied troops out of the city as reinforcements, converting a number of former Heavy Artillery regiments into regular infantry. Meantime, Hardin had met Early's men on the battlefield before, and knew that his own motley force was no match for such hardened veterans.[9]

Hardin also commanded able-bodied men from the 100-day Ohio militia, but they were raw recruits. Army Chief of Staff Major General Henry Halleck dismissed the lot as barely able to load and fire a musket.[10] The long-neglected Washington defensive ring was a hollow fortress that would crack like an egg before a determined assault by first-rate troops. And General Hardin knew as well as anyone that Early's ragged Confederate veterans were among the best infantry to appear in the war.[11]

Incredibly, the vulnerability of the Washington forts had been recognized as early as May 17, when Brigadier General Albion Howe, Inspector of Artillery, took stock of the situation. He reported that the undermanned forts were prey to "a sudden and covered dash upon the works."[12] No one of importance paid attention to Howe's warning. Perhaps, Halleck and the other Union generals were, as Lincoln's Attorney General Edward Bates believed, nothing but "helpless imbeciles."

Fiery radical Polish Count Adam Gurowski was also present in the Capital that July. This remarkable gadfly and intellect was even more scathing in his remarks regarding the lack of Union leadership before the impending crisis. This ardent Abolitionist, an opinionated but informed observer, wrote with a pen dipped in strychnine: "It is impossible to decide what is most revolting to witness here. Is it cowardice? Is it imbecility? The powers are scared out of their senses. We are taken by surprise like monks, nuns or chickens . . ."[13]

On July 9, Early's Confederates defeated a Union force of 9,000 men at the Monocacy River near Frederick, Maryland, commanded by Major General Lew Wallace. The victorious Rebel army was now only 50 miles away and poised to descend on Washington.[14]

The Capital's garrison scrambled to throw every available man into the forts and rifle pits; while the civilians came fairly close to panic. The streets were thronged with marching men, the gaslight shimmering on their naked bayonets and crowded with refugees from the Maryland countryside carrying their belongings in wagons, buggies or on their backs. Thousands of recently emancipated slaves were frightened that the oncoming Rebel army would recapture them and march them south. Historian Adam F. Colburn described the chaotic scene:

As the morning wore on, the evidences of trouble outside increased—scattering contrabands, some with bundles on their backs, some with chairs, buckets and wash-tubs on their heads, others with the family table. . . . These poor frightened people came trotting into the city over the Tennallytown and Brightwood roads, seeking a place of safety inside of the forts. The roads became blocked with all manner of rickety vehicles, many of them of the most primitive description, filled with the families and furniture of peaceable farmers, who had left their homes in fear of the approaching rebels. A more grotesque picture than was presented by this *anxious train* it is impossible to conceive.[15]

Rumors had floated through the city for more than a week about a possible Rebel attack, but were dismissed as "largely unworthy of notice," according to an angry Secretary of the Navy Gideon Welles. He bluntly stated that the approaching crisis was the result of Union "neglect, ignorance, folly, imbecility in the last degree. Stanton, Halleck and Grant are asleep or dumb."[16]

On late Sunday, July 10, newly promoted Brigadier General Hardin was inspecting the forts on the eastern edge of his northern perimeter on the far side of the Anacostia River bridge. His task was interrupted as a dispatch rider came galloping towards him, trailing a dusty plume behind his horse. Washington was sweltering in a drought 47 days long; oven-like temperatures hovered in the mid-90s even after the sun sank. Soldiers and citizens were continually bathed in sweat and irritation. Dust billowed everywhere.[17]

The rider brought momentous news from Hardin's superior, Major General Christopher Columbus Augur, commander of the Union XXII Corps, who was responsible for defending the city. Union cavalry some 20 miles north on the Rockville Pike were at that very moment skirmishing with Rebel horsemen, the advance elements of Early's Rebel army. Estimates of Confederate strength varied widely from 10,000 to 40,000— although the actual number was not more than 15,000.[18]

Hardin knew that mere numbers told only a part of the story. A little more than a month before, some of these very same Rebel soldiers had routed his Pennsylvanians at Bethesda Church. Hardin knew the quality of the approaching enemy troops, respecting them as "the very flower of the great Army of Northern Virginia."[19] The young Union General feared the ragtag garrison forces in Washington could not prevail against such men. Hardin was also thunderstruck by the news that Union General Wallace was falling back on Baltimore, leaving the door to Washington wide open. Hardin wrote:

> It was expected that Wallace would, if defeated, retreat in direction of Washington, so then the remnant of his army could be used to strengthen the garrison of that city. When the authorities in Washington heard that Wallace had not only been defeated, but that he retreated in the direction of Baltimore, and left the roads to Washington clear for Early they became, to put it mildly, somewhat alarmed . . . no portion of the Sixth Corps was in sight or in easy reach of Washington.[20]

There was really only one alternative for the Washington defenders in General Hardin's opinion. They must stage at least the appearance of a determined resistance. A bristling show of force might make Early hesitate before launching an attack on the impressive defenses. That would buy time for the expected arrival of Grant's Sixth Corps, now headed north on transports to rescue the imperiled city. The Nineteenth Corps was also on the way, having sailed from the Gulf and being redirected to the Capital instead of Petersburg. But would the reinforcements arrive in time?

No one on that Sunday was sure. If the Sixth Corps was delayed, they might be greeted with the sight of the smoldering ruins of Washington: the Treasury looted, the President and Cabinet members held prisoner or in ignominious flight, and the retiring Confederate Army freshly provisioned and armed.

The political and psychological impact of such a defeat—the loss of the Capital—this late in the war could endanger the Union cause and further erode civilian morale in the North. Ironically, Washington was rich in top military brass but poor indeed in private soldiers, men who could march, shoot and fight. General Halleck stated the case succinctly: "We have five times as many generals here as we want, but are greatly in need of privates. Anyone volunteering in that capacity will be thankfully received."[21] Such nightmarish possibilities must have clouded General Hardin's mind after he learned of Wallace's defeat at Monocacy on Saturday.

On Sunday afternoon one-armed General Hardin galloped west, clattering across the wooden bridge over Anacostia Creek bound for General Auger's headquarters on Pennsylvania Avenue to receive further orders.

Only six days had elapsed since his promotion to brigadier general. And now the 26-year-old was facing his greatest test of the war. Over the next two days, the crisis would require all his resolve, judgment and leadership abilities. And as he rode, the city's citizens were already in a frenzy as the wildest rumors spread. The *Frank Leslie's Illustrated News* reporter wrote of "The surprise, the panic, the smoke, the dust, the clamor and the confusion . . ."[22]

Awaiting Hardin at his headquarters was Major General Augur, a 43-year-old West Point graduate and former classmate of U.S. Grant. The cigar smoking regular soldier had served in the Mexican War and fought Indians in the Pacific Northwest during the early 1850s. At the outbreak of the Civil War, Augur was West Point Commandant.[23]

Like so many soldiers assigned to the Washington forts that summer, both Hardin and Augur had been badly wounded. Augur had been shot in the right hip at the Battle of Cedar Mountain, subsequently returned to the war much earlier than the surgeon advised, and led a division out west in the siege of Port Hudson in 1863. The undoubtedly brave regular soldier was deemed a reliable officer, if not an inspiring or dashing leader.[24]

When Hardin arrived at Augur's headquarters on Fourteenth Street and Pennsylvania Avenue, he was immediately briefed by his commander. Augur gave him details from recent dispatches sent by Major William H. Fry of the Sixteenth Pennsylvania Cavalry. This officer, in command of a heterogeneous collection of about 500 horsemen, was at that very moment shadowing Early's advance only a few hours march from the Capital. Earlier in the day, around 11 a.m., Fry's horsemen had been sharply repulsed by Rebel cavalry in a spirited skirmish north of Rockville, Maryland.[25] Perhaps Augur even read Fry's hastily written report to Hardin during their late afternoon meeting:

> About three miles from Rockville on the Frederick road, at a small village known as Garrradsville, my advance-guard met the advance

of Rebels. Skirmishing commenced at once, and upon riding to the skirmish line I could distinctly see a large column of cavalry moving along the road. I withdrew gradually through Rockville, and took a position about a mile from town, on a hill and dismounted my men, formed a skirmish line, which was held for an hour, when the enemy got a battery in position, and shelled my command so well that I was forced to retire.[26]

Augur told Hardin that Fry's horsemen were falling back on Fort Reno at Tennallytown on the western edge of the defensive line where they would make a stand. That sector of the front was held by the First Brigade of Hardin's Division, a force that hardly inspired confidence. By 4 p.m., Sunday, July 10, Fry's horsemen had already fallen back onto the thin outer picket-line of Hardin's Division at Fort Reno. The sound of enemy rifle fire was clearly heard for the first time in Washington's western outreaches after nearly three years of war.

General Augur ordered Hardin to report to Major General Alexander McCook, who would assume overall command of the northern defenses and act as Hardin's immediate senior. It was the first command change in what was soon to be a confusing and chaotic command structure involving a regiment of Union general officers from Chief of Staff Halleck to Quartermaster Montgomery Meigs.

The choice of Major General McCook as overall commander may have struck Hardin as odd, considering the former had absolutely no knowledge of the Washington defense lines. In fact, the Army of the Cumberland veteran had essentially been unemployed since his suspect performance at the Battle of Chickamauga, which led him to request a Court of Inquiry that spring in Washington. The court cleared his name, but McCook's future looked rather bleak. Now General Halleck, acting on the instructions of Secretary of War Stanton, had abruptly taken McCook off the shelf only hours before. McCook was thrust into the developing crisis with scant knowledge of the troops he commanded or the defenses.[27]

McCook was West Point, Class of 1852—graduating a year later than his peers due to a surplus of demerits and a serious deficiency in math. Before the war, he had campaigned against the Utes and Apaches in New Mexico before returning to West Point as an assistant instructor in infantry tactics, which included the grandiloquently titled course, "The Art of War." He and Cadet Hardin were present at the academy at the same time and probably remembered one another, although young Hardin's cadet status would have undoubtedly prevented them from forming any sort of familiarity.[28]

Early in the Civil War, General McCook was the youngest brigadier general in the army and commanded troops at Shiloh, Perryville and Stones River. The Ohio native was one of the "Fighting McCooks"—a combative clan of seven brothers and five cousins—five rising to the rank of general and three dying in combat. Alexander's 65-year-old father died resisting Rebel raider General John Hunt Morgan's incursion into Ohio in 1863.[29]

Although some doubted McCook's competence, few questioned his courage. Whatever Hardin's initial thoughts were on this score, he quickly developed a deep respect for the Ohio soldier. They agreed that the only salvation for Washington was for the undermanned garrison to put on a bold face and convince Rebel General Early that he faced a strong, aggressive and dangerous force. Later when the attacking Rebels appeared before the Washington defenses, General McCook telegraphed Augur's XXII Army Corps Headquarters, stating without much confidence: "My force is small but I will do my best."[30]

General Hardin now only commanded the northwestern forts from the Potomac River east to Fort Slocum. This line included Fort Sumner, Fort Bayard, Fort Reno, Fort De Russy and other undermanned strongpoints. Hardin at this early stage had less than 4,000 men available to cover a 20-mile stretch of front. Ominously in those early hours, General Augur told Hardin that his sector was expected to be the point of the Rebel attack the following morning.

The key to Hardin's western line of works was massive Fort Reno. The position was imposing, described by Hardin as "a large enclosed work . . . very strong, situated on high ground."[31] Observers atop the Fort Reno signal tower enjoyed a sweeping view of the western countryside and the crucial Rockford Pike and other key roads.

If only Hardin had adequate numbers of good, well-trained soldiers, he would have felt more confident. Fort Reno and the supporting forts and rifle pits bristled with cannons and were girdled by earthen ramparts. Unfortunately, Hardin lacked quality troops to adequately man the defenses.

He would make do with what he had and hoped for the early arrival of the veteran Sixth Corps. Those battle-tested veterans were crammed aboard Union transports at that very hour steaming north up the Potomac River. It was a race, and no one, in those anxious hours, could guess if the winner would be Early's Rebels or the Old Sixth Corps.[32]

Hardin did receive one good piece of news during the conference with Augur. His superior informed him that he had ordered a capable and veteran combat officer, Colonel John M. Warner, to assume command of Hardin First Brigade. The new commander would supplant Colonel John C. Marble, commanding officer of the 151st Ohio National Guard, a 100-day Ohio militia unit. Although Marble proved himself a brave soldier, he simply didn't have Warner's combat experience.[33]

Warner was in Washington that summer recovering from a severe wound suffered during Grant's summer campaign. Augur also told Hardin that his division would be reinforced by a company of the Ninth New York Heavy Artillery, tested veterans who would add backbone to the garrison. Other reinforcements on their way were of questionable quality. The Veteran Reserve Brigade (the old Invalid Corps) was expected to reinforce Hardin in the next few hours. They would soon be joined by a number of District of Columbia Volunteers—not high quality troops but all capable of firing a rifle and filling in those yawning gaps in the defensive network. Many of the trenches around the fort were entirely bare of defenders.[34]

At the conclusion of the Sunday afternoon briefing, General Augur instructed Hardin to meet with Major General McCook, who was currently establishing a reserve camp at Piney Branch Creek, behind Fort Stevens that guarded the Seventh Avenue Road leading into the Capital. The plan was to gather available units at the camp where they could be organized and dispatched to threatened sectors of the Washington defenses as needed.

"I rode around by the position where the supposed Reserve Camp would be," Hardin later recalled. "I was unable to see any troops, but encountered General McCook, accompanied by a few aides and a few orderlies. He was rather disgusted at finding no troops. He said he knew nothing about my First Brigade line. . . . He thought I had best hasten to Fort Reno and act entirely upon my own responsibility."[35] General Hardin didn't arrive at Fort Reno until around midnight, but he found preparations well under way, initiated by his capable subordinate, Colonel Warner. Hardin wrote:

> Leaving the camp on Piney Branch Creek about 11 p.m. (Sunday), I arrived at Fort Reno near Midnight. I found that our cavalry had been driven into the infantry picket line, about a mile and a half in front of the fort on the Rockville Turnpike. Colonel Warner had directed the cavalry to dismount and reinforce the infantry picket, which consisted . . . of about fifty one hundred days men; this reinforced line withstood the Rebel cavalry until daylight.[36]

Hardin's militia infantry and dismounted cavalry skirmished with the enemy's lead elements throughout the night and early morning of July 10 and July 11. He was directing those movements while still organizing and assigning fighting positions to the reinforcement that streamed in throughout the early morning hours. He later wrote: "We had good reason to suppose his {Early's} infantry would be up in ample time to make an attack at early daylight of the 11th {Monday}."[37]

Civilian refugees continued to stream in from the Maryland countryside with their wagons and carts, telling tales of Rebel marauders. "Some of our retreating cavalry had passed through Tennallytown carrying very alarming stories," Hardin recalled of that night of turmoil and apprehension.[38] Others in the Capital that night noted that Union dispatch riders were constantly galloping up and down the streets carrying messages to and from the various military headquarters and civilian departments. Their frantic movements apparently only increased the fear and alarm spreading through the city. Newspaper correspondent Noah Brooks described a city in panic:

> Washington was in a ferment; men were marching to and fro; able-bodied citizens were swept up and put into the District militia; and squads of department clerks were set to drilling in the parks. It was an odd sight to see men who had been thus impressed into the public service. . . . These sons of Mars were all under command of Brigadier General Bacon, a worthy grocer of Washington, who was the militia commander of the District of Columbia.[39]

Washington was totally unprepared for the coming Rebel assault, although some had anticipated this crisis long before. Major General E.A. Hitchcock, a veteran soldier and staff officer, had expressed his concern to President Lincoln that Halleck was indifferent to the gathering threat from Early's Confederates. On July 6, 1864, the increasingly apprehensive Hitchcock had written prophetic words in his diary: "An enterprising general could take the city."[40]

CHAPTER 20

GENERAL HARDIN MAKES A BRAVE SHOW

The early pre-dawn hours on that Monday, July 11 were incredibly busy for the newly promoted Brigadier General Martin D. Hardin. He worked against the clock scrambling to place as many riflemen on the picket lines and in the forts as possible.

Around 1 a.m., Monday morning, Colonel George W. Gile arrived with the first detachments of his Veteran Reserve Brigade; they were quickly posted to various points in front of Fort Kearny, Battery Terrill and Fort DeRussy. "They were instructed to take positions in the rifle-pits to strengthen those already out," Hardin later wrote.[1]

In those early morning hours, Hardin also ordered two artillery batteries stationed to the rear of Fort Sumner to move up and reinforce Forts Simmons, Mansfield and Bayard. Just before daylight, a regiment of District of Columbia Volunteers arrived and were assigned to the rifle pits protecting Fort Bayard.

Hardin was grateful for any help, even the wounded and crippled soldiers of the Veteran Reserve Corps, some of whom, unable to march any distance, arrived at Fort Reno in wagons during the early morning hours. Perhaps Hardin had heard the story making the rounds how a Veteran Reserve Corps officer had responded when asked if his men would fight. His response: "General, they can't run; they have to fight."[2]

General Grant in the lines outside Richmond and Petersburg appeared unconcerned about the Rebel threat to Washington, despite telegraphed requests for aid from President Lincoln and General Halleck. The latter, finally emerging from his lethargy, wrote frankly in one message his doubts about the quality of the troops manning the city's defenses: "What we have here are raw militia, invalids, convalescents from the hospitals, a few dismounted batteries and the dismounted and unorganized cavalrymen. But what can we do with such forces in the field against a column of 20,000 veterans? One half of the men here cannot march at all."[3]

Hardin was doing all he could. Unfortunately, he feared that it was not enough while the rattle of skirmishing ebbed and flowed out on the Rockville Pike. Despite his best efforts, the picket line was not continuous, and miles of rifle pits were empty of defenders. The massive, impressive forts and batteries were "insufficiently garrisoned to repel assault."[4] Their only hope was to continue the dangerous charade and deceive the oncoming Rebels into thinking they faced a strong, aggressive and determined enemy. If their true weakness was revealed, the veteran Rebel soldiers would quickly overwhelm the Union lines and move directly on the Capital itself.

When dawn came Monday, July 11, the firing on the picket line gathered intensity. Brig. General John McCausland's Rebel cavalry were present in force and fighting dismounted. Luckily, Hardin's outnumbered command received a significant reinforcement at almost the same time: the Second Massachsetts Cavalry Regiment commanded by Colonel Charles Russell Lowell.[5]

Lowell was a patrician New Englander and the nephew of famed poet James Russell Lowell. In addition to his three cavalry squadrons, Lowell brought with him a squadron of the Eighth Illinois Cavalry. Armed with breech-loading carbines, these combat-tested soldiers brought much needed firepower to Hardin's polyglot force of Veteran Reserves, convalescents and 100-day militia.

Lowell was a superb soldier and leader of men. In the hours and days ahead, General Hardin came to trust in this educated man of culture, refinement and wealth. He was that rare individual equally at home in running an iron foundry as he was speaking French, Italian and Spanish. At Harvard, Lowell was class valedictorian and socialized among Boston's elite families, the Ralph Waldo Emerson clan among them.[6] Before the war, the family doctor had predicted that his dormant tuberculosis would considerably shorten his life and predicted young Lowell would never see 30. The young man essentially ignored the advice and lived a strenuous life of intense activity, working on the railroad at one point and then supervising the workmen at the foundry.[7]

When he volunteered for cavalry service in 1861, Lowell claimed he could, "ride a horse as far and bring him as fresh as any other man."[8] Lowell was an Abolitionist whose brother had died during the Peninsula Campaign, and he exuded zeal and self-confidence. His enlisted men respected rather than loved Colonel Lowell. Early in the war he shot and killed a mutineer with a single pistol shot, for which he was exonerated. Despite his patrician bloodlines and a Harvard diploma, the young officer was also a killer, a useful trait in the brutal trade of war.

Not long after daybreak on Monday, July 11, Lowell's cavalry moved out on the Rockville Pike, acting upon General Hardin's orders. Around 6:40 a.m., they met up with Major Fry's mounted force just outside Old Tavern.[9] As senior officer, Lowell took command and led the united force toward the oncoming enemy. Fighting ensued almost immediately and would continue throughout the morning:

"He {Lowell} drove the enemy's advance back upon their main force, when he was, in turn, forced back to our picket-line on the Rockville road, where he dismounted his men and held the enemy in check with rapid fire from their breech-loading carbines," General Hardin wrote.[10] The Yankee cavalry put on that "show of force" that McCook and Hardin hoped would discourage any serious attack from the Rebels. On that day, the Yankee guard dog tried to conceal his lack of fangs with a loud and defiant bark.

At some point, early that morning, President Abraham Lincoln and a party of cabinet officers briefly visited the Tennallytown area where the Rebel blow was expected to fall. Unfortunately, the record is silent as to the specifics of what transpired. It seems likely that Lincoln would have met and discussed the situation with the son of his old Illinois friend, General Hardin. But whatever the facts, Lincoln's party was soon driving back into the city toward the Sixth Avenue Wharf where the Sixth Corps was expected to arrive very soon.[11]

General Hardin, if he had spoken with the President that morning, must not have had time for more than a few words. The enemy was advancing and the morning quiet dissolved into the steady pop of rifle fire on the skirmish line. Hardin was surely watching the unfolding events from the eminence of the Fort Reno signal tower, a solid 100-foot tall structure standing atop the Tennallytown heights—the highest elevation in Washington at 429 feet.[12]

From the top deck of the tower, General Hardin and his Signal Officer Captain L.A. Dillingham, 122nd New York Volunteers, enjoyed a panoramic view of the surrounding terrain. Any enemy movements they detected through spyglass or binoculars could be quickly forwarded to General Auger or General McCook by either flag signal or telegraph. In the fighting to come this vantage point played a key role. Early's troops could not make a move without being detected by the Yanks manning the Fort Reno signal tower.[13]

A telegraph line connected Hardin with Augur's XXII Army Corps Headquarters. Manning the key was Henry H. Atwater, who had been transferred from the U.S. Navy Yard on temporary duty by Major Thomas Eckert. Atwater did good service at Fort Reno during the next two days. During the skirmishing, his fellow telegraphist at Fort Stevens invited Atwater—perhaps in jest—to come up and take a pot-shot at the Rebel sharpshooters, but Atwater sensibly declined.[14]

Throughout Monday, General Hardin employed his heavy guns at Fort Reno and other strongpoints in raining shells on concentrations of enemy cavalry. This bombardment was part of the bold aggressive show, which Hardin hoped would conceal his weakness in infantry. During this spirited early morning skirmishing, Hardin ordered his riflemen to "appear first in one part, then in another of the works" to create the illusion of numbers.[15]

Hardin's superior, General McCook, abandoned the pretense of supervising reinforcements from the Piney Creek Reserve as early as 7:30 a.m., Monday. Hearing the rising crescendo of Rebel gunfire, McCook led what troops he had collected to Fort Stevens on the Seventh Avenue approaches. From generals to privates in the rifle pits, everyone expected and feared a full-scale assault.[16]

The skirmishing intensified all the while on Hardin's front, although the focus seemed to increasingly shift to his right flank around Fort DeRussy. Clouds of Rebel cavalry fought dismounted, and pressured the Yankee skirmish line at various points.

At around 9:20 a.m., Rebel artillery opened fire. Hardin telegraphed General Augur at XXII Corp Headquarters: "The enemy has a rifle gun on right of Rockville Road. They fire a shot about every 15 minutes. . . . I am anxious about the River and Aqueduct Roads."[17] All through the morning the skirmishing was brisk and interspersed with Union cannon fire directed from Fort Reno, Fort DeRussy and other Union strongpoints on the western edges of the city.

Very early it appeared that the enemy was drifting toward Hardin's right flank. They were actively probing the defenses. As of yet, Hardin hadn't identified Rebel infantry, but expected their appearance momentarily. General Augur cabled Hardin just before 10 a.m., asking if the Rebels had "broken ground in your front."[18] Hardin responded not long after: "The enemy have a short line formed, but I think are withdrawing. Quite a portion here made a move to the south. I have sent cavalry to watch them."[19]

Throughout the morning, Hardin kept Generals Augur and McCook apprised of the enemy strength and movements based on the observations made from the signal tower at Fort Reno. At 10:35 a.m., Hardin telegraphed Augur: "Signal officer thinks he can see army wagons in the distance where the dust is."[20]

Much of the action on Hardin's front centered on Fort DeRussy, commanded by Colonel John M.C. Marble of the 151st Ohio. On Marble's right was the Rock Creek valley, where Rebel riflemen were infiltrating their way south despite the obstructions placed in their path. They were also drawing fire from Fort Stevens on their left flank. The much-derided 100-day men appeared to be holding their own in this battle of skirmish lines. Colonel Marble reported:

> The infantry forces were immediately placed in the most commanding parts of the rifle pits. Noticing a heavy column moving to the right, we immediately opened on it with a 100-pounder Parrott, with apparently considerable effect. At the same time, the enemy commenced advancing through the fields, a little to the right of our front . . . to reinforce their skirmishers . . . in close proximity to this fort {DeRussy}. A few well-directed shots from our artillery, caused them to rapidly retire . . . leaving one man dead on the field.[21]

Hardin's defensive charade was apparently convincing. By mid-morning, McCausland reported to General Early that the Fort Reno front was strong and heavily defended. This intelligence was a major factor in Early's decision to shift the focus of attack eastward toward Fort Stevens, which guarded the Seventh Avenue approach to the Capital.

At noon Union transport ships steamed up to the Sixth Street Wharf and began disembarking General Horatio Wright's Sixth Corps while civilians ashore cheered. They were also greeted by President Abraham Lincoln who accompanied one of the regiments in his carriage when they began their march to Fort Stevens.

At 12:20 p.m., General McCook commanding that endangered sector informed Augur: "The enemy is advancing on my front with cavalry, artillery and infantry." Colonel C.H. Raymond, Augur's Assistant Adjutant General, responded a little later assuring McCook that a regiment and battery from Hardin's command was on the way, concluding: "If you need more force you can call on General Hardin for it, and in the event of an *urgent necessity* more troops will be sent to you."[22]

By 1:15 p.m., Hardin had sent a message to Augur's corps headquarters confirming the Rebel intentions: "The enemy are seen very plainly moving . . . in direction of {Fort} Stevens. Infantry and wagons or ambulances are plainly seen with a glass from signal station."[23] Colonel James A. Hardie, Inspector General of the XXII Army Corps, was with Hardin that morning at Fort Reno. He later telegraphed Augur: "I think the enemy's line of march clearly indicates that the main attack will be on the right of this post {Fort Reno}. . . . It is, I suggest, time to move the reserves up here toward the threatened portion of the front."[24]

A few minutes later, Colonel J.H. Taylor, Augur's Chief of Staff, responded unequivocally, ordering Hardin: "Send the Regiment to General McCook at once. Comply with any requisition he may make for reinforcements consistent with the safety of your position."[25] It remains unclear which specific regiment Taylor was requesting. Fearing an imminent Rebel assault on the Fort Stevens line, Colonel Taylor followed a few minutes later with another message, urgently ordering Hardin: "Move all your available men at once to the right."[26]

Civilian houses facing the Union works at Fort DeRussy and Fort Stevens soon became havens for Rebel sharpshooters, who, throughout the action, took a deadly toll of the Yank defenders. Early in the day, the Wilson house opposite Colonel Marble's men became a veritable nest of snipers.

"The sharpshooters in the house . . . became so troublesome to our advance line that we found it necessary to shell it," Marble reported.[27]

Artillery at Fort DeRussy under Captain John Norris, Second Provisional Pennsylvania Heavy Artillery, began lobbing 100-pound and 30-pound rifled Parrott shells at the Wilson house and several other structures serving as havens for the enemy sharpshooters. The huge cannon at Forts Reno, Bayard and Sumner fired all day at ranges from 1,700 to 4,200 yards. Union shells exploded all the way out to Silver Springs where, not long before, Early and his commanders had established their headquarters. Some of the Confederates later recalled jokingly how the "Yanks threw nail kegs and flour barrels at us that day."[28]

Although the heavy artillery fireworks show was certainly impressive—Fort DeRussy alone would fire more than 109 rounds over the next two days—the Rebel snipers continued to plague Hardin's men. Hardin responded by ordering a company of Veteran Reserves personally led by Colonel Gile to rout the snipers and fire their nest.

The Veteran Reserve moved out under a covering fire, but as they neared the Wilson house, they suffered a heavy fire from Rebel infantry concealed behind a "breastwork of logs and brush." Colonel Marble noted that when Gile's men retreated, the Rebs "commenced sending in reinforcements across the fields in plain view." Marble's artillerymen "opened on them," Marble wrote, and sent them streaming back to the Wilson house "in considerable confusion."[29]

Hardin's hodge-podge force was doing well, holding its own against Early's hardened troopers. However, these actions had been only a sparring match between skirmish lines. The Union position throughout the morning and early afternoon could still only be described as precarious.

One of the many thousands of civilians who heard the cannon thunder that Monday near Hardin's Fort Reno headquarters was Jane Grey Swisshelm. The newspaper correspondent, Abolitionist, and women's rights advocate wrote: " . . . our dwelling is in the Northern part of the city where the thunder of the cannon at Fort Reno was very plainly heard, and when the poor contraband women, all hanging in rags, with faces and voices full of wretchedness and fear, their babies clasped to their breasts and little ones clinging to their knees came to me to say, 'What do you think Missus? Will the Yankees be able to keep them out?'"[30]

Hardin's troops eventually burned out seven private homes occupied by Rebel skirmishers to the front of Fort Reno. A reporter for *Frank Leslie's Illustrated Newspaper* wrote: "These {sharpshooters} at one time had advanced to within less than 75 yards of the fort under cover afforded by the buildings and the immense undergrowth of bushes over the stumps of the first military clearings. . . . The Rebel sharpshooters appeared to be numerous & kept up a continual fire upon our men."[31]

As a division commander, Hardin could not simply assume that the skirmishing might not turn into a full-scale assault. The issue was certainly in doubt on that broiling hot July day. The Sixth Corps had not yet reached the Fort Stevens area, and would not do so in strength before late afternoon. In General Hardin's eyes, the Rebs had a wonderful opportunity to rush and overwhelm the thin line of defenders. Years later, Hardin wrote of that crisis point during the defense:

> As dilatory as the enemy had been in moving his infantry, he reached the ground between Rock Creek and Seventh Street Pike before there was any adequate force to check him. The enemy's skirmishers drove General McCook's light picket-line back to the rifle-pits on either side of Fort Stevens. The guns of Fort Stevens opened a very rapid fire upon every solid formation of the enemy, but of course could not check a skirmish-line. Having forced our pickets back to the line of entrenchments the enemy's efforts ceased. It was a fatal pause. Those were anxious moments for us.[32]

General McCook took decisive action, ordering the charge of 600 dismounted cavalry under Major G.G. Briggs, 7th Michigan Cavalry, which included the 25th New York Cavalry and contingents from various other units. This assault pushed the Confederates back to a line about 1,100 yards from Fort Stevens, where they remained through the heat of the late afternoon. The Rebels identified the attackers as veteran Union troops, not invalids or raw militia.[33] This probably was a factor in convincing Early that the Union Sixth Corps was already up manning the Union lines.

As the enemy's intentions became increasingly clear, General Augur ordered Hardin to forward units under his command to reinforce the line at Fort Stevens where the Rebels were concentrating. An attack was expected momentarily; and every man was needed to meet the anticipated enemy thrust.

Meanwhile along Hardin's front skirmishing continued all along the Union line the rest of the afternoon, but there were few signs of impending assault. Hardin informed General Augur at 3 p.m.: "I have ordered all the cavalry back on the infantry picket-line. I do not think the enemy have any infantry in front of Reno left of the Rockville Road, except a small force supporting the guns we have seen."[34]

Even so Hardin remained concerned about his weak defensive line. Reinforcing McCook's line on the right had left Hardin's front more vulnerable to a strong enemy push. His fears prompted a reassuring response from Lt. Colonel J.H. Taylor, Adjutant General, XXII Army Corps, at 4:35 p.m.: "Russell's division, Sixth Army Corps, will proceed to Reno as soon as it arrives. In the meantime, if troops are needed call upon General McCook, he has been reinforced from Sixth Corps."[35]

Five hours elapsed and no Sixth Corps. Once again Hardin grew apprehensive. His force, inadequate from the very first hour of the Rebel appearance before Washington, had been steadily diminished throughout the day to reinforce Fort Stevens. The promised reinforcements by troops from the Sixth Corps never materialized despite earlier assurances to the contrary. All the focus was on Fort Stevens.

We can't read Hardin's mind at the distance of more than a century, but we can make certain reasonable assumptions. It seems likely that Hardin worried the Rebels had deliberately weakened his front by demonstrating in front of Fort Stevens. That would set the stage to move units back to the Fort Reno front under cover of night and suddenly descend on Hardin's line in full force, either during the night or at break of day.

Although night attacks were rare in the Civil War, they were not unprecedented. Earlier that year, serving as a brigade commander with Crawford's Division at the Rappahannock Station fight, Hardin had witnessed a Union night attack that had quickly overrun a Confederate strongpoint on the north side of the river. That strongpoint, in fact, had been manned by part of Jubal Early's division.[36] Perhaps Hardin thought now that Early might be contemplating a similar night attack upon Fort Reno.

Hardin did what he could to prepare. He doubled the First Brigade picket line, but still fretted about the promised reinforcements. This prompted him to send another telegraph message to XXII Corps at about 9 p.m.: "None of the Sixth Corps have arrived. All quiet on our front. Camp fires are visible in direction of Seventh Street."[37] Hardin's suspicions that the enemy might still assault his front were expressed in a telegram sent to XXII Army Corps at 10:55 p.m., and later relayed to McCook, stating: "The chief officer of pickets says the enemy are apparently making every preparation for a grand assault, tearing down fences, bands playing. Cavalry is moving to our left. Cannot a part of the Sixth Corps be hurried up at once?"[38]

At 11:45 p.m. on Monday night, Hardin received a telegram from Augur, asking Hardin to keep him advised. Nothing was said about reinforcements. Apparently Augur didn't share Hardin's concern about an attack on that front. His attention was rightly focused on the Seventh Street Avenue approaches and Fort Stevens, in particular.

At midnight, Hardin sent another telegraph to Augur that documented the intensity of the skirmishing that had occurred along his line throughout the day: "Send for Second Massachusetts Cavalry, 16,000 rounds of ammunition for Sharps carbine and 16,000 rounds for Burnside carbine and forage for 450 horses, Major Fry's command. Send to Fort Reno."[39]

Major Henry Alvord of the Second Massachusetts Cavalry was stationed on the weak Union skirmish line from Fort Stevens to Fort Reno. He shared Hardin's fears of a determined Rebel assault and its possible consequences, writing: " . . . knowing that no veteran reinforcements of consequence had arrived, and that there was little but raw militia and a demoralized population in our rear, I felt then . . . that for the greater part of two days the City of Washington was absolutely at the mercy of the Confederates."[40]

Throughout the night and early morning General Hardin repeatedly asked for a contingent of the arriving Sixth Corps troops. At 6:15 a.m., Tuesday morning, XXII Corps Headquarters telegraphed the final word on the subject: "Fort Stevens is the real point of the attack. The enemy's movement in front of Reno being but a feint."[41]

Hardin relented. Actually, since the early morning hours he had been planning an aggressive move against McCausland's Confederate cavalry. The man who would carry that out was Colonel Lowell of the 2nd Massachusetts Cavalry. The Brahmin blueblood was an exemplary leader of courage and good judgment who had quickly won General Hardin's confidence.

Lowell and his mounted troopers had been very effective in fending off McCausland throughout the skirmishing on that first day. Hardin was also pleased with Colonel Lowell's accurate and timely intelligence reports on enemy movements and strength. His troops were tough and packed a powerful punch for cavalry. They had fought dismounted making good use of their rapid-fire breech-loading carbines. In effect, the troopers combined the mobility of cavalry with the staying power of infantry.

In the early hours of Tuesday, July 12, Colonel Lowell approached Hardin with a daring plan, the very audacity of which might multiply the small forces employed. The cavalry leader outlined his thoughts about launching a two-pronged, mounted pre-dawn assault. General Hardin approved the "bold operation" at around 2:30 a.m. and promptly set about preparing its execution.[42]

Lowell's plan was a classic pincer movement. Just before dawn he would lead two cavalry squadrons up the River Road and conceal his force in a wooded area on the enemy's right flank. Major Casper Crowinshield, his second-in-command, would lead two squadrons in a frontal assault. The major would attack when he heard gunshots signaling that Lowell's flanking movement was underway.[43]

Hardin remained alert through those early pre-dawn hours, though his fears of a Rebel attack never materialized. At 5:30 a.m. on Tuesday Hardin telegraphed General Augur at XXII Corps: "Rebel band playing, otherwise quiet." A half hour later, Hardin followed with an update: "Commanding officer of pickets on right of 1st Brigade reports the enemy is moving left{towards Fort Stevens}."[44]

Daylight brought the sound of heavy firing when Lowell's flanking force slammed into the Rebel position. A few minutes later, Crowinshield's men came shooting and hollering down the Rockville Pike, driving the enemy before them. Hardin's First Brigade Commander Colonel Warren reported that the enemy fell back in disarray for a mile-and-half, "throwing away arms, equipments, and retiring in great confusion."[45]

This success marked the beginning of the second day on Hardin's front. After that, the activity there diminished appreciably. There was some light skirmishing punctuated by an occasional shell from Hardin's heavy artillery. But, by now, he must have realized that the real point of the enemy attack had become Fort Stevens.

Hardin's men remained diligent through the day, but the skirmishing was nowhere near as intense as before. At 7:30 a.m. Hardin reported to XXII Corps: "The piece of artillery is still in position on Rockville Pike but has not fired today."[46]

Fort Reno and Fort DeRussy kept up their bombardment with 100 pounder and 30 pounder Parrott rifles, although the effectiveness of the shelling was problematic. Concerned about the civilians still remaining in the Tennallytown area near Fort Reno, Hardin telegraphed General Augur: "I think the citizens living within range of the guns of the forts should be notified to go into town with such articles as they can take."[47]

At one point that day, General Augur ordered Hardin to reinforce Fort Foote located on the city's southern frontier. This came about when Augur received intelligence that the Confedeates intended a bold raid on the Point Lookout prison camp on Chesapeake Bay utilizing Early's cavalry coordinating with a Naval landing force. The intent was to free and arm its 15,000 Rebel captives to assist in the attack on Washington. This would have doubled Early's force.[48]

The intelligence was indeed accurate. Confederate John Taylor Wood's small flotilla with the landing party aboard had departed its anchorage at Wilmington, North Carolina when they were called back.[49] The mission had been cancelled by President Jeffererson Davis, who had grown uneasy with the daring plan. Early was quickly informed of Jefferson's decision and, in turn, cancelled the proposed cavalry strike on Point Lookout.[50]

Throughout July 12, General Hardin kept a keen eye on enemy movements. He sent another message to Augur at 3 p.m., noting: "The enemy {doesn't} have any infantry except small force supporting guns." However, by 4:20 p.m., Hardin was concerned about Rebel activity on his extreme right flank: "The enemy have thrown up earthwork 3,500 yards, a little to the right and in front of Fort DeRussy, apparently for battery and rifle pits . . ."[51]

The major fight that day was in front of Fort Stevens where elements of General Wright's Sixth Corps pushed back the Confederate lines in an intense clash around dusk that claimed about 300 Union casualties. Hardin supported the attack with fire from the Fort DeRussy batteries. The Rebels were stubborn and only gradually fell back before the Union attack, which was witnessed by President Lincoln among others. This fight was to be the culminating event of Early's Raid.

Hardin was largely a bystander during the Tuesday fight at Fort Stevens. He was certainly not present for the event for which the raid is most remembered: President Lincoln's bold exposure to enemy fire while standing atop the walls of Fort Stevens. Like most of the city, and later the country, he later learned of Lincoln's deliberate exposure to enemy fire—a strong message to the Union troops that even the Chief Executive was willing to share their dangers. No wonder that the great majority of the army, including the often wounded General Hardin, loved this man and would vote overwhelmingly for his re-election to a second term only four months after the Raid.

General Jubal A. Early's Army of the Valley pulled out later that night. General Hardin received a message in the early evening from Major Ltc. Crowinshield of the 2nd Massachusetts Cavalry informing the commander: "There are no rebels in my front now. Shall I stay where I am, or shall I go on? My men have had hard work and are rather tired. I can go on, however, if ordered."[52]

Even so Hardin and his exhausted command spent the pre-dawn hours on Wednesday in the rifle pits with loaded weapons waiting for dawn and a possible resumption of the Rebel attack. Morning light told the tale. The Confederates were gone, and the Capital was saved.

CHAPTER 21

GARRISON SOLDIER IN WARTIME WASHINGTON

After the lapse of 150 years, historians still speculate whether or not Confederate General Jubal Early missed a golden opportunity by failing to attack the Washington defenses on the morning of July 11, or even later that day. In General Hardin's opinion there was no doubt. He believed Washington could easily have been taken at any time (a 36-hour window in Hardin's view) before Sixth Corps veterans arrived at Fort Stevens in the late afternoon of Monday, July 11. Thirty years after the battle Hardin presented a paper on the subject at a meeting of the Military Order of the Loyal Legion in Chicago, stating unequivocally: "I thank the God of Battles that He was not on this occasion 'on the side of the heaviest battalions,' and that a 'Stonewall Jackson' was not in command of the splendid Army that faced us."[1]

"The formidable appearance of this large fort {Fort Reno}, which was situated on a commanding eminence, dominating the country for miles in its front, had much to do with Early's failure to assault this fortified position," Hardin wrote on that occasion. In that statement we can understand Hardin being biased, as what he failed to mention was that Fort Reno had been originally named Fort Pennsylvania, and had been constructed at the beginning of the war by Hardin's own 12th Volunteer Infantry of the Pennsylvania Reserves. Hardin continued, writing as usual in the third person:

The writer . . . has no doubt that General Early's command could easily have carried these fortifications had it attacked before the arrival of the Sixth Corps, on account of the lack of defenders, the

Union line being held by a small force of hundred-day men, veteran reserves and convalescents, which force was posted on the picket line about a mile in front of the forts, there not being sufficient numbers to hold both the forts and picket line. A small detail to fire the hundred-pounder Parrott rifle, located in an angle of the fort, and some citizens, constituted the only garrison of this formidable looking fortification for nearly two days, whilst Early's veterans maneuvered in front of it.[2]

Confederate General John "Tiger" McCausland, who commanded the cavalry on Hardin's front, was also adamant that Early's army should have stormed the Washington forts as soon as they arrived. "I rode ahead of the infantry and arrived in sight of Fort Stevens on the road a short time after Noon, when I discovered that the works were but feebly manned." Supporting that view was General John Brown Gordon, who commanded an infantry division under Early, who claimed: "I myself rode to a point on those breastworks at which there was no force whatsoever."[3]

Union veteran turned author Frank Wilkerson vividly recalled Washington on Sunday July 10 when many of the inhabitants became fearful at the imminent arrival of Early's invaders. Wilkerson remembered widespread public drunkenness, poor discipline among the defending troops, and government clerks hastily packing boxes full of books, records and money preparatory to flight. In Wilkerson's view, Early's tested veterans "could break our line whenever he saw fit to strike it. I knew he would capture Washington in two hours."[4]

These views can be questioned. But what if Early's forces had stormed the forts and captured Washington in July of 1864? In such a scenario they would have either captured President Lincoln or forced him to flee ignominiously from the White House. They also might have burned the city, looted its records and absconded with millions in Greenbacks from the Treasury.

The Confederate coup would have come at a propitious time: The North was sick of war in the summer of 1864, the Presidential election loomed only four months in the future, and Grant's bloody campaign had yet to achieve victory over Lee's defiant army. The author believes the psychological and political fallout triggered by Early's capture of Washington might well have driven Northern morale to a tipping point, similar to the 1968 Tet Offensive, which dramatically changed American public opinion toward Vietnam. It's possible that, at the very least, Rebel seizure of the Capital, if only for a day, would have cost Lincoln the coming election and resulted in the negotiated peace advocated by the Democratic candidate, former General George B. McClellan.

From the Confederate point of view, the same sweltering, rainless summer suffered by the residents of Washington also contributed to saving the city. Early's men had been on the move since leaving the Cold Harbor lines on June 12, first to Lynchburg, then through the Shenendoah Valley, and in forced marches across Maryland since crossing the Potomac on July 5— a total of 300 miles. By the time the force reached Washington the men were exhausted, many of them having dropped out from heat stroke. The Rebel cavalry reached the forts first because the infantry column was strung out for miles on dust clogged roads behind them.

Dr. Franklin Cooling, the pre-eminent modern authority on Early's Washington raid, makes a sound case that the issue was actually decided at the Battle of Monocacy River on July 9, when Lew Wallace held up Early's force for a critical day. Although Wallace was beaten, the Confederates suffered nearly 700 casualties in the fight, and the battle further contributed to their exhaustion. When Early himself reached the Washington defenses on July 11 he saw that they were thinly manned and resolved to attack the next day once his army had closed up and was given a few hours' rest. By then, however, in the very nick of time, the Union Sixth Corps was seen to have arrived, followed by the Nineteenth Corps. With other Federal troops threatening to block the passes and fords behind him, Early felt he had no choice but to return to Virginia while he still could, at least having given Washington "a big scare."[5]

Certainly the July 11–12, 1864 battle for Washington was a small affair as regards forces engaged and casualties suffered. The Union forces suffered around 500 casualties, the great portion of which were incurred by the Sixth Corps troops during the July 12 fighting around Fort Stevens. Confederate losses were about 375, with at least half of those, mainly stragglers, captured. Hardin's Division incurred around 75 casualties. But this does not indicate the importance of this fighting, which could have had disastrous implications for the Union war effort. Historians have for many years called Picket's Charge at Gettysburg the high tide of the Confederacy, but a strong argument can be made that Early's near capture of Washington in 1864 was, in fact, the last authentic opportunity for the Confederacy to win independence.[6]

Although General Hardin ultimately played only a supporting role in the July 1864 drama, he could be proud of his performance. General Alexander McCook, his commanding officer, described Hardin as, "a gallant officer who never did himself more credit than on this occasion."[7] In those early hours of July 10–11, the new brigadier general had acted with coolness and dispatch preparing to receive the main assault of the oncoming Confederate army.

There is no more dramatic illustration of Hardin's merit as a man and soldier than the image of this many-times wounded, one-armed brigadier general resolutely awaiting Early's attack with a hodge-podge force of invalids, convalescents, raw militia, a handful of civilian volunteers, and artillerymen-turned-infantry. Hardin was representative of those men in blue who fought for the Union: steadfast, loyal and indomitable.

General Hardin was proud of his role. But most interestingly, he chose to share his experiences in a July 16, 1864 letter to his good friend Dolly Smith back in Saratoga Springs. The modern reader can't help being surprised at Hardin's decision to confide in a letter to a former black slave, who we assume must have been relieved for very personal reasons that Lincoln's capital had escaped Rebel capture. Hardin's letter is not patronizing, only a straightforward account written for a good friend, who in fact had been like an older sister to him since infancy:

> I had but little time to write, my health is tolerably good & I am enjoying myself about as well as one can in this city in summer, very warm and very dusty," General Hardin wrote the woman who had been like an older sister to him since infancy. I was put in command of the defenses north of the Potomac River just before the rebels came toward the city. The people were very badly scared. The Cavalry came to gun shot range of the forts in one place and some infantry in sight, but they made no attack on the city. Some of the 100 day troops fired a considerable amount at the few men they did see. Their main body of inf'y stopped some distance away,

and all retreated as soon as the old troops moved out as skirmishers. All is quiet here again. Five or six generals were sent to take
parts of my comd. While the enemy was in sight, leaving me, however, to commd. the front where the rebels showed their Artillery.
. . . Yours truly, MD Hardin[8]

There was, however, a prominent and influential man in Lincoln's government who wasn't impressed by the young brigadier general's performance during the late crisis.

Charles Anderson Dana (1819–1897), Assistant Secretary of War to the
powerful Edwin Stanton, was a well-connected former newspaperman who
had been one of Horace Greely's editors on the *New York Tribune*. During
the last half of the Civil War, he acted as Stanton's eyes in the field, sending
the Secretary of War coded telegraph reports containing frank, often critical
observations on the battlefield performance of general officers. Dana had
witnessed Early's raid, and during the July 11 skirmishing he sent a caustic
coded telegraph message to Secretary of War Stanton:

Gen. Augur commands the defenses of Washington with McCook
and a lot of Brigadier Generals. . . . But there is no head to the
whole and it seems indispensable that you should at once appoint
one. . . . General McCook is in command of Fort Stevens. . . . He
told me that the mass of the enemy's infantry was withdrawn from
his front. . . . A few rebel skirmishers still remained, McCook told
me, in a house about 1,200 yards distant and another body of them
in a wood about three thousand yard distant—He was firing thirty
pound Parrotts at the house—Br. Gen Hardin, who if possible is a
bigger fool than McCook notwithstanding his inferior rank, was
also firing thirty pound Parrotts from Fort Reno at the same sharpshooters—I think Hardin had a hundred pounder which he discharged occasionally. I was glad to notice that the fifteen inch
mortars had not yet been brought into use. . . . General Hardin
was also positive that the rebels had constructed a work thirty five
hundred yards distant to his front but I think that it exists nowhere
but in his imagination. . . . Along this part of the lines there was
no general commander—no real knowledge of what was in the

front—nothing but wild imagination and stupidity—From what I can hear the same system reigns throughout the whole length of the lines—I do not exaggerate in the least when I say that such a limitable want of intelligence, energy and purpose was never before seen in any command. . . . Halleck seems to be about as well informed as Augur and I judge that he contributes quite as much as the latter to the prevailing confusion & inefficiency.[9]

Stanton often shared the content of these secret Dana telegrams with President Lincoln. If he did in this case, we can only wonder what Lincoln's reaction was to Dana's disparagement of General Hardin. Then again, Lincoln was a man of his own mind and often took extreme criticisms of himself and others with a generous dose of salt. Certainly there is no evidence that he ever lost faith in Hardin's judgment as a commander and, in fact, in the last eight months of his life he met personally with the young general on several occasions.

The reader should also keep in mind that, although Dana was generally thought to be an astute observer and a sound judge of men, he was no military expert. He apparently ignored Hardin's need to put on a show of force to discourage Early's troops. Firing heavy cannon at distant formations of cavalry or clusters of snipers may sound like overkill; however, in this case, the cannonading, whatever its effectiveness, gave the desired impression that the Yankee garrison was strong, alert and aggressive. This was, of course, a crucial part of the charade.

Dana's other major criticism of Hardin implied that he was overly concerned about an enemy night attack on his sector, a "Nervous Nelly." Hardin's hunch that the Rebels were going to strike his lines proved incorrect, but it seems unfair to take a commander to task for being overly vigilant against a threat, no matter how unlikely.

We must concede at the same time, that Dana's call for a single head to direct the defenses of Washington and the surrounding area was valid. Right after Early's Raid, that confusing tangle of command was simplified to avoid future fiascos. Hardin, in his capacity as commander of Washington's northern defenses, still reported to General Augur. But the responsibility for the security of Washington now came under the overall command of Major General Phil Sheridan, who headed the newly created Middle Military Division created on August 7, 1864. From now on the capable "Little Phil" would be that one head to the whole demanded by Dana.[10]

Washington was still nervous in the weeks immediately following Early's Raid. That unease sparked a near panic that began during the last few days of July. The streets, hotels and saloons of Washington buzzed with the news that Colonel John Mosby, the Confederate "Gray Ghost," had recently crossed the Potomac with a large force, intending to link up with General James Longstreet's infantry corps and capture Washington.[11]

This new threat, although totally without foundation, sparked a repeat of the panic that had preceded the previous raid. Washington's streets filled with anxious crowds who exchanged the latest rumors and fed each other's fears with various scenarios of doom. The city's population of freed slaves were especially concerned, believing that a Rebel occupation would surely result in their re-enslavement.

General Hardin was among those in command who was alarmed by the wild rumors. After all, who could doubt that the legendary Confederate partisan Mosby was capable of nearly any deed, no matter how bold or risky. Therefore Hardin put his pickets on the alert and ordered a regiment of infantry to "move at once" to Fort Reno, and prepare to repel the expected arrival of a strong column of Rebel infantry.[12] Not long afterwards, General Halleck ordered all available troops to the threatened sector.

Hardin's men and their reinforcements formed a strong battle line that morning of August 1, 1864, awaiting the rrival of Mosby and Longstreet. They waited in the dust and heat for hours while mounted riders scoured the neighboring countryside for the unseen enemy. Gradually it became clear that the Yanks were bracing for the attack of a phantom army. Rumor and the power of Mosby's name had created another near panic in Washington. Hardin ordered his men back to their quarters. No doubt the enlisted men grumbled to each other about this latest waste of time.[13]

Washington gradually lapsed into its old routine. Now General Hardin's daily responsibilities were that of a rear-echelon garrison commander. His days were filled with troop inspections, military correspondence and frequent visits to the string of forts within his command to insure that fields of fire were kept free from brush.

Commanding a garrison of bored soldiers brought with it other concerns besides the unlikely threat of Rebel attack. Hardin's soldiers were prey to Washington's small army of pimps, whores, thugs, saloonkeepers and con-men. War correspondent Francis B. Wilkie regarded the over-crowded wartime capitol as" . . . the most pestiferous hole since the days of Sodom and Gomorrah."[14] City police records of that time back up his contention, noting the existence of 450 houses of prostitution within the city limits, bearing such evocative names as The Ironclad, Wolf's Den, The Haystack and Fort Sumter.

Due to his pervious service with the provost marshal, Hardin was well equipped to confront the temptations facing his garrison soldiers. He placed armed guards at brothels and gambling dens, declared the worst of them off-limits, and sent patrols though the streets to insure that a lone soldier returning from a night of revelry wasn't beaten and robbed by thugs. The division commander also tried to keep soldiers busy with incessant drills, inspections and guard duty. In the final analysis, however, General Hardin was limited as to what he could do to protect his men. Even a brigadier general's order could not alter human nature.

But General Hardin had other more important personal business to attend to in the fall of 1864 than hold inspections and train bored garrison troopers.

In November the young general felt comfortable enough in his new posting to request a leave, which was quickly granted. He traveled to Pine Grove in Saratoga Springs with the intent of marrying 17-year-old Estelle Graham, daughter of Major James Graham, and descended from an old and prominent Kentucky pioneer family. Young Hardin probably first made Estelle's acquaintance in his childhood when visiting Kentucky with his mother.

By this point, General Hardin had already converted to Roman Ca-tholicism, and Father Clarence Walworth, his stepbrother, conducted the religious service at St. Peter's Catholic Church in Saratoga Springs on November 15, 1864. Very soon after the ceremony, Hardin wrote his sister, Ellen, at the Bird's Nest in Louisville, notifying her that he and his new bride would soon be visiting.

This news stunned his older sister. Unknown to Martin, she was then hiding and nursing their wounded Confederate brother, Lemuel. During a skirmish with Union troops at Crockett's Grove, Virginia earlier that year, a Yankee bullet had smashed Lemuel's left leg. Since then, the crippled youngest brother had been living with Ellen at her home in Louisville, in Union occupied territory.[15]

Ellen Hardin Walworth faced a terrible dilemma. If Martin arrived to discover Lemuel living in the home, he would be duty bound to turn his Confederate brother over to the local Union authorities. That was unthinkable. She ultimately conceived a plan that, if successful, would preserve the freedom of Lemuel and simultaneously protect the honor of his brother, Union General Martin D. Hardin.

Realizing that Lemuel would never again be fit for active duty with the Confederate Army, she decided to spirit him out of the United States. Luckily, Lemuel's still boyish good looks allowed his older sister to dress him convincingly as a woman and put him aboard a train headed north into neutral Canada. There, he continued his convalescence among a group of Confederate expatriates living in Montreal.[16]

When Martin Hardin arrived at the Bird's Nest, his Confederate brother was gone. It seems likely that Ellen kept a discreet silence on Lemuel's whereabouts, at least for the time. We only know that Martin and Ellen enjoyed their reunion. The family bonds were undoubtedly strained during the war years, but never broke completely.

In the end, love triumphed over politics. Former slave Dolly Smith, as much a part of the family as anyone, proved this point when Confederate soldier Lemuel sent her a photo of him on crutches in Montreal. She wrote on the photograph: "My baby."[17]

Young Lemuel may have seen enough of war by the time he arrived in Canada and probably expressed to his mother a desire to return home and resume a normal life. Sarah Hardin Walworth once again turned to her old friend, President Abraham Lincoln, seeking a pardon for her youngest boy in a heartfelt letter posted December 15, 1864.[18]

The letter begins with a congratulatory note on the President's recent re-election to a second term, describing the President and Mary Todd as the best "Team" to guide the "destiny of a great nation." She then admits the purpose of her letter is to secure a pardon for her crippled son who had fought with Confederate John Hunt Morgan's Kentucky raiders, the same unit that had invaded southern Indiana and Ohio the year before. She wrote to Lincoln:

You have never refused me anything I have asked. I hope I have not been unreasonable or imposed on your naturally benevolent disposition. I have a young son, Lemuel S. Hardin, who has been a short time in the Southern army, has been severely wounded—he has made his way through the lines—and is now in Canada. He is crippled for life and is anxious to return to his home and family.

He has been a resident for the last three years in Louisville, Ky. . . . A few months since I was startled with the intelligence that he had gone off to join the command of "John Morgan" whose name has {illegible} magic sound for the youth of Kentucky. . . . Their imagination is laid low—the successful Scout, the hero of fair maiden and young men is no more. He has no longer power to entice . . . the flower of Kentucky's youth—his unfortunate followers are scattered and in broken bands suffering the penalty of their folly in abandoning home, friends, mother and sisters, sacrificing to a mistaken idea all their bright prospects . . .

I hoped that after your re-election—if matters {are} more favorable—an amnesty would be proclaimed for all such to return to {illegible} allegiance. If you think favorably of my petition for my son to return to his country and to his home and mother—'to be a good boy in the future'—you can make the conditions. I can see no good reason why he should not be allowed to return home (after he) has 'sown his wild oats' or has seen the Elephant . . .

In closing, Sara Walworth brings up the memory of her late husband, John J. Hardin, Lincoln's friend of youth and the man who had died in Mexico during the war while Lincoln went to the U.S. Congress. She played this trump card in the letter's final paragraph:

Mr. President—I claim your indulgence in favor of my petition—not on the merits of the case, but as an act of clemency to a wayward youth. My {Lemuel} is endowed with many of the good qualities of the noble man from which he came, both of head and heart.

Yours respectfully, S. E. Walworth[19]

Her oldest son, General Hardin, was now living with his new bride in the Capital, where they began what became a close and loving relationship. But even as a newlywed, Hardin must have been troubled at times like so many combat veterans. The war was still going on and was a constant reminder of what Hardin had endured for more than three years. He was a young man in transition, learning to cope each day with the memory of fallen friends.

Hardin was one of the survivors whose memory was populated with ghosts, the faces of young friends and acquaintances killed and maimed on a dozen battlefields. At times, Hardin must have wondered why he lived and they died. Those shadows were once flesh-and-blood human beings, friends with whom he had shared a pipe by the campfire, marched beside on the long road South, or fought with side-by-side. Hardin's list of lost comrades is a grim yardstick that measures, only in part, the young man's wartime ordeal.

During that fall of 1864, Hardin lost his West Point classmate, Confederate General Stephen Dodson Ramseur, who died of wounds at the battle of Cedar Creek in the Shenandoah Campaign. That same battle claimed Union cavalry leader Colonel Charles Russell Lowell, the man who had served Hardin so well during Early's raid on Washington; he, too, died of multiple wounds the next day following that bloody encounter.[20]

How many others were gone? A random artillery shell at Fredericksburg had killed Hardin's friend cavalry Brigadier General George D. Bayard. That terrific and senseless battle also saw the death of Hardin's former brigade commander, Brigadier General Conrad Feger Jackson, who fell leading a column of infantry against the Rebel works.[21]

A Rebel sharpshooter killed Hardin's idol, Major General John F. Reynolds, on the first day of Gettysburg. Enemy snipers also claimed Hardin's West Point friend, Captain Charles Hazlett, and Brig. General Stephen Hinsdale Weed, who fell at Little Round Top on the second day of that epic struggle. At Second Manassas, another friend, artillery Captain Mark Kerns, was mortally wounded only yards away from Hardin when the Chinn Ridge position was overrun. Union General Charles G. Harker, a class ahead of Hardin at West Point, died in action at the battle of Kennesaw Mountain in Georgia in another forlorn charge in 1864.[22] Lieutenant George Dare, who climbed Big Round Top with Hardin and his men, fell in action at the Wilderness.

In addition, four out of 22 graduates of Hardin's West Point Class of 1859 died in the Civil War: First Lieutenant Orlando G. Wagner died at Yorktown, April 1862; Captain Charles Collins, at Todd's Tavern, May 1864; Captain Roderick Stone died at Valverde, New Mexico, 1862; and Confederate Colonel Robert F. Beckham was killed at Columbia, Tenn. in December 1864.[23] (Five of Hardin's fellow graduates served with the Confederacy, most notably cavalryman General Joseph Wheeler, who achieved the rank of major general.)

All these friends were gone, swept away in the war that so many in 1861 had glibly predicted would be over in a few months.

Many ghosts lived on in Hardin's memory. Like thousands of other young soldiers, Hardin was an old man at 27, carrying into the future not only his physical scars, but mental pictures of what he had seen and endured during some of the war's most bitter fighting. War leaves its mark on a soldier; not only wounds to the body but invisible wounds to the soul. General Martin D. Hardin was one of those walking wounded, North and South.

In the spiritual sense, Hardin found refuge in his deep life-long commitment to the Roman Catholic Church, with its message of hope and redemption. Hardin would have great need of that faith upon returning to Washington in late 1864 where he would soon witness first-hand the cruel events of the war's final months; and strengthen his friendship with the sad, gaunt man in the White House, the faithful friend of his slain father who had become the nation's savior, President Abraham Lincoln.

CHAPTER 22

GOOD FRIDAY AT
FORD'S THEATER

Washington was a vibrant and exciting city in January of 1865 when General and Mrs. Hardin made their first home there. There was a certain feverish gaiety in the wartime Capital that persisted despite the daily reminders of the ongoing war.

General and Mrs. Hardin would grow accustomed to seeing thousands of wounded men from Grant's army who entered the city in long caravans of horse-drawn ambulances jolting their way to the Capital's more than forty crowded hospitals. Another spectacle was the shambling scarecrow Rebel prisoners herded down the avenues under the guard of Union rifle-men.[1]

On the crowded streets of the nation's Capital one might encounter a famous actress, an esteemed general officer, an arrogant Rebel officer on parole parading in full uniform, a senator, a spy, or a frowzy prostitute, a pimp, deserters from both armies, pick-pockets and strong-armed robbers. They were all part of Washington's passing parade in the final months of the Civil War.[2]

No matter. Many, if not most of Washington's civilians, in this fourth year of the war, had come to accept such scenes as everyday occurrence. This was the Capitol of the Union, and its denizens were busy with the often lucrative tasks of business, politics and war. Here at the seat of power decisions were being made with far-reaching impact and consequence, making some rich and sending others to their deaths in the trenches at Petersburg. History was being made and General and Mrs. Hardin were front-row spectators.

Brigadier General Hardin enjoyed the status and privilege which came with general rank, but one-star generals were plentiful in the streets of Washington. However, the Hardin family benefited from his mother's friendship with President Lincoln, First Lady Mary Lincoln, Secretary of State Seward, Senator Orville Browning and other powerful men. Mrs. Chancellor Walworth's son and his new bride had the credentials to open the doors of the city's most exclusive society.

Washington offered the privileged elite like General and Mrs. Hardin a wide variety of entertainment: fine dining establishments, grand balls, concerts, museums and professional theater presented by some of the most accomplished actors in America who performed at Grover's Theater and Ford's Theater. President Lincoln and the First Lady were enthusiastic play-goers and frequently attended performances featuring such famed actors as Edwin Booth and his younger brother, John Wilkes Booth.

There are no surviving letters describing General and Mrs. Hardin's days in Washington. However, we do have several clues contained in the diary of Hardin family friend Orville Hickman Browning.

This influential political powerbroker was one of Lincoln's closest Illinois friends and had also been a friend of General Hardin's parents, John and Sarah. The 58-year-old politician had been a key organizer of the Republican Party and had helped secure Lincoln's nomination in 1860. Browning came to Washington to fill out the term of Illinois Senator Stephen Douglas, who died of typhoid fever in 1861. He stayed to play the role of a lobbyist who had the ear of President Lincoln, who was pleased to have one of his oldest friends nearby. Browning had Lincoln's implicit trust. He knew his old Illinois friend would always tell him his true opinion, never betray him, or spill inside information to the press or political enemies.[3]

Browning often spent leisure time with Lincoln when they read their favorite poems to one another. He also attended church with them and supported the Lincoln family during the tragic illness and death of their son, Willie. Young General Hardin was also a friend of the influential insider. Browning noted in his diary entry for Monday, January 2, 1865: "Making calls all day in company with Senator Doolittle and Genl. M.D. Hardin."[4]

This cryptic entry provides us with a narrow window into Hardin's Washington tenure. His connection to Browning put him in powerful company. Certainly Wisconsin Senator James Rood Doolittle of Wisconsin was among the city's movers and shakers, and enjoyed easy access to his friend Lincoln.[5] On occasion, Doolittle even breakfasted with the President when they would discuss the issues of the day.

We don't know why General Hardin was asked to accompany Browning and Senator Doolittle that day; however, this diary entry does strongly suggest that Hardin was accepted within the inner circle around Lincoln and his administration, and supports his references to visiting the President in the White House during 1864 and 1865.

It would be fascinating to know what the General thought of Senator Doolittle, who was a true believer and an eloquent enemy of slavery. A powerful speaker, Doolittle once boldly announced: "Slavery is dying all around us. . . . The sword which it would have driven into the vitals of the Republic is parried and thrust back into its own. And, it will die without any sympathy of mine. Slavery, with all its abominations, may die and go into everlasting perdition."[6]

Browning's diary entry for March 28, 1865 is equally intriguing, but for a different reason: "At Departments in the morning. Emma started at 7 p.m. with genl (sic) & Mrs. Haskin and Gen & Miss Hardin, and other friends, to Point Lookout—Went on the Steamer Metamora."[7]

Point Lookout, Maryland was a Confederate prisoner-of-war camp containing around 11,000 captured Rebel soldiers who suffered great privation in captivity. The Rebel prisoners were thinly clad, ragged and dirty. They often endured insult and humiliation from their guards, most of whom were colored soldiers. Many lacked blankets and shoes; disease of every kind was prevalent and often fatal. Fresh water quality was poor and the supply inadequate. Camp Surgeon James H. Thompson officially protested that the overcrowding of the facility was inhumane.[8]

General Hardin and General Joseph Abel Haskin, Chief of Artillery for the Washington forts, were an interesting pair, both having lost their left arms in battle. During the Mexican War, Haskin, West Point Class of 1839, had his left arm amputated after being wounded in the storming of Chapultepec Castle. During Early's Raid, Haskin commanded Hardin's second brigade. Presumably these two combat veterans were inured to the sight of suffering, but that would certainly not have applied to Mrs. Hardin or Mr. and Mrs. Browning.

Most people in the modern era are probably appalled at the very thought of touring a prison camp as a holiday excursion. Yet in the 1860s this was not generally seen as out of the ordinary. In fact, curious civilians paid to observe the prisoners in Chicago's notorious Camp Douglas on Lake Michigan from the vantage point of wooden observation towers overlooking the camp wall.

The Hardin visit to Camp Lookout strikes most of us today as a rather morbid exercise in curiosity, similar in ways to modern zoo visitors. Unfortunately, Browning does not describe General and Mrs. Hardin's reaction to the spectacle. We can only hope that the sight of these suffering Confederate prisoners aroused their compassion rather than their amusement.

A more conventional outing was recorded in Browning's diary on May 31, 1865, several months after the conclusion of the war: " . . . Emma went today with Genl & Mrs. Hardin & others to Mount Vernon."[9] This excursion to the estate of President George Washington is in keeping with the Hardin reverence for America's past, and due to General Hardin's mother, who had played a key role in preserving and protecting the Mount Vernon estate.

On Friday, June 15, 1865, Browning again mentions General Hardin, writing: " . . . Last night Emma went in company with Judge Watts and his daughter & Mrs Atwood to Genl Hardin's Head Quarters to a party, and did not get back till day light this morning."[10] One month later, on July 15, 1866, Browning noted: "At Departments in the morning—Mrs. Chancellor Walworth and Genl Hardin & wife dined with us."[11]

In Washington, General Hardin and his lady resided in a comfortable two-story brick headquarters on the corner of Nineteenth Street and Pennsylvania Avenue, a short distance from the War Department. This was befitting his rank and position as commander of all the city's defenses north of the Potomac. And here they entertained the other members of their social clique.

Lt. Clarence Backus served as General Hardin's aide during this period, a position he won due to the fact that he was the nephew and namesake of the general's stepbrother, Father Clarence Walworth. In a brief post-war reminiscence, Backus mentioned that Hardin's headquarters on Pennsylvania Avenue was often visited by the most powerful men in the government, including Secretary of War Edwin Stanton and even President Lincoln.[12]

And of course, General Hardin was a visitor to the White House, a fact he mentioned many decades later during his speech made on the Centenary of Lincoln's Birthday in 1909 in St. Augustine, Florida. Considering Hardin's mother's ties to the Lincoln family and his father's friendship with Lincoln years before in Illinois, there is every reason to believe Hardin enjoyed a friendship with President Lincoln.[13] Incredible as it seems, however, General Hardin never wrote down his impressions of Lincoln or recorded their conversations which took place during multiple White House visits. We only know from Hardin's paraphrased remarks that he retained a deep veneration for Lincoln and remarked on the President's compassion and humanity, and his delight in telling humorous stories.

We do know that Hardin, despite his great admiration for Lincoln, did not subscribe to the notion that the great man was without flaws. He briefly noted years after the end of the war that Lincoln in the early part of the rebellion had been misled and, to some degree, manipulated by certain unscrupulous men in the political and military circles of Washington. Hardin describes a "military coterie which surrounded our noble President" but never mentions any specific members.[14]

> Few persons are acquainted with, and fewer still willing to acknowledge, the great difficulties of Mr. Lincoln's position, due principally to influential politicians and newspaper editors wishing to conduct the war, and jealous generals giving opposing counsels. The writer {Hardin} believes with Colonel Scott {compiler of the "Rebellion Records"} Lincoln gained great knowledge of the art of war, and that, if he had been permitted to act as he saw fit, many misfortunes would have been spared the Union forces.[15]

At another point in Hardin's 1890 history of the Twelfth Pennsylvania Reserve Regiment, the author digresses from the main narrative to pen a vigorous defense of President Lincoln's grasp of military tactics and strategy. This is in response to an article that had recently appeared in the Historical Society's publication, which categorized Lincoln as an amateur armchair general whose meddling was detrimental to the war effort. " . . . this criticism, though made and approved by a great historical society a generation after the close of the war, is too severe on Mr. Lincoln," Hardin wrote. "The writer's explanation or defense of Mr. Lincoln is that his better judgment was often over-ruled by the Committee on the Conduct of the War (whose representative in the Cabinet was Mr. Stanton, who controlled a two-thirds majority of Congress. This committee {was} backed up by the most powerful newspapers and popular orators."[16]

It seems likely that General and Mrs. Hardin were in the audience on that wet, windy March 4th day in 1865 when President Lincoln delivered his Second Inauguration Day speech on the east front of the Capitol. A vast crowd of fifty thousand slogged through muddy streets—in places mired ten-inches deep—to hear the President that day. As he had at Gettysburg, Lincoln delivered a brief speech, but one which has gone down as among the most powerful declarations ever uttered by an American President:

"Fondly do we hope—fervently do we pray—that this mighty scourge of war may speedily pass away," he said, but added a note of grim resolve: "Yet, if God wills that it continue, until all the wealth piled by the bond-man's two hundred and fifty years of unrequited toil shall be sunk, and until every drop of blood drawn with the lash, shall be paid by another drawn with the sword, as was said three thousand years ago, so still it must be said, 'the judgments of the Lord are true and righteous altogether.'"[17]

Lincoln ended with the soul-stirring words: "With malice toward none; with charity for all; with firmness in the right, as God gives us to see the right, let us strive on to finish the work we are in; to bind up the nation's wounds . . . to do all which may achieve and cherish a just, and a lasting peace, among ourselves, and with all nations."[18]

General Hardin, as well as the many thousands there, would have been horrified to know that the future assassin of President Lincoln was standing only a few feet away from him during the Inaugural, flanked by one of his key collaborators in the ongoing plot: a young, strong paroled Confederate soldier named Lewis Paine (aka: Powell). In a few months, all would become clear and General Hardin would ultimately discover new details about the deadly December 1863 ambush that had cost him his left arm.

A day after the Inauguration another Confederate agent slipped unob-trusively into the Capital on a secret mission, the nature of which has never been discovered. That man was Captain Benjamin Franklin Stringfellow, Mosby's favorite scout, and the man who had led the bushwhacking party at Catlett Station in December 1863 when Hardin was so severely wounded.[19]

In the weeks preceding Lee's surrender, Stringfellow lived under an assumed name in Washington, posing as a dentist, and even applying for a license. Perhaps Hardin and Stringfellow even passed each other on the street that spring of 1865, when every special edition of the *Washington Star* brought headlined news of another Union victory.

On April 1, Stringfellow re-crossed the Potomac, his unknown mission apparently completed, leaving to posterity only unanswered questions as to whether he had played a role in Booth's unfolding assassination plot. In the years of peace ahead, Hardin came to learn of Stringfellows's role in the December ambush and hear how his attacker had become a minister. This Hardin regarded as the height of hypocrisy. Until his death, Hardin believed his attackers at Catlett Station had acted as base assassins and not honorable soldiers.[20]

The news of General Robert E. Lee's surrender at Appomattox Courthouse on April 9, 1865 triggered a joyful night of fireworks, bonfires and army band concerts as Washington celebrated victory and the impending peace. General Hardin and his wife were present in the city that night and must have witnessed the joyous spectacle. " . . . the news spread like wildfire and the intelligence, first doubted, was speedily made certain of by the publication of thousands of newspapers 'extras' containing the news in bulletins issued from the War Department," remembered newspaper correspondent Noah Brooks. "In a moment of time the city was ablaze with an excitement the like of which had never been seen before."[21]

Secretary of War Stanton ordered the Union artillery to fire a 300-gun salute.[22] The General and his lady doubtless shared the crowd's joy at the news. For them and for most of the suffering nation, the alleged glory and grandeur of war had long ago proved an imposter. In General Hardin's case he must have felt much like the veterans memorialized in the lyrics of Walter Kittredge's popular tune "Tenting Tonight," which proclaimed: "We are tired of war on the old campground. Many are dead and gone. Of the brave and true who've left their homes. Others been wounded long."[23]

Then joy turned to shock and horror on that fateful Good Friday evening of April 14, 1865.

President Lincoln and First Lady Mary Todd Lincoln arrived at Ford's Theater late for a performance of "Our American Cousin," a popular comedy starring actress Laura Keene. Almost every American is familiar with the tragedy of that night, perhaps the worst night in American history, when actor John Wilkes Booth entered the Lincoln box and shot the unsuspecting President in the back of the head with his Derringer, slashed Major Henry Rathbone with his knife, and plunged twelve feet to the stage, breaking his leg.[24]

Booth then faced the stunned audience of a thousand, bloody blade in hand, and shouted, some claimed, "*Sic Semper Tyrannis*" ("thus always to tyrants"). The assassin then hobbled backstage to the alley where he mounted his horse and galloped off into the night and eternal infamy.

General Hardin, in his capacity as commander of Washington's northern defenses, was quickly alerted to the assassination attempt, probably within the hour, and reported to his headquarters where he would help direct the hunt for the assassin through the night.

Not long after, Hardin learned of the nearly simultaneous attempt on Secretary of State's William H. Seward's life. A crazed assassin stormed into the older man's bedroom where he was convalescing from a recent carriage accident, and slashed him with a Bowie knife after almost bludgeoning to death Seward's son, Frederick, with a heavy revolver after it misfired.[25]

This enraged giant then fled into the night crying out: "I'm mad! I'm mad!"[26] In his wake he left behind Seward and four others bleeding from wounds and blows. All this horror had been witnessed by the Secretary's gentle and frail 15-year-old daughter, Fanny.

The task of the soldiers stationed in Washington was to find and capture the assassins. Once the search started it became a frustrating exercise in misdirection, confusion, and false leads. The first act commenced when Major General Augur directed his two division commanders, General Hardin on the north of the river, and Brigadier General Gustavus DeRussy on the south, to rouse every available man, put them on the alert and seal off all avenues of escape. Augur's order read:

"Deploy your troops between the forts of your command and form a continuous line of pickets. Stop everyone from going out of the line. . . . Leave sufficient guard at each post. It is supposed one of the assassins is still in town."[27]

The well-known actor had been identified right from the beginning as the President's attacker. Unfortunately, for most of the night General Augur assumed that Booth remained in the city. But by the time the hunt was in full swing the President's murderer had already escaped.

One man in Hardin's command was doomed to inadvertently allow Booth's escape from the city. At approximately 11:40 p.m., Sergeant Silas Cobb, in command of the guard at the Washington Navy Yard Bridge, which spanned the Anacostia River to Maryland, observed a lone rider approaching.[28]

Cobb hadn't yet been alerted to Lincoln assassination. After questioning Booth, he let him pass over the river, despite being in violation of the 9 p.m. curfew. A little while later, Booth's accomplice, David Herold (who had recently deserted Lewis Paine at Secretary of State Seward's home) came riding up. He too, asked to cross, calling himself Smith. He told Cobb he was unaware of the curfew and was late in returning to his Maryland home because he had been dallying with a woman. The Sergeant let him pass as well. After all, the war was practically over; it probably seemed harmless enough to ease up on the strict curfew.[29]

Almost on the heels of Herold still another rider appeared at the bridgehead. Civilian stableman John Fletcher halted and explained to Sergeant Cobb that he was in pursuit of a man (Herald) who had stolen a rented horse. After Cobb told Fletcher he could cross the bridge but wouldn't be allowed to return to the city until daylight, the stableman gave up his pursuit. That decision may have saved his life.[30]

So it was that the Washington garrison force continued looking for Booth long after his escape. Part of the problem was the terribly slow process of spreading the word throughout the sprawling Capital surrounded by its 37-mile ring of forts, redoubts and gun emplacements.

A few minutes after midnight General Hardin ordered his division to seal off the city and seize and detain anyone trying to leave. The alert went out by flag signal, the message being forwarded by flagmen atop tall wooden signal stations located around the city's perimeter.[31] Augur also put out a series of telegraphic alerts through the night, but even "the lightning" proved frustratingly slow due to the cumbersome process of coding, receiving, duplicating and deciphering messages.[32]

At least an hour passed before all the troops in Washington were alerted to the assassination of Lincoln and the attempt on the life of Secretary of State Seward. The city was already buzzing with the news and a mob had formed outside the Petersen House where Lincoln lay dying. The streets of the city swarmed with double-timing infantrymen, rifles at the port, and clattering cavalry patrols; occasionally a mounted messenger galloped off into the night on some mission. Crowds of people began gathering at street corners discussing the various rumors.[33]

Out of the chaos one of the soldiers came upon a horse carrying an ornate saddle and immediately reported the fact to General Hardin. He, in turn, shared the news with the other commands in a telegram of great importance: "The horse and saddle of {the} supposed murderer have been found near Lincoln Hospital. Check all boats on the Eastern Branch and Potomac River to guard against crossing between bridges. Continue doing so throughout the night."[34]

Soon everyone was convinced that the horse and saddle was Booth's. The truth was that the animal had been ridden by Seward's attacker, Lewis Paine (Powell), who abandoned the horse near Lincoln Hospital when it fell apparently exhausted. The conspirator, confused and lost in a strange city, then set off on foot, wandering the unfamiliar streets until Monday, April 17. That's when the bedraggled conspirator walked into the hands of detectives at Madame Mary Surratt's boarding house with a shovel over his shoulder, and a flimsy cover story about being her hired man. Both were arrested and imprisoned as prime suspects.

During the early pre-dawn darkness of Saturday, April 15, Hardin's men spread through the city searching for the conspirators. At that point no one conducting the hunt even knew who Paine (the real name of Lewis Powell) was. But many witnesses at Ford's Theater had recognized the famous actor Booth as Lincoln's assassin. Soldiers soon found Powell's abandoned horse and saddle, bringing the latter to General Augur's headquarters. Not long afterward, stableman Fletcher appeared and told his story about pursuing Herold to the Navy Yard Bridge earlier that evening. He recognized the fancy saddle and told Augur it belonged to Booth.[35] This discovery convinced Augur and the others conducting the hunt that Booth and other conspirators still remained in the city.

Secretary of War Edwin Stanton had taken the reins of government firmly into his hands that night. While standing Lincoln's death watch at the Petersen House, Stanton was issuing orders and sending out telegraphic instructions. In those early hours he dictated a telegraph with information that electrified the nation: "Investigation strongly indicates J. Wilkes Booth as the assassin of the President. Whether it was the same or a different person that attempted to murder Mr. Seward remains in doubt. . . . Every exertion has been made to prevent the escape of the murderer. His horse has been found on the road, near Washington."[36]

Because of his friendship with President Lincoln, his father's old companion, General Hardin must have wondered during that long night if it wasn't all some sort of nightmare. The kind man who had been his mentor and benefactor was dying at the Petersen House and the search for his killer had so far been futile. Then stunningly, word came to Hardin's headquarters that a detachment of his troops had captured the assassin. Minutes later General Hardin sent out a telegram announcing the coup: "J. Wilkes Booth has been apprehended."[37]

The elation and satisfaction must have been intense for General Hardin. His men had run down the assassin of President Lincoln; at least justice could now be served. But the triumph was fleeting. Further investigation revealed that Hardin's soldiers had the wrong man in custody. It had all been a case of mistaken identity by over-zealous pursuers.

While General Hardin and his men continued in their fruitless search for the assassin, the life of President Abraham Lincoln was slowly ebbing away at the Petersen House. His long lank body lay crossways on a blood-soaked bed while the surgeons did what little they could. Lincoln's labored breathing stopped forever at 7:22 in the morning, April 15, 1865.[38] Within hours Washington was draped in black mourning and, according to the newspapers, paroled Confederates seemed to magically disappear from the streets fearing retribution. A steady drizzle of rain fell on a city in mourning.

Reporter Noah Brooks was present in the city on that gray, overcast morning of April 15, 1865 observing what he later described as "an extraordinary spectacle": "They were suddenly crowded with people—men, woman and children thronging the pavements and darkening the thoroughfares. It seemed as if everybody was in tears. Pale faces, streaming eyes, with now and again frowning countenance, were on every side."[39]

The Great Emancipator, the savior of the Union, Abraham Lincoln, would no longer regale his friends with funny stories, recite his favorite lines from Shakespeare's plays, share his favorite poems, or laugh at Tad Lincoln's childish deviltry. Secretary of War Stanton allegedly said, "Now he belongs to the Ages."[40]

General Hardin's immediate reaction to Lincoln's death was not re-corded. We do know that he next appears in the sad aftermath to the assas-sination on Monday, April 17, when he visited the White House. He was probably there to convey his sympathies to Mary Todd Lincoln and her sons, Robert and Tad. It seems highly unlikely that General Hardin met with the widow at that time because she remained secluded upstairs, deep in mourning and inconsolable.

Preparations were being made for the great funeral scheduled two days hence. During his visit to the White House that day General Hardin took a few minutes to write his mother, Mrs. Chancellor Walworth, with the terrible news.

Executive Mansion Washington D.C.
April 17, 1865

My Dear Mother,
Here in the presence of the mighty dead, I write you these few lines. Our good, Honest President is dead! Just as he was making peace throughout our unfortunate Country he is taken from amongst us by the fanatical hand of the assassin. Oh how I shall pray that our Country may not be again the scene of fratricidal Strife; I am Sick at heart! The investigations have disclosed so much villainy, it's impossible to tell what to expect next . . . Oh! Mother what Sad, Sad times we live in . . . !
Truly Yours, Love in haste MD Hardin[41]

On the following afternoon General Hardin had the delicate task of escorting Miss Fanny Seward and her brother, Major Augustus Seward, to the Navy Yard anchorage where the man calling himself Paine was being held chained and hooded in the bowels of the monitor U.S.S. *Saugus*. The grim ironclad was anchored several hundred yards off the landing and guarded by armed Navy picket boats. Below decks, the conspirator was manacled and wore a ball and chain, and his head was covered with a canvas hood, on the express orders of Secretary of War Edwin Stanton.[42]

A frail, sensitive and bookish teenager, Miss Seward had been exposed to the horrible violence perpetuated that Good Friday when the suspect had gained entrance to the Seward home claiming to be a courier delivering medicine for her father. Paine's attack was timed to occur at around 10:15 p.m., Good Friday, April 15, almost simultaneously with John Wilkes Booth's attack on President Lincoln. Secretary of Steward was in an upstairs bedroom recovering from a recent accident when he was thrown from his carriage, breaking an arm and fracturing his jaw.[43]

When the stranger came to the door, Seward's daughter Fanny was seated at his bedside reading aloud from a book. Family servant William Bell answered the door and confronted the tall and surly stranger. Paine claimed he brought medicine for the injured man and had been told by the family doctor to deliver it personally to the Secretary.

Bell instinctively knew something was amiss and offered to take the medicine up himself. The stranger brusquely refused and pushed on past the servant. He ignored Bell and began walking up the stairs to the second floor. On the landing outside Seward's bedroom door, he was questioned by Fanny's brother, Frederick, his father's assistant at the State Department.[44]

"He's asleep," Frederick told the insistent courier. At that instant, Fanny Seward cracked open the bedroom door announcing to her brother's irritation: "Fred, father is awake now." Paine asked in a demanding tone: "Is the Secretary asleep?"

"Almost," Fanny responded. As his sister retreated back into the bedroom, Frederic quickly closed the door, and told Paine he would take the medicine in for him.[45] The big man turned away as if to leave, but with catlike speed, his hand dove beneath his jacket and produced a large Army revolver, which he pressed to Frederic's Seward's temple. Snap! The handgun misfired.

Now the powerful Paine began using the heavy revolver as a bludgeon against Fred Seward, hammering his skull with all his strength. Hearing the commotion, Fanny opened the bedroom door and the intruder brushed past her, now with a large Bowie knife in his hand. He confronted Private Robinson, the male Army nurse, and slashed him several times before moving towards the helpless Secretary of State. The injured man could only roll away from the oncoming attacker, and slid part way down between the bed and the wall.[46]

Payne repeatedly stabbed the helpless man in the face and neck drawing great gouts of blood until he was pulled away by the nurse and the two Seward brothers. After a wild struggle, the crazed giant was pinned to the floor. But when Augustus Steward stood up to go and retrieve his revolver from his bedroom, Paine flung off nurse Robinson, quickly regained his feet, and bolted out onto the landing.[47]

At that moment Department of State messenger Emrick Hansell was coming up the stairs and attempted to block the assassin's escape. Paine knocked him down, stabbed him in the back, and resumed his flight. He ran out the door into the night, shouting: "I'm mad! I'm mad!"[48] He dashed across the street to his horse, leapt into the saddle and galloped off. The assassin known as Paine left bloody chaos in his wake.

Dr. Tullio S. Verdi, the family doctor, arrived soon after and literally waded through a thick puddle of blood on the bedroom floor as he approached the badly wounded Secretary of State.[49] "Blood was streaming from an extensive gash in his swollen cheek, the cheek was now laid open, and the flap hung loose on his neck," Dr. Verdi remembered in an 1873 newspaper article. "The gash commenced from the high cheek bone down to the neck in a semi-circular form toward the mouth; it was probably five inches long and two inches deep. It was a frightful wound."[50]

Despite the horrific nature of the wounds, Paine's knife blade had narrowly missed severing the jugular and carotid arteries. The Secretary of State would survive. His son Frederick, however, appeared mortally wounded. The attacker's terrible blows left Frederick's skull cracked, exposing part of his brain. "I feared these wounds would prove fatal," Dr. Verdi later confessed. Army nurse George F. Robinson was also bleeding from multiple slashes and cuts. Major Augustus Steward was cut on his forehead and right hand, although Verdi described the wounds as superficial. Emerick Hansell was wounded in the back near the spine.[51]

Four days following the brutal assault, with the life of their brother Frederick still hanging in the balance, Fanny and Augustus, escorted by General Hardin, boarded a Navy launch to take them to where Paine was being held aboard the monitor *Saugus*. Although he had already been identified by servant William Bell, additional confirmation was thought prudent.[52]

Yeoman William H. Howard aboard the *Saugus* duly noted the visit of General Hardin and the Sewards in the ship's log dated April 18, 1865: "In the afternoon Commander Montgomery, major of marines, two gentlemen (Augustus Seward and General Hardin) and Miss Seward came aboard. One of the citizens (Augustus Seward) was cut in the assault on Secretary Seward. He wore bandages about his head and arm. The prisoner was stripped and dressed in sailor's clothes. Blood was found on his undergarments."[53]

Another witness who saw General Hardin escort Fanny and Augustus Seward aboard the *Saugus* that day was Henry Harrison Atwater, a civilian telegraphist who worked at the Navy Yard. This was the same Atwater who had manned the telegraph at Fort Reno less than a year before for General Hardin during the July 1864 Confederate raid on Washington.[54]

"While Paine was confined on the monitor, Miss Fanny Seward, daughter of the Secretary, was escorted by General Hardin, my old commander at Fort Reno," Atwater said. "They came down to identify Paine, who it will be remembered, rushed past her and into Sec. Seward's room, where he committed the murderous deed."[55]

The dramatic encounter between Miss Fanny Seward and the alleged attacker was later described by Dr. Tullio Verdi for the Juanita (Pa.) *Sentinel*. On June 25, 1873 the front page story was featured under the headline: "'The Assassination of the Sewards' by T.S. Verdi, the family doctor."[56] Dr. Verdi wrote:

> Next morning I accompanied Miss Fanny and Augustus Seward to the Monitor, where Paine was held a prisoner. What a feeling must have pervaded the bosom of this girl while she was going to meet the assassin who before her own eyes, had so brutally assaulted, and all but killed her father. She had seen him in a dimly lighted room, under great excitement. Would she recognize him now? The idea of meeting this man face-to-face although where he was harmless, would have excited vain fears in many a girl's heart; but she was composed, and her demeanor expressed only the dignity of her own strange position. She met the naval officer on the Monitor with the same calm and gentle manners so natural to her. . . . Paine gradually rose from the hatchway . . . showing a serious if not stolid face, and colossal frame he stood unmoved before the frail girl, who would not even utter a curse upon him. God alone knew what passed in those two hearts at that moment.

Strangely quiet, they stood before each other. . . . The scene was a solemn one, too solemn—too solemn for man to utter a sound; a silence broken only by the hissing wind and surging waves.[57]

Fanny Seward could not say for certain this was the same man who had wreaked such havoc in their home four days earlier. However, her brother, Augustus, had no doubts. This was the man, he announced.

General Hardin then escorted Augustus and Fanny ashore, not realizing that Paine had recognized him as one of the Union officers he and the other members of Captain Stringfellow's raiding party had ambushed December 14, 1863 near Catlett Station. Perhaps the prisoner who had so savagely wounded Secretary of State Seward had also fired the revolver bullet that shattered Hardin's left arm.

For the time being, the hulking prisoner in irons remained silent. During his incarceration and trial, however, he confessed his role in the ambush to his chief jailor, General Frank Hartranft. At some point before Paine's hanging, General Hartranft shared the startling revelation with General Hardin, who later wrote: "If that is fair warfare the writer {Hardin} is unable to understand what is fair."[58]

Although Lewis Paine/Powell along with four others—including Mary Surratt, the owner of the conspirators' boarding house—were sent to the gallows, John Wilkes Booth evaded the noose. Trapped by Union soldiers at a Virginia farm on April 26, he refused to surrender, and after the barn in which he hid was set on fire, a soldier caught sight of him through the smoke and shot him dead, despite orders to take him alive.

During the formal funeral service for President Lincoln conducted in the early afternoon of Wednesday, April 19, General Hardin waited outside the White House with the rest of the military escort which would accompany the President's coffin to the Capitol where it would lie in state in the rotunda for public viewing.

Inside the White House, Rev. Dr. Phineas Burley of the New York Avenue Presbyterian Church gave the eulogy before a ticketed crowd of Washington's ruling classes. Among the mourners: Robert Todd Lincoln representing the family, President Andrew Johnson, General Grant, Secretary of War Stanton, the Supreme Court Justices, Admiral David Farragut, Major-General Henry Halleck, and Hardin family friend Oliver H. Browning. The President's widow and young Tad, his father's favorite, remained upstairs at the White House too distraught to attend.[59]

"Probably no man since the days of Washington was ever so deeply and firmly enshrined in the very hearts of the people as Abraham Lincoln," the Reverend Doctor Phineas Gurley of the New York Avenue Presbyterian Church remarked during his funeral address.[60] General Grant was in tears as were many others attending.

About 2 p.m., a contingent of twelve sergeants from the Veteran Reserve Corps (formerly Invalid Corps) lifted the casket and carried it out to the specially constructed funeral hearse, drawn by six white horses, each with a black feathered plume bobbing above its head. All the while the city's church bells rang a farewell salute accompanied by the bark of minute guns.[61]

Brigadier General Hardin rode at the side of his immediate supervisor, Major General Christopher Columbus Augur. Each officer wore a black mourning band around one arm and their sword hilts also bore a black crepe band. The President's coffin was placed atop the hearse's raised platform allowing the crowd a clear view as the procession marched more than a mile down Pennsylvania Avenue to the Capitol. A groom led Lincoln's saddled gray horse with boots in the stirrups.[62]

Colonel George W. Gile, the same officer who had fought under Hardin during Early's Raid, led the honor guard that day, which consisted of 100 men from the Ninth and Tenth Veteran Reserve Corps regiments, who flanked the hearse. Upon the order the procession began, marching at a slow pace with arms reversed. A drum corps sounded the death march with muffled drums and the 25-member U.S. Marine Band played various funeral airs.[63]

People of every class and background had been pouring into the city for several days by train, buggy, wagon, on horseback and on foot determined to witness the great and solemn historical event. More than 100,000 spectators now crowded the sidewalks, peered down from upper story windows, or observed from atop rooftops. Some men and boys had climbed into the branches of the trees lining the avenue for a better view. For the most part, the crowd was silent and somber as the grim procession passed by.[64]

The death pageant concluded in front of the U.S. Capitol where the honor guard of Veteran Reserve Corps sergeants carried Lincoln's casket and set it atop a catafalque at the center of the rotunda under the magnificent, newly constructed dome. Throughout the war, Lincoln had insisted the Capitol building's construction work continue as a symbol of the sacred Union's continued survival.

Lincoln remained in the Rotunda on public view until Friday morning when the coffin was taken to the Washington railroad station. The nine-car train was drawn by a locomotive displaying a portrait of the slain president framed by American flags. Millions of Americans would watch from trackside as the funeral train carried Lincoln west on his final 1,700 mile journey.[65]

Abraham Lincoln, the friend and mentor of Brigadier General Martin D. Hardin, was finally going home to Illinois where he and Martin's father, John J. Hardin, had long ago met as militia volunteers.

CHAPTER 23

COMMANDING FORMER ENEMIES IN RALEIGH

I remember the first I heard of the Yankees was when young master came in and says, 'Lord Pa, the Yankees are in Raleigh!' That evening I was drawing water when all of a sudden I looks up the road, and the air is dark with Yankees. I never seen so many men, horses and mules in my life. The band was playing and the soldiers were hollering and the horses were prancing high.—Former slave John Coggin, in a 1938 interview[1]

I n the era we remember as Reconstruction, Brigadier General Martin D. Hardin was assigned to command occupying Union troops in Raleigh, North Carolina in late summer 1865. In this dismal aftermath of a lost war, the white South was, for the most part, sullenly resigned to the presence of Federal troops.

Nevertheless, many Southerners still resented and held in contempt the Yankee occupiers. Despite General and Mrs. Hardin's strong ancestral ties to Kentucky, they too were only tolerated by most of Raleigh's embittered former Confederates when they arrived in early August 1865. Yet, in an October 1865 letter to his mother in Sarasota Springs, General Hardin, not yet married a year, told his mother that he and Estelle were "happy as mortals can be."[2] The young husband boasted of his wife's skill as a hostess and joked how they had already entertained more people for dinner than resided in all of Raleigh.

However, later in that same letter, Hardin confessed that few of their dinner guests were local Southerners. "We have had one or two only from the resident population," he wrote his mother. "The people of Raleigh are not given to hospitality to Yankees."[3] In the eyes of most local whites, General Hardin was the commander of an occupying army, and they never welcomed him into their social circle.

Southern white women often appeared more hostile than their male companions and relatives. Laura Craven was one who never bothered concealing her hostility to the Northern invaders. She came to visit her aunt in Raleigh during General Hardin's tenure as Union commander, and Miss Craven was mortified upon learning that Yankee officers were among the residents of her aunt's boarding house:

"I got into a real nest of Yankees last week," Craven wrote an acquaintance, explaining how her aunt's Bluecoat boarders, a colonel, his wife and a lieutenant, invited over at least another seven or eight Yankees for the evening. She then related how she, several female friends and "several confed boys" had "formed ourselves into a party in one corner, had our own music, conversation, and amusements. It was real laughable."[4] Miss Craven apparently enjoyed shunning the Federals and their ladies, remarking in her letter, "the fact that there is not alkali enough in the south to make water and oil mix was plainly demonstrated that night."[5]

Another Raleigh belle, Catherine Ann Edmonston, was appalled and outraged by the white Union soldiers attending nightly balls at the Guion Hotel, where she claimed, "the *Yankee Officers* dance with the *negro women!*"[6]

· White North Carolina was full of Unreconstructed Rebels like Miss Edmonston. They were outraged at the social revolution taking place around them following the demise of slavery. From almost the beginning of the official peace, these reactionary white elements vowed to limit the freedom of the former slaves. To that end, they employed murder, whippings, lynching and mob rule.

For a conservative man with strong Kentucky roots, Hardin was remarkably open-minded about race and the Freedmen of the South. While commanding at Raleigh he seems to have done his best to help the former slaves achieve their rights under law as American citizens. At the same time, he tried to give the defeated white Confederates justice as well.

General Hardin in the months ahead proved to be a fair man attempting to establish a middle ground between the newly liberated slaves and their former masters. Despite the enormous challenge of Reconstruction, General Hardin was perhaps too optimistic in a letter written to his mother during his Raleigh assignment: "There is but one reason now for keeping any troops in the State—that is the inability of the Negro to testify in the Courts of Justice. If any arrangement can be made, by which the Freedman can be tried the same as white men, that is have the same rights of protection to life and property as white men, there will no longer {be a} need of troops in the State."[7]

Like many other Union officers assigned to occupation duty in the former Confederacy, General Hardin learned from the beginning that his efforts would be strongly challenged by the white establishment, determined, if not to resurrect slavery, to impose racially segregated Jim Crow society with one standard of justice for whites and an inferior, prejudicial standard for blacks. The dark side of Reconstruction is dramatically illustrated by a newspaper account of an outrage committed by whites in a community near Raleigh just after General Hardin reported there for duty. *The Philadelphia Daily Evening Bulletin*, in its September 13, 1865 edition proclaimed in a bold, three-deck headline:

NORTH CAROLINA
A FREEDMAN PUNISHED BY THE OLD SLAVE CODE
Murderous Assault in Court—The Freedman Finally Missing[8]

The newspaper story was based on a report of the episode compiled by Dexter H. Clapp, who headed the Freedman's Bureau in the Raleigh area at the time. This former Union officer investigated the case of ex-slave Richard Cotton who was allegedly whipped and tortured in Chatham County, not far away from Raleigh.

Chatham County was, according to Reconstruction historians, a stronghold of the Ku Klux Klan where they operated with impunity right after the Civil War. One former slave, a free African-American named Essic Harris, witnessed many whippings and atrocities in Chatham County during the Reconstruction years, claiming that many had been whipped and run off by white vigilantes.[9]

Freedman Richard Cotton was one of the victims, the individual who allegedly struck a white man, James Camell, according to the Philadelphia newspaper account. Not long after, Cotton was run down by a white mob and turned over to the justice of the peace. During the questioning that followed, the victim of the assault, Camell, pistol-whipped the colored man right in court. Jailor John T. Mallory then stepped between them, preventing the enraged white man from "booting the negro as seemed his intention."[10]

Justice of the Peace Thomas Long, Magistrate, ordered Mallory to take Cotton to the city whipping post and apply ten lashes, leave him tied there for two hours, and then apply nine more lashes. Long also had the Negro tied by the thumbs for two hours with his feet barely touching the ground before the whippings commenced.[11]

To his credit, Jailor Mallory told Long that Cotton, who had severe head injuries from the pistol whipping, would probably not survive the punishment. Mallory refused to carry out the sentence unless provided with a written order. "Can't I let him off after tying him up?" Mallory asked. But again the magistrate refused and threatened to jail Mallory if he refused to carry out the sentence as ordered.[12]

At some point afterwards Mallory noted the presence of a white mob outside the jail and feared they might seize the prisoner and murder him. Mallory was quoted in the Philadelphia newspaper saying, " . . . threats were made by the mob that they would take the keys from me, seize the prisoner and lynch him."[13]

Mallory told Freedman Bureau investigators he later carried out Cotton's punishment under duress. "I did these things from compulsion," and added: "The Negro has been missing; I don't know where he is."[14]

The details of the case were presented to General Hardin in Raleigh, who immediately ordered Justice of the Peace Long and another county official to report and answer for their actions. A month later, however, the victim, Richard Cotton, remained missing. It was an open question as to whether he was hiding out of fear of white retaliation or had been murdered by the vigilantes.[15]

The final disposition of the case is unknown. The victim may have simply vanished and the other witnesses chose silence rather than risk violent retribution from the Klan. The episode dramatically illustrates the difficulties confronting General Hardin in trying to apply justice to freed slaves.

General Hardin's efforts at reconciliation between the races didn't go unnoticed. Dexter Clapp of the Raleigh Freedman's Bureau testified on February 21, 1866 before the Joint Committee on Reconstruction during the first session of the Thirty-Ninth Congress, praising General Hardin:

"In the immediate vicinity of military posts things are in a very good condition," Clapp told Congress. "They are a great deal worse in some sections than others. General Hardin, commanding the district, has been very constant and efficient in his labors to maintain order and insure justice to all classes."[16]

This was high praise indeed considering Clapp, a native New Yorker, had served during the recent war as lieutenant colonel of the Thirty-Eighth United States Colored Troops.

Clapp, however, did not share General Hardin's optimism about the future. He told the Committee that withdrawing Federal troops from North Carolina at that time would, "be very disastrous indeed." Asked his opinion on whether white southerners in the Raleigh area desired another civil war, Clapp answered: "They have no indication of opposing the government by open war any further. I think they have no more love for the government than at any time during the rebellion. The more sensible . . . intend to make the best they can of it."[17]

General Hardin served four months in Raleigh, at a time when he was at a crossroads in his life and career. Soon, he would revert to his regular army rank of captain with a commensurate reduction in pay and privileges. Despite his continued ambition to practice law, he finally decided to remain in the army for the present. But, he also asked his mother to use her connections to secure him a "majority in the line or in some corps," frankly admitting, "You have plenty of friends and I have a few, but I do not know how to get any of them to look out for me."[18]

On January 15, 1866, Hardin left his post at Raleigh and commenced a three-month leave of absence, on the same date as he was mustered out as Brigadier-General of Volunteers. From April to October 1866, Captain Hardin was in Chicago on recruiting service. During this assignment, he and Estelle enjoyed a number of sightseeing expeditions around the city, which had grown enormously since Martin had visited there in 1851.[19]

General and Mrs. Hardin also renewed acquaintances with President Lincoln's widow and her young son, Tad. On May 8, 1866, Estelle wrote her mother-in-law, Sarah (Hardin) Walworth in Saratoga Springs, ending the note with a postscript documenting their recent contacts with Mary Todd Lincoln: "Mrs. L. speaks of you on all occasions with the greatest affection & admiration. Always asks about you & talks a great deal of you.

She had been very kind lately {handwriting eligible} if we don't call every few days, says 'why don't come an afternoon and see me.' I expect she misses D's [Martin's] cheerful laugh."[20]

In July of 1866, presumably due to his mother's influence, the 28-year-old Hardin was promoted major in the regular army and assigned to the Forty-third United States Infantry. He spent the fall and winter of 1866–1867 in Detroit on regimental recruiting service. And, in the spring of 1867, was Acting Judge-Advocate, Headquarters Department of the Lakes, Detroit.[21] This assignment focusing on military justice was probably a welcome one because Hardin never entirely abandoned his long-term interest in the law.

On November 27, 1867, Chancellor Reuben Hyde Walworth passed away at age 79 in Saratoga Springs, leaving behind both an estimable career and a considerable inheritance for his children and stepchildren.

During a year's leave of absence 1867/1868, General and Mrs. Hardin traveled in Europe with an unidentified maid who was probably Dolly Smith. We know nothing about the specifics of their itinerary, except for a surviving photo of Estelle taken in London.[22] Upon returning, Hardin transferred to the First United States Infantry and, for brief periods of time, commanded at Fort Porter in Buffalo, New York and Fort Gratiot in Michigan, where he was given a medical discharge on account of his war injuries. He retired at age 33 on half-pay with the rank of brigadier-general, the youngest retired general officer in the country.

Finally Martin Hardin was free to pursue his first love, the law. There in the booming city by Lake Michigan he set out to make-up for a decade of lost time. Ahead beckoned a new life with prospects untold in that mad scramble for wealth remembered as America's Gilded Age.

CHAPTER 24

THE GILDED AGE DAWNS, TAD
LINCOLN DIES, CHICAGO BURNS

C hicago had been transformed from when the teenage Hardin had visited in the early 1850s, undergoing phenomenal growth. In 1852, the city's population was around 38,000; by 1870, that number had grown by a factor of nearly ten, standing at around 300,000. Half the population consisted of foreign immigrants, mainly German and Irish, poorly housed in ramshackle wooded firetraps, teeming with rats, pimps, prostitutes, pick-pockets and strong-arm robbers.

This was not the Chicago in which General and Mrs. Hardin lived, however, when they moved there in 1870. They lived on the near north side and were shielded by their class, education and social connections, far removed from the other Chicago: the city of poverty, crime and soul-destroying manual labor. Hardin's pension as a brigadier general and his inheritance from Chancellor Walworth in 1867 provided sufficient income to insure a comfortable and protected life.

Sharing their Chicago home was Estelle's younger sister, Grace Graham. She married Captain Leopold Oscar Parker, U.S. Army, on January 2, 1872 at St. James Catholic Church on Wabash Avenue. General and Mrs. Hardin were witnesses to the ceremony. Born in Missouri and raised in Virginia by an uncle, Leo Parker was a staunch Union man during the war. His military career began as a Second Lieutenant with the Second Regiment, United States Volunteer Infantry in Virginia during the final months of the Civil War.[1]

After the war, Parker saw extensive service in the Indian campaigns out West. Most notably, he was adjutant to Colonel Ranald Mackenzie of the

Fourth Cavalry during a daring raid across the Mexican border in May 1873. This bold violation of Mexican sovereignty was to chastise Kickapoo and Lipan Indians then using Mexico as a safe haven between raids on Texas settlements. Parker served for many years at various times in Texas, Kansas, New Mexico and the Dakota Territory.[2]

Later, in the early 1880s, Parker was stationed at Fort Bowie, Arizona Territory, guarding Apache Pass during the Apache wars.[3] His wife and children moved back in with General and Mrs. Hardin in Chicago for several years. Being childless, perhaps Martin and Estelle enjoyed having young children in their home. During the '70s and '80s General Hardin also continued to play the doting uncle to his sister's children, at one point purchasing a pony for her oldest son, Frank Hardin Walworth, and later befriending his younger brother, Tracy Walworth, a strange, withdrawn child, who enjoyed visiting his Uncle Dee during winter holidays in St. Augustine.

General Hardin thrived in the City by the Lake, energized by its pulsing energy and capitalizing on the many opportunities afforded a son of Colonel Hardin and the former protégé of President Lincoln. Not surprisingly, Hardin began his law career in the offices of Scammon, McCagg & Fuller on Chicago's Water Street. The prestigious firm was headed by 58-year-old Johnathan Young Scammon, an early political backer and close personal friend of Lincoln; and was a force to be recognized in booming Chicago.[4] Only a few years before Hardin's arrival, the President's oldest son, Robert Todd Lincoln, began his own legal career in Scammon's office.

Scammon was a classic American success story. He had come to Chicago from Maine in 1835, only two years after its incorporation as a city, and immediately became a key player in its dramatic expansion. He made his mark as a lawyer, alderman, banker, railroad builder and founder of *The Chicago Journal* newspaper. Rumor had it that he had been a conductor on the Underground Railroad, smuggling Southern slaves to freedom in the North. He was known as a progressive possessing an impeccable personal reputation, and a pioneer advocate for free public schooling. Scammon's success was inextricably linked to the early history of Chicago, now the second most populous city in the United States.[5]

Early on, General Hardin was welcomed by Chicago's political and social elite, providing the young attorney with a rich source of potential clients and contacts. In the years ahead, we know that Hardin's law services were utilized by many of the rich and the powerful, including his former commander, General Philip Sheridan, and Mrs. Bertha Honore Potter, wife of hotel and real estate magnate Potter Palmer.[6] His Chicago friends included both the former President's son, Robert Lincoln, and Fred Grant, the son of the former Union commander in chief. In modern parlance the 33-year-old retired brigadier general and attorney was well connected.

General and Mrs. Hardin remained close to the Lincoln family. When the President's widow returned from Europe in 1871, the Hardins resumed their friendship. Tad was now a teenager and well liked, a far cry from the pesky scamp who ruled his father's heart during the war years. During General Hardin's visits with President Lincoln in the White House in 1864–1865, he probably became well acquainted with young Tad.

Mrs. Lincoln was still ravaged by unrelenting grief at this time. Already wounded by the childhood deaths of her boys, Willie and Eddie, she had barely survived the subsequent murder of her husband. She clung to her husband's favorite child, Tad, who had matured into a caring and responsible young man and become her closest companion. Tad was his mother's security and refuge from the black plague of depression that had descended since the assassination on Good Friday, April 14, 1865.

Tad had undergone a personal transformation following his father's death. Lincoln's personal secretary John Hay remembered the boy as a terribly undisciplined brat with a contempt for books and learning. But Hay totally reversed his opinion upon Tad's return from Europe, describing him as a "cordial, frank, warm-hearted boy."[7] Perhaps the terrible emotional impact of his father's assassination and his mother's deep-seated grief had inspired Tad to throw off his impetuous nature and assume a dignified maturity.

In the summer of 1871, Mary and Tad Lincoln were living in Room 21 at the Clifton House in Chicago. Ever since returning from the Continent, the 18-year-old had been ill and suffered from a nagging cough, but still attended school and enjoyed the society of his young friends. But that summer his health deteriorated drastically, to the great alarm of Mrs. Lincoln and his older brother, Robert.[8]

General Hardin's wife, Estelle, wrote her mother-in-law, Mrs. Chancellor Walworth, back in Saratoga Springs a letter dated June 18, 1871, explaining the serious nature of Tad Lincoln's affliction: "Mrs. Lincoln and

Tad have been boarding here for a month, The Clifton House. Mrs. Lincoln asked about you and sends her love. Tad is very ill now with dropsy {probably pleurisy} on the lungs and the doctors despair of his recovery. I feel so sorry for Mrs. Lincoln. She is almost distracted with grief. She is so devoted to Tad and it seems so hard that she should have to give him up. Martin and I have been helping to nurse him. He suffers a great deal but is very patient."[9]

Chicago's most eminent physicians attended Tad in those last days, but they were helpless to treat the viral infection, which was probably a symptom of tuberculosis contracted years before. This would have explained his frequent bronchial complaints and bouts of sickness that had gone on for some time.

Tad Lincoln suffered intensely, but bore his trials with a commendable stoicism. Supreme Court Judge David Davis, his father's old friend and the executer of his will, visited the boy during his final days, writing: "Tadd {sic} Lincoln is dangerously ill. If he recovers, it will be almost a miracle. The disease is dropsy on the chest. He has been compelled to sit upright in a chair for upwards of a month. His mother is in great affliction. I saw him and her on Saturday—it made me feel very sad. He seems a warm hearted youth."[10]

At 4:30 a.m., Saturday, July 15, 1871, Tad's condition perceptibly worsened. His older brother, Robert, was called from his Wabash home. He stood by the bed with his mother, Mary Todd, and the Reverend D. John Howe Brown, past of the Presbyterian Church. Concerned friends and neighbors, perhaps including General Hardin and his wife, crowded the parlor, hallways and staircase.

At 7:30 a.m., Tad "suddenly threw himself forward . . . and was gone."[11]

Looking back on how President Lincoln had so loved Tad, former secretary John Hay wrote a moving tribute in the pages of the *New York Tribune* dedicated to the "tricky little sprite who gave to that sad and solemn White House of the great war—the only comic relief it knew."[12]

General and Mrs. Hardin, had barely recovered from the tragedy of Tad's death when they and the other 300,000 residents of Chicago were confronted with a calamity of much greater proportions. A fire began in a barn on the city's south side and quickly spread, feeding on the wooden shacks of the poor. The lake winds whipped up the flames and the city's volunteer fire companies were nearly helpless in the face of the firestorm.[13]

Even the Chicago River failed to block the progress of the insatiable inferno. The lake wind carried a storm of sparks and burning debris across the river to the north bank, igniting the houses and businesses there, which soon burned like torches. The city's downtown business district and the residences of the wealthy were now at risk. General Hardin's mentor, Jonathan Youth Scammon's palatial mansion overlooking the lake on Terrace Row, was just one residence consumed in the flames. Luckily, his wife, Maria, had piled many of their valuable books and other treasures into wagons before fleeing from the oncoming blaze.

Before the fire finally died out, General Hardin's friend Robert Lincoln was one of thousands who lost their homes to the conflagration. *The Chicago Tribune* offices, the Tremont Hotel, and the famed Palmer House Hotel all burned. Thousands of Chicagoans—perhaps including Mary Todd Lincoln—sought refuge on the beaches fronting Lake Michigan. Frantic to escape the incredible oven-like heat, some families waded or swam out into the water. Others actually burrowed into the sand in their desperation.

The survivors, including General and Mrs. Hardin, awoke to total devastation. More than half the city was smoldering ruins, a mile wide and four miles in length. Approximately 18,000 buildings were destroyed, 300 people died, and three out of every four Chicagoans were homeless. "Our beautiful city is in ruins," William H. Carter, president of the city's board of public works, wrote his brother. "It went up in a cloud of fire, and desolation is all around us."[14]

Robert Todd Lincoln lost his entire law library and his comfortable home at 635 Wabash. Landmarks like the Crosby Opera House were burned to the ground. The *Chicago Tribune* offices went up in flames, and two days passed before they could print an edition reporting the Great Chicago Fire of 1871.[15]

Not only had General Hardin's residence and State Street office been burned out, but the flames had destroyed a valuable commemorative sword presented to Martin as a boy by the State of Illinois honoring his father's death in the Battle of Buena Vista. But the like the city of Chicago itself, General Hardin and his wife put the great fire behind them and began rebuilding the dream.

Chicago rose from the ashes like the Phoenix of old. A new, bigger and more modern city took shape in a few short years, bold and full of braggadocio, and teeming with ambitious, industrious people consumed in pursuit of the American dream. This was not the Puritan vision of a "city on a hill" but a crass, vulgar and ostentatious society where money ruled supreme. It was the age of the Robber Baron and the Sweat Shop.

General and Mrs. Hardin were a part of that Gilded Age world that rose up from the ashes of the great fire, with the right social credentials to thrive in the new environment. Hardin's family connections, his status as a wounded hero of the Civil War, and his rank as a retired one-star general, gave him a passport to Chicago's inner circles where fortunes were to be made. He and his wife became members of the elite who ruled the new post–Civil War America, an indulgent epoch which took its name from the 1873 book by Mark Twain and Dudley Pope, *The Gilded Age*.[16]

Although General Hardin never enjoyed the wealth of this inner ring of industrial giants, his lucrative law practice throughout the 1870s provided him with a very comfortable life. He became a member of the exclusive Chicago Literary Club, the Chicago Historical Society, the Chicago Catholic Library Board, the Chicago Saddle and Cycle Club and the Metropolitan Club. These were exclusive institutions whose membership included the cream of Chicago's society.[17]

General Hardin stood, in one sense, apart from many of his contemporaries because of his war service and sacrifice. Certainly, the great business titans of the Gilded Age had been, for the most part, bystanders during the war, in which they reaped millions in profits manufacturing guns, selling grain and beef, and making uniforms for the troops. These Robber Barons became fabulously wealthy while the rest of their generation fought, bled and died from Bull Run to Five Forks.

Financier J.P. Morgan, railroad king Jay Gould, Chicago's meat-packing millionaire Philip Armour, oil-man John D. Rockefeller, future president Grover Cleveland, and railroad car manufacturer George Pullman were among the many wealthy elite who had paid $300 for a substitute during the draft to legally avoid service. In the post-war years, these men built pleasure palaces at Newport and played croquet on manicured lawns, while thousands of crippled, limbless or blind veterans begged for pennies on the streets of Chicago, New York and Philadelphia.

Hardin was poised to benefit from his associations with all the right people, and the promise of the good life beckoned. However, this pleasant dream was soon to dissolve into a terrible nightmare of murder involving his beloved sister and her family. Newspapers across the nation reported every detail of the lurid scandal called The Walworth Parricide.[18]

CHAPTER 25

MADNESS, MURDER
AND SCANDAL, 1873

"HAVE SHOT FATHER THIS MORNING.
LOOK AFTER MOTHER. FRANK
WALWORTH."[1]

This stunning ten-word telegram was sent June 3, 1873 and addressed to Father Clarence Walworth in Albany, New York, and to General Martin D. Hardin in Chicago. The sender, their 19-year-old nephew, Frank Hardin Walworth, had only minutes before murdered his father, Mansfield Tracy Walworth, in a New York City hotel room.

General Hardin departed Chicago almost immediately by train to meet with his distraught widowed sister, Ellen, and other members of the Hardin/Walworth clan in New York City. Frank Walworth was being held in a notorious prison called The Tombs prior to his trial for murder. The family came together to deal with this incredible tragedy and its potentially fatal denoument. Soon they learned the stark and terrible details of what had transpired.

Around 6:20 a.m., Tuesday, June 3, the hotel desk clerk at New York City's Sturtevant House Hotel heard loud voices, then four shots in succession, followed by the cry, "Murder!"

Frank Walworth appeared at the front desk directly afterwards, saying calmly: "I have shot my father, and want a policeman."[2]

The incredulous desk clerk responded: "You don't mean you have shot your father?"

"Yes, I have shot him four times," Frank Walworth replied in a composed voice.³ A bellboy was sent for the police who arrived minutes later. Taking a revolver from his jacket pocket, Frank handed it to the officer, saying: "This is the pistol I shot him with."⁴

Before Frank had taken the train from Saratoga Springs to New York City, he had written a letter to to his uncle, Clarence Walworth in Albany. His father's older brother had been like a father to Frank, and he had only recently asked him to accompany him on a projected trip around the world. Frank's letter read in part: "It would be neither safe nor wise to leave mother unproteced from father's acts, and I think that her condition is far from safe. . . . I am going to New York in the morning to try to see him, and I may add, without informing mother, for she would feel very uneasy. My trip will determine any question in regard to my trip to Europe."⁵

For many months Frank had been intercepting threatening letters written by his father who appeared dangerously psychotic. Much of his rage was directed at his late father, Chancellor Walworth, who Mansfield felt had shortchanged him in his will in 1867. As he brooded about this alleged injustice he became obsessed, convinced that his wife, Ellen, was turning the children against him. Increasingly, he saw all the Hardin family—Ellen, Martin and Lemuel—as enemies acting in concert to rob him of his inheritance and the love of his children.⁶

Frank's fateful trip to New York was triggered by the contents of his father's most recent letter, in which he had written: "God is my lawyer!" Mansfield threatened Ellen repeatedly in these letters, saying, "Keep Frank Walworth out of my way; You have taught him to hate me."⁷ In another brutal note, the brooding Mansfield made an even more explicit threat: "You are pushing your doom. . . . All the intensity of hate in my life is centered on you. Listen for the crack of the pistol."⁸

Mansfield Tracy Walworth was determined to intimidate Ellen into signing a legal settlement giving him access to the Chancellor's inheritance. "I went to kill you . . . ; that door chain alone saved you. If you do not sign the papers your lawyer says he sent you . . . I shall shoot you. You are dealing with a despairing, demoniacal murderer, or whatever despair makes a man. Sign damn quick."⁹

Nineteen-year-old Frank took these threats seriously and pledged to defend his mother's honor and physical safety. That astute observer of the age, George Templeton Strong, had practiced law in Chancellor Walworth's court, and knew that son whom he dismissed as, " . . . an unprecedented compound of lunatic, beast, and devil."[10]

It was a blessing that the old Chancellor didn't live to witness the final chapter of his youngest son's life. Never very emotionally stable, Mansfield sank deep into madness, obsessing on what he perceived as his father's betrayal. In his delusional state, Mansfield focused his violent hatred on his wife, Ellen, and the Hardin family. He became convinced they had all conspired with the Chancellor and his older brother, Clarence, to defraud him of his inheritance. As always Mansfield was simultaneously the hero and victim of his own story.

The son of the esteemed Last Chancellor of New York, the handsome novelist and lady's man was also delusional and dangerous.

Outside of Ellen, no one had more direct knowledge of that chilling fact than Mansfield's stepbrother, General Hardin. Early in 1871, he came to Saratoga Springs to assist his sister in obtaining a limited divorce. This followed an episode during which Mansfield had beaten Ellen and then bit one of her fingers to the bone. Teenager Frank had intervened and probably saved his mother from even more serious injury.[11]

The savage attack was a watershed. Ellen now wanted a divorce, no matter that during that time, place and social circle, such an act was rarely countenanced by polite society no matter what the reason. Her brother, General Hardin, soon came to Saratoga Springs and took rooms at the Hoffman House Hotel. Upon his sister's request, he assembled a team of lawyers to draw up the necessary papers.

At 4 a.m., General Hardin was sleeping in bed while the lawyers continued their discussion. That's when they heard loud pounding on the door. One lawyer opened the door and Mansfield Walworth strode into the room and moved quickly toward Martin's bed. Now wide awake, the General sat up and saw the agitation on the face of his unstable brother-in-law.[12]

Pulling a revolver from under his coat, Mansfield demanded to know the whereabouts of his wife and children. The man was in the throes of a terrible frenzy. Mansfield had Hardin by the collar and pressed the gun barrel against his neck, shouting threats. Suddenly, the one-armed general punched Walworth and the revolver flew out of his hand. While Walworth scrambled to retrieve the gun, Hardin bolted for the door.[13]

The General tried to slam the bedroom door shut behind him, but

Mansfield shoved it open. Hardin then ran down the hall shouting, closely pursued by Walworth, pistol in hand. Luckily, a policeman and a porter heard the shouting, seized Walworth, and disarmed him.

Roused from their sleep by the commotion, the hallway was soon crowded with people. Mansfield was taken into temporary custody, and apparently the family was able to keep the incident out of the newspapers. Surely Saratoga Springs gossips quickly spread the details of this shocking family drama, but the hubbub was nothing compared to what followed several years later.[14]

One can't help but assume that Martin Hardin must have looked back on this close call with a certain irony. How strange that a soldier who had twice been on death's door from combat wounds should then come so perilously close to being murdered by his deranged stepbrother and brother-in-law? The incident certainly proved beyond doubt that Mansfield Walworth was a very dangerous man.

The courts granted Ellen a limited divorce on April 8, 1871. But the likelihood of further violence from Mansfield was an ever-present danger. Soon he began writing her the threatening letters.

Having been a principal agent in the divorce proceedings, it's hard to believe that General Hardin was totally shocked when he received his nephew's telegram less than two years later confessing to patricide. Hardin would support his sister and nephew in this crisis and endure with them the embarrassment of seeing the family tragedy spread across the nation's newspapers. The Walworth Patricide was heavily covered by the *New York Times*, *Brooklyn Eagle*, *New York Tribune*, *New York Sun*, the *Nation*, *Frank Leslie's Illustrated Newspaper* and *Harper's Weekly*.

Spectators jammed the courtroom when Frank's trial began, eager to enjoy the high drama of two socially prominent families entangled in a web of sex, madness, murder and adultery. Some of the regulars hadn't missed a murder trial in a decade. They came today to see Mrs. Mansfield Hardin Walworth, the widow of the murder victim and the mother of the accused murderer, appear on center stage in a drama worthy of Shakespeare. She sat, straight and proud each day with her older brother General Hardin, step-brother Father Clarence Walworth, younger brother, attorney Lemuel Hardin of Louisville, various other family members, and, of course, Dolly Smith, the faithful family retainer.[15]

Presiding from the bench was Justice John Noah Davis. Young Frank Walworth was represented by a three-lawyer defense team led by Charles O'Conor, a long-time friend and political ally of the late Chancellor Walworth. Leading the prosecution was District Attorney Benjamin Phelps assisted by Daniel Rolins. These were all tested veterans of the legal wars and familiar to the judicial aficionados who thronged to the high profile trial.[16]

Defense attorney O'Conor had firsthand knowledge of the slain Mansfield Hardin's character and held a deep contempt for the Chancellor's youngest son: "I knew {Mansfield} Walworth well . . . It was scarcely possible to conceive of a worse man; he was bad in grain, and his badness was the more contemptible because it was united to a character that was very frivolous and inane."[17]

Right from the beginning, Defense Attorney O'Conor set about putting the murder victim on trial, knowing that his only hope was to convince the jury that the murder victim was a maniac who deserved killing. Achieving that end was made much easier when O'Conor was allowed to enter into evidence the threatening letters the man had sent his wife over the past several years. Fellow defense attorney Edward Beach described them accurately as demonic.[18] For two and a half hours Mansfield's letters were read in open court, creating a sensation among the listeners. The effect was as if the demented Mansfield Tracy Walworth were present in court testifying at his trial from the grave.

Ellen Hardin Walworth became increasingly distraught at hearing her husband's crazed threats read aloud in public. Before O'Conor finished reading, she left the courtroom on the arm of her servant, Dolly Smith. Few present that day could not have felt pity for this woman who bore with resolute dignity the incredible humiliation and invasion of privacy.

The audience was stunned when they heard the dead man's threats:

"The pistols are loaded. I shall blow out your brains, and my own, too."

"I am hungry to lap my tongue in salt blood."[19, 20]

On and on, the jury and those present were mesmerized by the words of the madman read by Defense Attorney O'Conor. They heard Mansfield threaten to "spatter her brains," condemn his own father as a "dead scoundrel dog!" and swear to murder his children in revenge upon the Chancellor and his wife for their betrayal.[21]

This was in stark contrast to the portrait of the madman's son presented by the defense. One character witness for Frank Hardin Walworth told the judge and jury that the accused possessed, "amiability, pleasantness of temper and great affection for his mother."[22] Father Walworth, the well-known and respected Catholic clergyman and uncle of the accused, also testified: "He has been very kind, very gentle and courteous."[23]

General Hardin was also called to the witness stand where he answered questions about the Saratoga Springs Hotel incident when Mansfield Walworth burst into his room with gun in hand, "very much excited." Martin's younger brother, Lemuel, the former Confederate soldier, also appeared on the witness stand swearing to his nephew's high character, describing him as "the best boy I ever knew."[24]

The prosecution countered with various witnesses who testified that they had found the late Mansfield Tracy Walworth to be a gentleman and a respected member of the literary world. At the same time, several newspaper reporters presented the alleged murderer in an extremely negative light. Notably the *Brooklyn Eagle* was most severe in its description of young Frank: "A disdainful, haughty look rests upon his features continually. His general appearance conveys the impression that he is an excessively egotistical and conceited youth, who imagines he is a moral hero."[25]

O'Conor simultaneously pursued another strategy, calling to the stand various witnesses who testified to Frank Walworth's recent forgetfulness, distracted behavior, loss of interest in favorite pursuits, night terrors, frothing at the mouth, convulsions and symptoms of epilepsy. Finally, O'Conner asked expert witness Dr. Grant: "Under the influence of epileptic mania is there consciousness or will?" The answer: "Not when fully under the influence of the mania."[26]

The defense then called Dr. John Gray, superintendent of the State Lunatic Asylum at Utica, New York, and editor of the *American Journal of Insanity,* as an expert witness. Both the defense and prosecution questioned Dr. Gray for several hours with mixed results. On one hand, Gray stated that the condition brought with it, in certain cases, homicidal mania. At the same time, when asked by the prosecution directly if he thought Frank Walworth had killed his father during an epileptic fit, Dr. Gray equivocated, pointing out he lacked the ability to diagnose Frank's symptoms on the morning of the murder.[27]

Defense Attorney O'Conor was under no illusions about Frank Walworth's chances. He was fighting an uphill battle to save the boy from the hangman. Many people were deeply revolted at the very idea of a son shooting down a father in cold blood, no matter what the provocation. The sin of patricide threw a dark shadow over the entire proceeding.

O'Conor knew that he had to impress upon the jury that Mansfield Tracy Walworth had never been a father, in the normal definition of the word. He was, instead, a Frankenstein who was stalking young Frank's beloved, often brutalized mother.

"From the time of the separation Frank only knew his father as a fierce, desperate man, there being no evidence that his father had ever addressed to him one single kind word, or even did a single act of affection or regard for his son. He knew him not as a father, except by report. He had never received a father's treatment from him."[28]

In his three hour and thirty-three minute closing argument to the jury, O'Conor stressed that there was no evidence indicating that Frank had gone to New York City with cold-blooded intent to murder his father. He hammered home on the theme that the boy was only concerned about his mother's safety and knew full well his father's violent tendencies and his habit of going armed. He also reminded the jury that if they had the least doubt of Frank's sanity at the time of the murder, they must acquit.

District Attorney Phelps took two and a half hours in his final statement. He reminded the jury to look beyond obfuscations, which he claimed never addressed the uncontested fact that the son had cold-bloodedly and without remorse shot his father to death. The prosecutor went on to dismiss Mansfield's threatening letters, claiming that no one in the Hardin/Walworth family took them seriously. And regarding suggestions of Frank Walworth's insanity or epilepsy, Phelps noted that these remained unproven.[29]

The defense, Phelps stated, had made much of young Frank's positive virtues as compared with his father's obvious character flaws, but contended strongly that these facts were irrelevant to the charge of murder. The Prosecutor pleaded with the jury to keep their eyes focused on the simple, uncontested facts of the case: An unarmed man had been shot to death in cold blood by his son and the killer must pay the penalty.

Judge Davis was not to be outdone and spent three hours reviewing the case, explaining the intricate details of insanity as a defense, the laws of self-defense, and—most importantly—explained in detail a new state law allowing the jury to convict the accused of second-degree murder. The judge emphasized that this new law could be applied if the jury believed there had been no deliberation or premeditation.[30]

After Judge Davis charged the jury, they departed the courtroom at 4:30 p.m. to deliberate, returning around 7 p.m. with their judgment. The defendant sat next to his mother, with his little brother Tracy at his side. Clustered around were General Hardin, Lemuel Hardin, Father Walworth and other family members.

"Guilty in the second degree," the jury foreman announced.

The court clerk, asked: "Guilty of what?"

"Of murder in the second degree."[31]

Frank Walworth was saved from the hangman. Reporters noted that he smiled at the news and that his mother seemed intensely relieved. Some days later, they returned to the courtroom to hear Judge Davis pronounce the sentence: "The sentence of the Court is that you be imprisoned in the State Prison at Sing Sing, at hard labor, for the full term of your natural life."[32]

From that day forward, Frank's mother never relented in her efforts to secure her son's freedom. In August 1877, New York Governor Lucius Robinson, who had practiced in Chancellor Walworth's court years before, unconditionally pardoned Frank Walworth.[33]

Incredibly, General Hardin's long-abused and suffering sister, Ellen, rbegan to flourish after the humiliation of the murder trial and her son's subsequent imprisonment. In the decades to come she made a mark as an attorney, educator, author, Spanish-American War nurse, historian and suffragette. In 1891 she was one of the four founders of the Daughters of the American Revolution (DAR) and was the first editor of the DAR publication, *American Monthly Magazine*.[34]

Perhaps her crowning, overarching success was serving as an eloquent and passionate advocate for the preservation of historic places and the creation of an American national archives. In many ways, General Hardin's sister proved his equal in courage, conviction and resilience. After all, she was a Hardin and her father's favored child. Getting by was always a challenge. Ellen had meantime transformed the Pine Grove Mansion into a boarding school for the privileged, acting as teacher and principal.

After securing his freedom, Ellen's son taught sporadically at his mother's school and earned a degree in law, but never seriously practiced. He did devote a great deal of time to archery and ultimately won national recognition for his skill; he also became an enthusiastic "Wheelman" (bicyclist), peddling for hours at a time about the New York countryside.

Frank Hardin Walworth married Corinne Bramlette, the daughter of Kentucky's wartime governor, on December 20, 1883. Three years later, Corinne gave birth to Clara Grant Walworth. The new father died in October of the same year of Clara's birth, the cause being acute bronchitis. In his mother's eyes Frank, in the final analysis, was a disappointment, a purposeless idler who never achieved his potential. Frank's death came a few years after his younger brother, Tracy Walworth, Jr., suffered a nervous breakdown; he, too, was unsuited to the world and, became increasingly unstable with tragic consequences in the distant future.[35]

By now, Ellen was morally repelled both by Father Clarence Walworth and the Roman Catholic religion. She was outraged when her daughter, Clara, entered the convent to become a nun, convinced that the young girl had been manipulated into that life by Father Walworth. The widow of Mansfield Tracy Walworth was certain that the charismatic priest had stolen Clara's sister, Ellen "Nelly" Hardin, from her as well, when that daughter chose to devote her life to Uncle Clarence, acting as life companion, secretary, nurse and, finally, biographer.[36]

Despite her public successes as a historian, educator, attorney and historic preservationist, Ellen was increasingly isolated and alienated from all her children except for the youngest girl, Reubena Hyde Walworth, an apparently charming, talented and educated woman who became her mother's joy. This happiness, as events soon revealed, would also succumb to misfortune.

General Hardin occasionally provided his sister with financial assistance and befriended her children, but certainly didn't share her detestation of Father Walworth and the Roman Catholic Church.[37] But, whatever their differences, the brother and sister apparently never severed their ties of affection; they remained close until Ellen, a bitter, lonely old woman in black, died in 1915.

After the trial of his nephew Frank in New York City, General Hardin returned to Chicago to resume his post-war career. No doubt he hoped that the future held the hope of better times for the entire family. During the next tumultuous decades, his hopes became reality. General and Mrs. Hardin enjoyed a happy and prosperous life in the booming city by the lake.

CHAPTER 26

GENERAL HARDIN—
GILDED AGE PRINCE

Attorney Hardin began a steady climb in Chicago's legal circles. The affable and handsome retired brigadier general knew all the best people, belonged to all the right clubs, and was recognized as the heroic protégé of the martyred President Lincoln. Even in civilian clothes, Hardin's empty left sleeve gave mute but eloquent testimony to his battlefield heroics, and served as a passport to the highest circles of Chicago's Gilded Age elite.

The Hardin family persevered and, if anything, became closer in the wake of Mansfield Tracy Walworth's murder. This was very much a family of writers. Ellen Hardin Walworth wrote an unpublished novel, but was more successful with her non-fiction efforts. The youngest sibling, attorney Lemuel Smith Hardin, eventually left the practice of the law to embark on a full-time editorial career in agricultural journalism.[1]

General Hardin's niece, "Nelly" Walworth, became a writer when she was still her in her teens. After her brother Frank's trial. Nelly took his place at Father Walworth's side during the projected trip around the world. The 15-year-old sent back regular descriptive letters of her travels each week, which her mother arranged to be published as an ongoing series in the *Albany Sunday Press*. These travel letters were later published in book form under the title, *An Old World As Seen Through Young Eyes or Travels Around The World*.[2] In early 1877, with Father Walworth's encouragement and oversight, Nelly, only 19, wrote a biography of a Catholic Native-American Saint: *The Life and Times of Kateri Tekakwitha: The Lilly of the Mohawks*.[3]

General Hardin was delighted with his niece's literary success and set about helping her market the book in the Midwest. He wrote his sister to that effect from his office at the Tribune Building on June 6, 1877:

> Some of my acquaintances—book dealers—advised me to get T.D. Lautry of this city to interest himself in the tale of Nellie's book, he having good facilities for disposing of such a book through canvassers. . . . He is principal dealer in Catholic books in this city & has connections in Milwaukee. . . . I saw Mr. Lautry today. He said he would be very glad to take hold of the book if he could make satisfactory terms with Sadlier & Co. {New York publishers} to whom he said he would write at once. . . . Of course I am not acquainted with the book business but it seemed to me that this was a fair opportunity for getting Nellie's book before the people in this part of the country. . . . Please send me {reviews?} as soon as any are printed in the Eastern papers. Love to all, Your Affectionate Brother, M.D. Hardin.[4]

Meanwhile Hardin's career as an attorney gained momentum. Within a few years he left the law firm of Scammon, McCagg and Fuller and became a full partner in the firm of Caufield, Hardin and Patton. Later this law firm became Hardin and Patton, Attorneys At Law. Initially, General and Mrs. Hardin resided at 1426 State Street; later they moved to 538 State Street, both addresses in the very heart of Chicago's business district.

Religion was central to General and Mrs. Hardin. They were very active in the Chicago Catholic community, and faithfully attended Sunday Mass at the city's cavernous Holy Name Cathedral. Hardin also served as attorney for the Chicago Arch-Diocese, a prestigious and well-paid position, and did volunteer work for the Catholic library system. Even his mother, Sarah Hardin Walworth, who had expressed her dislike and distrust of Rome's corps of priests and nuns, eventually converted to Roman Catholicism.[5]

Many of attorney Hardin's legal clients were military men stationed at what later came to be called Fort Sheridan in the northern Chicago suburbs. These included General Philip Sheridan, the famed Union cavalry leader, and his younger brother, Colonel Michael Sheridan. Hardin was particularly close to Michael, and the two went on to enjoy a friendship long into the next century. Fred Grant, the son of General and President U.S. Grant, was another Hardin acquaintance. Martin's journal of Friday, November 14, 1879, includes this notation: "Attended reception at Fred Grant's at Chicago Club."[6]

Most prominently in the circle of Hardin's Chicago friends was fellow attorney Robert Todd Lincoln. This connection had only grown stronger when Martin and his wife helped nursed Robert's younger brother, Tad, during his terminal illness. General Hardin's relationship with Lincoln's surviving son was close enough that he made the following note in his office journal: "Told Robt. Lincoln to propose my name for member of Chicago Historical Society."[7]

The Chicago Historical Society membership list was a microcosm of the city's business and government elite. Membership could unlock the doors to personal advancement for a young attorney like Hardin. Aside from Robert Lincoln, some of the more prominent members included Mrs. Potter Palmer, Mrs. George M. Pullman, famed retailer Marshall Field, Philip D. Armour, James Deering and General Mason Brayman. J. Young Scammon, Hardin's original legal mentor in the city, had helped found the Society in 1856.

Thanks to Robert Todd Lincoln's sponsorship, General Hardin became a member of the Society on November 22, 1879, and would remain a member until his death 45 years later. Hardin didn't join simply for the social and business contacts; he harbored a decided interest in American history throughout his life, not surprisingly since many of his ancestors had played important roles in the story of the nation.

In 1880 General Hardin sent out a form letter to various Hardin family members soliciting information preparatory to publishing a family geneal-ogy. This appears to have been a joint project with his sister Ellen. Unfor-tunately, the projected genealogy was never completed. But Hardin did eloquently express in the Jan. 1, 1880 letter to extended family members his deep pride in their shared American ancestry:

> The Hardins have been foremost as settlers of the Great West. Towns and counties in many of the Western States have been named for them. As planters, lawyers, soldiers and honest politi-cians, they have, for more than a hundred years, held an enviable

place in the annals of our country. That they still retain the traits of the original founder Le Hardi, the bold, the courageous, the venturesome, with the corresponding traits of truthfulness and honesty is proved by the distinguished positions held by many of them in our day.[8]

Ellen Hardin Walworth came to Chicago in the winter of 1879 to research a projected biography of their father, Colonel John J. Hardin, and a history of the Hardin family. Her brother noted in his journal for December 4 how he and Ellen visited the *Chicago Journal* editorial offices and borrowed the bound volumes for 1844, 1845 and 1846 for that purpose. Ellen took several volumes to her room at the Palmer House to study at leisure.[9] Although Ellen went on to publish a number of books and historical articles, she never succeeded in her long-term goal to write a biography of her father.

Four days after visiting the newspaper offices with his sister, Martin noted in his journal: "Called on Gordon {sometime spelled Gurdon} Hubbard & had a talk about history of Ills {Illinois}."[10] This interview was probably General Hardin's effort to assist his sister's research on the life of their father. Gordon Hubbard, 77 when interviewed by General Hardin, had served in the Black Hawk War at the same time as his father. Hubbard also served as an aide to one of John J. Hardin's closest friends, Illinois Governor Duncan. Hubbard doubtless knew the elder Hardin at that time, or later when they served in the Illinois legislature.[11]

What stories Hubbard might have told General Hardin that day. The old man had come to Chicago at age 16 in 1818 as an employee of the American Fur Company, when the settlement consisted only of Fort Dearborn and two or three log cabins outside the palisade. Over the next decade young Hubbard endured "privations, toils and certain perils" in the Illinois Country where he became legendary for "wonderful courage, judgment and skill," according to an early Chicago history.[12]

A few days later, General Hardin recorded further historical investigation in his journal, writing: "Worked at making list of books of history of northwest. Was told that Genl. Sheridan called in my absence."[13] Some years earlier, attorney Hardin had investigated the reputation of a family renting a home from Sheridan, whose character had been called into question. For many years he was also the attorney for Bishop Foley, Catholic Bishop of Chicago.

A century before the invention of the term "networking," General Hardin was apparently adept in its practice. He was a joiner, and over the years became active in the Chicago Saddle and Cycle Club, the Chicago Literary Society, the Union League, Chicago Art Institute, the Grand Army of the Republic (GAR), the Chicago Historical Society and the Military Order of the Loyal Legion of the United States (MOLLUS). In the spring of 1879, Hardin became Commander of the Illinois MOLLUS chapter. He also became the Illinois GAR State Commander in 1882. Later affiliations included: the St. Augustine Yacht Club, the St. Augustine Country Club, Owentsia Country Club in Lake Forest, Illinois, the Army and Navy Club of Washington, D.C., as well as Washington's Metropolitan Club.[14]

Although General Hardin enjoyed society and felt at home in the world of bridge parties, golf, concerts, balls and formal dinners, he had another more studious side. That aspect of his persona led the General to join the Chicago Literary Society in 1877 where members met weekly to discuss literature and history, and also to benefit from lectures on the important economic, political and scientific issues of the day.

The Chicago Literary Society was among the most selective clubs in the city. Founded in 1874, it immediately attracted a stellar membership, eventually including educator William Rainey Harper, publisher/bookseller Alexander McClurg, Robert Todd Lincoln, General Sheridan, and reaper manufacturer Cyrus McCormick. Club historian Frederick William Gookin asserted that the club quickly "acquired the reputation of being the most exclusive and difficult to gain access to of any city."[15]

One didn't just apply to be a member. Only a serving member could sponsor a new member for consideration, and—even then—some were turned away. General Hardin was nominated for membership in 1877 and remained active in the Society until his death. Over the years, Hardin presented a variety of papers including: "The Failure of the American System of Education and Its Cause," Political and Social Life in Illinois in the Thirties," "The Labor Question," "Life On A Remote Army Post in 1860," "The Treatment of Malaria," and "Army Experiences."[16]

Following Hardin's death in 1923, one of his fellow Chicago Literary Club members recalled him as, " . . . a man of keen intelligence and always deeply interested in current social and economic questions . . . noted for his military bearing, affability, and steady independence of mind."[17] In the early 1880s, Hardin embarked on a course of self-improvement, outlining a rigorous curriculum including Spanish, history, philosophy, the Roman Catholic Church, Latin classics and English literature. At the same time, the West Point graduate kept up with the latest developments in military tactics and armaments.

His life as a lawyer and a prominent member of society fed off each other in a mutually beneficial manner. Mrs. Bertha Mathilde Honore Palmer, the reigning "Queen of Chicago Society," was both a friend and a client. This formidable woman was the young wife of millionaire Potter Palmer, owner of the Palmer House Hotel, real estate magnate, and war profiteer. Mrs. Palmer was partial to the military and this may have been a major factor in her decision to employ General Hardin in regard to several legal matters.[18] As the first lady of Chicago, Mrs. Palmer enjoyed dazzling the public with her expensive jewelry displayed while in the company of distinguished officers wearing stars on their shoulders.

"The military note was strong in Mrs. Palmer's circle," wrote her biographer, Ishbel Ross. "Generals were much in evidence at her gatherings. General Phil H. Sheridan was always an honored guest and on more than one occasion she led the main column of the Charity Ball on the arm of General Nelson A. Miles." It certainly didn't hurt Hardin's standing in Mrs. Palmer's eyes that he was friends with both Miles and Sheridan.[19]

Mrs. Palmer was also a Kentucky native who had come to Chicago from Louisville in 1855 and apparently never completely lost her Southern accent. She and Hardin were fellow Southerners making their way in a Yankee metropolis. This too may have been a bond. And, it didn't hurt that another Hardin friend was Captain Fred Grant, son of the President, who married Honore's sister, Ida Honore, in a lavish ceremony on October 24, 1874.[20]

Although General Hardin enjoyed society and, in time, became very at home in that rarified world, he had another more studious side. He continued to be an author specializing in military topics whose works appeared in a number of periodicals. One of his more interesting articles, titled "Across The New Northwest in 1860," was featured in the May and August 1888 issues of the *U.S. Service Magazine.*

Interestingly enough these articles were lifted almost verbatim from an abandoned autobiography Hardin had written in 1882. The surviving handwritten 110-page manuscript is preserved in the Hardin Family Archives at the Chicago Historical Society. The narrative is lively and filled with fascinating anecdotes of Hardin's life from his childhood in Jacksonville to his arrival at Fort Umpqua in Oregon Territory in 1860 after crossing the continent. For some unexplained reason, Hardin abandoned the autobiography, and never wrote, at least in detail, of his wartime exploits or his close relationship to President Lincoln and the Lincoln family. This omission is puzzling, indeed incomprehensible, especially since Hardin was very historically minded and considered himself a professional writer.[21]

General Hardin did author several monographs presented before the Illinois Commandery of the Military Order of the Loyal Legion of the United States. "The Defense of Washington Against Early's Attack in July 1864" was featured in an 1894 volume entitled, *Military Essays and Recollections, Papers Read Before the Military Order of the Loyal Legion of the United States.* Although the article provided a great deal of factual information about the raid, it ignored the human element and failed to impart to the reader the urgency and near-desperation in Washington when General Jubal Early's army appeared on its doorstep in July of 1864.[22]

Defending the military records of officers he respected was certainly a motivating factor in several of Hardin's post-war articles. "Gettysburg Not A Surprise," which appeared in the *Military Essays and Recollections: Papers Read Before the Commandery of the State of Illinois.* 1907, was a spirited defense of General Gordon Meade and the slain General John F. Reynolds. Both were Hardin's superiors and friends. As the title clearly implies, Hardin challenged the prevailing notion that the battle at Gettysburg had been essentially a blind collision of the two armies. Hardin makes a solid and strong argument that the key crossroads was considered by General Meade early on in the campaign as a likely site of the battle. Hardin's article also asserts that General Reynolds' death on the first day was the primary reason for the initial Confederate success.[23]

One of the more interesting periods during Hardin's post-war years may well have been a two-month journey to the Far West in company with his friend and former commander, General Phil Sheridan. Hardin's file at the West Point states he accompanied General Sheridan on an inspection tour in July and August of 1881, including visits to the Custer Battlefield at the Little Big Horn and to Yellowstone Park. Unfortunately, the author was unable to learn any more beyond a statement to that effect included in a January 5, 1924 letter from Major H.B. Lewis, West Point Adjutant, written to long-time Hardin friend, Nelson Thomasson of Chicago.

1882 proved a transitional year for General and Mrs. Hardin. At this point, he apparently concluded his legal career, at least as a full-time occupation. Several sources indicate this indirectly by stating his law career was only 12 years in length from its beginning in 1870. This can only be partially true since other records indicate he kept a law office in Chicago's Loop up until around 1904. The author believes that Hardin continued practicing law into the early 20th century, but only on a part-time basis.[24]

What is clear is that General Hardin's health had been, at least intermittently, poor, and significantly so in 1882 when he suffered a bout of ague (malaria), originally contracted during the Peninsula Campaign in 1862. This recurring malady led Hardin to at least taper off his legal career, and travel south each winter to rest and recuperate. At some point, his wife became chronically ill and may have contracted tuberculosis, although the exact nature of her illness remains unclear.

St. Augustine, Florida, the oldest city in the United States, became the Hardin's winter refuge in the early 1880s where they stayed at one of the hotels then catering to convalescents, many suffering from tuberculosis. It was said that the visitor to St. Augustine in those days could never get away from the sound of coughing or the sight of a patient in a wheelchair. Historian Dr. Thomas Graham of St. Augustine's Flagler College graphically described the little community as "one large sanatorium." That, however, was all about to change, and the Hardins would be witnesses to that transition brought about by oil tycoon and Rockefeller partner, Henry Flagler.

We do know that General and Estelle Hardin began leasing a modest winter cottage at 22 St. Francis Street, St. Augustine for $15 a month in 1885. The quaint two-and-a-half story corner residence was a survivor of the Spanish colonial era and had once been occupied by a Spanish army officer. The Tovar House, as it is called today, is one of the oldest structures in St. Augustine.[25]

General Hardin's health soon improved following the move. In fact, he seems to have enjoyed a robust constitution during the middle and late years of his life. In 1890, at age 53, he wrote, not without a trace of pride: "He {Hardin} is also an accomplished horseman, a good shot, an ardent and successful fisherman, and an excellent swimmer, and {fond} of mountain climbing."[26]

Their St. Augustine hideaway featured a second-floor open balcony from where the couple could sit and enjoy melodies played by the U.S. Army band across the street at the St. Francis Army Barracks. Like many St. Augustine winter residents, they surely enjoyed walking down the seawall located only a few short blocks from their cottage.

In 1885, captive Apache prisoners, including a wife of Geronimo, were installed at the nearby Castillo San Marcos, now designated Fort Marion. Old-timers recalled how the sound of the Apache dirges echoed through the old city at night. " . . . the Indians were quartered in Sibley army tents pitched side-by-side on the terreplein. At night weird and mournful sounds of Indian chants could be heard drifting over the battlements," wrote Dr. Thomas Graham in *The Awakening of St. Augustine: The Anderson Family and the Oldest City 1821–1924.*[27]

This rustic, little town was about to change thanks to a man who came there about the same time as General and Mrs. Hardin. Standard Oil partner Henry Flagler (1830–1913), began his career as an Ohio teenage store clerk sleeping under the counter. By 1885, he was one of John D. Rockefeller's major partners and a man of fabulous wealth. He was also a visionary who saw the sleepy backwater town becoming a national resort, the Newport of the South.

On December 1, 1885, Flagler and Mayor Anderson of St. Augustine presided at a ceremony commencing construction of the Ponce de Leon Hotel. This opulent structure was intended by Flagler to be the flagship resort in his grand scheme to build a string of fabulous hotels along Florida's east coast, linked together by his own personal railroad. Slumbering St. Augustine was awakening to a new era.[28]

At about the same time, General Hardin was working on his own more modest construction project. He was refurbishing Tovar House, and during the renovation he discovered several cannon balls buried in the house's masonry walls, relics of the British siege of 1740. This was especially ironic considering Hardin's own background as an artillery officer and graduate of the school of artillery at Fort Monroe, Virginia. Most fittingly, General

Hardin christened his winter residence "Casa del Canonaza" (Cannonball House).[29]

A Washington scandal almost brought General Hardin out of his pleasant semi-retirement. The management of the Soldiers' Home in Washington had come under Congressional investigation for improprieties. Secretary of War Robert Todd Lincoln, Hardin's old friend from Chicago, needed someone to clean up the mess, a man of high integrity and ideals. He turned to General (Ret.) Martin D. Hardin, the old friend of the Lincoln family.

The *Saratoga Daily Journal* ran a story in its August 29, 1886 announcing that Secretary of War Lincoln had appointed General Hardin as the new Governor of the Soldiers Home. After a brief review of Hardin's brilliant war record, the story informed readers that the stepson of the late Chancellor Walworth and son of slain Buena Vista hero Colonel John J. Hardin, "was retired after the war, and has since lived quietly at Chicago, engaged mainly in literary pursuits."[30]

In closing, the story gave what amounted to a resounding approval of Hardin's appointment: "He is a person of uncompromising integrity fitted for the position assigned him at this critical period in the history of the Soldiers' Home, the management of which, it will be remembered, was the subject of congressional investigation last winter."

Not long afterwards, Secretary of War Lincoln withdrew the nomination and retained the current Governor, despite the strong indications that wrongdoing had occurred. Politics certainly must have been at play in the decision to reverse the appointment. General Hardin once again faded back into his post-war private life.

In one sense, this incident was all to the good. General Hardin was now preoccupied with his wife's "delicate health" that slowly began eroding in the latter part of the 1880s. St. Augustine acquaintances were touched by the crippled veteran's consideration for his ailing partner. Unfortunately, Estelle Graham Hardin was terminally ill. The end came August 24, 1890 at Highland Falls, New York, a small community near West Point on the Hudson. Mrs. Hardin was taken to Saratoga Springs for burial in the family plot.[31]

Parting with his companion of 26 years was, in Hardin's own words, "a terrible blow" that left him badly shaken. He wrote a moving tribute to his late wife in 1890:

Mrs. Hardin was one of the most beautiful and intellectual women, and one of the loveliest characters of her day. She was remarkably well-read and by means of her extraordinary memory was never amiss on a quotation or a work of art. Although so usually well-informed—on account of her gentle, modest and retiring nature—few but her friends (all who knew her were friends) were aware of her accomplishments.[32]

General Hardin's close friend from his days as commander of the Twelfth Pennsylvania Reserve Regiment, Major Chill Hazzard of Monongahela City, Pennsylvania, had just returned from a reunion of the Pennsylvania Reserves in Gettysburg where he had learned of Mrs. Hardin's recent death. On September 12, 1890 Hazzard wrote his old commanding officer:

Dear General: I had received notice of the death of Mrs. Hardin from Col. Sinclair's wife at Gettysburg. She told me of it, and coupled it with such kind remarks of her whom you loved, and in such high appreciation of your devotion that I am sure the fragrance of her life and your love must have diffused itself amongst all your friends. I need not say how much I sympathize with you in this bereavement. You were anxiously asked for at Gettysburg; many of the boys were there, and many officers whose friendship you have. It was a glad occasion. . . . Did you ever recall in contemplating your bereavement of the old Oriental story, viz: A gardener once went into his vineyard, and observing that the very last of the fruit, was taken, asked angrily, "Who hath taken it?" And they said to him—"the Master, the owner of the vineyard." Now he was content. For the owner may do what he will with his own. Very sincerely yours, Chill Hazzard[33]

In his grief and mourning, General Hardin took refuge in his family. In the spring of 1892, he invited his sister, Mrs. Ellen Hardin Walworth, and her youngest daughter, Miss Reubena Hyde Walworth, to spend a holiday with him at Cannonball House in St. Augustine. They were joined by his brother Lemuel's daughters, Evelyn Hardin of New York and Mrs.

Bessie Hardin Ranney of Elizabeth, New Jersey. This family reunion was highlighted with an old-fashioned square dance held upstairs at General Hardin's winter home. The gala event was reported in the March 5, 1892 edition of St. Augustine's society newspaper, *The Tattler*:

> One of the prettiest parties given in this city in recent years was the ball given by General M.D. Hardin, in honor of his Shrove Tuesday night. The quaint old house of the General's—one of the oldest if not the very oldest—has been repaired and made thoroughly comfortable without changing any of its distinguished structures, consequently the long room used for dancing had . . . stained rafters, plain white walls, and the bare floor. . . . The other rooms and quaint old staircase are just as built one hundred years ago. These rooms were tastily decorated with flowers and ferns, adding to their quaintness.[34]

The affair was attended by a group of Army officers from nearby St. Francis Barracks, with other guests including prominent St. Augustine residents hotelier J. Arthur Seavey and John T. Dismukes, a local banker, former Confederate soldier, and a longtime friend of General Hardin. Festivities commenced at 11 p.m. with a late snack of coffee and sandwiches followed by ices and cakes. The guests "grew gay" as the evening concluded with an energetic old-time Virginia reel that, the reporter noted, "only ended as Ash Wednesday dawned."[35]

General Hardin's sister was enchanted by the little house near the ocean, which inspired her to write a poem about how "past ages whisper still" there in the old Spanish city. This piece was later published in the *New York Home Journal*. During Ellen's visit much was made of her youngest daughter Reubena, who was a striking, slender and elegant woman of ethereal beauty. Her proud mother called her, "My Little Puritan." *The Tattler* account described Reubena and her cousins as "maidens fair to see" during their visit to Uncle Martin, "that grand old veteran."[36] But Reubena was more than pretty; she was a serious-minded intellectual who earned a degree at Vassar College and was a sketch artist of decided talent.

Perhaps Ellen spoke to her brother Martin on that visit about her pride in Reubena (Ruby) and her growing bitterness toward Father Walworth, a man she once idealized but now demonized. Ellen was convinced that Father Walworth had stolen her family through manipulation and deceit.

Against Ellen's wishes, her daughter Clara Walworth had taken holy vows as a Catholic nun. Nelly, the successful young author, spent her entire life totally dedicated to Father Walworth, serving as caretaker, amanuensis and, ultimately, biographer. Her son, Tracy Mansfield, seemed a happy little fellow but with the passage of years became increasingly strange and alienated, never at home in the world. Although he attended college and was intelligent, Tracy spent years working as a caretaker at his mother's boarding school. He became withdrawn, socially awkward and lacking in goals and ambition.[37]

Ellen was convinced that her brother-in-law, the sainted Father Walworth, was in many ways just as controlling and manipulative as his murdered brother, Mansfield, her late husband and persecutor. What General Hardin felt about this development is unknown. However, it seems likely that he retained his admiration for Father Walworth. Certainly Hardin retained his own deep-seated attachment to the Catholic Church while his sister, Ellen, in her final years seems to have largely abandoned her faith.

In the face of sorrow, Ellen Hardin Walworth remained indefatigable. Ahead still lay some of her most productive years. She would eventually move to Washington where she further established a reputation as a strong, independent woman. Her sterling achievements, however, never sufficed to shield her from the effects of personal disappointment, including one final tragedy that descended with devastating consequences.

CHAPTER 27

BATTLES REFOUGHT WITH
PEN, INK AND PAPER

During his long life, General Hardin devoted significant time
and effort to historical research and writing articles, usually
on military subjects. His greatest single project was a history of his old
outfit, the Twelfth Pennsylvania Reserve Volunteer Regiment. This task
involved searching out comrades from the war and tapping the official
records then still undergoing compilation in Washington.

Like many old soldiers General Hardin was motivated by the desire to
memorialize the names, heroic actions and terrible sacrifices made by the
men he had known and led in the late war. The end result was a volume
Hardin self-published in New York City in 1890 with the rambling title:
*History of the Twelfth Regiment, Pennsylvania Reserve Volunteer Corps (41st Reg-
iment of the Line) From Its Muster into the United States Service, August 10th,
1861, to Its Muster Out, June 11, 1864.*

The 230-page history is a rare source of information on the regiment
and includes an excellent biographical section devoted to the unit's key
officers. In that sense, the work is a valuable contribution to the military
history of the Civil War, and a resource for descendants of soldiers who
served in the Twelfth Regiment. However, the work falls short as historical
narrative, and remains a "cut and paste" job of quoting official reports and
other sources at great length.

Perhaps most revealing is the author's digression in the very first pages
of his regimental history to elaborate on the significance of Confederate
General Jubal Early's raid on Washington when his army stood at the gates
of the Capital on July 11 and July 12, 1864. This episode had very little

connection with the history of the Twelfth Pennsylvania Reserve Regiment; they had been mustered out more than a month previously. It did, of course, have much to do with General Hardin, who led a division in defense of Washington; the only time as a general officer he directed troops in battle.

The only connection is that the men of the Pennsylvania Reserve Division did, in the early days of the war, construct Fort Pennsylvania on the western edge of Washington. This large fortification was later renamed Fort Reno in honor of a Union general fallen at the Battle of South Mountain. During Early's raid, General Hardin made Fort Reno his headquarters, and this fact allowed him to diverge from the regimental narrative to editorialize on why he thought that Early failed when he refrained from not attacking the Washington forts. It was almost boasting on behalf of his old regiment when he wrote: "The formidable appearance of this large fort, which was situated on a commanding eminence, dominating the country for miles in its front, had much to do with Early's failure to assault this fortified position."[1]

The remainder of the regimental history provides a detailed account of the unit's battles and marches with very little in the way of human interest. However, in certain isolated passages, the narrative does provide us with valuable insight into the author's opinions about the reasons for the war. He places a great deal of blame on the Abolitionists, viewing them as an extremist minority willing to make any sacrifice to eradicate slavery. Hardin emphasizes that the rank and file of the Union army, the men who answered the call after Fort Sumter's fall in 1861, fought to save the Union. Liberating the slaves, in Hardin's recollections, only gradually became a Union war aim.[2] In the context of his time, General Hardin was essentially a moderate on issues of slavery and race.

"Never was there greater unanimity amongst a people than existed throughout the whole North immediately after the fall of Fort Sumter," Hardin wrote. "The first military as well as political blunder of the new Administration was the failure to take advantage of this enthusiasm, that is, if the Administration were honest in its expressed desire to suppress the Rebellion as quickly as possible. So much has been written by the close friends of the Administration since the war, in regard to the freeing of the slaves, and so little in relation to the preservation of the Union, that latter always being spoken of as incidental or subordinate to the former, suspicion arises as to the honest desire of the Administration to have had the Rebellion suppressed suddenly, which, of course, would have left slavery still existing."[3]

Hardin's point is well taken. Ending slavery only became a Union priority after the intensity and length of the contest made it a military necessity. By striking at slavery, the Union undermined the very economic foundation of the Confederacy. Only with the passage of time did the North embrace anti-slavery as a higher cause and justification for the war's terrible cost. At the same time there is a greater historical awareness that the slaves played a key role in self-liberation. Long before the Emancipation Proclamation, tens of thousands of slaves abandoned their plantations and sought refuge in Union camps where they were put to work as "contrabands of war." By that very act, these slave refugees helped transform a war to preserve the Union into a revolutionary struggle for human freedom.[4]

That General Hardin held this conspiratorial view of Lincoln as late as 1890 is surprising. It seems especially incongruous since Hardin had personally known and admired Lincoln. Yet he apparently believed, or at least thought it plausible, that Lincoln refused McClellan additional troops for the Peninsula campaign only as a stalling tactic to delay the suppression of the rebellion long enough to transform the war into an anti-slavery crusade. Lincoln was certainly a shrewd politician, but hardly capable of such duplicity.

As regards, the military sphere, Hardin is essentially an apologist for his former commander, George B. McClellan. Despite being well aware of McClellan's failures as a commander and as a man—his overly cautious nature, his willingness to believe the enemy always outnumbered him, and his contempt for President Lincoln—Hardin remained convinced that the "young Napoleon" could have ended the Rebellion if he had only been provided more men. Perhaps Hardin, like so many of McClellan's soldiers, was so dazzled by the man's charisma that he excused his many flaws. The fact remains: no other commander of the Army of the Potomac ever commanded such loyalty from the troops as "Little Mac."[5]

In describing the battle of Mechanicsville outside Richmond in 1862, Hardin again emphasized that McClellan had been denied sufficient troops to accomplish the task of taking the Rebel Capital. He totally ignored his own experience at Yorktown when Hardin contended, quite rightly, that the enemy's position could have been taken by immediate assault rather than the lengthy siege ordered by his commander. "Who now doubts that if McClellan had had the reinforcements he might have received without injury to any interest, the battle of Mechanicsville would have been the prelude to the destruction of Jackson's force?"[6]

With the passage of time, General Hardin along with the other leaders of the Civil War generation, were increasingly focusing on remembering and commemorating the great struggle. The veterans in blue and gray were taking on an almost iconic stature in the national consciousness. For many, the suffering and ugly horror of the real war was fading, replaced by a pristine image of gallant soldiers embattled in a glorious crusade.

In 1888, General Hardin returned to the Gettysburg battlefield with other veterans of the Pennsylvania Reserves to dedicate various monuments to the units that fought during the pivotal battle, which resulted in nearly 50,000 casualties over three days.[7] Hardin climbed to the summit of Big Round Top where the Twelfth Pennsylvania Reserve Regiment, under his command, was entrenched on the third day of the climactic battle.

General Hardin addressed the veterans and members of their families, presenting them with an overview of the struggle, taking particular care to praise the efforts of two of his favorite commanders, the late General John Reynolds, who fell on the first day,[8] and the victor of the battle, General George Gordon Meade.[9] Both, of course, had come up through the ranks of the Pennsylvania Reserves Division, having commanded a brigade and then the division before assuming corps and army command. Many of the veterans present that day remembered both men fondly and with respect.

> It was most fortunate for the Union side that it had such intelligent and energetic generals in advance as Reynolds and Buford, generals who had the confidence of the army commander. General Meade giving General Reynolds (a fighting general) his advance with three corps proved to that general, as to the world, that General Meade was not attempting to avoid a battle, but was only anxious that the fight, which must take place, should be a defensive one on his side, if possible.[10]

330 | LINCOLN'S BOLD LION

After describing General Reynolds' tragic death on the field, Hardin told his listeners that the fallen hero "had already seized this good position, and had given such an impetus to his command, that it went on without a break, in carrying out his designs, under his able fighting successor, General Doubleday. Reynolds had planted the advance of the Union army in Lee's route, he had secured a position across all the roads leading east of the mountains at this point, a point where the Confederate army must assemble. . . . He acted as the prompt and intelligent soldier that he was."[11]

In his closing remarks, General Hardin turned to his former commander, General George Gordon Meade, praising his management of the battle, but also defending Meade against the charges that he was too timid in his pursuit of Lee's wounded army and allowed it to escape, practically unmolested, back across the Potomac River. "The criticism of General Meade for not attacking the Confederate army after Gettysburg, was refuted by subsequent events. What chance had General Meade with a force no larger than the enemy, when General Grant with more than double the enemy's force in his repeated assaults {referring to Grant's 1864 Overland Campaign} suffered such heavy losses and accomplished so little?"[12]

Only a few years later, on October 7, 1891, General Martin D. Hardin participated in Chicago's grand celebration of the unveiling of General Grant's equestrian statue in Lincoln Park overlooking Lake Michigan.[13]

The celebration began with a grand parade of more than 20,000 who marched five miles through the city to Lincoln Park. They included Regular Army units led by General Nelson A. Miles, hero of the Civil War and the post-war campaigns against the Native American tribes, and Illinois National Guard units, many civic organizations, and a vast contingent of the Grand Army of the Republic (GAR).

The streets were jammed thick with several hundred thousand cheering spectators. Cavalry soldiers pranced in review, marching bands played "Rally Round The Flag," squads of pipers squealed the martial airs of Scotland, and cannon fire rumbled in the background. American flags and patriotic bunting decorated the parade route. A contingent of 200 aging Confederate veterans marched as a unit, a symbol of the re-united nation. This was a celebration of a new nation forged in the fires of the Civil War.[14]

"The sky was gray and as cold as a soldier's fare on a forced march," the *Tribune* reporter wrote. "It was a mass of colors, natural hues principally, but with a dash of yellow, with just a little green in the hats of the Hibernian companies and the orange of the North of Ireland. Following the city police came the chief marshal, General Miles and his staff, resplendent in plumes and gold braid, and jingling with brass and steel. General Miles had beneath him a big chestnut horse . . ."[15]

The marchers formed on the right of the statue and formed ranks. General Hardin was seated with other dignitaries, including General John Schofield, Illinois Governor and former General Richard Oglesby, former General and current Illinois Senator John Logan, General Dan Butterfield, and General Horace Porter. Judge Walter Gresham gave the commemoration speech.

The colossal eight-ton bronze statue stood swathed in drapery atop a massive three-level pedestal of solid granite. The pedestal rose 42 feet from the ground; the statue itself measured eight and a half feet from the base to the crown of General Grant's campaign hat. The sculptor was Italian immigrant Louis Rebisso. His massive work was the "largest ever cast in this country."[16]

Guest of honor for the unveiling was General Grant's widow, Julia, seated immediately in front of her husband's statue beside Mr. and Mrs. Potter Palmer, who were hosting her at their palatial lakeside mansion. On the day General Grant died, July 23, 1885, Mr. Palmer had pledged $5,000 for a statue in his memory. Within four days, one hundred thousand Illinois residents pledged a total of $65,000.[17]

Out on Lake Michigan was a fleet of perhaps 200 vessels, large and small: U.S. Navy warships manned by sailors in dress uniforms, excursion steamers, tugboats streaming black plumes of smoke, fancy yachts, schooners under sail. Spectators lined the railings of this colorful flotilla.

General Grant's widow and the Palmers sat together in the immediate front of the statue, which stood nearly fifty feet above the ground. Men from Grant's first Civil War command, the Twenty-First Illinois Volunteer Infantry Regiment, were seated right behind them, their frayed and bullet-torn flag proudly carried by one of the veterans.[18] An intermittent rain spattered the crowd throughout the afternoon but failed to suppress their enthusiasm. Finally, at 4 p.m., the long-awaited unveiling occurred as vividly described by a reporter from the *Chicago Tribune*:

When the drapery that hid the statue of General Grant fell away, the warships sent forth volley after volley from their batteries, and hundreds of whistles screamed and groaned, bells rang, and the fireboats *Geyser* and *Yosemite* spouted great streams of water with a rushing, roaring sound.[19]

Julia Grant was overwhelmed with tears as she gazed at the great bronze silent soldier seated atop a magnificent steed, his eyes fixed on the distant horizon. "Mrs. Grant bowed in full view of the huge multitude," the *Tribune* reporter wrote. "The tears were running down her cheeks. She lifted to her red eyes a handkerchief bordered with black. She looked directly down from the stand where her husband's old comrades of the 21st were gathered around their historical and battered colors."[20]

After the interminable speeches, the great mass of spectators gradually dispersed. Chicago's hundreds of saloons rang with many toasts that night to General Grant and the Boys in Blue. At 50 and in good health, General Hardin could look forward to living another two or even three decades. But surely, like so many of his contemporaries, General Hardin must have concluded by then that his greatest moments, and greatest adventures, were largely relegated to the past.

CHAPTER 28

GHOST HUNTING IN OLD MEXICO

At some point, probably in 1891, General Hardin began court-ing a 28-year-old woman, Amelia McLaughlin, the daughter of Chicago's millionaire coffee dealer, William F. McLaughlin. The father was one of the resilient Chicagoans who lost so much during the Great Fire and yet rebounded in a few short years. The McLaughlins were a prominent Irish Catholic family, and the prospective bride and groom shared a deep devotion to the church.

At 7 p.m. on October 25, 1892, General Hardin and Amelia McLaugh-lin were married in a private ceremony at Chicago's Holy Name Cathedral, presided over by Cardinal James Gibbons of Baltimore, the most famous and influential Catholic prelate in the United States. The best man was Colonel Francis Crilly of Philadelphia, Hardin's West Point classmate and lifelong friend.[1] The wedding rated extensive coverage in the society section of the *Chicago Tribune*:

> The bride's gown was of heavy white satin made with a full train, a high bodice and full long sleeves. Her tulle veil was fastened with a star and aigrette of diamonds and she carried a bouquet of roses. . . . A reception was held at the residence of the bride's parents, No. 97 Rush Street, from 8 until 10 o'clock. Mrs. McLaughlin received in a gown of pearl gray silk maiden high and trimmed with point lace. Her ornaments were diamonds. Cardinal Gibbons received with Mrs. McLaughin.[2]

The reception guest list reflected the social standing of the couple.

Most prominent was Army General Nelson A. Miles, one of the outstanding "boy generals" of the Civil War, and victor of the wars against the Nez Pierce, Sioux and Apaches. In 1894, Miles would win mixed reviews when he commanded troops sent to Chicago to quell the Pullman riots.[3]

The participation of the Irish-born Cardinal James Gibbons in the Hardin wedding was another great coup. He was then and would remain for thirty years the most respected Catholic in America. His exalted place in American Catholic history was based on his acceptance of separation of church and state, his respect for all faiths, and his patriotic espousal of democratic values. Interestingly enough he had heard General Hardin's stepbrother, Father Clarence Walworth, preach and was moved by the former Paulist's eloquence.[4]

Although not famous at the time, another Hardin wedding guest would become quite well known more than a century later thanks to BBC Television. H.G. Selfridge, a partner of Marshal Field, the great Chicago retailer, was a talented and ambitious man who later moved to London where he established the incredibly successful Selfridge's Department Store.[5] He was credited, among many retail innovations, with implementing the marketing slogan: "Only {so many} days left until Christmas!" Selfridge later became the subject of a popular television series broadcast by the BBC, and later on by the American Public Broadcasting System (PBS).

Less famous, but still a powerful figure in Illinois, was Chief Justice of the Illinois Supreme Court Benjamin D. Magruder, a graduate of Yale University and a Mississippi native. He had presided over the appeal of the Haymarket Square anarchists a few years earlier, upholding the death sentences of the accused. The defendants were later pardoned by Illinois Governor Peter Atgeld, in a controversial move much resented by those who believed Magruder had "sustained the majesty of the law."[6]

If General Hardin had been financially comfortable before his marriage to the coffee heiress, he now qualified as a bona-fide member of the Gilded Age plutocracy. He and his young wife would continue spending winters in St. Augustine, but not at the modest cottage on St. Francis Street. Now they rented rooms at the palatial Ponce de Leon Hotel and socialized with the likes of Mrs. Henry Flagler, the wife of the fabulously wealthy partner of John D. Rockefeller. But before returning to winter in St. Augustine in 1893, the newly married couple set out for a six-week tour of Mexico.

Although described as a honeymoon, the trip was also a pilgrimage for Martin D. Hardin. This was a middle-aged man's effort to follow the footsteps of the father he barely remembered. Luckily, Mrs. Amelia (McLaughlin) Hardin faithfully kept a daily handwritten record of their Mexican journey, titled *Our Mexican Trip—Diary (1893)*.[7] This journal provides us not only with a record of their travels but with a few clues about General Hardin's search for his fallen father.

The trip began January 4, 1893, when Amelia's mother, father and sister, Florence, saw the couple off at the station. The travelers were surrounded by luggage, small bundles, a hat box, a lunch basket, satchels and other impedimenta. Hour after hour the steam locomotive chugged through Iowa and the Midwest, and then across Indian Territory (Oklahoma) and down to San Antonio where Martin's father had bivouacked nearly a half-century before on his way to Mexico. General Hardin and Amelia booked into a hotel and toured the sights, including the hallowed shrine of the Alamo.[8]

Martin was probably unaware during his tour of the Alamo that his father had visited the same shrine to American heroism nearly 45 years earlier. On April 27, 1846, Colonel John J. Hardin had written his sister, Martinette (Hardin) McKee in Lancaster, Kentucky, reflecting on the sad condition of the "most magnificent" ruins where the heroes of the Texas Revolution had died a decade earlier. "Think of the Alamo which Travis and Crocket have rendered immortal being used by the U.S. Gov't for blacksmith and wagon shops," he wrote.[9]

By January 9, General and Mrs. Hardin had arrived at Monterey, Mexico where they remained for several days. "Spent the morning visiting the churches, many of which are very interesting," Amelia noted in her journal. "The General had several conversations with some Jesuits who are splendid, gentlemanly men." Mrs. Hardin, however, was much taken when they witnessed an upper class bridal party emerge from the great cathedral onto the stone steps garlanded with tropical blossoms. To her, Monterey seemed a community of ancient churches set amidst a great crown of brilliantly colored flowers.[10]

Their next stop was Saltillo, where General Hardin's father and the First Illinois Volunteers under his command had bivouacked so many decades before. On that occasion, the elder Hardin had written his daughter, Ellen, noting that the ancient town was "marked by features of decay" and "built in a narrow pass or valley said to be the coldest, and most visited by high winds of any other place in Mexico."[11]

Instead of marching as did his father so long before, General and Mrs. Hardin rode the iron rails high into the mountain country of Saltillo. Amelia Hardin described the scenery as "perfectly beautiful" during the climb into the clouds. She jotted in her journal: " . . . the conductor . . . was so ragged with no shoes or stockings and great holes in his hat, that the Americans refused to hand him their fare, claiming that he was not the conductor."[12] After the General and Amelia settled into their hotel room in Saltillo, she confided to her journal that the couple "thought we were in another world and that the centuries had rolled back . . ."[13]

That evening General Hardin arranged to rent a carriage, horses and driver to carry them further south the next day to the Buena Vista battlefield, located to the south in what was essentially wilderness. On the next morning they set out traveling that same primitive road that had been taken by Martin's father and the First Illinois Regiment back in 1847. As they drove their rented buggy south through a stark and desolate landscape, Amelia reported, "The dust was blowing in sheets that we could hardly see the road before us. We were jolted over a rocky road, on the other side of which stretched the plains, so barren, so desolate, and so wild that your heart stood still."[14]

At one point General and Mrs. Hardin glimpsed in the distance riders coming directly towards them, closing the distance rapidly until Ameila could see "two fierce looking Mexicans galloping towards us." She was certain they were bandits who often did ride these bleak, forsaken badlands which seemed to her a perfect stage "for deeds of terror and crime."[15] Fortunately the bandits proved to be nothing more than two hard-working Vaqueros rounding up wild horses. Relieved, the General and Mrs. Hardin continued their jarring carriage drive though a largely uninhabited land of harsh beauty. "Occasionally we would pass a lonely looking hacienda with the Sierra Madre rising behind it, and cactus growing all around it," Amelia wrote.[16]

Finally, they arrived at the edge of the old battlefield where Martin's father had been cut down by Mexican lancers. The terrain was a stark desert, an arid moonscape riven with gullies and ravines. In Mrs. Hardin's words, the Buena Vista battlefield was "a most dreadful looking place. . . . How they ever fought there is hard to understand for the plains are very rocky; great deep gulches cut it up in every direction."[17]

In this austere, forbidding place, General Hardin sought the spirit of his fallen father, the national hero of his youth. We can only wonder at the thoughts that went through his mind, recalling his dimly remembered parent, the subject of that romantic and heroic Currier and Ives print depicting his death. Like most boys whose fathers die when they are very young, General Hardin probably retained an unrealistic image of the perfect parent and the perfect soldier.

"We climbed to the top of one of the (illegible) hills and took a photograph of the battlefield," his wife wrote. "Very glad was I to get back to the carriage and shut out the whole dismal scene."[18] They rode back to Saltillo, and if the General spoke of his visit to the battlefield, the words went unrecorded in Amelia's journal. They went to bed early in order to catch the 3 a.m. train to Mexico City. When they drove to the station in the pre-dawn, the streets were almost deserted: "As we passed through the silent streets that night we would meet now and then a figure shrouded in his serape, and carrying in his hand a lantern of a pattern that they must have used centuries ago," Amelia wrote. "It was the guardian of the peace keeping his watch on the silent city."[19]

After a day's journey by train, General and Mrs. Hardin entered the great capital of Mexico City where they spent a full week touring the grand palaces and museums, and making a special visit to Chapultepec Castle, now a Mexican national memorial dedicated to the young military cadets who defended the strongpoint to the death against the American assault in 1847. They also viewed the grand carriage of the Emperor Maximilian, the brother of Franz Joseph, Emperor of Austria-Hungary, who met death by firing squad at the end of his brief, disastrous reign.

The next leg of the journey took the Hardins by train past the great volcanoes surrounding Mexico City and to the historic city of Puebla. Amelia wrote in her diary, "The city looks prosperous, and is very clean and pretty. We went to the Hotel del Jardin (Garden), which is nicely kept, and where they set the best table of any hotel we have found in Mexico."[20]

They journeyed on to Vera Cruz on the Gulf of Mexico, a squalid place of poverty and slums Amelia found repelling. Upon leaving the port where

General Winfield Scott's little army had landed in the Mexican War, she vowed she would "never see it again!"[21] They then pushed south into the tropical region around the snow-covered heights of Orizaba. This fantastic, lush tropical garden kingdom delighted Mrs. Hardin who wrote at length of its beauty.

In her forty-page handwritten account of the Mexican trip the reader is most struck by the repeated references to attending Mass, confession, communion, meeting priests and bishops, and touring dozens of chapels, cathedrals, and holy shrines. Their honeymoon seemed in part to be a religious pilgrimage documenting the married couple's strong Roman Catholic faith.

They returned to the United States after their six-week Mexican tour, traveling back along the iron road north and looking forward to married life. That coming fall, they would be among the untold thousands who would marvel at the Great White City that had risen as if by a magic spell in Chicago's Jackson Park on the south side. Before its closing, nearly 27 million people visited the Chicago Columbian Exposition of 1893, featuring 65,000 exhibits in 200 buildings.[22]

The Columbian Exposition, dedicated to celebrating the 500-year anniversary of Christopher Columbus's first voyage to the New World, was epic in the history of the city and the nation, and become an icon of the Gilded Age. President Grover Cleveland opened the fair by touching an ivory and gold button which activated the many fountains and unfurled the various American flags and banners: "In the sunlight the white palaces shone like marble. Sunbeams glanced on the waters of the lagoon on which red, blue, or gold gondolas floated lazily back and forth," the *New York Times* reporter wrote on the fair's opening day. He proclaimed in the front-page story that the fairgrounds in Chicago's Jackson Park were "Athens and Venice and Naples in one."[23]

For General Hardin, the Columbian Exposition would mark a triumph of his long-suffering sister, Ellen Hardin Walworth. She was slated to make a historically important presentation at the Woman's Pavilion on the need for a national archive. This event was a vindication for Ellen as a woman who had devoted her life to historical scholarship and preservation.

She delivered her presentation, "The Value of a National Archives to a Nation," on July 12, 1893 to the American Historical Association meeting.

General Hardin and his wife were in attendance and invited members of the audience to attend a reception for Ellen later that day at their residence, 528 North State Street. This was undoubtedly a very happy time for the entire family who, long ago, had largely put behind them the terrible family scandal of 1873.[24]

Another presenter that day on the same stage as Ellen was Dr. Frederick Jackson Turner of the University of Wisconsin, who spoke on "The Significance of the Frontier in American History." His frontier thesis was groundbreaking, and must have been of special interest to the Hardin family members who had grown up hearing of their ancestors' dramatic roles in the westward expansion.[25]

This day in Chicago was probably the high point in Ellen Hardin Walworth's life, but at the end of the decade popularly remembered as "The Gay Nineties," she suffered an emotional blow that stole joy from the final years of her life like a bandit in the night.

At the onset of the Spanish-American War in 1898, Mrs. Walworth's youngest child, Reubena Hyde Walworth, was working as an art teacher with a degree from Vassar College. A frail, almost ethereal sprite, she soon volunteered to serve as a nurse, first at Fort Monroe in Virginia (her uncle's former duty post a half-century before), and then at Camp Wykoff, Montauk Point, Long Island. She felt compelled to volunteer and continue the Walworth-Hardin's century-plus tradition of wartime service. "I can't go and fight, but at any rate I can nurse, and I will," Ruby announced. Her mother, Ellen, also served as Directress-General of the Women's War Relief Association.[26]

Camp Wykoff on Long Island became a vast army tent hospital when thousands of soldiers came back from Cuba suffering from a battery of tropical diseases. Disease was destined to kill far more American soldiers than combat. Unfortunately, the U.S. Army Medical Corps was not up to the challenge of caring for 10,000 ill soldiers. "One hundred and fifty graves have been filled already, and the grave diggers are working steadily each day," one reporter wrote under the headline: "DAILY SCENES AT CAMP WIKOFF: The Camp Graveyard." Other reporters filed dozens of stories condemning the incompetent management of the camp, which they characterized as a national scandal. "More men Killed By Spoils System than By Spanish Bullets," headlined an editorial in the *Brooklyn Daily Eagle*, in which the author stated that the United States Army "is honeycombed with politics. Instead of being a fighting machine it has been a reservation for the friends of the men in high office."[27]

Despite her mother's pleas, Reubena volunteered to serve in the dangerous isolation ward where the worst fever cases were housed. Ellen couldn't even visit her daughter, only drive by the off-limits tent camp and wave from a distance. On this medical battlefield, General Hardin's niece showed the kind of resolve and bravery that he would have applauded. Tragically, her sterling courage led this altruistic young woman with the gentle heart of the artist to an early death. A reporter from the *New York Herald* memorialized Reubena Walworth on October 19, 1898:

> Miss Walworth refused to leave her post until the last patient had gone his way. Then she told her mother that she, too, was ill. Mrs. Walworth brought her daughter home . . . for several days, and it was then thought best to remove her to the Presbyterian Hospital. There Miss Walworth's illness developed into typhoid fever in its malignant form. Not one dreadful pang of that fearful scourge was spared her, and her suffering was very great. The courage that had sustained her while ministering to the sufferings of others did not desert her as she lay slowly dying and she was cheerful to the end . . . Her mother was with her when she died . . . [28]

Another story featured a woodcut of Nurse Walworth and declared she was descended from, "A FAMILY OF FIGHTERS":

> No hero of the war demonstrated his patriotism with more unflinching courage than did Miss Walworth. She comes of fighting stock. Her grandfather, Chancellor Reuben Walworth, the last of the Chancellors of New York, fought in the War of 1812. Her maternal grandfather, General {John J.} Hardin, was killed at the Battle of Buena Vista. Her uncle, another General {Martin D.} Hardin, was crippled for life in the civil war.[29]

Reubena's body was taken to the family plot in Saratoga Springs, where she was buried alongside her namesake grandfather, Reuben Hyde Walworth, and other members of the family. The little graveyard now was the last resting place for General Hardin's lamented first wife, Estelle Graham, his mother, his stepfather Chancellor Walworth, his friend from childhood, Dolly Smith, and his nephew, Frank Hardin Walworth. The Daughters of the American Revolution erected a monument to Reubena Hyde Walworth, but it was scant consolation for her mother Ellen, who faced a bleak and dark future without her "Little Puritan."

Hardin's good friend, Anna Marcotte, had met his sister and Reubena during their visit to St. Augustine in 1892. The editor of St. Augustine's social newspaper, *The Tattler*, eulogized Reubena, who was one of thirteen nurses who died of typhoid and yellow fever while nursing soldiers during the Spanish-American War.

> Many St. Augustine visitors and residents will recall Miss Reubena Hyde Walworth, who was here several years ago with her uncle, General Martin D. Hardin, and who gave her bright young life to her country, dying of a fever contracted at Montauk Point a year ago while nursing sick soldiers. Recently the Daughters of the American Revolution erected a monument to her memory in Greenridge Cemetery, Saratoga {Springs}, New York. . . . Mrs. Walworth was chiefly instrumental in organizing the Daughters of the American Revolution, and also was prominent in the work of aid for soldiers at Montauk.[30]

Ellen Hardin Walworth never totally recovered from the loss of her daughter, and spent the remaining 17 years of her life in black mourning: bereft, saddened and inconsolable. She described her life in the wake of Reubena's death as "a horrible waking dream."[31]

CHAPTER 29

LAY DOWN YOUR SWORD
AND SHIELD

With the turn of the new century, General Martin D. Hardin, was increasingly defined by the past and not the future. The great adventures of his youth, exploring the Far West and fighting in the Civil War, were receding in the national memory and taking on the patina of myth and legend.

General Hardin's old world was rapidly being replaced by a newer one, a veritable avalanche of progress and change. Silent films became all the rage, intrepid aviators flew flimsy kite-like aircraft high above the St. Augustine beach before crowds of gaping spectators, and young women reveled in the syncopated rhythms of Ragtime and danced the Tango. Prohibition arrived and brought with it the reign of the Bootleggers and Gangsters.

Life, however, continued much the same for General and Mrs. Hardin, despite the transformation of the nation with the arrival of a brash new century. He was witness to all the constant change but no longer a part of the process. The wounded Civil War hero, the friend and protégé of Abraham Lincoln, was a living anachronism long since sliding into comfortable obscurity.

American writer Edith W. Wharton might well have been writing about General and Mrs. Hardin and their world when she wrote these lines in her 1920 Pulitzer Prize-winning novel, *The Age of Innocence*: "Theirs was a leisured life filled with teas and dinner parties, banquets and balls, openings of operas, art and literature, polo matches and yacht races undergirded by rigid mores of propriety, ritual and fashion. . . . Commerce, not custom, is king. The old fashioned age of innocence is passing . . ."[1]

General and Mrs. Hardin led a privileged life spent summering in Chicago and wintering in St. Augustine. The winter resort was General Hardin's favorite playground. He and his young wife indulged themselves in a gilded routine of formal balls, picnics on Anastasia Island beach, sailing jaunts, horseback riding, golfing, concerts, cake walks, theater, charity benefits, and endless rounds of bridge.

They were regular winter guests at Henry Flagler's flagship hotel, the sprawling and massive Ponce de Leon, an evocation of Imperial Spain featuring the latest creature comforts for the privileged classes. Here General and Mrs. Hardin often dined with friends and finished the evening with a convivial hand of bridge, followed perhaps by a pleasant nighttime stroll down the seawall along Matanzas Bay.[2] Flagler's ornate palace was reminiscent of a boy's impressions of the Arabian Nights. Upon its opening a Vogue writer wrote: "It is as if some modern Haroun-Al-Rachid deserted his own palace and turned it into a hotel."[3]

Even as a young West Pointer, General Hardin conceded he had a taste for the good life. Certainly following his marriage to Chicago coffee heiress Amelia McLaughlin, he could afford to indulge his fancy. Meals were always a high point of the day and the chefs at the Ponce de Leon were renowned for their culinary talents.

A typical evening meal might feature up to ten courses with various options to please even a jaded Gilded Age palette. A Ponce de Leon menu from January 31, 1893 offered diners the choice of Blue Point Oysters or Little Neck Clams as an appetizer. This was followed by either a bowled of Chicken Giblet soup in heavy cream or Consomme Macaroni with noodles. Then, the diner could enjoy a Canape Madison along with sliced tomatoes, olives, salted almonds and sliced cucumbers.[4]

This was simply preparatory to the fish course featuring Boiled Sheepshead with an egg sauce complimented by Parisienne potatoes sautéed in butter, garlic and parsley. Of course, this only whetted the appetite for a serving of boiled ham in cream sauce. Now the diner could enjoy at leisure either roast loin of pork with shaker apple sauce or roast ribs of beef with a dish gravy, or roast capon with chestnut stuffing, served with green peas, boiled potatoes, sweet potatoes, sweet corn or mashed potatoes.[5]

The seventh course of the evening offered a choice of sirloin of beef, a la Flamande, Grandine of lamb, or Chicken Provençale in a delectable sauce. Now the diner was ready to cleanse the tired palette with a European liquor in preparation for the ninth and main course of Broiled English snipe on toast served with lettuce salad and red currant jelly.[6]

Diners were presented with a splendid array of desserts to complete their dining adventure: Queen Pudding, Peach Pie, or a delectable Washington Pie (Similar to Boston cream pie, but even more delectable, this sugary confection consisted of four thin layers of cake, with cooked custard between layers and topped with fresh fruit and fancy kisses); Maizena cake, Baba au Rhum (a small yeast cake soaked in rum and stuffed with whipped cream), or macaroons with vanilla ice cream.[7]

Like the other members of their class, General and Mrs. Hardin lived apart from the sordid reality of America's Gilded Age. They lived a life of indulgence and pleasure when, for most of the population, it was a time of scarcity, want and unrest. These people of the abyss, a phrase coined by novelist Jack London, lived in a different America. Their world was one of sweat shops, urban ghettos, bindle-stiffs, strike-breakers, Jim Crow, mob lynchings, 14-hour work days, and factories guarded by armed Pinkerton detectives.

Whether General or Mrs. Hardin were aware of that other America or cared about the people who lived there remains an open question. Nothing in the surviving documentation reveals a particular concern on their part, even as they lived at the time of Chicago's Hay Market Square bombing, the violent Homestead Steel Strike, the national railroad strike of 1877, and the rise of organized labor. All the glitter and gloss of the Gilded Age could not conceal the deep suffering and injustices throughout American society. Henry Adams, the descendant of two American Presidents, contemptuously dismissed the "mauve decade" toward the end of the century as a gauche and pointless era of materialism and excess.[8]

The winter society pages of the New York, Boston and Chicago newspapers from 1893 to 1923 serve as a window into the social lives of General and Mrs. Hardin. They are repeatedly mentioned in news briefs about the social gatherings held at the famed Florida resort city. The stories describing lunches, bridge tournaments, charity events and theater parties usually include a list of participants. A close study of these articles allowed the author to determine the membership of the social circle to which the General and his wife belonged. It is a list representing St. Augustine's elite.[9]

They were especially close to Dr. and Mrs. Andrew Anderson, town mayor and the confidant of Henry Morrison Flagler, the Yankee business tycoon who literally created Gilded Age St. Augustine, making it the hub of his new railroad and hotel empire eventually stretching all the way down Florida's east coast to Key West.[10] Together, Flagler—a savvy business partner of John D. Rockefeller—and Anderson, the progressive mayor and community booster, masterminded the transformation of a small town primarily patronized by invalids into the Newport of the South: a fabulous winter mecca attracting some of the richest and most powerful people in the country.

General Hardin also befriended a Flagler lieutenant, James Edmundson Ingraham. This Wisconsin native and Racine College graduate came to Florida in 1874 and quickly became a key mover in developing the state as it grew from a frontier backwater to a magnet for Northern vacationers. Always a good judge of talent, Flagler ultimately hired Ingraham away from his West Coast rival Henry B. Plant to manage his East Coast Railroad and oversee land acquisition. The handsome, mustached Ingraham was not only an astute businessman but a man of action who led a historic pioneer exploration of the Everglades in 1892 and later survived a terrible ordeal at sea following the sinking of the yacht *Yuma* off the Florida coast.[11]

Another Hardin friend was John Louis Ketterlinus, a Philadelphia printer who pioneered color lithography in the 1870s and amassed a large fortune in the process. He and his wife, Elizabeth, lived in a rambling St. Augustine Mansion called the Warden Castle. The estate was later converted into the Hotel Warden in the 1940s by author Marjorie Kinnan Rawlings. The building currently houses "Ripley's Believe It Or Not."[12]

Banker and philanthropist John H. Hewson of Washington married the young widow of Major General John Schofield, Georgia (Kilbourne) Schofield following the General's death in 1906. They became quite close to General and Mrs. Hardin. The Hewsons were bona fide members of high society and listed in the Washington and New York Social Registers (1918 and 1914, respectively).

Mr. Hewson was a deeply religious man with a social conscience. His charities included the Society of St. Johnland in King's Park, New York, a refuge home for "friendless children" and destitute elderly men.[13] Other wealthy and famous benefactors included James Roosevelt, the father of

Franklin Delano Roosevelt and financier J.P. Morgan; A Hewson was also a fundraiser for Lincoln Memorial University in Harrowgate, Tenn., chartered in 1897 for the purpose of providing higher education opportunities to the white underclass in the impoverished eastern part of the state. East Tennessee provided many volunteers to the Union cause during the Civil War, and President Lincoln had expressed his desire to reward them for their loyalty at the conclusion of the war.[14]

Another interesting member of the Hardin social set in St. Augustine was Charles M. Swift. This Detroit entrepreneur and investor purchased a government franchise in 1903 to build and operate an electric tramway system in Manila, the Philippines, recently acquired as a colony by the United States.[15] Mrs. George Fletcher of rural Rutland, Vermont was also frequently in company with General and Mrs. Hardin; her brother, Robert Murray, managed the Ponce de Leon Hotel for 35 years.[16]

Ironically, one of Hardin's closest companions in St. Augustine was a former Confederate soldier, banker John T. Dismukes. Their relationship illustrated General Hardin's commitment to national reconciliation following the Civil War. Dismukes was the wealthy and respected President of the Union Bank in St. Augustine and a philanthropist whose generosity funded a free dental clinic for the poor in the city. Seventeen-year-old Dismukes had enlisted in the Confederate Army in 1864 and served as an artillerist until the war's conclusion. However, the former Rebel and the one-armed Union officer never let the past sabotage their long and enduring friendship. Upon General Hardin's death in 1923, Dismukes was one of his pallbearers.[17]

Beginning in 1894, General and Mrs. Hardin began to regularly sail aboard one of the modern steam liners to Europe visiting at various times England, Spain, France, Austria and Italy. General Schofield, then the ranking general in the United States Army, provided Hardin with letters of introduction to the U.S. Ambassadors of all the major European capitals, requesting they extend Mr. and Mrs. Hardin every courtesy. In 1906 the *New York Sun* reported that General Hardin, with another American tourist, hosted a reception in Rome for American Archbishop John Ireland following his audience with Pope Pius X after gaining the Pontiff's "full favor and esteem."[18]

Returning from Europe in August of that year, General and Mrs.

Hardin were aboard the RMS *Caronia* of the Cunard Line when she passed by a "huge iceberg." The gigantic ice island left a strong impression on all those aboard. No doubt, the General and Mrs. Hardin recalled the incident only six years later when the ill-fated *Titanic* struck a similar berg with enormous loss of life in April of 1912.[19]

St. Augustine was where the Hardins felt most at home, perhaps in part because, as the *New York Times* described in a March 17, 1912 article, it was a "a popular rendezvous for retired Army men." On that occasion, the reporter noted the presence of General Hardin among a gaggle of socializing retired brass. "What stories they could tell?" the article wondered.[20]

Even as the young rich began to flee the old city for Palm Beach Island and other posh resorts farther south, the old guard remained, epitomized by General and Mrs. Hardin, and kept up their rituals and routines. The social circle in St. Augustine became increasingly gray and feeble, living relics of another age and world. The *New York Tribune* ran a brief article on the military tone of the southern resort in its February 14, 1915 edition: "Each season St. Augustine proves a rendezvous for interesting retired army and navy officers and their wives . . . Major General John R. Brooke and Mrs. Brooke are annual patrons at the Alcazar. . . . Another interesting member of the army coterie is Brigadier General Hardin who with Mrs. Hardin, occupies Villa Schofield and entertains delightfully."[21]

That great epic event of their youth, the Civil War, was slowly fading from memory. The ranks of the Boys in Blue and Gray were thinning each year. Survivors who had known the turmoil and tragedy of those years seemed to cling together against the cold winds of time and change. One such friend and contemporary of General Hardin was Union General Adelbert Ames, who visited St. Augustine with his wife in the spring of 1910 as houseguests of the Hardins. The two men had been cadets together at West Point, although Ames graduated in 1861, two years after Hardin. Ames had distinguished himself as an artillery officer at First Bull Run where he refused to abandon his cannon despite serious wounds. His greatest triumph came in the spring of 1865 when he helped win the Union victory at Fort Fisher in North Carolina. The capture of the mighty Rebel fortress sealed off the port of Wilmington to blockade runners and pounded another nail into the Confederacy's coffin.[22]

Following the war, Ames joined the political battles as a Radical Republican, serving as Governor of Mississippi during Reconstruction. Interestingly enough, in 1876, Ames was also present in Northfield, Minnesota during the infamous Jesse James gang's failed bank robbery attempt. Although unharmed in the shoot-out, the former Union army general coached a nervous civilian in the procedure of loading and firing his weapon at the gang members riding up and down the street.[23]

The Hardin social circle also included Admiral Winfield Scott Schley, the celebrated victor of the 1898 naval battle of Santiago. Admiral Schley was a dinner guest of the Hardins at the Ponce de Leon Hotel. He commanded the American fleet when Admiral Cervera's blockaded warships attempted to make a dash from Santiago Harbor. The Spanish ships were all sunk in a resounding victory that virtually ended the Spanish-American War. In his youth, Schley had sailed aboard a Union blockader off the Southern coast.[24]

Probably the most colorful of Hardin's military coterie in St. Augustine was Admiral Henry Walton Grinnell, famed as the Mikado's "Yankee Admiral" for his service aboard a Japanese battleship during the 1895 Battle of the Yalu in the Sino-Japanese war, which ended with the destruction of the antiquated Chinese armada. This scion of a wealthy family had also served with Admiral David Farragut during the 1864 Battle of Mobile Bay. In 1904, the old sailor married a young lady less than half his age.[25]

Captain Henry Marcotte was especially close to General and Mrs. Hardin during their yearly winter sojourns in St. Augustine. Marcotte was an Italian-American who had come to the United States at age six, lost a leg in the Civil War, but despite the handicap later served as a war correspondent for the *Army-Navy Journal* in Cuba during the Spanish-American War. He was embedded with a Gatling Gun Battery in the thick of the fighting outside Santiago. Young soldiers admired the 60-year-old, crippled veteran for his coolness under fire and willingness to endure with them the ordeal of short rations, brutal tropical heat, and the ever-present threat of disease.[26] Marcotte and his wife, Anna, were frequent bridge partners of General and Mrs. Hardin in St. Augustine.

The Captain's wife had led an equally fascinating life. "She . . . married Capt. Henry Marcotte, U.S.A, and served with him in Dakota prior to 1873, frequently having to defend herself against attacks of Sioux Indians at Forts Rice and Lincoln, and in those troubled and dangerous times, she proved that she could handle a rifle with as much skill and courage as any soldier possessed," wrote a reporter for the *New York Herald* in 1896. "Mrs. Marcotte was the first white woman who ever crossed the plains from Fort Lincoln to where the city of Fargo now stands. . . . this remarkable journey of 235 miles was accomplished in sleighs, camping at night in whatever favored spot fortune might provide; it is only necessary to state that the mercury during the whole trip ranged from 28 degrees to 48 degrees below zero."[27]

St. Augustine was certainly a pleasant change from the wintery plains of the Dakotas. There Mrs. Marcotte edited the social newspaper, *The Tattler,* worked for the *St. Augustine News,* and was a stringer for several New York papers providing them with society news from the Ancient City. Her husband was the St. Augustine correspondent for the *Jacksonville Times-Union* newspapers. They were a popular couple during the heyday of Flagler's resort city during the Gilded Age. Captain Marcotte cut a gallant figure at the Alcazar and Ponce de Leon hotels, often in the company of Mrs. Henry Flagler and the other social lions of the age. He died in St. Augustine in January 1923, about ten months before the death of General Hardin.

There is a strong possibility that Captain Marcotte and Anna knew General and Mrs. Hardin earlier when all four were living in Washington in the last year of the Civil War. The Captain, a wounded veteran of many battles with the Army of the Potomac, was seriously injured at Chancellorsville and assigned to the Veteran Reserve Corp in the Capital, which came under General Hardin's command. He probably met his future wife, Anna M. (Hughes) Rhodes, who moved there to work at the U.S. Treasury following the death of her first husband, Lt. Amos B. Rhodes of the Seventh Pennsylvania Cavalry.[28]

Even more intriguing is that Anna encountered President Lincoln on several occasions while walking to her Treasury office. On one memorable excursion, she went to one of the army hospitals to visit an acquaintance and was startled to find President Lincoln at the boy's bedside holding his hand. It seems logical and likely that Anne and General Hardin, during their long post-war friendship, shared with one another their mutual reminiscences of the martyred President.

Another close retired military friend of General and Mrs. Hardin was General John Rutter Brooke, who had graduated two classes back of Hardin at West Point. During the Civil War, the young officer was awarded the Medal of Honor for heroism and was severely wounded during the Battle of Gettysburg. He later served on the Western frontier, trained troops during the Spanish-American War, and was appointed military governor, at different times, of Cuba and Puerto Rico. He and his wife lived in Philadelphia, but became regular winter residents at the Alcazar Hotel beginning in 1900.[29]

Around 1911, General and Mrs. Hardin moved from their downtown Chicago residence at 538 State Street after building a new home in the Dutch Colonial Revival style on two acres in the fashionable suburb of Lake Forest. Their residence at 1145 North Green Bay Road featured two distinctive black-tipped chimneys, which inspired the name "Two Chimneys." Years later, William Foote McLaughlin, nephew of General and Mrs. Hardin, recalled how Aunt Melly commuted every day from Lake Forest to downtown Chicago in her antiquated Baker electric car.[30]

General Hardin was a member of the nearby Owentsia Country Club whose exclusive membership list included Robert Todd Lincoln, Major-General Fred Grant, Mrs. Honore Potter and Cyrus McCormick, among other notables.[31] General Hardin's brother-in-law, Frederick McLaughlin, also a member, told his son years later that the handicapped general shot a very competitive game of billiards despite having only one arm. Owentsia, founded in 1896, still remains a bastion of Chicago's social elite where money alone does not guarantee membership. The name of the club supposedly means a "gathering of braves" in some forgotten Indian dialect.[32]

The old soldier remained alert and very active even as he reached his sixty-third year in 1900 to witness the birth of a new century. As the brash 20th century progressed, General Hardin began to see his old soldier friends and contemporaries answer the final roll call. The Civil War generation was fading fast. In 1906, his classmate, Confederate General Joseph Wheeler died.[33] His brother, former Confederate private Lemuel S.Hardin, died of complications of his war wound in 1909.[34] The next year saw the loss of Hardin's friend and contemporary, General Wesley Merritt, who had commanded the American expedition to the Philippines in the Spanish-American War.[35] His sister, Ellen Hardin Walworth, died at her Washington home in 1915, still mourning her martyred daughter, Spanish-American War nurse, Reubena H. Walworth.[36]

In 1914, one of the General's oldest friends from Chicago, Phil Sheridan's brother, Colonel Michael Sheridan, wrote him at General and Mrs. Hardin's new winter home at 20 Valencia, St. Augustine, thanking them for their sympathy note upon the recent death of his wife: "My Dear Hardin . . . I thank both you and Mrs. Hardin for your sincere sympathy. When I saw you in Fall I was indeed much discouraged about my dear wife's condition, yet I had hopes of her recovery because of her most excellent health {thru?} our long companionship of nearly forty-four years. But the great reaper was too much for her and I am a very lonely old man."[37]

Perhaps the most crushing emotional blow to fall upon General Hardin in his final years was the death of Colonel Crilly, his old West Point roommate and the Best Man at his 1892 Chicago wedding to Amelia. Early on Hardin had come to admire Crilly for his moral courage in practicing his Roman Catholic faith at West Point in an era of extreme prejudice. When Crilly died at age 71 in Philadelphia on January 25, 1908, Hardin's grief at the loss of "my dear, dear old friend" was palpable.

General Hardin authored Colonel Crilly's obituary for the West Point alumni publication printed June 12, 1908, in which he praised his close friend's accomplishments as a quartermaster officer dealing with railroad transportation and repair during the Civil War, and his 40-year post-war career as a Philadelphia bank president and director of the board overseeing the Catholic High School of that city. "Colonel Crilly was not only a thoroughly good and successful business man, but a consistent member of the Catholic Church," General Hardin wrote. "He was of a most cheery and sociable disposition, devoting much of his time to kind works for his friends and neighbors. His hospitality was famous and he was extremely popular in all his clubs and associations. He was a most 'clubable' man . . ."[38]

His memoriam honoring his dearest friend could have been easily served to define Hardin's own affable and outgoing nature. They were in their faith and personality very similar. Although Hardin would live for another 15 years, he probably never filled the void left by Francis J. Crilly, the son off Irish immigrants, who like thousands of other newcomers had by hard work and discipline transformed himself into a fine American citizen.[39]

During those long, pleasant years of leisure, the Hardins witnessed a passing parade of the most notable and powerful people of the age. Locals were known to remark that if you lived in St. Augustine long enough you would over the years meet the world's richest and most famous citizens who came to reside for the winter in one of Flagler's fabled hotels. Many of those celebrities became friends of the convivial General and Mrs. Hardin. They became known as one of the "city's hosts."

New York Senator Chauncey Depew often enjoyed the hospitality offered by General Hardin and his young wife. The sociable politician and popular speaker was a fixture in St. Augustine society for many years. During World War I, he and General Hardin shared the stage during a rally supporting the war effort and, after the death of the general, Mrs. Hardin was a guest at the Senator's New York estate.

Largely forgotten today, Depew was a leading Republican power-broker who, in 1898, nominated Spanish-American War hero Theodore Roosevelt for governor of New York. He was a gifted orator who spoke at the dedication of the Statue of Liberty in 1886, the centennial celebration of George Washington's presidential inauguration in 1889, and at the opening ceremonies of the Columbian Exposition in Chicago in 1893.[40]

One wonders what General and Mrs. Hardin thought when the well-liked New York senator came under the relentless scrutiny of the reformers. Their friend, who began his career as a manager for a railroad magnate, was attacked as a tool of the moneyed classes, ruled by rapacious Robber Barons like J.P. Morgan and John Rockefeller.[41] *McClures Magazine* displayed Senator Chauncey Depew's picture with a caption reading: "Here is the archetypal Face of the Sleek, Self-Satisfied American Opportunist in Politics and Plunder." General Hardin must have been shocked and outraged when the article described his friend, Senator Depew, as owned "mentally and morally" by railroad kings Cornelius and William Vanderbilt. He was characterized as a "boodler," "robber," "coward" and "sniveling sycophant."[42]

Long-time winter residents at St. Augustine's palatial Ponce de Leon Hotel, General and Mrs. Hardin, decided around 1916 to lease the former residence of the late General John Schofield at 20 Valencia Street, referred to as Villa Schofield. This would be their home until the general's death seven years later. The Hardin-Schofield residence, now called the Union General's House, is owned by Flagler College, and houses administrative offices.[43]

In those final St. Augustine years, General and Mrs. Hardin welcomed into their conservative social circle a rather exotic denizen of the artistic crowd. This was the famous dancer, Irene Castle of Vernon and Castle fame: the Fred Astaire and Ginger Rogers of their generation. Following the death of her husband and dance partner, Vernon Castle, in an airplane crash at a Texas training field in 1918, the widow spent time as a guest of General and Mrs. Hardin at 20 Valencia Street. The Bohemian dancer and silent film star popularized short hair, shorter dresses and suggestive dances like the Tango.[44] After General Hardin's death, the dancer married Amelia Hardin's brother, Frederic McLaughlin of Chicago, a World War I veteran and volatile owner of the Chicago Black Hawks hockey team.

The aging General Hardin must have increasingly felt like a flesh-and-blood Rip Van Winkle, suddenly awakening in a strange, often outlandish world far removed from the one he knew as a youth. The steamboats, covered wagons, and canal boats of the past had been replaced with flying machines, automobiles and high-speed luxury passenger trains. Jazz music poured from phonographs and the young flocked to see Valentino and Mary Pickford perform in the movies. Prohibition was in full-swing; gangsters defended their turf with Thompson sub-machine-guns; and young girls, called Flappers, smoked cigarettes in public, drank bathtub gin and danced "The Charleston."

The aging General Hardin remained remarkably resilient and active. His health remained good even in his eighties, and he was engaged both physically and mentally. Bridge kept his mind alert and his body benefited from swimming, fishing trips, sailing, horseback riding and golf. In a 1911 profile in *The American Catholic Who's Who*, General Hardin was described as, "an accomplished horseman, a good shot, and ardent and successful fisherman and excellent swimmer, even after losing one arm."[45] He was also a member of the St. Augustine Yacht Club and an enthusiastic sailor, a sport he first enjoyed on Chesapeake Bay in 1859 as a young officer posted at Fort Monroe. Although there is no record of Hardin owning a yacht, at least four of his closest St. Augustine friends did and presumably invited him aboard on various occasions.[46]

In September 1923, during a visit to New York, the old soldier experienced severe abdominal pain. After a month, General and Mrs. Hardin returned to St. Augustine where his condition worsened and was diagnosed as terminal stomach cancer. Pain became General Hardin's faithful companion day and night.

Catholic Father John Francis Conoley, 39, a World War I Army Chaplain, was an intimate friend during the General's final years. He recalled that the old soldier suffered horribly in the final weeks of his life, fighting against intense pain "even he could hardly bear."[47] Death was merciful when it finally came on December 12, 1923. Eighty-six-year-old General Martin Davis Hardin, the last living member of the West Point Class of 1859, answered his final roll call.

Mrs. Amelia Hardin could have buried the Civil War hero at Arlington National Cemetery, but instead, knowing how much the old soldier loved the city by the sea, she chose the National Cemetery in St. Augustine to be his final resting place.

The Right Reverend Patrick Barry, Bishop of the Diocese of St. Augustine, officiated at the Requiem Mass conducted at the St. Augustine Cathedral where General and Mrs. Hardin had worshipped every Sunday. The funeral service filled the Cathedral with mourners including General Hardin's closest friends who were named honorary pallbearers: Dr. Andrew Anderson, the old Confederate artilleryman John T. Dismukes, John A. Ingraham, John H. Hewson, W.W. Dewhurst and J.L. Ketterlinus.[48] The honor guard was commanded by General J.C.R. Foster, chief of the Florida National Guard, and Father John Conoley, General Hardin's dear friend, gave the eulogy:

> This is our sad and honorable duty today: to inter with Christian rites the body of one who eminently deserves the two-fold title, Christian gentleman, American soldier, for as unbelievable as it may be to us, who knew him so long, so intimately, Martin D. Hardin, Brigadier General of the United States' armies, lies dead on the field of honor.
>
> My Brethren, here was a man who combined intrepid courage with the simplicity of a child; great intelligence with the humility of a Saint; profound judgment with a charity that was as large as his heart was sympathetic. . . . His military record you know. It is a stupendous narrative of sacrificial effort in behalf and in defense of those fundamental liberties and traditions we now enjoy. . . . He

carries to the grave not only the uniform of his high office in our national service, but many honorable scars as pledges of his heroism.[49]

In closing, Father Conoley emphasized that General Hardin had been a sterling representative of the Civil War generation, now fading so fast from the American scene: those intrepid souls who saved the Union and eradicated the awful specter of slavery. The priest described the late General Hardin as "this son of a generation, who built what yet endures as our county—united, free . . ."[50]

Father Conoley told the mourners that General Hardin had confronted and vanquished death with the same courage and the same Christian faith that had seen him safely through a score of bloody Civil War battles: And so, beholding his last enemy approach to bear him away . . . he made haste to meet him "having on the shield of faith. . . . Thus he met death. Standing so long upon the walls of life, he took off his armor, like a watch-worn and weary sentinel, to lie down at last to sleep, to rest."[51]

IN THE DAYS THAT FOLLOWED

A few months after General Hardin's death, his good friend and eulogist, Father John Conoley, was kidnapped by Ku Klux Klansman in Gainesville and taken to some isolated location where he was badly beaten and castrated. His attackers drove the bloodied clergyman to Palatka and dumped his body in front of the Catholic Church. This act of terror was carried out because Father Conoley had established a youth ministry at the University of Florida, and the Klan feared he would convert the primarily Protestant student body.[1]

Mrs. Amelia Hardin continued her oversight of the renovation of Le Leche Chapel in St. Augustine, located on the grounds of the Mission Nombre De Dios where the first Roman Catholic Mass was celebrated in what is now the United States.[2] The renovated chapel was dedicated to the memory of General Martin D. Hardin and includes a small statue of St. Martin. On the outside wall the memorial plaque quotes Psalm 26:8:

IN MEMORIUM
GENERAL M. D. HARDIN
'I have loved O' Lord the beauty of thy house
And the place where thy glory dwelleth.'

General Hardin had been among the last surviving Union general officers. On May 15, 1925, 86-year-old General Nelson A. Miles, who had attended Hardin's second wedding in 1892, took his grandchildren to the circus in Washington where he had a fatal heart attack. The Medal of Honor recipient was the last survivor of the Civil War to hold the rank of major general. He was interred in a mausoleum of his own design at Arlington National Cemetery.[3]

On September 5, 1926, Hardin's old friend, General John R. Brooke, died at 88 years of age in Philadelphia.[4] Only one Union general remained alive: Adelbert Ames, who had been a frequent guest of the Hardins in St. Augustine. On April 13, 1933, Ames died at his winter home in Ormond Beach, Florida, at age 97. He was the last surviving Union general.[5]

General Hardin's nephew, Mansfield Tracy Walworth, Jr., called Tracy, had long before the death of his uncle become a recluse, living the life of a hermit obsessed with religion in a secluded forest near Glen Carlyn, Virginia. People at the time described his refuge as a "woodland forest." On December 2, 1928, this lost soul slashed his throat with a hunting knife.[6]

On Memorial Day, 1935, General Hardin's widow was present at the National Cemetery in St. Augustine where a patriotic ceremony was held dedicated to the memory of her late husband.[7] She died in 1939 and was buried at General Hardin's side. The grave is marked with a large cross that dwarfs its neighbors, inscribed with the General's name and the epitaph "Christian. Soldier. Gentleman." (Only a few feet away are three distinctive stone pyramids containing the remains of American soldiers killed in the Seminole War of 1836–1842.)

Visitors to modern-day St. Augustine can visit the chapel dedicated to General Hardin's memory, tour the Tovar House which he and his first wife leased in the 1880s, visit the Alcazar Hotel where Hardin spoke on the Centennial of Lincoln's birth in 1909, and marvel at the splendor of Flagler's Ponce de Leon Hotel where General Hardin and his second wife enjoyed bridge parties and balls. Only a few blocks away stands the Union Generals Home on 20 Valencia Way where Hardin died on December 12, 1923.[8] At the National Cemetery of St. Augustine, occasionally a visitor places a small American flag by General Hardin's cross in memory of one of America's forgotten heroes, a man who knew Lincoln, fought at Gettysburg, and explored the Far West.

Gone from the American scene was a remarkable soldier, Christian gentleman, and witness to American history, a good man who deserves to be remembered. General Martin Davis Hardin saw the city of Chicago in its infancy when pedestrians crossed the Chicago River via a rope ferry. As a boy, he watched his father's regiment board a steamboat and depart for the Mexican War, traveled by canal boat and stage coach, and listened fearfully to ghost stories told in the slave quarters of his Uncle Abram Smith's Mississippi plantation.

During his lifetime, Hardin met many of America's great men and women, and knew them not as icons from a distance, but as flesh and blood human beings. These included War of 1812 hero and conqueror of Mexico General Winfield Scott, Secretary of State William Seward, the great novelist Washington Irving, stage actor Junius Brutus Booth, Presidents Franklin Pierce, Abraham Lincoln and Grover Cleveland, western explorer Captain Bonneville, Gettysburg victor General George Gordon Meade, American historian Frederick Jackson Turner, Lincoln's oldest son, Robert Todd Lincoln, and the bejeweled doyen of Chicago high society in The Gilded Age, Mrs. Potter Palmer.

In Hardin's days as a West Point cadet that venerable institution was presided over by Colonel Robert E. Lee, the future commander of the Confederate's fabled Army of Northern Virginia. Cadet Hardin attended classes with Custer, Merritt, Ramseur, Wheeler and other future generals of the Union and Confederate armies. Lt. Hardin was present at Harper's Ferry when Abolitionist John Brown was captured and the fuse lit for the coming Civil War. This young man journeyed into the Far West when the wild Indian tribes, the buffalo and the Grizzly Bear still ruled a vast and magnificent wilderness. This was the now legendary great American frontier in its final days during the time of the Pony Express, steamboats, wagon trains and lonely army posts. In a few years this wilderness world vanished, replaced seemingly overnight with railroads, telegraph lines, towns, churches, schools, colleges and farms.

During the Civil War—our American Iliad—Hardin fought with distinction in a dozen battles including Gettysburg, where he personally witnessed Pickett's Charge, later lost an arm in a guerrilla ambush, suffered with Grant's army in the bloody spring of 1864, and won promotion to brigadier general by personal order of friend and mentor President Abraham Lincoln. In those memorably tragic April days of 1865, General Hardin helped coordinate the search and pursuit of the Lincoln-Seward conspirators, and later escorted President Lincoln's coffin from the White House to the Capitol rotunda in a solemn procession watched by silent thousands.

After the war, General Hardin did his utmost to provide justice to the newly freed slaves and their former masters in Raleigh, befriended Lincoln's widow, Mary Todd, and helped nurse Tad Lincoln during his final days at the Clifton House in Chicago. A few months later, General Hardin watched while the Great Chicago Fire consumed the city and drove many thousands from their homes. And, he was among those stalwart souls who rebuilt their lives from the ashes and smoking rubble of that epic conflagration, living to see Chicago rise again to take its place as the nation's second city.

In his long life General Hardin beheld many of the most dramatic and significant events in America's history, knew many of its most famous men and woman, and always played his role in the great drama with a deep and abiding sense of duty and honor. Although it would be imprecise to call General Martin D. Hardin a great man; he was certainly a very good man, whose storied life can admirably serve as an inspiration and model for all Americans.

NOTES

ABBREVIATIONS

Chicago History Museum (CHM) 2. United States Library of Congress (LOC) 3. St. Augustine Historical Society Research Library (SAHSRL) 4. Saratoga Springs History Museum (SSHM) 5. Dictionary of American Biography (DAB) 6. Pennsylvania Volunteer Reserve Corps Historical Society (PVRC) 7. War of the Rebellion: A Compilation of the Official Records of the War of the Rebellion (ORs) 8. American National Biography (ANB)

INTRODUCTION: AN EPIC LIFE

1. King James Bible, Cambridge Edition.
2. Ezra Warner. *General In Blue: Lives of the Union Commanders,* p. 205.
3. Ibid, p. 205, 206.
4. William Harding Carter. "Martin D. Hardin, Class of 1859," *Annual Report of the West Point Association,* June 11, 1924, p. 97–100; Thomas E. Stephens. "Senator Martin D. Hardin, June 21, 1780–October 8, 1823," *American National Biography* (ANB), Vol. 10, p. 60; Stephen L. Hansen. "John J. Hardin, January 6, 1810–February 23, 1847," *ANB,* Vol. 10, p. 57, 58.
5. Tom Day (editor). "Papers, letters, and documents relating to the Hardin Family of Virginia, Kentucky, and Illinois," St. Augustine Historical Society Research Library (SAHSRL), February 2011; "Hardin Family Papers," Chicago History Museum (CHM) archive; Wiley Sword. *President Washington's Indian War: The Struggle for the Old Northwest, 1790–1795,* p. 77, 94–97, 109–111, 140, 211–212, 238.
6. Stephen Aron, "Benjamin Logan, 1742–11 Dec. 1802," *ANB,* Vol. XIII, p. 832.
7. Charles Gano Talbert. *Benjamin Logan: Kentucky Frontiersman,* p. 300.
8. Estelle Graham Hardin letter datelined Chicago to her mother-in-law, Mrs. Chancellor Ellen (Hardin) Walworth, Saratoga Springs, N.Y. regarding Tad Lincoln's illness, June 18, 1871. Walworth-Hardin Family Archive, Saratoga Historical Museum (SHM), Saratoga Springs, N.Y.
9. Amy S. Greenberg. *A Wicked War: Polk, Clay, Lincoln, and the 1846 Invasion of Mexico,* p. xiv, 52–54, 86–90, 181; Stephen L. Hansen. "John J. Hardin, January 6, 1810–February 23, 1847, *ANB.* Vol. 10, p. 57–58; Paul David Nelson. "John Hardin, October 1, 1753–May 1792," *ANB.* Vol. 10, p. 56, 57.
10. Ibid, p. 48–49, 251–252, 157–158.

11. George W. Cullum. *Biographical Register of the Officers and Graduates of the United States Military Academy at West Point, N.Y. since its establishment in 1802*, p. 84.
12. William Harding Carter. "Martin D. Hardin, Class of 1859," *Annual Report of the West Point Association*, June 11, 1924, p. 99.
13. Michael W. Kauffman. *American Brutus: John Wilkes Booth and the Lincoln Conspiracies*, p. 59, 62, 69.
14. Anonymous, "Historic Chapel: General Hardin Memorial Blessed at St. Augustine," Jan. 23, 1926, *Catholic Southern Cross Magazine*.

PROLOGUE: LINCOLN REMEMBERED, 1909
1. Anonymous. "Lincoln Program at Hotel Alcazar," *St. Augustine Evening Record*, Feb. 13, 1909.
2. James A. Woodburn and Samuel B. Harding. *Lincoln Centenary Guide for Indiana Schools.* (Indianapolis: Indiana Department of Education, 1908). Francis D. Tandy. "To Celebrate Lincoln's Centenary" letter to the *New York Times*, Jan. 23, 1908. Anonymous. "Washington's Day Somewhat Overshadowed by Lincoln Centenary," *New York Times*, Feb. 22, 1909.
3. Nathan William MacChesney. *Abraham Lincoln: The Tribute of a Century*, p. 3, 185, 256 and 492.
4. William Harding Carter. "Martin D. Hardin, Class of 1859," *West Point Annual Report*, June 11, 1924), p. 97–100.
5. Anonymous. "Lincoln Centenary Observed at Alcazar Hotel," *St. Augustine Evening Record*, Feb. 13, 1909.
6. Anonymous. "When Lincoln Was Born," *St. Augustine Evening Record*, Feb. 14, 1909.
7. Ibid.
8. Martin D. Hardin. *Reminiscences.* Hardin Family Papers, 1882–1943, CHM, p. 1. (105–page unpublished handwritten autobiography covering the period of 1843 to 1860)
9. Anonymous. "Lincoln Centenary Observed at Hotel Alcazar," *St. Augustine Evening Record*, Feb. 13 and 14, 1909.
10. Ibid.
11. Anonymous. "Lincoln Centenary Observed at Hotel Alcazar," *St. Augustine Evening Record*, Feb. 13, 1909.

CHAPTER 1: LITTLE BOY AFRAID OF GHOSTS
1. Martin D. Hardin. *Reminiscences*, p. 1.
2. Stephen L. Hansen. "John J. Hardin," *American National Biography* (ANB), (New York: Oxford University Press, 1999), Vol. 10, p. 57–58.
3. Thomas E. Stephens. "Martin D. Hardin," *ANB*, Vol. 10, p. 60.
4. Ibid.
5. Jack Hardin, Jr. *History of the Hardin Family in the Early Settling of Kentucky*, p. 1–17; Thomas M. Greene. *Historic Families of Kentucky*, p. 177–188, 120–141, 225.; Thomas E. Stephens. "Senator Martin D. Hardin, June 21, 1780–Oct. 8, 1823," *ANB*. Vol. 1, p. 60; Paul David Neeson. "John (Indian Killer) Hardin, Oct. 1, 1753–May 1792," *ANB*. Vol. 10, p. 56, 57; G. Glen Clift. *Remember The Raisin: Kentucky and Kentuckians in the Battles and Massacre at Frenchtown, Michigan Territory, War 1812.*

6. Martin D. Hardin. *Reminiscences*, p. 8.
7. Evelyn Britten. Chronicles of Saratoga, p. 201–202.
8. Martin D. Hardin. *Reminiscences*, p. 8.
9. Ibid., p. 9
10. Ellen Hardin Walworth. "Earliest Recollections," undated typed article at Saratoga Historical Museum SHM; Donald M. Roper. "Ellen Hardin Walworth, October 20, 1832–June 23, 1915," *ANB*. Vol. 22, p. 594, 595; Stephen L. Hansen. "John J. Hardin, Jan. 6, 1810–Feb. 23, 1847," *ANB*. Vol 10, p. 57–58.
11. Don Harrison Doyle. *The Social Order of a Frontier Community, Jacksonville, Illinois 1825–1870*, p. 33.
12. "Underground railroad committee of the Morgan County Historical Society," Internet:
13. Ellen Hardin Walworth. "Earliest Recollections," undated typed article at Saratoga Historical Museum, Saratoga Spring, N.Y., *SSHM*, p. 7; Donald M. Roper. "Ellen Hardin Walworth, Oct. 20, 1832–June 23, 1915," *ANB*. Vol. 22, p. 594, 595.
14. Ibid.
15. Ibid.
16. Geoffrey O'Brien. *The House of Walworth: Murder and Madness in Gilded Age America*, p. 92.
17. Stephen L. Hansen. "John J. Hardin," *ANB*, Vol. 10, p. 57, 58.
18. Ibid.
19. Dorothy Ford Wulfeck. *Hardin and Harding of Virginia and Kentucky*, p. 34, 35, 40.
20. Ellen Hardin Walworth. "Earliest Recollection," undated copy of typed article at *SSHM*.
21. Bernard Mayo. *Henry Clay: Spokesman of the New West*, p. 134.
22. Ellen Hardin Walworth. "Earliest Recollection," undated copy of typed article at *SSHM*.
23. Ibid.
24. Ibid.
25. Ibid
26. Ibid.
27. Ibid.
28. Martin D. Hardin. *Reminiscences*, p. 2.
29. Ibid, p. 1.
30. Ibid, p. 5.
31. Ibid, p. 2–3.
32. Ibid, p. 17.
33. Ibid.
34. Ibid, p. 6–7.
35. Ibid, p. 3.
36. Ibid.
37. Ibid. 1–3.
38. Ibid, p. 1.
39. Ibid, p. 1–2.
40. Geoffrey O'Brien. *The House of Walworth: Murder and Madness in Gilded Age America*, p. 93.

41. Martin D. Hardin. *Reminiscences*, p. 18.
42. Ibid.

CHAPTER 2: THE LINCOLN CONNECTION
1. Hardin Funeral Details, *St. Augustine Evening Record*, Dec. 12, 13, 14, 15, 1923.
2. Stephen L. Hansen. "John Hardin," *ANB*, p. 57–58.
3. Carl Sandburg. *Lincoln*, p. 25–26.
4. Letters to author from Morgan County Historian and former Jacksonville, Il. Mayor Ron Tendrick, June 28 and Aug. 12, 2012.
5. Amy S. Greenberg. *A Wicked War*, p. 53.
6. Willard L. King. Lincoln's *Manager David Davis*, p. 46; Stephen L. Hansen. "John J. Hardin," ANB, p. 57–58.
7. Karen L. Cox. *The Life of John J. Hardin* (1964 master's thesis at University of Miami at Ohio), p. 11.
8. Ibid, p. 9, 10.
9. Ibid, p. 18.
10. Michael Burlingame. *The Inner World of Abraham Lincoln*, p. 214.
11. Karen L. Cox. *The Life of John J. Hardin* (1964 master's thesis, University of Miami At Ohio), p. 6, 11.
12. Ibid, p. 6.
13. Paul Simon. Lincoln's *Preparation for Greatness: The Illinois Legislative Years*, p. 310; David Hebert Donald. *Lincoln*, p. 124–125.
14. Karen L. Cox. *The Life of John J. Hardin* (1964 master's thesis at University of Miami at Ohio), p. 11.
15. Harold Holzer. *Lincoln As I Knew Him*, p. 242–243.
16. David Hebert Donald. *Lincoln*, p. 84.
17. Justin G. Turner, Editor. *Mary Todd Lincoln: Life and Letters*, p. 295.
18. Ibid.
19. Marietta H. Brown. "A Romance of Lincoln," *Lincoln Herald* scholarly journal, Lincoln Memorial University, Harrowgate, Tenn. 97:2 (Summer 1995.
20. Ibid.
21. Ibid.
22. Letter from Martinette Hardin to her brother John Hardin, Jan. 22, 1841; and letter by Martinette to John Hardin, Jan. 26, 1841. Hardin Family Collection. CHM.
23. Ibid.
24. Michael Burlingame. *The Inner World of Abraham Lincoln*, p. 99.
25. David Herbert Donald. *Lincoln*, p. 90–92.
26. Ida M. Tarbell. *The Life of Lincoln*, p. 189.
27. Carl Sandburg. *Abraham Lincoln: The Prairie Years & The War Years*, p. 77; "Lincoln Duel," *Springfield Illinois State Journal*, April 27, 1860.
28. Ibid.
29. Karen L. Cox. *The Life of John J. Hardin* (1964 master's thesis at University of Miami at Ohio), p. 46.
30. David Herbert Donald. *Lincoln*, p. 80–81.
31. Karen L. Cox. *The Life of John J. Hardin* (1964 master's thesis at University of Miami at Ohio), p. 7.

32. Stephen L. Hansen. "John Hardin," *ANB*, p. 57–58.
33. Ibid.
34. Maurice G. Baxter. Orville H. Browning: Lincoln's Friend and Critic, p. 48.
35. Lee M. Pearson. "The Princeton and the Peacemaker, *Technology & Culture*. Vol. 7, No. 2. (Spring 1966), p. 163–189; Ann Blackman, *Fatal Cruise of the Princeton*, Naval Institute, Annapolis, MD, 1956.
36. Karen L. Cox. *The Life of John J. Hardin* (1964 master's thesis at University of Miami at Ohio), p. 7.
37. JJH letter to law partner David Smith in Jacksonville, Il, Feb. 8, 1844. Hardin Family Papers, *Chicago History Museum* (CHM).
38. Bruce Flanders. *Nauvoo: Kingdom on the Mississippi*, p. 308.
39. Bernard DeVoto. *The Year of Decision 1846*, p. 83. Note: John J. Hardin's daughter, Ellen Hardin Walworth, spent many years researching her father's life in preparation to write a biography, which she never completed. Her notes and copies of letters survive in the Hardin Papers at the St. Augustine Historical Society Research Library. A note on the Morman crisis reads: "The influences of religion are, together with the influences of race, the strongest motive found . . ."
40. John E. Halwas and Roger D. Launius. *Cultures In Conflict: A Documentary History of the Mormon War in Illinois*, p. 310–311.
41. Bernard DeVoto. *Year of Decision 1846*, p. 88.
42. Robert W. Johnson, Editor. *The Letters of S. A. Douglas*, p. 120.
43. Bruce Flanders. *Nauvoo: Kingdom on the Mississippi*, p. 307.
44. Harold Holzer. *Lincoln As I Knew Him*, p. 112–115.
45. William Lee Miller. *Lincoln's Virtues: An Ethical Biography*, p. 158.
46. Ida M. Tarbell. *The Life of Lincoln*, p. 205.
47. Martin D. Hardin. *Reminiscences*, p. 4.
48. Ellen Hardin Walworth. "The Battle of Buena Vista," *Magazine of American History*. (December 1879) Vol 3. No. 12, p. 709.
49. Amy S. Greenberg. *A Wicked War*, p. 154–155, 177, 179.
50. Geoffrey O'Brien. *The Fall of the House of Walworth*, p. 93.
51. Karen L. Cox. *The Life of John J. Hardin* (master's thesis), p. 187.
52. John Wool. (General). *Narrative of the Army of Chihuahua, Commanded By Brigadier General Wool*. P 126.
53. Thomas Reilly. *War With Mexico: America's Reporters Cover the Battle Front*, p. 92; Ellen Hardin Walworth. "The Battle of Buena Vista," *Magazine of American History*. (December 1879) Vol. 3. No. 12, p. 734–735.
54. Ibid, p. 96.
55. Stephen L. Hansen. "John J. Hardin," *ANB*, p. 58.
56. Amy S. Greenberg. *A Wicked War*, p. 180.
57. Evelyn Barrett Britten. *Chronicles of Saratoga*, p. 247.
58. Willard L. King. *Lincoln's Manager David Davis*, p. 57.

CHAPTER 3: HOMECOMING FOR A DEAD HERO

1. Harry E. Pratt, Editor. "Illinois As Lincoln Knew It: A Boston Reporter's Record of a Trip in 1847," *Papers in Illinois History and Transactions for the Year 1937*. Reprinted for the Abraham Lincoln Association, Springfield, Il, p. 40–43.

2. Ibid.
3. Ibid.
4. Ibid.
5. Ibid.
6. Ibid.
7. Anonymous. "The Funeral of Col. John J. Hardin, Killed at Buena Vista, Mexico. Buried at Jacksonville, Illinois," *Journal of the Illinois State Historical Society*. Vol XL. No. 2. June 1947, p. 223–224.
8. Richard Yates. *Obsequies of Col. John J. Hardin at Jacksonville, Illinois, July 14, 1847*. Copy in Hardin papers at St. Augustine Historical Research Library, St. Augustine, Fl.
9. Ibid.
10. Ibid.
11. Martin D. Hardin. *Reminiscences*, p. 20.
12. John J. Hardin. "The Last Will of John J. Hardin, June 20, 1846," Hardin-Walworth Archive, *SSHM*.
13. Ibid.
14. Martin D. Hardin. *Reminiscences*, p. 20.
15. Dolly Hardin letter
16. Martin D. Hardin. *Reminiscences*, p. 19, 20.
17. Ibid.
18. Ibid, p. 19.
19. Ibid, p. 27.
20. Ibid, p. 26.
21. Ibid.
22. Ibid, p. 25.
23. Ibid.
24. Ibid, p. 21.
25. Ibid, p. 22.
26. Ibid.
27. Ibid.
28. Martin D. Hardin. *Reminiscences*, p. 21.
29. Ibid.
30. Evelyn Barrett Britten. *Chronicles of Saratoga*, p. 305–315; George Baker Anderson. *Our County and Its People: A Descriptive and Biographical Record of Saratoga County, 1899*. Patrick W. Carey. "Clarence Augustus Walworth, May 30, 1820–Sept. 19, 1900," *ANB*. Vol. 22, p. 593, 594. Donald M. Roper. "Reuben Hyde Walworth, October 25, 1788–November 28, 1867," *ANB*. Vol. 22, p. 595–597.
31. Ibid.
32. Ibid.
33. Ibid.
34. Geoffrey O'Brien. *The Fall of the House of Walworth*, p. 61, 84, 86, 103, 119.
35. Ibid, p. 90, 91.
36. Letter from Reuben Hyde Walworth, Saratoga Springs, N.Y. to Mrs. Sarah Hardin, Harrodsburg, Ky., Nov. 26, 1850. Hardin-Walworth Archive. *SSHM*.
37. Letter from Mrs. Sarah Hardin, Harrodsburg, Ky. to Reuben Hyde Walworth,

Saratoga Springs, N.Y. , December 2, 1850. Hardin-Walworth Archive. *SSHM*.

38. Letter from Reuben Hyde Walworth, Saratoga Spring, N.Y. to Mrs. Sarah Hardin, Harrodsburg, Ky., Dec. 23, 1850. Hardin-Walworth Archive. *SSHM*.

39. Letter from Mrs. Sarah Hardin, Harrodsburg, Ky. to Reuben Hyde Walworth, Saratoga Springs N.Y., Feb. 10, 1851. Hardin-Walworth Archive. *SSHM*.

40. Ibid.

41. Ibid.

42. Ibid.

43. Letter from Reuben Hyde Walworth, Saratoga Springs, N.Y. to Mrs. Sarah Hardin, Harrodsburg, Ky., March 22, 1851. Hardin-Walworth Archive. *SSHM*.

44. Letter from Mrs. Sarah Hardin, Harrodsburg, Ky. to Reuben Hyde Walworth, Saratoga Springs, N.Y., March 9, 1851. *SSHM*.

CHAPTER 4: SARATOGA SPRINGS: ENTER SAINT AND SINNER

1. Letter from Ellen Hardin, Peoria, Il. to Mary "Molly" Duncan, Jacksonville, Il., April 30, 1851. Hardin-Walworth Collection, *SHM*.

2. Martin D. Hardin. *Reminiscences*, p. 39.

3. Ibid.

4. Ibid, p. 23.

5. Ibid.

6. G. Glenn Clift. *Remember The Raisin: Kentucky and Kentuckians in the Battles and Massacre at Frenchtown, Michigan Territory in the War of 1812*, p. 113–116, and 207.

7. Martin D. Hardin. *Reminiscences,* p. 23.

8. Evelyn Barrett Britten. *Chronicles of Saratoga,* p. 305–315.

9. Clarence A. Walworth. *The Walworths of America*, p. 112, 119.

10. Hugh Bradley. *Such Was Saratoga*, p. 111–112.

11. Evelyn Barrett Britten. *Chronicles of Saratoga*, p. 463–474; Nathaniel Bartlett Sylvester. History of Saratoga County (1878).

12. Geoffrey O'Brien. *The Fall of the House of Walworth*, p. 61, 79–83, 279.

13. Ibid, p. 80–81.

14. Ibid.

15. Ibid.

16. Ibid.

17. Ibid.

18. Ibid.

19. Ibid, p. 99.

20. Ibid, p. 101–102, 107.

21. Ibid, p. 107–109, 99 and 154.

22. Ibid, p. 98, 107–109, 120.

23. Ibid, p. 98.

24. Ibid, p. 71, 75.

25. Evelyn Barrett Britten. *Chronicles of Saratoga*, p. 345–348.

26. Ibid, p. 346; Ellen ("Nelly") Walworth. *Life Sketches of Father Clarence Walworth*, 1907; Patrick W. Carey. "Clarence Augustus Walworth, May 30, 1820–September 19, 1900," *ANB*. Vol. 22, p. 593, 594.

27. Evelyn Barrett Britten. *Chronicles of Saratoga*, p. 346–347.

28. Ellen "Nelly" Walworth. *Life Sketches of Father Clarence Walworth.*
29. Geoffrey O'Brien. *The Fall of the House of Walworth*, p. 73.
30. Evelyn Barrett Britten. *Chronicles of Saratoga*, p. 227.
31. Geoffrey O'Brien. *The Fall of the House of Walworth*, p. 74.
32. Ibid, p. 78.
33. Ibid, p. 103.
34. Sarah Bond Hanley. "In The Early Days," *Journal of the Illinois State Historical Society.* Vol. XXII. No. 4, p. 665.
35. Geoffrey O'Brien. *The Fall of the House of Walworth*, p. 103.

CHAPTER 5: SHADOWS IN THE FOREST
1. "Exhibition of the Industry of All Nations," Internet Website: *www.crystalpalaemu seum.org.uk/*
2. Ibid.
3. Ibid.
4. Evelyn Barrett Britten. *Chronicles of Saratoga*, p. 201.
5. Geoffrey O'Brien. *The Fall of the House of Walworth*, p. 105.
6. William L. Stone. Reminiscences of Saratoga and Ballston, p. 354.
7. Ibid, p. 354, 357.
8. Ibid.
9. Geoffrey O'Brien. *The Fall of the House off Walworth*, p. 143–144.
10. Walter Stahr. *Seward: Lincoln's Indispensable Man*, p. 149.
11. Geoffrey O'Brien. *The Fall of the House of Walworth*, p. 104.
12. Ibid.
13. Ibid, p. 278–279.
14. Martin D. Hardin. *Reminiscences*, p. 28.
15. Ibid, p. 28, 29.
16. Ibid.
17. Ibid.
18. Ibid.
19. Martin D. Hardin *Report Card.* Ballston Spa Institute, Sept. 30, 1851. *SSHM.*
20. Martin D. Hardin *Report Card.* Ballston Spa Institute, Jan. 31, 1854.
21. Martin D. Hardin. *Reminiscences*, p. 132.
22. Ibid.
23. Ibid.
24. Ibid, p. 34, 35.
25. Ibid.
26. Ibid.
27. Ibid.
28. Evelyn Barrett Britten. *Chronicles of Saratoga*, p. 229–233.
29. Ibid.
30. Tom Carlarco. *The Underground Railroad in the Adirondack Region*, p. 164.
31. Geoffrey O'Brien. *The Fall of the House of Walworth*, p. 85–86.
32. Ibid.
33. Martin D. Hardin. *Reminiscences*, p. 30.
34. Letter from Martin D. Hardin, Ballston Spa Institute, to his mother, Sarah Hardin

Walworth, Saratoga Springs, N.Y., Jan. 31, 1854. *SHM*.
35. Ibid.

CHAPTER 6: WEST POINT: NO PLACE FOR WEAKLINGS (1854–1859)
1. Martin D. Hardin. *Reminiscences*, p. 36.
2. Ibid, p. 38.
3. Ibid, p. 40.
4. George Crocket Strong. *Cadet Life At West Point, With A Descriptive Sketch of West Point*, p. xvii, 1, 2, 10, 55.
5. Martin D. Hardin. *Reminiscences*, p. 41, 45.
6. Ibid; William Warner Hoppin. *The Peace Conference of 1861 At Washington: A paper read before the Rhode Island and New Haven Historical Society, 1889–90*.
7. George Crocket Strong. *Cadet Life At West Point, With a Descriptive Sketch of West Point*, p. 153–154.
8. George G. Kundahl. *Bravest of the Brave: The Correspondence of Stephen Dodson Ramseur*, p. 32.
9. Ibid, p. xvii.
10. Letter from Major H. B. Lewis, Adjutant, United States Military Academy at West Point to one of Hardin's close post-war friends, Nelson Thomasson, Chicago, Jan. 5, 1924. Hardin Papers. SAHSRL.
11. Martin D. Hardin. *Reminiscences*, p. 42.
12. Ibid, p. 41.
13. George Crocket Strong. *Cadet Life At West Point, Wish a Descriptive Sketch of West Point*, p. 93.
14. Ibid, p. 92.
15. Morris Schaff. *Spirit of Old West Point*, p. 81.
16. Martin D. Hardin. *Reminiscences*, p. 41.
17. Ibid, p. 46.
18. Ibid, p. 44.
19. Ibid.
20. Letter from West Point Cadet Martin D. Hardin to his brother, Lemuel Smith Hardin, Saratoga Spring, N.Y., Nov. 12, 1855. *SHM*.
21. Ibid.
22. Ibid.
23. Ibid.
25. Ibid.
26. Morris Schaff. *Spirit of Old West Point*, p. 58.
27. Martin D. Hardin. "Francis Crilly, Class of 1859," *Annual Report of the West Point Association 1908*. USMA Library, West Point.
28. Ibid.
29. Ibid.
30. Martin D. Hardin. *Reminiscences,* p. 42.
31. Ibid.
32. Ibid, p. 50.
32. Martin D. Hardin. *Reminiscences*, p. 48; Ronald B. Frankum, Jr. "Ben Hardin, February 29, 1784–September 1852," *ANB*. Vol. 10, p. 54, 55.

33. Elizabeth Brown Pryor. *Reading The Man: A Portrait of Robert E. Lee Through His Private Letters,* p. 215.
34. Ibid.
35. Martin D. Hardin. *Reminiscences,* p. 49.
36. Ibid, p. 50.
37. Ibid, p. 45.
38. Ibid, p. 46.
39. Ibid, p. 47.
40. Gerard A. Patterson. *From Blue to Gray: The Life of Confederate General Cadmus W. Wilcox.*
41. Martin D. Hardin. *Reminiscences,* p. 45.
42. Ibid, p. 51, 52.
43. Ibid.
44. Ibid, p. 47.
45. Morris Schaff. *The Spirit of Old West Point,* p. 122.
46. Ibid.
47. Ibid, p. 59.
48. Letter from Cadet Martin D. Hardin, USMA at West Point, to Dolly Smith, Saratoga Springs, N.Y., Feb. 21, 1859. SHM.
49. Ibid.
50. Ibid.
51. Ibid.
52. Richard P. Weinert, Jr. and Colonel Robert Arthur. *Defender of the Chesapeake—the story of Fort Monroe,* p. 87.
53. Martin D. Hardin. *Reminiscences,* p. 53.
54. Ezra J. Warner. *Generals In Blue,* p. 214–215.
55. Martin D. Hardin. *Reminiscences,* p. 57.
56. Ibid, p. 54.
57. Thomas E. Williams (Gunnery Sergeant, Ret., USMC). "At All Times Ready: The Marines at Harper's Ferry and the John Brown Raid, October 1859," *Leatherneck Magazine.* Sept., 2009.
58. Karen Whitman. "Re-evaluating John Brown's Raid at Harpers Ferry," *West Virginia History.* Vol 34. No. 1 (October 1972), p. 46–84.
59. Martin D. Hardin. "John Brown Raid in the Fall of 1859," a handwritten, undated note written after the war. Hardin Papers, CHM.
60. Morris Schaff. *The Spirit of Old West Point,* p. 142.
61. Ibid.

CHAPTER 7: ADVENTURES FAR WEST

1. Martin D. Hardin. *Reminiscences,* p. 59.
2. Albert T. Watkins. "The Oregon Recruit Expedition," *Collections of the Nebraska State Historical Society.* Vol. XVII. (1913).
3. Martin D. Hardin. *Reminiscences,* p. 60.
4. Martin D. Hardin. "Across The New Northwest In 1860, Part One," *The United States Service Magazine.* (May 1882), p. 576.
5. Albert T. Watkins. "The Oregon Recruit Expedition," *Collections of the Nebraska State*

Historical Society. Vo. XVII. (1913).

6. Martin D. Hardin. "Across the New Northwest In 1860, Part One," *The United States Service Magazine*. (May 1882), p. 578.

7. Ibid, p. 576.

8. Albert T. Watkins. "The Oregon Recruit Expedition," *Collections of the Nebraska Historical Society*. Vol. XVII. (1913), p. 130.

9. Anonymous. "From The Upper Missouri," *New York Times*, Aug. 1, 1860.

10. Martin D. Hardin. "Across The New Northwest In 1860, Part One," *The United States Service Magazine*. (May 1882), p. 577.

11. Ibid, p. 579.

12. Lawrence G. Kautz. *August Valentine Kautz, USA: Biography of a Civil War General*, p. 60.

13. Ibid, p. 52.

14. Ibid, p. 52, 53.

15. Martin D. Hardin. "Across The New Northwest In 1860, Part One," *The United States Service Magazine*. (May 1882), p. 578.

16. Ibid.

17. Ibid, p. 587.

18. Ibid.

19. Eugene Coan. *James Graham Cooper: Pioneer Western Naturalist*, p. 1–25.

20. Robert Taft. *Artists and Illustrators of the Old West 1850–1900*, p. 36, 37, 38.

21. Eugene Coan. *James Graham Cooper: Pioneer Western Naturalist*, p. 91, 92.

22. Robert Taft. *Artists and Illustrators of the Old West 1850–1900*, p. 39.

23. Eugene Coan. *James Graham Cooper: Pioneer Western Naturalist*, p. 92.

24. Martin D. Hardin. "Across The New Northwest in 1860, Part One," *The United States Service Magazine* (May 1882), p. 579.

25. Ibid.

26. Ibid, p. 579, 580.

27. Ibid, p. 580, 581.

28. Martin F. Schmitt (Editor). "From Missouri to Oregon in 1860: The Diary of August V. Kautz," *Pacific Northwest Quarterly* (July 1946), p. 210.

29. Martin D. Hardin. "Across The New Northwest in 1860, Part One," The United States Service Magazine, p. 581.

30. Ibid.

31. Ibid, p. 583, 586.

32. Ibid, p. 581.

33. Ibid.

34. Ibid.

35. Ibid.

36. Ibid.

37. Ibid, p. 582.

38. Ibid, p. 584.

39. Ibid.

40. Ibid.

41. Ibid, p. 583.

42. Ibid, p. 584.

3. Ibid.

44. Anonymous. "Blazing the Mullan Road," *Mineral County Pioneer* (Vol. 6), published by the Mineral County Historical Society, Mineral County, Montana. (2010), p. 14. (mineralcountyinfo/BlazingTheMullanRoad.htm)

CHAPTER 8: AN AMERICAN EDEN

1. Ray Allen Billington (Editor). *Frontier and Section: Selected Essays of Frederick Jackson Turner*, p. 5.
2. Martin D. Hardin. "Across The New Northwest in 1860, Part One," *The United States Service Magazine*. (May 1882), p. 585.
3. Martin D. Hardin. "Across The New Northwest in 1860, Part Two. (Aug. 1882) *The United States Service Magazine*, p. 85.
4. Ibid.
5. Ibid.
6. Martin D. Hardin. "Across The New Northwest in 1860, Part One," *The United States Service Magazine*. (May 1882), p. 585, 586.
7. Ibid, p. 586.
8. Martin D. Hardin. "Across The New Northwest in 1860, Part Two," *The United States Service Magazine*. (Aug. 1882), p. 186.
9. Ibid. Hardin. "Across The New Northwest in 1860, Part One," *The United States Service Magazine*. (May 1882), p. 587.
10. Martin D. Hardin. "Across The New Northwest in 1860, Part Two," *The United States Service Magazine*. (Aug. 1882), p. 187.
11. Ibid.
12. Ibid.
13. Ibid, p. 188.
14. Ibid.
15. Ibid, p. 189.
16. Ibid.
17. Ibid.
18. Ibid.
19. Ibid, p. 190.
20. Ibid, p. 191.
21. Ibid.
22. Ibid, p. 192.
23. Ibid, p. 192, 193.
24. Ibid, p. 193.
25. Ibid.
26. Ibid, p. 194.
27. Ibid.
28. Ibid.
29. Ibid.
30. Ibid, p. 195.
31. Ibid.
32. Ibid, p. 196.
33. Ibid.

34. Ibid, p. 197.
35. Ibid.
36. Ibid.
37. Stephen Dow Beckham. "Lonely Outpost: The Army's Fort Umpqua," *Oregon Historical Quarterly*. (Sep. 1969); Janice Marschner. *Oregon 1859: A Snapshot In Time*, p. 217–218.

CHAPTER 9: ARMAGEDDON BECKONS
1. Stephen Dow Beckham. "Lonely Outpost: The Army's Fort Upqua," *Oregon Historical Quarterly* (Sept. 1969), p. 233, 245.
2. Ibid.
3. Martin D. Hardin. Letter from Fort Umpqua, Oregon Territory to his mother in Saratoga Springs, N.Y., Jan. 4, 1861. Hardin-Walworth Papers, SHM; Geoffrey O'Brien. *The Fall of the House of Walworth*, p. 113.
4. Ibid.
5. Carl Sandburg. *Lincoln: The Prairie Years and The War Years*, p. 182.
6. William Warren Hoppin. *The Peace Conference of 1861 at Washington (Part 3)*.
7. Anonymous. "The Peace Conference of 1861," *The New York Times*, June 18, 1865; Alfred H. Guernsey and Henry M. Alden. *Harper's Pictorial History of the Civil War*, p. 47 (note).
8. Reuben Hyde Walworth. Letter to Nicholas Rainey, St. Louis Mo., published in the *New York Times*, March 21, 1861.
9. Evelyn Barrett Britten. *Chronicles of Saratoga*, p. 244.
10. David Herbert Donald. *Lincoln*, p. 283–284.
11. Evelyn Barrett Britten. *Chronicles of Saratoga*, p. 244.
12. Carl Sandburg. *Abraham Lincoln: The Prairie Years and The War Years*, p. 189.
13. Letter from Mrs. Sarah Hardin Walworth, Saratoga Springs, N.Y., to President-Elect Abraham Lincoln, December 6, 1860. Abraham Lincoln Collection, Library of Congress.
14. Ibid.
15. Lincoln letter.
16. Ibid. Lincoln appoints McKee to Panama.
17. Evelyn Barrett Britten. *Chronicles of Saratoga*, p. 245.
18. Ernest B. Furgurson. *Freedom Rising—Washington in the Civil War*; Margaret Leech. *Reveille in Washington: 1860–1865*.
19. Julia Ward Howe. *Reminiscences, 1819–1899*, p. 269.
20. Evelyn Barrett Britten. *Chronicles of Saratoga*, p. 246.
21. Anonymous. "General Sumner's Panama Expedition. Aboard Orziba," *New York Times*, Nov. 16, 1861; *ORs*, Ser. 1, Vol. 50, Part 1, p. 526. Other officers aboard who were to figure in Hardin's Civil War battlefield career included: Lt. Phil H. Sheridan, Capt. Christopher C. Augur and Capt. George E. Pickett. Hardin served under Sheridan and Augur, and witnessed Pickett's Charge at Gettysburg.
22. Ezra J. Warner. *Generals In Blue*, p. 489–490.
23. Ibid.
24. *OR*, Series 2. Vol 2. Chapter 2, p. 1009.
25. Mark M. Boatner. "J. Lancaster Bent, 1826–1905," *The Civil War Dictionary*, p. 83;

Hubert Howe Bancroft. *History of California*, p. 239; H. D. Barrows. "J. Lancaster Bent," Publication of the Southern California and of the Pioneers of Los Angeles County, *Historical Society of Los Angeles County* V5; "William M. Gwin, 1805–1885," *Biographical Directory of the U. S. Congress* (bioguide.congress.gov/scripts/biodisplay. pl?index_goo540).

26. Elijah R. Kennedy. *The Contest for California in 1861*, p. 227–229.
27. Anonymous. "General Sumner's Panama Expedition. Aboard Orziba," *New York Times*, Nov. 16, 1861.
28. Reuben Hyde Walworth. Letter from R. H. Walworth, Saratoga Springs, N.Y. to President Abraham Lincoln, Washington, D.C., Nov. 18, 1861. Abraham Lincoln Collection, *Library of Congress*.
29. Ibid. Separate cover note from Chancellor Walworth addressed to Mary Todd Lincoln, Nov. 18, 1861.

CHAPTER 10: TRAITOR IN THEIR MIDST
1. Uzal W. Ent. *The Pennsylvania Reserves in the Civil War*, p. 1, 2. Dr. Josiah R. Sypher. *History of the Pennsylvania Reserve Corps, 1865*.
2. Martin D. Hardin. *History of the Twelfth Regiment, Pennsylvania Reserve Corps*, p. 21.
3. Ibid, p. 23.
4. Ezra J. Warner. *Generals In Blue*, p. 26.
5. Letter from J. F. Speed, Louisville, Ky. to Mrs. Sarah Hardin Walworth, Saratoga Springs, N.Y., Jan. 16, 1862. Hardin-Walworth Papers, SHM.
6. Letter from General John Wool, Washington, D.C. to Mrs. Sarah Hardin Walworth, n. d., Hardin-Walworth Papers, SHM.
7. Geoffrey O'Brien. *The Fall of the House of Walworth*, p. 119.
8. Ibid, p. 118.
9. Ibid, p. 117.
10. Ibid, p. 118–119.
11. Ibid, p. 121.
12. Ibid, p. 13.
13. Allison P. Bennett. *Saratoga Sojourn: A Biography of Ellen Hardin Walworth*, p. 81.
14. Major General William Harding Carter. "Martin D. Hardin, Class of 1859," *Annual Report by the United States Military Academy Association of Graduates*, June 11, 1924, p. 97.
15. Martin D. Hardin. *History of the Twelfth Regiment, Pennsylvania Reserve Corps*, p. 1–2.
16. Geoffrey O'Brien. *The Fall of the House of Walworth*, p. 120.
17. Ibid, p. 121–122.
18. Ibid, p. 122–123.
19. Ibid, p. 122.
20. Reuben Hyde Walworth. *Hyde Genealogy Or, The Descendants, in the Female as Well as in the Male Lines, From William Hyde of Norwich (1864)*.
21. Geoffrey O'Brien. *The Fall of the House of Walworth*, p. 125.
22. Ibid, p. 124.
23. George Templeton Strong. (Allan Nevins and Milton H. Thomas, Editors). *The Diary of George Templeton Strong: Post War Years, 1865–1875*, p. 169–170.
24. Ezra J. Warner. *General In Blue*, p. 242–243; Edward G. Longacre. *The Man Behind*

The Guns: A Biography of General Henry Jackson Hunt, Chief of Artillery, Army of the Potomac.

CHAPTER 11: THE HEAVENS RAIN FIRE AND IRON

1. Stephen W. Sears. *To the Gates of Richmond: The Peninsula Campaign.* P 24, 35.
2. Russell H. Beattie. *Army of the Potomac*, p. 275.
3. Stephen W. Sears. *To the Gates of Richmond: The Peninsula Campaign*, p. 36–38.
4. Ibid, p. 42.
5. Martin D. Hardin. *History of the Twelfth Regiment, Pennsylvania Reserve Volunteer Corps*, p. 26.
6. Stephen W. Sears. *To the Gates of Richmond: The Peninsula Campaign*, p. 99.
7. Martin D. Hardin. *History of the Twelfth Regiment, Pennsylvania Reserve Volunteer Corps*, p. 26.
8. Stephen W. Sears. *To the Gates of Richmond: The Peninsula Campaign*, p. 65.
9. Martin D. Hardin. *History of the Twelfth Regiment, Pennsylvania Reserve Volunteer Corps*, p. 32.
10. Ibid.
11. Mark M. Boatner III. *The Civil War Dictionary*, p. 272–274.
12. Ibid.
13. Ibid, p. 441.
14. Douglas Southhall Freeman. *R. E. Lee.*
15. James R. Arnold. *The Armies of U.S. Grant*, p. 274.
16. Mark M. Boatner III. *The Civil War Dictionary*, p. 54–542.
17. Ibid, p. 321.
18. Martin D. Hardin. *History of the Twelfth Regiment, Pennsylvania Reserve Volunteer Corps*, p. 49.
19. Mark M. Boatner III. *The Civil War Dictionary*, p. 721, 722.
20. Martin D. Hardin. *History of the Twelfth Regiment, Pennsylvania Reserve Volunteer Corps*, p. 53–75.
21. Ibid, p. 57.
22. Uzal W. Ent. *The Pennsylvania Reserves in the Civil War*, p. 86.
23. Martin D. Hardin. *History of the Twelfth Regiment, Pennsylvania Reserve Volunteer Corps*, p. 60.
24. Ibid, p. 63; Brian K. Burton. *Extraordinary Circumstances: The Seven Days Battles*, p. 308.
25. Ibid, p. 66.
26. Mark M. Boatner III. *The Civil War Dictionary*, p. 914–916.
27. Uzal W. Ent. *The Pennsylvania Reserves in the Civil War*, p. 100.
28. Mark M. Boatner III. *The Civil War Dictionary*, p. 914–916.
29. Stephen W. Sears. *To the Gates of Richmond: The Peninsula Campaign*, p. 103.
30. Ibid, p. 340; Mark M. Boatner III. *The Civil War Dictionary*, p. 504–507.
31. Mark M. Boatner III. *The Civil War Dictionary.* P 504; Martin D. Hardin. *History of the Twelfth Regiment, Pennsylvania Reserve Volunteer Corps*, p. 76.
32. Ibid, p. 504–507.
33. Edward G. Longacre. *The Man Behind the Guns: A Military Biography of General Henry J. Hunt*, p. 113–117.

34. Brian K. Burton. *Extraordinary Circumstances: The Seven Days Battles*, p. 357.
35. Martin D. Hardin. *History of the Twelfth Regiment, Pennsylvania Reserve Volunteer Corps*, p. 77–78.
36. Mark M. Boatner III. *The Civil War Dictionary*, p. 506.
37. Ibid.
38. Martin D. Hardin. *History of the Twelfth Regiment, Pennsylvania Reserve Volunteer Corps*, p. 78.
39. Ibid.
40. Ibid, p. 80.
41. Ibid, p. 79.
42. Ibid.
43. Ibid.
44. Ibid, p. 80.
45. Letter from Sergeant Thomas W. Dick, Co. H., Twelfth Pennsylvania Reserve Regiment from Harrison's Landing, Virginia to his brother in the North, August 1, 1862. *Pennsylvania Reserve Volunteer Corps Historical Society (PRVC) website: www.pareserves.com*
46. Letter from Lieutenant Chill H. Hazzard, Co. F, Twelfth Pennsylvania Reserve Regiment from Harrison Landing, Virginia to his father in the North, July 4, 1862. *Pennsylvania Reserve Volunteer Corps Historical Society (PRVC) website: www.pareserves.com*
47. Sergeant Major William Meyers letter to the brother of Private Alexander Rankin from Harrison's Landing, Virginia informing of the family of his death in combat, July 4, 1862. *Pennsylvania Reserve Volunteer Corps Historical Society (PRVC) website: www.pareserves.com*
48. Uzal W. Ent. *The Pennsylvania Reserves in the Civil War*, p. 104.
49. "Harrison's Landing Bombardment Recalled," *The National Tribune*, September 9, 1881.
50. Uzal W. Ent. *The Pennsylvania Reserves in the Civil War*, p. 104.
51. Ezra J. Warner. *Generals in Blue*, p. 442, 443; Martin D. Hardin. *History of the Twelfth Regiment, Pennsylvania Reserve Volunteer Corps*, p. 80.
52. Ibid, p. 376–377.
53. Martin D. Hardin. *History of the Twelfth Regiment, Pennsylvania Reserve Volunteer Corps*, p. 81.
54. Ezra J. Warner. *Generals in Blue*, p. 246–247; Uzal W. Ent. *The Pennsylvania Reserves in the Civil War*, p. 113; Francis Augustin O'Reilly. "Busted Up and Gone To Hell: The Assault of the Pennsylvania Reserves at Fredericksburg," *Civil War Regiments: A Journal of the American Civil War*. Vol. 4. No. 4, p. 1–27.
55. Martin D. Hardin. *History of the Twelfth Regiment, Pennsylvania Reserve Volunteer Corps*, p. 82.
56. Ibid.
57. Ibid.
58. Ibid.
59. Ibid.
60. Ibid, p. 83.
61. Ibid, p. 84.

62. Ibid.
63. Ibid.
64. Ibid.
65. Uzal W. Ent. *The Pennsylvania Reserves in the Civil War*, p. 106; Ezra J. Warner. *Generals in Blue*, p. 376,377.
66. Mark M. Boatner III. *The Civil War Dictionary*, p. 103.
67. Ibid.
68. Ibid.
69. Martin D. Hardin. *History of the Twelfth Regiment, Pennsylvania Reserve Volunteer Corps*, p. 86.
70. Uzal W. Ent. *The Pennsylvania Reserves in the Civil War*, p. 111.
71. Ibid, p. 112.
72. Martin D. Hardin. *History of the Twelfth Regiment, Pennsylvania Reserve Volunteer Corps*, p. 87.
73. Ibid, p. 89.
74. Ibid. Martin D. Hardin. *History of the Twelfth Regiment, Pennsylvania Reserve Volunteer Corps*, p. 113.
75. Ibid, p. 89, 90.
76. Ibid, p. 90.
77. Ibid.
78. Ibid.

CHAPTER 12: THE SUN NEVER SET ON A BRAVER MAN

1. Report of Brigadier General John F. Reynolds, commanding Third Division (Pennsylvania Reserves), McDowell's Corps, Army of Virginia, during the Second Battle of Bull Run, September 5, 1862, camp near Munson's Hill, Virginia. PRVC Website: pareserves.com
2. Martin D. Hardin. *History of the Twelfth Regiment, Pennsylvania Reserve Volunteer Corps*, p. 93, 94.
3. Ibid, p. 94.
4. Ibid.
5. Ibid.
6. Ibid, p. 95.
7. Ibid.
8. Ibid.
9. Ibid.
10. Ibid.
11. Ibid.
12. Ibid, p. 96.
13. Ibid, p. 92.
14. Ibid, p. 97, 98.
15. Ibid, p. 99.
16. Ibid.
17. Ibid, p. 100.
18. Scott C. Patchan. *Second Manassas: Longstreet's Attack and the Struggle for Chinn Ridge*, p. 10.

19. Martin D. Hardin. *History of the Twelfth Regiment, Pennsylvania Reserve Volunteer Corps*, p. 100.
20. Ibid.
21. Donald Bridgman Sanger and Thomas Robson Hay. *James Longstreet*, p. 88, 89.
22. John J. Hennessy. *Return to Bull Run: The Campaign and Battle of Second Manassas*, p. 373.
23. Ibid, p. 371.
24. Martin D. Hardin. *History of the Twelfth Regiment, Pennsylvania Reserve Volunteer Corps*, p. 100.
25. Ibid, p. 101.
26. John J. Hennessy. *Return to Bull Run: The Campaign and Battle of Second Manassas*, p. 370.
27. Jack D. Welsh. *Medical Histories of Union General*, p. 151, 152.
28. Martin D. Hardin. *History of the Twelfth Regiment, Pennsylvania Reserve Volunteer Corps*, p. 101.
29. Uzal W. Ent. *The Pennsylvania Reserves in the Civil War*, p. 125, 126; John J. Hennessy. *Return to Bull Run: The Campaign and Battle of Second Manassas*, p. 375–377.
30. Ibid, p. 128.
31. Edward H. Bonekemper III. "General Disobedience: 'Little Mac' lets John Pope twist in the wind," *Civil War Times*, (December 2010)
32. September 7 1862 letter home by Sergeant David Shirk, Co. G, Twelfth Pa. Reserve Regiment, later published in the September 7, 1862 edition of the *Shirleysburg (PA) Herald*. PRVC Historical Society Website: *www.pareserves.com*
33. Ibid, p. 98. Joseph W. A. Whitehorne. *Self-Guided Tour: The Battle of Second Manassas*, p. 7, 11. Donald Bridgman Sanger and Thomas Robson Hay. *James Longstreet*, p. 88; Mark M. Boatner. *The Civil War Dictionary*, p. 101–105. Note: More than 3,000 soldiers died at Second Manassas. Union killed, wounded and captured totaled 16,054 for a casualty rate of 21 percent. Confederate casualties totaled 9,197 for a 19 percent rate. Source: Mark M. Boatner III. *The Civil War Dictionary*, p. 105.

CHAPTER 13: SLAUGHTERED FOR NOTHING

1. Letter from Sarah (Hardin) Walworth of Sarasota Spring, N.Y. to her daughter, Ellen (Hardin) Walworth at Bird's Nest near Louisville, Ky., December 11, 1862. Hardin-Walworth Collection, SSM.
2. Mark M. Boatner III. *The Civil War Dictionary*, p. 245, 246.
3. Martin D. Hardin. *History of the Twelfth Regiment, Pennsylvania Reserve Volunteer Corps*, p. 101.
4. Ibid, p. 102.
5. Ibid, p. 101.
6. Ibid, p. 112; Uzal W. Ent. *The Pennsylvania Reserves in the Civil War*, p. 131.
7. Uzal W. Ent. *The Pennsylvania Reserves in the Civil War*, p. 130.
8. Ibid, p. 132; Mark M. Boatner III. *The Civil War Dictionary*, p. 17.
9. Mark M. Boatner III. *The Civil War Dictionary*, p. 20.
10. Martin D. Hardin. *History of the Twelfth Regiment, Pennsylvania Reserve Volunteer Corps*, p. 118.
11. Mark M. Boatner III. *The Civil War Dictionary*, p. 20.
12. Ibid, p. 17–21.

13. Ibid, p. 21.

14. Martin D. Hardin. *History of the Twelfth Regiment, Pennsylvania Reserve Volunteer Corps*, p. 126; Uzal W. Ent. *The Pennsylvania Reserves in the Civil War*, p. 130–159.

15. Letter from Sgt. Thomas W. Dick, Co. H, Twelfth Pa. Reserve Regt. near Belle Landing, Va., to his parents in Pennsylvania, January 3, 1863. *Pennsylvania Reserve Volunteer Corps Historical Society (PRVC)* website: *www.pareserves.com*

16. Uzal W. Ent. *The Pennsylvania Reserves in the Civil War*, p. 178.

17. Ibid.

18. Ibid, p. 184.

19. Ibid, p. 176.

20. Ibid, p. 184.

21. Martin D. Hardin. *History of the Twelfth Regiment, Pennsylvania Reserve Volunteer Corps*, p. 137.

22. Ibid, p. 135; Ezra Warner. *Generals In Blue*, p. 26.

23. Ibid, p. 137.

24. Ibid.

25. Mark M. Boatner III. *The Civil War Dictionary*, p.136–140.

26. Stephen W. Sears. *Chancellorsville*, p. 442–447.

27. Martin D. Hardin. *History of the Twelfth Regiment, Pennsylvania Reserve Volunteer Corps*, p. 137.

28. Ibid; Letter from Sgt. Thomas Dick, Co. H, Twelfth Pa. Reserve Regt., to his brother, Feb. 22, 1863. *Pennsylvania Reserve Volunteer Corps Historical Society (PRVC)* website: *www.pareserves.com*

29. Ibid, p. 138.

30. Ibid, p. 137.

31. Letter from Sgt. Thomas W. Dick, Co. H, Twelfth Pa. Reserve Regt., near Belle Landing, Va., to his parents in Pennsylvania, January 3, 1863. *Pennsylvania Reserve Volunteer Corps Historical Society (PRVC)* Website: *www.pareserves.com*

32. Letter from Sgt. Frank D. Stevens, Co. I, Twelfth Pa. Reserve Regt., near Miner's Hill, Va., to his father in Pennsylvania, March 22, 1863. *Pennsylvania Reserve Volunteer Corps Historical Society (PRVC)* Website: *www.pareserves.com*

CHAPTER 14: LONG, HOT, DUSTY ROAD TO GETTYSBURG

1. Martin D. Hardin. *History of the Twelfth Regiment, Pennsylvania Reserve Volunteer Corps*, p. 199.

2. John D. Nicholson (Editor). *Pennsylvania At Gettysburg: Ceremonies at the Dedication of Monuments*, p. 287. Martin D. Hardin. *History of the Twelfth Regiment, Pennsylvania Reserve Volunteer Corps*, p. 140.

3. Private A. D. Benedick. *Extracts from E. D. Benedick Diary.* (June 28, 1863 entry) Hardin Family Papers, CHM.

4. Richard Wagner. *For Honor, Flag, and Family: Civil War Major General Samuel W. Crawford, 1827–1892*, p. 20, 69; Ezra Warner. *Generals In Blue*, p. 99, 100; William Marvel. "Thorn In The Flesh," *Civil War Times Illustrated*. Vol.XLI. No.3. (June 2002).

5. Ibid, p. 91, 98, 99.

6. Ibid, p. 140.

7. Bradley M. Gottfried. *Brigades of Gettysburg: The Union and Confederate Brigades of the*

Battle of Gettysburg, p. 269–284; Martin D. Hardin. *History of the Twelfth Regiment, Pennsylvania Reserve Volunteer Corps*, p. xvi, 7, 182.

8. Larry Tagg. *Generals At Gettysburg*, p. 44; Stephen R. Taafe. *Commanding the Army of the Potomac*, p. 293.

9. Robert I. Girardi. *The Civil War Generals: Peers, Rivals (in their own words)*, p. 49–50.

10. Stephen R. Taafe. *Commanding the Army of the Potomac*, p. 203.

11. Richard Wagner. *For Honor, Flag, and Family: Civil War Major General Samuel W. Crawford, 1827–1892*, p. 131.

12. Letter from Sarah (Hardin) Walworth, Saratoga Springs, NY.

13. Martin D. Hardin. *History of the Twelfth Regiment, Pennsylvania Reserve Volunteer Corps*, p. 140, 141.

14. Ibid, p. 141; John D. Nicholson (Editor). *Pennsylvania At Gettysburg: Ceremonies at the Dedication of Monuments*, p. 287.

15. Uzal W. Ent. *The Pennsylvania Reserves in the Civil War*, p. 2.

16. Letter from Sgt. Thomas W. Dick, Twelfth Pennsylvania Reserve Regiment, Falls Church, Va., to his brother in Pennsylvania, March 6, 1863. *Pennsylvania Reserve Volunteer Corps Historical Society (PRVC)* website: *www.pareserves.com*

17. Martin D. Hardin. *History of the Twelfth Regiment, Pennsylvania Reserve Volunteer Corps*.

18. John D. Nicholson (Editor). *Pennsylvania At Gettysburg: Ceremonies at the Dedication of Monuments*, p. 287.

19. Martin D. Hardin. *History of the Twelfth Regiment, Pennsylvania Reserve Volunteer Corps*, p. 143.

20. Ibid.

21. Ibid, p. 144.

22. Ibid, p. 148.

23. Ibid, p. 144.

24. Larry Tagg. *Generals At Gettysburg*, p. 44.

25. Robert I. Girardi. *The Civil War Generals: Peers, Rivals (in their own words)*, p. 176.

26. Martin D. Hardin. *History of the Twelfth Regiment, Pennsylvania Reserve Volunteer Corps*, p. 144.

27. Private A. D. Benedick. *Extracts from E. D. Benedick Diary.* (July 1, 1863 entry) Hardin Family Papers, CHM.

28. Harry W. Pfanz. *Gettysburg, The Second Day*, p. 52.

29. Edwin B. Coddington. *The Gettysburg Campaign: A Study in Command*, p. 335; Jeffrey F. Sherry. "The Terrible Impetuosity," *Gettysburg Magazine*. No. 16. (January 1997); D. Scott Hartwig. "John Reynolds," *ANB*. Vol. 18, p. 382, 383; Martin D. Hardin. "Gettysburg Not A Surprise," *Military Essays and Recollections: Papers Read Before the Commandery of the State of Illinois (1892)*, p. 265–275. Military Order of the Loyal Legion of the United States. (MOLLUS)

30. John D. Nicholson (Editor). *Pennsylvania At Gettysburg: Ceremonies at the Dedication of Monuments*, p. 288–300.

CHAPTER 15: BIG ROUND TOP: EVERY MAN A COWARD IN THE DARK

1. Martin D. Hardin. *History of the Twelfth Regiment, Pennsylvania Reserve Volunteer Corps*, p. 144.

2. John D. Nicholson (Editor). *Pennsylvania At Gettysburg: Ceremonies at the Dedication*

of Monuments, p. 287; Martin D. Hardin. *History of the Twelfth Regiment, Pennsylvania Reserve Volunteer Corps*, p. 152.

3. Mark Adkin. *The Gettysburg Companion: The Complete Guide to America's Most Famous Battle*, p. 271; Ezra Warner. *Generals In Blue*, p. 446, 447.

4. Ibid, p. 407–442.

5. Mark Adkin. *The Gettysburg Companion: The Complete Guide to America's Most Famous Battle*, p. 442.

6. Ibid, p. 419, 420; Ezra J. Warner. *Generals In Blue*, p. 541, 542.

7. Ibid, p. 413–417; Mark M. Boatner III. *The Civil War Dictionary*, p. 336–337.

8. Martin D. Hardin. *History of the Twelfth Regiment, Pennsylvania Reserve Volunteer Corps*, p. 153.

9. Ibid.

10. Ibid.

11. Ezra J. Warner. *Generals In Blue*, p. 547, 548; Mark Adkin. *The Gettysburg Companion: The Complete Guide to America's Most Famous Battle*, p. 171, 175, 325, 415, 419.

12. Bradley M. Gottfried. "Fisher's Brigade at Gettysburg: The Big Round Top Controversy," *Gettysburg Magazine*. No. 19 (1998), p. 84–93; Uzal W. Ent. *The Pennsylvania Reserves in the Civil War*, p. 215, 216; Mark Adkin. *The Gettysburg Companion: The Complete Guide to America's Most Famous Battle*, p. 420; Harry W. Pfanz. *Gettysburg: The Second Day*, p. 393, 396–398.

13. Richard Wagner. *For Honor, Flag, and Family: Civil War Major General Samuel W. Crawford, 1827–1892*, p. 164, 165.

14. Martin D. Hardin. *History of the Twelfth Regiment, Pennsylvania Reserve Volunteer Corps*, p. 154. (magazine article on Crawford)

15. Bradley M. Gottfried. "Fisher's Brigade at Gettysburg: The Big Round Top Controversy," *Gettysburg Magazine*. No. 19 (1998), p. 90.

16. Ibid.

17. Ibid.

18. Martin D. Hardin. *History of the Twelfth Regiment, Pennsylvania Reserve Volunteer Corps*, p. 154, 155.

19. Ibid.

20. Bradley M. Gottfried. "Fisher's Brigade at Gettysburg: The Big Round Top Controversy," *Gettysburg Magazine*. No. 19 (1998), p. 91; John Pullen. *The Twentieth Maine: A Volunteer Regiment in the Civil War*, p. 130, 131.

21. Martin D. Hardin. *History of the Twelfth Regiment, Pennsylvania Reserve Volunteer Corps*, p. 155.

22. Private A. D. Benedick. *Extracts from E. D. Benedick Diary.* (July 2, 1863 entry) Hardin Family Papers, CHM.

23. Martin D. Hardin. *History of the Twelfth Regiment, Pennsylvania Reserve Volunteer Corps*, p. 155.

24. Bradley M. Gottfried. "Fisher's Brigade at Gettysburg: The Big Round Top Controversy," *Gettysburg Magazine*. No. 19 (1998), p. 92, 93.

25. Martin D. Hardin. *History of the Twelfth Regiment, Pennsylvania Reserve Volunteer Corps*, p. 155.

26. Private A.D. Benedick. *Extracts from E.D. Benedick Diary.* (July 3, 1863 entry) Hardin Family Papers, CHM.

27. Martin D. Hardin. *History of the Twelfth Regiment, Pennsylvania Reserve Volunteer Corps,* p. 156, 157.
28. Ibid, p. 156.
29. Mark M. Boatner III. *The Civil War Dictionary,* p. 339.
30. David Herbert Donald. *Lincoln,* p. 462.
31. Report of Colonel Joseph W. Fisher, Third Brigade, Third Division (Pennsylvania Reserves), July 9, 1863. *OR* 27 (1), p. 43; Martin D. Hardin. *History of the Twelfth Regiment, Pennsylvania Reserve Volunteer Corps,* p. 162.

CHAPTER 16: ATTACK, RETREAT, ENDURE
1. Mark Adkin. *The Gettysburg Companion: The Complete Guide to America's Most Famous Battle,* p. 530–532.
2. Mark M. Boatner III. *The Civil War Dictionary,* p. 273, 274.
3. David Herbert Donald. *Lincoln,* p. 446.
4. Uzal W. Ent. *The Pennsylvania Reserves in the Civil War,* p. 230.
5. Martin D. Hardin. *History of the Twelfth Regiment, Pennsylvania Reserve Volunteer Corps,* p. 165.
6. Ibid.
7. Ibid.
8. Tom Huntington. *Searching for George Gordon Meade, the Forgotten Victor of Gettysburg,* p. 204–217; Adrian G. Tighe. *The Bristoe Campaign: General Lee's Last Strategic Offense with The Army of Northern Virginia, October 1863,* p. 205.
9. Martin D. Hardin. *History of the Twelfth Regiment, Pennsylvania Reserve Volunteer Corps,* p. 167.
10. Adrian G. Tighe. *The Bristoe Campaign: General Lee's Last Strategic Offense with The Army of Northern Virginia, October 1863,* p. 245–265.
11. Martin D. Hardin. *History of the Twelfth Regiment, Pennsylvania Reserve Volunteer Corps,* p. 167; Adrian G. Tighe. *The Bristoe Campaign: General Lee's Last Strategic Offense with The Army of Northern Virginia, October 1863,* p. 245–265.
12. James I. Robertson. *General A.P. Hill: The Story of a Confederate Warrior,* p. 112, 234–240, 242, 247. Ibid, p. 169; Uzal W. Ent. *The Pennsylvania Reserves in the Civil War,* p. 231, 232.
13. Martin D. Hardin. *History of the Twelfth Regiment, Pennsylvania Reserve Volunteer Corps,* p. 168.
14. Mark M. Boatner III. *The Civil War Dictionary,* p. 88.
15. Douglas Southhall Freeman. *Robert E. Lee,* p. 327. Vol. 3.
16. Martin D. Hardin. *History of the Twelfth Regiment, Pennsylvania Reserve Volunteer Corps,* p. 169.
17. Adrian G. Tighe. *The Bristoe Campaign: General Lee's Last Strategic Offense with The Army of Northern Virginia, October 1863,* p. 309.
18. Martin F. Graham and George F. Skoch. *Mine Run: A Campaign of Lost Opportunities,* p. 16–18; Ezra J. Warner. Generals In Blue, p. 167, 168; Uzal W. Ent. *The Pennsylvania Reserves in the Civil War,* p. 231.
19. Martin D. Hardin. *History of the Twelfth Regiment, Pennsylvania Reserve Volunteer Corps,* p. 170, 171.
20. Mark M. Boatner III. *The Civil War Dictionary,* p. 680, 681.

21. Stephen E. Ambrose. *Upton and the Army*, p. 24–26; Ezra J. Warner. *Generals In Blue*, p. 519, 520.

22. Mark M. Boatner III. *The Civil War Dictionary*, p. 680, 681.

23. Ibid.

24. Nicholas Smith. *Stories of Great National Songs*, p. 155.

25. Letter by First Sergeant Frank D. Stevens, Co I, Twelfth Pa. Reserve Regt., Miner's Hill, Va., to friends in Pennsylvania, March 22, 1863. *Pennsylvania Reserve Volunteer Corps Historical Society (PRVC)* website: *www.pareserves.com*

26. Martin F. Graham and George F. Skoch. *Mine Run: A Campaign of Lost Opportunities*, p. 36, 45–59; Mark M. Boatner III. *The Civil War Dictionary*, p. 680, 681.

27. Martin D. Hardin. *History of the Twelfth Regiment, Pennsylvania Reserve Volunteer Corps*, p. 171; Ezra J. Warner. *Generals In Blue*, p. 541, 542; Martin F. Graham and George F. Skoch. *Mine Run: A Campaign of Lost Opportunities*, p. 57–75.

28. Martin D. Hardin. *History of the Twelfth Regiment, Pennsylvania Reserve Volunteer Corps*, p. 172, 173.

29. Ibid, p. 173.

30. Uzal W. Ent. *The Pennsylvania Reserves in the Civil War*, p. 233.

31. David. M. Jordan. *Happiness Is Not My Companion: The Life of General G. K. Warren*, p. 144, 171, 316; Ezra J. Warner. *Generals In Blue*, p. 541, 542.

CHAPTER 17: BUSHWHACKED: LITTLE HOPE OF RECOVERY

1. Martin D. Hardin. *History of the Twelfth Regiment, Pennsylvania Reserve Volunteer Corps*, p. 173.

2. James G. Ramage. *Gray Ghost: The Life of Col. John Singleton Mosby*, p. 1.

3. Martin D. Hardin. *History of the Twelfth Regiment, Pennsylvania Reserve Volunteer Corps*, p. 174; J. R. Sypher. *History of the Pennsylvania Reserves*, p. 502.

4. Letter from Reuben Hyde Walworth, Saratoga Springs, N.Y. to his wife, Sarah Hardin Walworth, Washington, D.C., Dec. 15, 1863. Hardin-Walworth Papers, SSHM.

5. Letter from Sarah Hardin Walworth, Ebbett House, Washington, D.C. to her husband, Reuben Hyde Walworth, Saratoga Springs, N.Y., Dec. 17, 1863. Hardin-Walworth Papers, SSHM.

6. Letter from Sarah Hardin Walworth, Ebbett House, Washington, D.C. to her husband, Reuben Hyde Walworth, Saratoga Springs, N.Y., Dec. 20, 1863. Hardin-Walworth Papers, SSHM.

7. Ibid.

8. Letter from Mrs. Reuben Hyde Walworth, Saratoga Springs, N.Y. to President Abraham Lincoln, White House, Jan. 7, 1864. Abraham Lincoln Collection, Library of Congress.

9. Geoffrey O'Brien. *The Fall of the House of Walworth: A Tale of Madness and Murder in Gilded Age America*, p. 123.

10. Ibid, p. 38, 132, 137–138, 156–159, 162.

11. Patrick W. Carey. "Clarence Augustus Walworth, 1820–1900," ANB. Vol. 22, p. 593–594.

12. Geoffrey O'Brien. *The Fall of the House of Walworth: A Tale of Madness and Murder in Gilded Age America*, p. 133.

13. Ibid, p. 136–137, 154–155, 185–186.
14. Letter from Major H. B. Lewis, Adjutant, USMA at West Point to Nelson Thommasson of Chicago (close friend of the late General M. D. Hardin), Jan. 5, 1924. Hardin Papers, SAHSRL.
15. Letter from Sarah Hardin Walworth, Washington, D.C. to her daughter, Ellen "Nelly" (Hardin) Walworth, Louisville, Ky., March 6, 1864. Hardin Papers, SAHSRL; General Assembly of Kentucky. "Biographical Sketch of the Honorable Lazarus W. Powell, Governor of the state of Kentucky from 1851–1855 and a senator in Congress from 1859–1865," Frankfort, Ky., 1868. Note: Powell was a conservative Democrat, a critic of Lincoln, and anti-Negro rights.
16. Ibid.
17. Ibid.
18. Ibid; Ezra J. Warner. *Generals In Blue*: (Gen. Alexander Stewart Webb), p. 544–545, (Bvt. Gen. John I. Curtain), p. 584, (Gen. John Wilson Sprague), p. 468–469.
19. Letter from Sarah Hardin Walworth, Pittsburgh, Pa., to her husband, Reuben Hyde Walworth, Saratoga Springs, N.Y., May 22, 1864. Hardin-Walworth Papers, SSHM.
20. Ibid.
21. Dr. Josiah R. Sypher. *History of the Pennsylvania Reserve Corps*, p. 527, 528.

CHAPTER 18: EVEN BRAVE MEN RUN: FIGHTING WITH GRANT'S ARMY
1. Uzal W. Ent. *The Pennsylvania Reserves in the Civil War*, p. 254.
2. Mark M. Boatner III. *The Civil War Dictionary*, p. 925.
3. David Herbert Donald. *Lincoln*, p. 515.
4. Mark M. Boatner III. *The Civil War Dictionary*, p. 788, 799.
5. Uzal W. Ent. *The Pennsylvania Reserves in the Civil War*, p. 262.
6. Ibid, p. 254, 258.
7. *History of the Bucktails: Kane Rifle Regiment of the Pennsylvania Reserve Corps (13th Pa. Reserves, 42nd of the Line)*, p. 307, 308.
8. Martin D. Hardin. *History of the Twelfth Regiment, Pennsylvania Reserve Volunteer Corps*, p. 183.
9. Ibid.
10. Ibid.
11. Ibid.
12. Ibid.
13. Ibid.
14. Ibid.
15. Ibid.
16. Ibid, p. 183, 184.
17. J. Michael Miller. "Strike Them A Blow: Lee and Grant at the North Anna River," *Blue & Gray Magazine*. Vol X. No. 4. (April 1993), p. 13.
18. *History of the Bucktails: Kane Rifle Regiment of the Pennsylvania Reserve Corps (13th Pa. Reserves, 42nd of the Line)*, p. 311–313.
19. Ibid, p. 318–320.
20. Ibid.
21. Noah Andre Trudeau. *Bloody Roads South: The Wilderness to Cold Harbor, May–June 1864*, p. 228, 229.

22. Charles S. Wainwright. (Allan Nevins, Editor) *A Diary of Battle: The Personal Journals of Colonel Charles S. Wainwright, 1861, 1865*, p. 384.

23. Martin D. Hardin. *History of the Twelfth Regiment, Pennsylvania Reserve Volunteer Corps*, p. 186. J. Michael Miller; "Strike Them A Blow: Lee and Grant at the North Anna River," *Blue & Gray Magazine*. Vol X. No. 4. (April 1993), p. 71, 72.

24. Ibid.

25. J. Michael Miller. "Strike Them A Blow: Lee and Grant at the North Anna River," *Blue & Gray Magazine*. Vol X. No. 4. (April 1993), p. 45.

26. Ibid.

27. Martin D. Hardin. *History of the Twelfth Regiment, Pennsylvania Reserve Volunteer Corps*, p. 187.

28. Ibid.

29. Ibid.

30. Ibid; Ezra J. Warner. *Generals in Blue*, p. 57, 58.

31. Gordon C. Rhea. *To The North Anna River: Grant and Lee, May 13–25, 1864*, p. 323, 323, 353.

32. Ibid, p. 323.

33. Noah Andre Trudeau. *Bloody Roads South: The Wilderness to Cold Harbor, May–June 1864*, p. 239; J. Michael Miller. "Strike Them A Blow: Lee and Grant at the North Anna River," *Blue & Gray Magazine*. Vol X. No. 4. (April 1993), p. 12, 13.

34. J. Michael Miller. "Strike Them A Blow: Lee and Grant at the North Anna River," *Blue & Gray Magazine*. Vol X. No. 4. (April 1993), p. 54, 55.

35. Uzal W. Ent. *The Pennsylvania Reserves in the Civil War*, p. 277–283.

36. *History of the Bucktails: Kane Rifle Regiment of the Pennsylvania Reserve Corps (13th Pa. Reserves, 42nd of the Line)*, p. 318–320.

37. Martin D. Hardin. *History of the Twelfth Regiment, Pennsylvania Reserve Volunteer Corps*, p. 188.

38. Ibid, p. 189.

39. Ibid.

40. Charles S. Wainwright. (Allan Nevins, Editor) *A Diary of Battle: The Personal Journals of Colonel Charles S. Wainwright, 1861, 1865*, p. 393.

41. Martin D. Hardin. *History of the Twelfth Regiment, Pennsylvania Reserve Volunteer Corps*, p. 189.

42. Gordon C. Rhea. "Butchery at Bethesda Church," *America's Civil War Magazine*. (January 2002), p. 52.

43. Ibid, p. 50.

44. Martin D. Hardin. *History of the Twelfth Regiment, Pennsylvania Reserve Volunteer Corps*, p. 190; Gordon C. Rhea. "Butchery at Bethesda Church," *America's Civil War Magazine*. (January 2002), p. 52.

45. Gordon C. Rhea. "Butchery at Bethesda Church," *America's Civil War Magazine*. (January 2002), p. 53.

46. Ibid, p. 52.

47. Mark M. Boatner III. *The Civil War Dictionary*, p. 360, 361.

48. Gordon C. Rhea. "Butchery at Bethesda Church," *America's Civil War Magazine*. (January 2002), p. 53; Anonymous. "Bethesda Church Battle," *New York Times*, June 4, 1864.

49. Ibid.
50. Charles S. Wainwright. (Allan Nevins, Editor) *A Diary of Battle: The Personal Journals of Colonel Charles S. Wainwright, 1861, 1865*, p. 394.
51. Gordon C. Rhea. "Butchery at Bethesda Church," *America's Civil War Magazine*. (January 2002), p. 53.
52. Gordon C. Rhea. *Cold Harbor: Grant and Lee, May 26–June 3, 1864*, p. 130, 139–143, 145, 438n68.
53. Robert E. Eberly, Jr. *Bouquets from the Cannon's Mouth: Soldiering with the Eighth Regiment of the Pennsylvania Reserves*, p. 193.
54. Gordon C. Rhea. "Butchery at Bethesda Church," *America's Civil War Magazine*. (January 2002), p. 54.
55. O.R. Howard Thomson and William H. Rauch. *History of the Bucktails: Kane Rifle Regiment of the Pennsylvania Reserve Corps (13th Pa. Reserves, 42nd of the Line)*, p. 320.
56. Richard Wagner. *For Honor, Flag, and Family: Civil War Major General Samuel W. Crawford, 1827–1892*, p. 211, 212; ORs (1)Vol. 36 (i), p. 158.
57. Gordon C. Rhea. "Butchery at Bethesda Church," *America's Civil War Magazine*. (January 2002), p. 54.
58. Richard Wagner. *For Honor, Flag, and Family: Civil War Major General Samuel W. Crawford, 1827–1892*, p. 212, 213.
59. Letter of recommendation for Brigadier General Martin D. Hardin from General George Gordon Meade, Army of the Potomac, June 1863. Hardin Family Papers. CHM.

CHAPTER 19: DESPERATE HOURS: REBEL RAIDERS MENACE WASHINGTON

1. Evelyn Britten. *Chronicles of Saratoga*, p. 244–261.
2. Ibid, p. 305–315; Ellen Hardin Walworth. "Reuben Hyde Walworth, The Last of the New York Chancellors," *The New York Genealogical and Biographical Record*. Vol. 26. No. 3 (July 1895), p. 109.
3. Evelyn Britten. *Chronicles of Saratoga*, p. 251–253; Original note written on the back of an envelope by President Lincoln nominating Colonel Martin D. Hardin for promotion to brigadier general, June 30, 1864. SSHM; *Record of General Hardin's Military Career* annotated in a January 5, 1924 letter from Major H. B. Lewis, Adjutant, United States Military Academy at West Point, written in response to an information request from Nelson Thomasson, a long-time Chicago friend of the late General Hardin. Hardin Papers, SAHSRL.
4. Ibid, p. 253.
5. Letter from Sarah Hardin Walworth, Washington, D.C. to Chancellor Reuben Hyde Walworth, Saratoga Spring, N.Y., July 4, 1864. Walworth-Hardin Papers, SSHM.
6. Benjamin Franklin Cooling. *Jubal Early's Raid on Washington*, p. 232.
7. Ibid, p. 193.
8. Jack E. Schairer. *Lee's Bold Plan for Point Lookout: The Rescue of Confederate Prisoners That Never Took Place*, p. 74.
9. Benjamin Franklin Cooling. *Jubal Early's Raid on Washington*, p. 93.
10. Joseph Judge. *Season of Fire: The Confederate Strike On Washington*, p. 218–219; Jack E. Schairer. *Lee's Bold Plan for Point Lookout: The Rescue of Confederate Prisoners That Never Took Place*, p. 83.

11. Martin D. Hardin. "The Defense of Washington Against Early's Attack In July 1864," *Military Essays and Recollections: Papers Read Before Commandery of the State of Illinois, Military Order of the Loyal Legion of the United States.*

12. Jack E. Schairer. *Lee's Bold Plan for Point Lookout: The Rescue of Confederate Prisoners That Never Took Place*, p. 74.

13. Count Adam Gurowski. *My Diary.* Vol 3. (1864–1866), p. 277.

14. Benjamin Franklin Cooling. *Monocacy: The Battle That Saved Washington.*

15. F. Colburn Adams. *Siege of Washington (written expressly for little people)*, p. 101, 106.

16. Gideon Welles. *Diary of Gideon Welles, Secretary of the Navy Under Lincoln and Johnson.* Vol. 2.(1864–66), p. 73.

17. Benjamin Franklin Cooling. *Jubal Early's Raid on Washington*, p. 98–100.

18. Ibid.

19. Martin D. Hardin. "The Defense of Washington Against Early's Attack In July 1864," *Military Essays and Recollections: Papers Read Before Commandery of the State of Illinois, Military Order of the Loyal Legion of the United States.*

20. Ibid.

21. Benjamin Franklin Cooling. *Jubal Early's Raid on Washington*, p. 90.

22. Anonymous. *Frank Leslie's Illustrated News* (July 30, 1864), p. 290, 296.

23. Ezra J. Warner. *Generals In Blue*, p. 12.

24. Ibid.

25. *ORs.* (1) Vol. 37. Part One (Reports). Report of Brigadier General M. D. Hardin, Commanding Northern Defenses, July 19, 1864, p. 236–237.

26. *ORs.* (1) Vol. 37. Part One (Reports). Report of Major William H. Fry, Sixteenth Pa. Cavalry, July 26, 1864, p. 248.

27. Wayne Fanebust. *Major General Alexander McCook, USA: A Civil War Biography*, p. 29, 74; *Whitelaw Reid. Ohio In The War: Her Statesmen, Generals and Soldiers.* Vol. 2, p. 807–808; Ezra J. Warner. *Generals In Blue*, p. 294–295.

28. Ibid.

29. Ibid.

30. Ibid, p. 225–238.

31. Martin D. Hardin. "The Defense of Washington Against Early's Attack In July 1864," *Military Essays and Recollections: Papers Read Before Commandery of the State of Illinois, Military Order of the Loyal Legion of the United States.*

32. Benjamin Franklin Cooling. *Jubal Early's Raid on Washington*, p. 87.

33. Ibid, p. 120; Benjamin Franklin Cooling. *The Day Lincoln Was Almost Shot: The Fort Stevens Story*, p. 131, 133, 138, 141, 146–147, 166–167.

34. Byron Stinson. "The Invalid Corps," *Civil War Times Illustrated.* Vol. 10. No. 2. (May 1971); Edward J. Stackpole. "The Day the Rebels Could Have Marched into the White House," *Civil War Times Illustrated.* No. 10. (February–March 1961)

35. Martin D. Hardin. "The Defense of Washington Against Early's Attack In July 1864," *Military Essays and Recollections: Papers Read Before Commandery of the State of Illinois, Military Order of the Loyal Legion of the United States.*

36. Ibid.

37. Ibid.

38. Ibid.

39. Noah Brooks. *Washington In Lincoln's Time*, p. 174.

40. Ethan Allen Hitchcock. *Fifty Years In Camp and Field*, p. 463.

CHAPTER 20: GENERAL HARDIN MAKES A BRAVE SHOW

1. Martin D. Hardin. "The Defense of Washington Against Early's Attack In July 1864," *Military Essays and Recollections: Papers Read Before Commandery of the State of Illinois, Military Order of the Loyal Legion of the United States.*
2. Byron Stinson. "The Invalid Corps," *Civil War Times Illustrated*. Vol. 10. No. 2. (May 1971)
3. John F. Marszalek. *Commander of All Lincoln's Armies: A Life of General Henry W. Halleck*, p. 205–213.
4. Martin D. Hardin. "The Defense of Washington Against Early's Attack In July 1864," *Military Essays and Recollections: Papers Read Before Commandery of the State of Illinois, Military Order of the Loyal Legion of the United States.*
5. James McLean. *California Sabers: The Second Massachusetts Cavalry in the Civil War*, p. 91–95; Benjamin Franklin Cooling. *Symbol, Sword, and Shield: Defending Washington During The Civil War*, p. 194.
6. Edward W. Emerson. *Life and Letters of Charles Russell Lowell*, p. 321–329, 405.
7. Ibid, p. 14–17.
8. Ibid, p. 16.
9. Martin D. Hardin. "The Defense of Washington Against Early's Attack In July 1864," *Military Essays and Recollections: Papers Read Before Commandery of the State of Illinois, Military Order of the Loyal Legion of the United States.*
10. Ibid.
11. Benjamin Franklin Cooling. *The Day Lincoln Was Almost Shot: The Fort Stevens Story*, p. 148.
12. Benjamin Franklin Cooling. *Jubal Early's Raid on Washington*, p. 110.
13. Ibid, p. 262.
14. Ibid, p. 168.
15. Martin D. Hardin. "The Defense of Washington Against Early's Attack In July 1864," *Military Essays and Recollections: Papers Read Before Commandery of the State of Illinois, Military Order of the Loyal Legion of the United States.*
16. James McLean. *California Sabers: The Second Massachusetts Cavalry in the Civil War*, p. 92; Jack E. Schairer. *Lee's Bold Plan For Point Lookout: The Rescue of Confederate Prisoners That Never Happened*, p. 205–206.
17. ORs. (1) Vol. 37. Part Two (Correspondence), p. 198.
18. ORs. (1) Vol. 37. Part Two (Correspondence), p. 238.
19. Ibid.
20. ORs. (1) Vol. 37. Part Two (Correspondence), p. 199.
21. ORs. (1) Vol. 37. Part One (Reports), p. 241–242.
22. ORs. (1) Vol. 37. Part Two (Correspondence), p. 197.
23. ORs. (1) Vol. 37. Part Two (Correspondence), p. 200.
24. ORs. (1) Vol. 37. Part Two (Correspondence), p. 200.
25. Ibid.
26. Ibid.
27. ORs. (1) Vol. 37. Part One (Reports), p. 241.
28. Benjamin Franklin Cooling. *Jubal Early's Raid on Washington*, p. 120–121.

29. ORs. (1) Vol. 37. Part One (Reports), p. 241; Jack E. Schairer. *Lee's Bold Plan for Point Lookout: The Rescue of Confederate Prisoners That Never Took Place*, p. 190–191, 198–199.

30. Jane Grey Swisshelm. (Arthur L. Larsen, Editor) *Crusader and Feminist: Letters of Jane Grey Swisshelm, 1858–1865*, p. 273–274.

31. Anonymous. *Frank Leslie's Illustrated News* (July 30, 1864), p. 290, 296.

32. Martin D. Hardin. "The Defense of Washington Against Early's Attack In July 1864," *Military Essays and Recollections: Papers Read Before Commandery of the State of Illinois, Military Order of the Loyal Legion of the United States*.

33. Benjamin Franklin Cooling. *Jubal Early's Raid on Washington*, p. 118–120, 123.

34. ORs. (1) Vol. 37. Part Two (Correspondence), p. 201.

35. ORs. (1) Vol. 37. Part Two (Correspondence), p. 201.

36. Jefrey Wert. "Rappahannock Station," *Civil War Times Illustrated*. (December 1976)

37. ORs. (1) Vol. 37. Part Two (Correspondence), p. 201.

38. ORs. (1) Vol. 37. Part Two (Correspondence), p. 198.

39. ORs. (1) Vol. 37. Part Two (Correspondence), p. 199.

40. Jack E. Schairer. *Lee's Bold Plan for Point Lookout: The Rescue of Confederate Prisoners That Never Took Place*, p. 181.

41. ORs. (1) Vol. 37. Part Two (Correspondence), p. 237.

42. Martin D. Hardin. "The Defense of Washington Against Early's Attack In July 1864," *Military Essays and Recollections: Papers Read Before Commandery of the State of Illinois, Military Order of the Loyal Legion of the United States*.

43. Benjamin Franklin Cooling. *Jubal Early's Raid on Washington*, p. 138.

44. ORs. (1) Vol. 37. Part Two (Correspondence), p. 237.

45. Martin D. Hardin. "The Defense of Washington Against Early's Attack In July 1864," *Military Essays and Recollections: Papers Read Before Commandery of the State of Illinois, Military Order of the Loyal Legion of the United States*.

46. ORs. (1) Vol. 37. Part Two (Correspondence), p. 237.

47. Benjamin Franklin Cooling. *Jubal Early's Raid on Washington*, p. 171.

48. Jack E. Schairer. *Lee's Bold Plan for Point Lookout: The Rescue of Confederate Prisoners That Never Took Place*, p. 23–28, 130–135, 141, 146, 164, 168–169.

49. Ibid.

50. Ibid, p. 135.

51. ORs. (1) Vol. 37. Part Two (Correspondence), p. 239.

52. ORs. (1) Vol. 37. Part Two (Correspondence), p. 239.

CHAPTER 21: GARRISON SOLDIER IN WARTIME WASHINGTON

1. Martin D. Hardin. "The Defense of Washington Against Early's Attack In July 1864," *Military Essays and Recollections: Papers Read Before Commandery of the State of Illinois, Military Order of the Loyal Legion of the United States*.

2. Ibid.

3. Jack E. Schairer. *Lee's Bold Plan for Point Lookout: The Rescue of Confederate Prisoners That Never Took Place*, p. 179–180.

4. Frank Wilkerson. *A Private Soldier in the Army of the Potomac*, p. 218.

5. Benjamin Franklin Cooling. *The Battle of Monocacy*.

6. Mark M. Boatner III. *The Civil War Dictionary*, p. 255–257.

7. Jack E. Schairer. *Lee's Bold Plan for Point Lookout: The Rescue of Confederate Prisoners That Never Took Place*, p. 206.
8. Letter from General Hardin, Washington, D.C. to Miss Dolly Smith, Saratoga Springs, N.Y., July 11, 1864. Hardin-Walworth Collection, SSHM.
9. John Simon. (editor) *The Paper of Ulysses S. Grant*. Vol. 2 (June 1, 1864 to August 15, 1864), p. 228–232, 231n; Janet E. Steele. "Charles Anderson Dana, 1819–1897," *ANB*. Vol. 6, p. 55–58. (See also: Janet E. Steele. *The Sun Shines On All: Journalism and Ideology in the Life of Charles Anderson Dana*.)
10. Benjamin Franklin Cooling. *Jubal Early's Raid on Washington*, p. 221–223; Paul Andrew Hutton. *Phil Sheridan and His Army*, p. 10–27.
11. James A. Ramage. *Grey Ghost: The Life of Col. John Singleton Mosby*, p. 18.
12. ORs. (1) Vol. 37. Part 2, p. 560–563; "Mosby," *New York Times*, Aug. 3, 1864.
13. Ibid.
14. Mike Wright. *What They Didn't Teach You About the Civil War*, p. 147–148.
15. Ron Tendick. "Time Line: the Life of Lemuel Smith Hardin (1840–1909)," Note: This is an annotated time-line provided the author by Mr. Tendick, a local historian in Jacksonville, IL.
16. Evelyn Britten. *Chronicles of Saratoga*, p. 248–249.
17. Photograph of Lemuel Smith Hardin taken in Montreal, Canada (1864–65). Hardin-Walworth Collection. SSHM.
18. Letter from Sarah Hardin Walworth, Saratoga Springs, New York to President Abraham Lincoln, Washington, D.C., Dec. 15, 1864. Abraham Lincoln Collection, Library of Congress.
19. Ibid.
20. Edward Waldo Emerson and Joan Waugh. *Life and Letters of Charles Russell Lowell*, p. 62–65, 376, 475; Ezra J. Warner. *Generals In Blue*, p. 284–285.
21. Uzal W. Ent. *The Pennsylvania Reserves in the Civil War*, p. 178; Ezra J. Warner. *Generals In Blue*, p. 26.
22. A. B. Bernard. *Reminiscences of West Point in the Olden Time*, p. 36–37; "Death of General Harker," *Harper's Weekly*, Jun 23, 1864, p. 467.
23. Ibid.

CHAPTER 22: GOOD FRIDAY AT FORD'S THEATER

1. Ernest B. Furgurson. *Freedom Rising: Washington in the Civil War*, p.14, 78, 144–145, 159, 191, 206–208, 214, 262, 361.
2. Ibid.
3. Brian J. Kenny. "Orville Hickman Browning, 1806–1881," *ANB*. Vol. 3, p. 769–770; David Herbert Donald. *Lincoln*, p. 273, 285, 293–294, 296, 316–317, 402–403.
4. Orville Hickman Browning. *The Diary of Orville Hickman Browning*, p. 1
5. Lawrence P. Gooley. "North County Abolitionist James Rood Doolittle, *An Adirondack Almanack* Website: www:andirondackalmanack.com
6. Ibid.
7. Orville Hickman Browning. *The Diary of Orville Hickman Browning*, p. 15.
8. Jack E. Schairer. *Lee's Bold Plan for Point Lookout: The Rescue of Confederate Prisoners That Never Took Place*, p. 95.

9. Orville Hickman Browning. *The Diary of Orville Hickman Browning*, p. 31.

10. Ibid, p. 33; Frederic Ray, "General Hardin ... A Little Larger," *Civil War Times Illustrated Magazine*. No. 10. (July 1971), p. 40–41. Note: Ray's articles deals with a photograph of General and (presumably) Mrs. Estelle Hardin in front of his downtown Nineteenth Street, Washington headquarters in April of 1865.

11. Ibid, p. 38.

12. Reverend Clarence Walworth Backus. "Closing War Scenes," *The Magazine of History*. Vol. XX. No. 6. (June 1915).

13. Evelyn Barrett Britten. *Chronicles of Saratoga*, p. 244–261.

14. Martin D. Hardin. *History of the Twelfth Regiment, Pennsylvania Reserve Volunteer Corps*, p. 141.

15. Ibid.

16. Ibid, p. 29.

17. David Herbert Donald. *Lincoln*, p. 565–568.

18. Ibid.

19. Tidwell, William A. and James O. Hall. *Come Retribution: The Confederate Secret Service and The Assassination of Lincoln*, p. 411.

20. Martin D. Hardin. *History of the Twelfth Regiment, Pennsylvania Reserve Volunteer Corps*, p. 174.

21. Noah Brooks. *Washington In Lincoln's Time*, p. 244.

22. Ibid.

23. Nicholas Smith. *Stories of Great National Songs*, p. 155.

24. Michael W. Kauffman. *American Brutus: John Wilkes Booth and The Lincoln Conspiracies*, p. 70–21.

25. Ibid, p. 22–24.

26. Ibid, p. 24.

27. Ibid, p. 59.

28. Ibid, p. 75, 227–228, 257, 273, 349.

29. Ibid.

30. Ibid.

31. ORs. (1) Vol. 46 (3), p. 1041.

32. Michael W. Kauffman. *American Brutus: John Wilkes Booth and The Lincoln Conspiracies*, p. 69–70.

33. Ibid, p. 33.

34. Ibid, p. 62.

35. Ibid, p. 58, 59, 75.

36. Ibid, p. 62.

37. Ibid, p. 59.

38. Carl Sandburg. *Abraham Lincoln: The Prairie Years and The War Years*, p. 587–588.

39. Noah Brooks. *Washington In Lincoln's Time*, p. 231.

40. Ibid.

41. Letter written in the White House by General Hardin to his mother, Sarah (Hardin) Walworth, Saratoga Springs, New York, April 17, 1865 two days after Lincoln's death. Hardin Collection. CHM.

42. John E. Elliott & Barry Cauchon. "13 Days Aboard the Monitors," *A Peek Inside The Walls: The Final Days of the Lincoln Conspirators*, p. 5, 6, 8.

43. David Herbert Donald. *Lincoln*, p. 579, 580–581; Carl Sandburg. *Abraham Lincoln: The Prarie Years and The War Years*, p. 585–587.

44. Michael W. Kauffman. *American Brutus: John Wilkes Booth and The Lincoln Conspiracies*, p. 22–23.

45. Ibid.

46. Ibid.

47. Ibid.

48. Ibid.

49. Tullio S. Verdi. "The Assassination of the Sewards by T. S. Verdi, the family doctor," *Juanita Sentinel*, Mifflintown, Pa., June 25, 1873.

50. Ibid.

51. Ibid.

52. Michael W. Kauffman. *American Brutus: John Wilkes Booth and The Lincoln Conspiracies*, p. 267.

53. John E. Elliott & Barry Cauchon. "13 Days Aboard the Monitors," *A Peek Inside The Walls: The Final Days of the Lincoln Conspirators*, p. 5, 6, 8.

54. "Tragedy of April 14, 1865 As Recalled By Eight Survivors of the U.S. Military Telegraph Corps," *Washington Post*, April 11, 1915.

55. Ibid.

56. Tullio S. Verdi. "The Assassination of the Sewards by T. S. Verdi, the family doctor," *Juanita Sentinel*, Mifflintown, Pa., June 25, 1873.

57. Ibid.

58. Martin D. Hardin. *History of the Twelfth Regiment, Pennsylvania Reserve Volunteer Corps*, p. 174.

59. Carl Sandburg. *Abraham Lincoln: The Prairie Years and The War Years*, p. 605–606.

60. Allen Culling Clark. *Abraham Lincoln in the National Capitol*, p. 117.

61. Ibid.

62. "The Funeral," *The Washington Evening Star*, April 20, 1865, p. 1.

63. Noah Brooks. *Washington In Lincoln's Time*, p. 261–266.

64. Ibid.

65. Carl Sandburg. *Abraham Lincoln: The Prairie Years and The War Years*, p. 606–611.

CHAPTER 23: COMMANDING FORMER ENEMIES IN RALEIGH

1. Federal Writers Project. *Slave Narratives: A Folk History of Slavery in the United States From Interviews With Former Slaves (1936–1938)*. Vol. XI. Part 1, p. 1.

2. Letter from General Hardin in Raleigh, North Carolina to his mother Sarah (Hardin) Walworth, Saratoga Springs, New York, October 1865. Hardin-Walworth Papers. SSHM.

3. Ibid.

4. Mark Bradley. *Bluecoats and Tar Heels: Soldiers and Civilians in Reconstruction North Carolina*, p. 52.

5. Ibid.

6. Ibid, p. 53, 87.

7. Letter from General Hardin in Raleigh, North Carolina to his mother Sarah (Hardin) Walworth, Saratoga Springs, New York, October 1865. Hardin-Walworth Papers. SSHM.

8. "NORTH CAROLINA. A Freedman Punished by the Old Slave Code," *Philadelphia Daily Evening Bulletin*, September 13, 1865.
9. Ibid.
10. Ibid.
11. Ibid.
12. Ibid.
13. Ibid.
14. Ibid.
15. Ibid.
16. Testimony of Dexter H. Clapp on February 21, 1866 before The Joint committee On Reconstruction, Thirty-Ninth Congress, Washington, D.C.
17. Ibid.
18. Undated letter from General Hardin, Raleigh, North Carolina, to his mother Sarah (Hardin) Walworth, Saratoga Springs, New York, 1865 or 1866. Hardin Walworth Collection. SSHM.
19. Letter from Major H. B. Lewis, Adjutant, United States Military Academy at West Point in response to an information from Hardin long-time friend, Mr. Nelson Thomasson of Chicago, January 5, 1924. Note: Contains a detailed military history of General Hardin's career.
20. Letter from General Hardin's first wife, Estelle Graham Hardin, Chicago to her mother-in-law, Sarah (Hardin) Walworth, Saratoga Springs, New York, May 8, 1866. Hardin Walworth Collection. SSHM.
21. Letter from Major H. B. Lewis, Adjutant, United States Military Academy at West Point in response to an information from Hardin long-time friend, Mr. Nelson Thomasson of Chicago, January 5, 1924. Note: Contains a detailed military history of General Hardin's career.
22. Digital copy of Estelle Graham Hardin's London photo was thoughtfully provided to the author by Ms. Laurie Nesbitt of Lovettsville, Virginia, a great, great, granddaughter of Estelle's sister, Grace (Graham) Parker; Letter from Major H. B. Lewis, Adjutant, United States Military Academy at West Point in response to an information from Hardin long-time friend, Mr. Nelson Thomasson of Chicago, January 5, 1924.

CHAPTER 24: THE GILDED AGE DAWNS, TAD LINCOLN DIES

1. Michael Ellis and Laurie Parker. "Military History of Leopold Oscar Parker," (General Hardin's brother-in-law) *Twenty-Second Infantry Website*: 1-22infantry.org/commanders/Parker3.htm.22infantry.org/commanders/Parker3.htm.
2. Ibid. Note: Parker was cut from the same cloth as General Hardin. He served as an infantry officer in the U.S. Army and saw combat in the Civil War, against the Comanche, Apaches and other hostile tribes in Kansas, New Mexico and Dakota Territory, fought in Cuba during the Spanish American War of 1898, and served later in the Philippine Insurrection, 1899–1902. He won special praise for his role in Colonel Ranald Mackenzie's bold raid into old Mexico in May of 1873 against renegade Kickapoo and Lipan Indians who had been using Mexico as a safe haven to conduct raids on the Texas frontier. Colonel and Mrs. Parker are buried in Arlington National Cemetery.

3. Ibid.
4. Mabel McIlvaine. *Reminiscences of Early Chicago*, p. 28, 29, 172; Charles Lachman. *The Last Lincolns: The Rise & Fall of a Great American Family*, p. 167.
5. "Jonathan Young Scammon," *Dictionary of American Biography*. 8:2, p. 407–408; John Palmer. (Editor) *The Bench and Bar of Illinois: Historical and Reminiscent*. Vol. 1, p. 155. Vol. 2, p. 987–989.
6. Martin D. Hardin. "Letter Book, 1879–1880," Hardin Papers, SAHSRL; Letter from Mrs. Potter Palmer and receipts, Hardin Family Papers, CHM.
7. Charles Lachman. *The Last Lincolns: The Rise & Fall of a Great American Family*, p. 164, 166.
8. Ibid, p. 157–161.
9. Letter from General Hardin's first wife, Estelle (Graham) Hardin of Chicago to her mother-in-law, Sarah (Hardin) Walworth, Saratoga Springs, New York, June 18, 1871. Hardin-Walworth Collection. SSHM.
10. Charles Lachman. *The Last Lincolns: The Rise & Fall of a Great American Family*, p. 164.
11. Ibid, p. 165.
12. Ibid, p. 166.
13. Robert Cromie. *The Great Chicago Fire*, p. 12, 88–120, 141–142, 168; *Chicago Tribune*, October 11, 1871; *The Nation Magazine*, November 1871. .
14. Carter Henry Harrison. *Growing Up With Chicago: an Autobiography*, p. 47.
15. Charles Lachman. *The Last Lincolns: The Rise & Fall of a Great American Family*, p. 170–173.
16. Mark Twain and Charles Dudley Warner. *The Gilded Age: A Tale of Today*. (1873)
17. *Chicago Historical Society: 1908–1909*. (listing of members of the society, brief history and related) Published by the Chicago Historical Society, 1909.
18. Thomas O'Kane. *The Walworth Parricide*.

CHAPTER 25: MADNESS, MURDER AND SCANDAL, 1873

1. Geoffrey O'Brien. *The House of Walworth: A Tale Murder and Madness in Gilded Age America*, p. 20.
2. "The Walworth Tragedy," *The New York Times*, June 16, 1873.
3. Ibid.
4. "Walworth Trial, *The New York Times*, June 27, 1873.
5. Geoffrey O'Brien. *The House of Walworth: A Tale Murder and Madness in Gilded Age America*, p. 9–10., 26–27, 38, 119–120, 166–169, 173–175, 182–183, 200, 201, 204.
6. Ibid, p. 26–27, 38, 119–120, 166–169, 173–175, 182–183, 200, 201, 204.
7. Ibid, p. 182.
8. Ibid, p. 166.
9. Ibid, p. 167.
10. George Templeton Strong. *The Diary of George Templeton Strong: Post-War Years, 1865–1875*, p. 486.
11. Geoffrey O'Brien. *The House of Walworth: A Tale Murder and Madness in Gilded Age America*, p. 160.
12. Allison P. Bennett. *Saratoga Sojourn: A Biography of Ellen Hardin Walworth*, p. 123–124.
13. Ibid.
14. Geoffrey O'Brien. *The House of Walworth: A Tale Murder and Madness in Gilded Age*

America, p. 160.

15. "Walworth Trial, *The New York Times*, June 27, 1873.

16. Geoffrey O'Brien. *The House of Walworth: A Tale Murder and Madness in Gilded Age America*, p. 189.

17. Ibid, p. 33.

18. Ibid, p. 194–195

19. "Walworth Trial," *The New York Times*, June 29, 1873.

20. Ibid.

21. Ibid.

22. Ibid.

23. Ibid.

24. Geoffrey O'Brien. *The House of Walworth: A Tale Murder and Madness in Gilded Age America*, p. 208.

25. Ibid, p. 191.

26. Ibid, p. 209.

27. Ibid, p. 209–210, 215.

28. "Walworth Trial," *The New York Times*, July 2, 1873.

29. Geoffrey O'Brien. *The House of Walworth: A Tale Murder and Madness in Gilded Age America*, p. 215–219.

30. Ibid, p. 219–221.

31. Ibid, p. 222; "Walworth Trial," *The New York Times*, July 2, 1873.

32. Ibid, p. 225.

33. Ibid, p. 257–258.

34. Edward T. James. *Notable American Women: 1607–1950*

35. Geoffrey O'Brien. *The House of Walworth: A Tale Murder and Madness in Gilded Age America*, p. 267, 274–275, 286.

36. Ibid, p. 264, 268, 271, 273.

37. Ibid, p. 261–262.

CHAPTER 26: GENERAL HARDIN—GILDED AGE PRINCE

1. Ron Tendick. "Time Line: the Life of Lemuel Smith Hardin (1840–1909)," Note: This is an annotated time-line provided the author by Mr. Tendick, a local historian in Jacksonville, IL.

2. Geoffrey O'Brien. *The House of Walworth: A Tale Murder and Madness in Gilded Age America*, p. 237–239.

3. Ibid, p. 277–280.

4. Letter from General Hardin, Chicago to his sister, Ellen Hardin Walworth, Saratoga Springs, New York, June 6, 1877. Hardin-Walworth Collection. SSHM.

5. Martin D. Hardin. *Letter Book, 1879–1880*. Hardin Papers. SAHSRL.

6. Ibid.

7. Ibid.

8. Form letter from General Hardin, Honore Building, 204 Dearborn St., Chicago, June 1, 1880, to Hardin family members requesting information for a genealogical history. Hardin Family Collection. CHM.

9. Martin D. Hardin. *Letter Book, 1879–1880*. Entry for Dec. 4, 1879. Hardin Papers. SAHSRL.

10. Ibid. Entry for Dec. 8, 1879.
11. Edward Mason and Edward Mackinac. *Early Chicago and Illinois History*, p. 9–26, 187, 191; "Journey of Gurdon S. Hubbard," *Pioneer Collections: Report of the Pioneer Society of Michigan.* No. 3. (1881).
12. Ibid.
13. Martin D. Hardin. *Letter Book, 1879–1880*. Hardin Papers, entry for December 11, 1879. SAHSRL.
14. Letter from Major H. B. Lewis, Adjutant, United States Military Academy at West Point in response to an information from Hardin long-time friend, Mr. Nelson Thomasson of Chicago, January 5, 1924. Note: Contains a detailed list of Hardin's club memberships and affiliations.
15. Frederick William Gookin. *The Chicago Literary Club: a history of its first fifty years.*
16. Ibid.
17. Ibid.
18. Correspondence from Mrs. Potter Palmer of Chicago to General Hardin. Hardin Family Papers, CHM.
19. Isabel Ross. *Silhouette In Diamonds: the Life of Mrs. Potter Palmer*, p. 57.
20. Martin D. Hardin. *Letter Book, 1879–1880*, entry for October 24, 1879: "Attended reception of Fred Grant's at Chicago Club. Hardin Papers. SAHSRL.
21. Martin D. Hardin. "Reminiscences." Manuscript found among Hardin Family Papers. CHM.
22. Martin D. Hardin. "The Defense of Washington Against Early's Attack In July 1864," *Military Essays and Recollections: Papers Read Before Commandery of the State of Illinois, Military Order of the Loyal Legion of the United States*, p. 265–275.
23. Ibid.
24. Martin D. Hardin. *History of the Twelfth Regiment, Pennsylvania Reserve Volunteer Corps*, p. 193–196.
25. David Nolan and Jean E. Fitzpatrick. *The Houses of St. Augustine*, p. 49.
26. "Funeral of Late Gen. M.D. Hardin Largely Attended," *St. Augustine Evening Record*, Dec. 15, 1923.
27. Thomas Graham. *The Awakening of St. Augustine: The Anderson Family and the Oldest City 1821–1924*, p. 164.
28. Ibid, p. 168.
29. David Nolan and Jean E. Fitzpatrick. *The Houses of St. Augustine*, p. 49.
30. "Hardin Named to Head Soldier's Home," *The Saratoga Daily Journal*, August 29, 1886.
31. "Martin D. Hardin," the *National Cyclopedia of American Biography*. Vol. XII, p. 146–147.
32. Martin D. Hardin. *History of the Twelfth Regiment, Pennsylvania Reserve Volunteer Corps*, p. 196.
33. Letter from Chil Hazard of Monongahela City, Pa., an old army comrade of Hardin's, to General Hardin, 20 St. Frances Street, St. Augustine, Florida, September 12, 1890. Hardin Family Papers. CHM.
34. "General Hardin Hosts Ball," *The Tattler* (St. Augustine society newspaper), March 5, 1892. SAHSRL.
35. Geoffrey O'Brien. *The House of Walworth: A Tale Murder and Madness in Gilded Age America*, p. 267.

36. Ibid, p. 274–275.
37. Ibid, p. 286–289.

CHAPTER 27: BATTLES FOUGHT WITH PEN, INK AND PAPER
1. Martin D. Hardin. *History of the Twelfth Regiment, Pennsylvania Reserve Volunteer Corps*, p. 6.
2. Ibid, p. 1–2.
3. Martin D. Hardin. *History of the Twelfth Regiment, Pennsylvania Reserve Volunteer Corps*, p. 2.
4. David Herbert Donald. *Lincoln*, p. 342–348, 417–418, 362–369.4 Martin D. Hardin.
5. Stephen W. Sears. *George B. McClellan: The Young Napoleon*, p. 97–98, 202–203, 247, 260, 262, 271.
6. Martin D. Hardin. *History of the Twelfth Regiment, Pennsylvania Reserve Volunteer Corps*, p. 40.
7. John P. Nicholson. (Editor/Compiler) *Pennsylvania at Gettysburg: Ceremonies at the Dedication of the Monuments*, p. 288–300.
8. Scott Hartwig. "John F. Reynolds, 1820–1863," *ANB*. Vol. 18, p. 382–383; Edward J. Nichols. *Towards Gettysburg: A Biography of General John F. Reynolds*.
9. Ezra J. Warner. *Generals In Blue*, p. 315–317.
10. "Gettysburg Not A Surprise," *Military Essays and Recollections: Papers Read Before the Commandery of the State of Illinois (1892)*, p. 265–275. Military Order of the Loyal Legion of the United States. (MOLLUS)
11. Ibid.
12. Ibid.
13. "General Grant Statue Dedicated," *Chicago Tribune*, Oct. 8, 1891. Front Page.
14. Ibid.
15. Ibid.
16. Ibid.
17. "Palmer of Chicago Pledges $5,000 for General Grant statue," *The New York Times*, October 7, 1891.
18. "General Grant Statue Dedicated," *Chicago Tribune*, Oct. 8, 1891. Front Page.
19. Ibid.
20. Ibid.

CHAPTER 28: CHASING A GHOST IN OLD MEXICO
1. "Hardin-Mclaughlin Wedding: Cardinal Gibbons Performs the Ceremony, *Chicago Tribune*, Oct. 25, 1892.
2. Ibid.
3. Ibid.
4. John Tracy Ellis. *The Life of James Cardinal Gibbons, Archbishop of Baltimore 1834–1921*, p. 28, 376.
5. Lindy Woodhead. *Shopping, Seduction & Mr. Selfridge*, p. 1–25.
6. John M. Palmer. *The Bench and Bar of Illinois* (Vol. 1), p. 65–67.
7. Amelia (McLaughlin) Hardin. *Our Mexican Trip: Diary 1893*. Jan. 4, 1893 entry.
8. Ibid.
9. Letter from Colonel John J. Hardin, First Illinois Volunteer Infantry, San Antonio,

Texas to his sister, Martinette (Hardin) McKee in Kentucky, April 27, 1846. Hardin Papers. SAHSRL.

10. Amelia (McLaughlin) Hardin. *Our Mexican Trip: Diary 1893*. Jan. 9, 1893 entry.

11. Letter from Colonel John J. Hardin, First Illinois Volunteer Infantry, San Antonio, Texas to his daughter, Ellen Hardin, Jacksonville, Illinois, n.d., 1847. Hardin Papers. SAHSRL.

12. Amelia (McLaughlin) Hardin. *Our Mexican Trip: Diary 1893*. Jan. 10, 1893 entry.

13. Ibid.

14. Ibid.

15. Ibid. Jan. 11, 1893.

16. Ibid.

17. Ibid.

18. Ibid.

19. Ibid. Jan. 12, 1893.

20. Ibid. Jan. 16, 1893.

21. Ibid. Jan. 17, 1893.

22. "Chicago Columbian Exposition of 1893," *The New York Times*, Nov. 1, 2003.

23. "Grover Cleveland Opens Chicago Fair," *The New York Times*, May 2, 1893.

24. Article about Ellen (Hardin) Walworth's role at the Columbian Exposition in Chicago. *The American Monthly Magazine* (Official publication of the Daughters of the American Revolution). Vol. 3. (July 1893), p. 61.

25. Frederick Jackson Turner. *The Significance of the Frontier in American History*. Reubena Hyde Walworth obituary, *The New York Times*, Oct. 19, 1898. Note: It's possible that General Hardin's niece, Reubena H. Walworth, may have nursed Colonel Leo Parker's son at Camp Wikoff. Parker was Hardin's brother-in-law from his first marriage with Estelle Graham Hardin. Oddly enough, Annie Laurie Early Wheeler, a daughter of Confederate General Joe Wheeler was also a nurse at Camp Wikoff. Her father and Hardin were both members of the West Point Class of 1859; Annie later visited Hardin's wife in St. Augustine following the General's death in 1923. Tragically, General Wheeler son, Naval Cadet Thomas H. Wheeler, drowned while swimming in the ocean off Camp Wikoff during this period. (See, Jeff Heatley. *BULLY: Colonel Theodore Roosevelt, The Rough Riders & Camp Wikoff*, p. 119–121, 289–292, 297–298,

26. Jeff Heatley. (Editor) *BULLY! Colonel Theodore Roosevelt, The Rough Riders & Camp Wikoff: A Newspaper Chronicle with Roosevelt's Letters*, p. 303–306.

27. Ibid, p. 446–447.

28. "Miss Walworth, a War Martyr," *The New York Herald*, Oct. 19, 1898.

29. Philip A. Kallisch. Heroines of '98: Female Army Nurses in the Spanish-American War," *Nursing Research Journal*. Vol. 24. Issue 6, p. 423.

30. "Death of Reubena Hyde Walworth," *The Tattler* (St. Augustine society newspaper), Jan. 6, 1900.

31. "Ellen Hardin Walworth Journal." Hardin-Walworth Collection. SSHM.

CHAPTER 29: LAY DOWN YOUR SWORD AND SHIELD

1. David Richards. "The Gilded Age: A Tale of Today," an Internet book discussion presented by the Maine Humanities Council, 2007.

2. Virginia Edwards. *Stories of Old St. Augustine*, p. 47.
3. Ibid, p. 27.
4. Robert Nawrocki. "Fine Dining in St. Augustine," *El Escribano: The St. Augustine Journal of History*. Vol. 49. (2012), p. 30–34.
5. Ibid.
6. Ibid.
7. Ibid, p. 31, 32.
8. Sean Dennis Cashman. *America In The Gilded Age: From the Death of Lincoln to the Rise of Theodore Roosevelt*, p. 2, 4, 5, 214.
9. Thirty-five articles appearing from 1889 through 1922 in the society pages of the *New York Times, New York Herald, Washington Post, Chicago Tribune*, and *New York Tribune*.
10. Joe Knetsch. "The Business System of Henry Flagler," *El Escribano: The St. Augustine Journal of History*. Vol. 40. (2003), p. 68–92; Thomas Graham. *The Awakening of St. Augustine, The Anderson Family and the Oldest City: 1821–1924*, p. 168–169, 205–206, 209–210, 212–213, 216–218.
11. Barbara A. Poleo. "James Edmundson Ingraham: Florida, Flagler, and St. Augstine," *El Escribano: The St. Augustine Journal of History*. Vol. 40. (2003), p. 93–118.
12. Dr. Bronson's St. Augustine History Website: *www.drbronsontours.com.html*; Karen Harvey. *Legends and Tales: Remembering St. Augustine*. Vol. 2.
13. "The Society of St. Johnland Report for the Twenty-six Year Ending St. John's Day, Dec. 27, 1896."
14. "Need of Lincoln University," *The New York Times*, Feb. 6 1910.
15. Secretary of War. *Fourth Annual Report of the United States Philippine Commission for 1903*. Prepared by the Secretary of War, Bureau of Insular Affairs. Washington, D.C.: U.S. Government Printing Office, 1904.
16. Dr. Bronson's St. Augustine History Website: *www.drbronsontours.com.html*
17. Ibid.
18. Letter from General John Schofield, Headquarters of the Army, Washington, D.C. to General Martin D. Hardin, Room 44, 99 Randolph St., Chicago, Sept. 17, 1894. Hardin Family Papers. CHM.
19. Newspaper article
20. "St. Augustine Popular Among Military Men," *The New York Times*, March 17, 1912.
21. "News From The Southern Resorts," *New York Tribune*, Feb. 14, 1915.
22. Ezra J. Warner. *Generals In Blue*, p. 5, 6.
23. Ibid.
24. "Delightful Dinner for Mrs. Booth," *St. Augustine Evening Record*, Feb. 18, 1910.
25. "Admiral Grinnell marries at 74," *The New York Times*, July 26, 1910.
26. John H. Parker. *The Gatlings at Santiago*, p. 59–61.
27. "Anna M. Hughes: The Chief traits of this Remarkable Woman Are Described," *New York Herald*, Jan. 18, 1896. (See *St. Augustine Genealogy Homepage: www.rootsweb. ancestry.com/~flsags/marcotte.htm*)
28. Thomas Graham. *Mr. Flagler's St. Augustine*, p. 218–219.
29. Ezra J. Warner. *Generals In Blue*, p. 46–47.
30. Telephone conversation and exchange of email messages with the late Mr. William Foote McLaughlin (1929–2012), a nephew by marriage to General Hardin. Mr.

McLaughlin related many stories he had heard from his Aunt "Melly" Amelia (McLaughlin) Hardin (1863–1939) about General Hardin; *Lake Forest* published by the Communities Association, Chicago, 1916, p. 72. Copy at the University of Illinois Library, Urbana, IL.

31. Owentsia Country Club, Lake Forest, Illinois. "Club Regulations and Memberships (1909)," CHM.
32. Stephen Richard Higley Rowman. *Privilege, Power and Place: The Geography of the American Upper Class*, p. 54.
33. Ezra J. Warner. *Generals In Gray*, p. 184.
34. Ron Tendick. "Timeline: The Life of Lemuel Smith Hardin (1840–1909)." Copy provided by Mr. Tendick, former three-time mayor of Jacksonville, Illinois and local historian.
35. Ezra J. Warner. *Generals In Blue*. 321–322.
36. Donald M. Roper. "Ellen Hardin Walworth (1832–1915)," *ANB*. Vol. 22, p. 594–595.
37. Letter from Colonel Michael Sheridan, Chicago to General Martin D. Hardin, St. Augustine, Jan. 25, 1914. Hardin Family Papers. CHM.
38. Martin D. Hardin. "Memoriam: Francis J. Crilly, Class of 1859," *Annual Report by the United States Military Academy Association of Graduates*, June 12, 1908.
39. Ibid.
40. Jon C. Teaford. "Chauncey M. Depew, 1834–1928," *ANB*. Vol. 6, p. 459–460.
41. "Honor St. Patrick: Hotel Alcazar in St. Augustine," *New York Sun*, March 19, 1918.
42. Jon C. Teaford. "Chauncey M. Depew, 1834–1928," *ANB*. Vol. 6, p. 459–460.
43. David Nolan, Jean E. Fitzpatrick, and Ken Barrett. *The Houses of St. Augustine*, p. 49, 45–60; Robert Redd, *St. Augustine in the Civil War*, p. 138.
44. David Nolan. "Lincoln Tie to St. Augustine," Special article for the *St. Augustine Record* internet edition, March 23, 2004.
45. Georgina Pell Curtis. (Editor) *The American Catholic Who's Who*, p. 272.
46. St. Augustine Yacht Club file (membership list) at SAHSRL; Karen G. Harvey. *Legends and Tales: Remembering St. Augustine*. Vol. II.
47. "Funeral of Late Gen. M.D. Hardin Largely Attended," *St. Augustine Evening Record*, Dec. 15, 1923.
48. Ibid.
49. Ibid.
50. Ibid.
51. Ibid.

EPILOGUE: IN THE DAYS THAT FOLLOWED

1. Stephen R. Prescott. "White Robes and Crosses: Father John Conoley, the Ku Klux Klan and the University of Florida," *Florida Historical Quarterly*. Vol. 71. No. 1. (July 1992)
2. Letters (1923–1925) to Mrs. Amelia Hardin relating to the renovation of the La Leche Chapel on the grounds of the Mission Nombre de Dios in St. Augustine. On file at the archives, Sisters of St. Joseph, 241 St. George St., St. Augustine, Florida; Irene Castle. *Castles in the Air*. (Told to Bob and Wanda Duncan.)
3. Ezra J. Warner. *Generals In Blue*, p. 322–323.

4. Ibid, p. 45–46.
5. Ibid. 5–6.
6. Geoffrey O'Brien. *The House of Walworth: Murder and Madness in Gilded Age America*, p. 286–287.
7. "1935 Memorial Day Program," National Cemetery, St. Augustine, Florida. Copy on file at the Florida State Archives, Tallahassee, Florida. General M. D. Hardin file.
8. Robert Redd. *St. Augustine In The Civil War*, p. 138; David Nolan and Jean Fitzpatrick. *Houses of St. Augustine*, p. 45–60.

BIBLIOGRAPHY

Adkin, Mark. *The Gettysburg Companion: The Complete Guide to America's Most Famous Battle*. Mechanicsburg, PA.: Stackpole Books, 2008.

Alberts, Don E. *Brandy Station to Manila Bay: A Biography of General Wesley Merritt*. Austin: Presidial Press, 1980.

Alleman, Tillie Pierce. *At Gettysburg or What a Girl Heard and Saw of the Battle, A True Narrative*. New York City, Archeron Press, 1889.

Allen, Johnson & Malone, Dumas. Editors. *Dictionary of American Biography*. New York: Charles Scribner's Sons, 1930.

Altsheler, Brent. "C.C. Graham, M. D., 1784–1885, Historian, Antiquarian, Rifle Expert, Centenarian," *Filson Club History Quarterly*. Vol. 7, April, 1933.

Andreas, A. T. *History of Chicago*. Chicago: A. T. Andreas Co., 1886.

Andrews, J. Cutler. *The North Reports* The Civil War. Pittsburgh: The University of Pittsburgh Press, 1955.

Anonymous. *Owentsia Golf Club 1909: Officers, Membership, Charter.* Chicago: n.p., 1909.

Arnold, James R. *The Armies of U.S. Grant*. New York: Arms and Armour Press, 1995.

Athearn, Robert G. *Forts of The Upper Missouri*. Lincoln: University of Nebraska Press, 1972.

Barton, William E. *The Paternity of Abraham Lincoln: Was He The Son of Thomas Lincoln*, an essay on the chastity of Nancy Hanks. New York: George Doran and Co., 1920.

Basler, Roy P. *The Collected Works of Abraham Lincoln*. (8 vol.) New Brunswick: New Jersey: Rutgers University Press, 1953.

Bates, Edward. *The Diary of Edward Bates, 1859–1866.* Edited Howard K. Beal. New York: DaCapo Press, 1971.

Bates, Samuel P. *Martial Deeds of Pennsylvania.* Philadelphia: T. H. Davis & Co. Publishers, 1876.

———. *History of the Pennsylvania Volunteers, 1861–65. (5 vols.)* Harrisburg, Pa.: Publisher unknown, 1869.

Baxter, Maurice G. *Orville H. Browning, Lincoln's Friend and Critic.* Bloomington: University of Indiana Press, 1957.

Beatie, Russel H. *Army of the Potomac: McClellan's First Campaign, March–May 1862.* El Dorado Hills, CA: Savas-Beatie, 2007.

Beckham, Stephen Dow. "Lonely Outpost: The Army's Fort Umpqua," *Oregon Historical Quarterly.* Vol. 70. No. 3. (September 1969).

Bennett, Allison P. *Saratoga Sojourn: A Biography of Ellen Hardin Walworth.* Danbury: Rutledge Books, Inc., 2002.

Bernard, A. B. *Reminiscences of West Point in the Olden Time.* East Saginaw: Evening News Printing and Publishing House. 1886.

Bernstein, Steven. *The Confederacy's Last Northern Offensive: Jubal Early, The Army of the Valley, and the Raid on Washington.* Jefferson, N.C.: McFarland & Co. Publishers, 2011.

Beveridge, Albert J. *Abraham Lincoln. 1809–1858* (Vol. 1) Boston: Houghton Mifflin Publishers, 1928.

Billington, Ray Allen. (Editor) *Frontier and Section: Selected Essays of Frederick Jackson Turner.*

Boatner, Mark Mayo, *The Civil War Dictionary.* New York: David McKay Company, Inc., 1959.

Bonekemper, Edward H. "General Disobedience: 'Little Mac' lets John Pope twist in the wind," *Civil War Times,* December 2010.

Books, Kirtis. *The History of Peoria County, Containing A History of the Northwest.* Chicago: Johnson & Company, 1880.

Boyer, Paul, James, Edward, James Janet, Editors. *Notable American Women, 1607–1950: A Biographical Dictionary.* (3 vols.) Cambridge, Mass.: Harvard University Press, 1971.

Birkhimer, William E. "The Third Regiment of Artillery," *Journal of the Military History* (October 30, 2002). U.S. Army Center of Military History.

Bradley, Mark L. *Bluecoats & Tar Heels: Soldiers and Civilians In Reconstruction North Carolina.* Lexington: The University Press of Kentucky, 2009.

Britten, Evelyn Barrett. *Chronicles of Saratoga*. Saratoga Springs: Privately Published, 1959.

Brooks, Noah. *Washington D.C. in Lincoln's Time*. Edited by Herbert Mitgang. Washington, D.C., Century Co., 1895.

Brown, R. Shepard. *Stringfellow of the Fourth*. New York: Crown Publishers, Inc., 1960.

Browning, Orville Hickman. *The Diary of Orville Hickman Browning*. (vol 2, 1865–1881). Edited by Theodore Calvin Pease and James G. Randall. Champaign: the University of Illinois Press, 1925.

Buhoup, Jonathan W. *Narrative of the Central Division of the Army of Chihuahua, Commanded by Brigadier General Wool*. Pittsburgh: M. P. Morse Publishers, 1847.

Bundy, Carol. *The Nature of Sacrifice: A Biography of Charles Russell Lowell, Jr., 1835–1864*. New York: Farrar, Strauss and Giroux Publishers, 2005.

Burton, Brian K. *Extraordinary Circumstances, The Seven Days Battles*. Bloomington and Indianapolis: Indiana University Press, 2001.

Cable, Mary. *High Society From the Gilded Age to the Roaring Twenties*. New York: Antheneum Press, 1984.

Calarco, Tom. *The Underground Railroad in the Adirondack Region*. Jefferson, N.C.: McFarland & Co., Inc., 2004.

Carey, Patrick W. "Clarence Augustus Walworth, 1820–1900," ANB. Vol. 22, p. 593–594.

Carhart, Tom. *Sacred Ties: From West Point Brothers To Battlefield Rivals: A True Story of the Civil War*. New York: The Penguin Group, 2010.

Cashman, Sean Dennis. *America In The Gilded Age: From the Death of Lincoln to the Rise of Theodore Roosevelt*. New York and London: New York University Press, 1984.

Castle, Irene. *Castles in the Air*. Told to Bob and Wanda Duncan. Garden City, NY: Doubleday Press, 1958.

Castledon, Louis D. *The Early Years of the Ponce de Leon Hotel*. Pamphlet, N. P, N. D., St. Augustine Historical Society Research Library, St. Augustine, FL.

Catton, Bruce: *Grant Moves South*. Boston & Toronto: Little, Brown & Co., 1960.

Chicago Historical Society. *Chicago Historical Society Annual Report For The Year Ending Oct. 31, 1918*. Chicago: Published by the Chicago Historical

Society, 1919.

Clift, G. Glenn. *Remember The Raisin! Kentucky and Kentuckians in the Battles and Massacre at Frenchtown, Michigan Territory, in the War of 1812*. Baltimore: Genealogical Publishing Col., Inc, 2002.

Coan, Eugene. *James Graham Cooper: Pioneer Western Naturalist*. Boise: The University Press of Idaho, 1981.

Coddington, Edwin B. *The Gettysburg Campaign: A Study in Command*. New York: Charles Scribner's and Sons, 1968.

Connelley, William Elsey. Coulter, Ellis Merton. (Editor: Judge Charles Kerr). *History of Kentucky (Vol. 1)*. Chicago and New York: The American Historical Society, 1922.

Cooling, Benjamin Franklin. *Jubal Early's Raid on Washington*. Tuscaloosa: The University of Alabama Press, 1989.

——. *Symbol, Sword and Shield: Defending Washington During the Civil War*. Washington: White Mane Publishing, 1991.

——. *Monocacy: The Battle That Saved Washington*. Washington: White Mane Publishing Co., 1996.

——. *The Day Lincoln Was Almost Shot: The Fort Stevens Story*. Lanham, MD: Scarecrow Press, 2013.

Cooper, Major James Graham. "Dispatches From The Blakeman Expedition," *Century Magazine*. New York: (Summer 1860).

Coughenour, Kavin L. (Lieutenant Colonel, U.S. Army). "The Mine Run Campaign—An Operational Analysis of Major General George G. Meade," *U.S. Army War College*, Carlisle Barracks, PA., March 1, 1990.

Cozzens, Peter. *General John Pope: A Life for the Nation*. New York, 2000.

Chamberlain, Joshua Lawrence. *Joshua L. Chamberlain: A Life In Letters*. Edited by Thomas Desjardin. Harrisburg, Pa.: National Civil War Museum Publishers, 2012.

Cromie, Robert. *The Great Chicago Fire*. Nashville: Rutledge Hill Press. 1958.

Cullum, George W. *Biographical Register of the Officers and Graduates of the U.S. Military Academy at West Point*, N.Y. (Reprint of 1891 original) Charleston, S. C.: Nabu Press, 2010.

Currey, J. Seymour. *Chicago: Its History and Its Builders*. (5 vols.) Chicago: S. J. Clarke Publishing Co., 1912.

Curtis, Georgina Pell. (Editor). *The American Catholic Who's Who*. St. Louis:

B. Herder Publishers. 1911.

Dana, Charles A. *Recollections of the Civil War.* New York: D. Appleton and Company, 1902.

Davis, Carl L. *Arming The Union: Small Arms In The Civil War.* New York and London: Kennikat Press, 1973.

Dickey, Jerry. "Flagler-Era Stage Entertainments at the Alcazar Casino," *El Escribano: The St. Augustine Journal of History.* St. Augustine Historical Society. Vol. 49. 2012.

Donald, David Herbert. *Lincoln.* New York: Blank Press, 1995.

Doubleday, Abner. *My Life in the Old Army—The Reminiscences of Abner Doubleday.* Edited by Joseph E. Chance. Fort Worth: Collection of the New York Historical Society, 1998.

Douglas, Stephen A. *The Letters of Stephen A. Douglas.* Edited by Robert W. Johannsen. Urbana: University of Illinois Press, 1961.

Dyer, John P. *"Fightin' Joe" Wheeler.* Baton Rouge: Louisiana State University Press, 1941.

Eberly, Robert E., Jr. *Bouquets from the Cannon's Mouth: Soldiering with the Eighth Regiment of the Pennsylvania Reserves.*

Edwards, Virginia. *Stories of Old St. Augustine.* Jacksonville, Fl.: Paramount Press, 1973.

Eicher, John H., and Eicher, David J. *Civil War High Commands.* Stanford, Cal.: Stanford University Press, 2001.

Elliott, John E. and Cauchon, Barry M. *Inside The Walls: The Final Days of the Lincoln Conspirators, The Mystery of John Wilkes Booth's Autopsy Photo.* Self-published monograph by authors for the Surratt House Museum Conference on the Lincoln assassination, 2011.

———. *Special Supplement: A Peek Inside The Walls: The Final Days of the Lincoln Conspirators.* Self-published monograph by authors for the Surratt House Museum Conference on the Lincoln assassination, 2011.

———. *A Peek Inside The Walls: 13 Days Aboard the Monitors: the Early Incarceration of the Conspirators, the Mug Shot Photo Sessions and the Truth About the Hoods.* Self-published monograph by authors for the Surratt House Museum Conference on the Lincoln assassination, 2012.

Ellis, John Tracy. *The Life of James Cardinal Gibbons, Archbishop of Baltimore 1834–1921.* Two Vol. Milwaukee: 1952.

Emerson, Edward Waldo and Joan Waugh. *Life and Letters of Charles Russell*

Lowell. Boston and New York: Houghton, Mifflin and Co., 1907.

Ent, Uzal W. *The Pennsylvania Reserves in the Civil War: A Comprehensive History*. Jefferson, N.C.: McFarland & Co., Inc., 2014.

Fanebust, Wayne. *Major General Alexander M. McCook, USA: a Civil War Biography*. Jefferson, N.C., and London: McFarland and Company, Inc. Publishers, 2013.

Flanders, Robert Bruce. *Nauvoo: Kingdom On The Mississippi*. Champaign-Urbana: University of Illinois Press, 1965.

Fleischner, Jennifer. *Mrs. Lincoln and Mrs. Keckley: the remarkable story of the friendship between a first lady and a former slave*. New York: Broadway Books, 2003.

Freeman, Douglas Southall. *LEE: An abridgment in one volume*. New York: Charles Scribner's Sons, 1961.

Furgurson, Ernest B. *Not War But Murder: Cold Harbor, 1864*. New York: Random House, 2000.

———. *Freedom Rising—Washington in the Civil War*. New York: Vintage Civil War Library, Division of Random House, Inc., 2004.

Gallagher, Gary W. *Stephen Dodson Ramseur: Lee's Gallant General*. Chapel Hill and London: University of North Carolina Press, 1985.

Gernon, Blaine Brooks. *The Lincolns in Chicago*. Chicago: Ancarthe Publishers, 1934.

Gibbs, Joseph. *Three Years in the Bloody Eleventh, The Campaigns of a Pennsylvania Reserves Regiment*. University Park, Penn.: Pennsylvania State University Press, 2002.

Girardi, Robert I. *The Civil War Generals: Peers, Rivals (in their own words)*.

Goff, John S. *Robert Todd Lincoln: A Man in His Own Right*. Norman: University of Oklahoma Press, 1969.

Goodwin, Doris Kearns. *The Bully Pulpit: Theodore Roosevelt, William Howard Taft, and the Golden Age of Journalism*. New York and London: Simon and Schuster, Inc., 2013.

Gookin, Frederick William. *The Chicago Literary Club*, a history of its first fifty years. Chicago: 1926.

Gooley, Lawrence P. "North County Abolitionist James Rood Doolittle," *Adirondack Almanac*. (May 21, 2012).

Gottfried, Bradley M. *Brigades of Gettysburg: the Union and Confederate Brigades at the Battle of Gettysburg*. Cambridge, MA: DaCapo Press, 2002.

———. "Fisher's Brigade at Gettysburg: The Big Round Top Controversy," Gettysburg Magazine, Issue 19.

Graham, Martin F. and Skoch, George F. Mine Run: A Campaign of Lost Opportunities. Lynchburg: H. E. Howard, Inc., 1987.

Graham, Thomas. The Awakening of St. Augustine: The Anderson Family and the Oldest City: 1821–1924. St. Augustine, Saint Augustine Historical Society Publishers, 1978.

———. Mr. Flagler's St. Augustine. Gainesville: University of Florida Press, 2014.

———. "Opening Season for the Hotel Ponce de Leon: January through May 1888," El Escribiano: The St. Augustine Journal of History. St. Augustine Historical Society. Vol. 49. (2012).

———. "Henry Flagler's St. Augustine," El Escribano: The St. Augustine Journal of History. St. Augustine Historical Society. Vol. 40. (2003).

Grant, Julia Dent. The Personal Memoirs of Julia Dent Grant. Edited by John Y. Simon. New York: George P. Putnam's Sons Publisher, 1975.

Grant, Ulysses S. The Papers of U.S. Grant. (11 vols.) Edited by John Y. Simon. Carbondale: Southern Illinois University Press, 1984.

Greenberg, Amy S. A Wicked War: Polk, Clay, Lincoln, and the 1846 U.S. Invasion of Mexico. New York: Alfred Knopf Publishers, 2012.

Greene, Thomas Marshall. Historic Families of Kentucky. Cincinnati: Clarke & Co., Publishers, 1880.

Grier, Williams Hayes. "Diary excerpts regarding battle of Gettysburg," Gettysburg Compiler (July 2, 1913).

Grose, Edward F. Centennial History of the Village of Ballston Spa, Including the Town of Ballston and Milton. Ballston, New York: Ballston Journal Publisher, 1907.

Guernsey, Alfred H. and Alden, Henry M. Harper's History of the Civil War. New York: Fairfax Press, 1866.

Gurowski, Adam (Count). My Diary. Vol. 3 (1864–66).

Hardin, Amelia (McLaughlin). Our Mexican Trip—Diary, 1893. A 40-page handwritten journal of her Mexico honeymoon with husband General Martin D. Hardin. St. Augustine (FL) Historical Society Research Library Archive.

Hardin, Martin Davis. History of the Twelfth Regiment, Pennsylvania Reserve Volunteer Corps (41st Regiment Of The Line) From Its Muster into the United

States Service, August 10th, 1861, Until its Muster Out, June 11, 1864. New York: Published by the author, 1891.

——. "In Memoriam: Col. Francis J. Crilly, *Annual Report of the Association of the Graduates of the U.S. Military Academy.* (June 1908).

——. "The Defense of Washington Against Early's Attack in July 1864," *Military Essays and Recollections; Papers Read Before the Commandery of the State of Illinois, Military Order of the Loyal Legion of the United States.* Chicago, 1894.

——. "Across the New Northwest in 1860," *U.S. Service Magazine.* (Two installments). (May, 1888 and August 1888).

——. "Gettysburg Not A Surprise," *Military Essays and Recollections: Papers Read Before the Commandery of the State of Illinois, Military Order of the Loyal Legion of the United States.* Chicago, 18—.

——. "Address by Brig-Gen. Martin D. Hardin: Dedication of Monument, 41st Regt. Inf. (12th Reserves)." *Pennsylvania At Gettysburg: Ceremonies at the Dedication of the Monuments.* Editor/Compiler Ltc. John P. Nicholson. Harrisburg: Wm. Stanley Ray State Printer, 1914.

Harvey, Karen G. *Legends and Tales: Volume II: Remembering St. Augustine.* Cleveland: Horizon Books, 2012.

Heidler, David S. and Heidler, Jeanne T. (Editors). *Encyclopedia of the American Civil War, A Political, Social, and Military History.* Denver, Oxford, and Santa Barbara: W.W. Norton & Co., 2000.

Heatley, Jeff. Editor. *Bully! Colonel Theodore Roosevelt, The Rough Riders & Camp Wikoff: A Newspaper Chronicle.* Montauk: Montauk Historical Society, Pushcart Press, 1998.

Helm, Judith Beck. *Tenleytown, D.C.: Country Village into City Neighborhood.* Washington, D.C.: Tennally Press, 1981.

Hennessy, John J. *Return to Bull Run—The Campaign and Battle of Second Manassas.* New York: MacMillan, 1993.

Henry, Robert Selph. *The Story of Reconstruction.* New York: Bobbs-Merrill Co., 1938.

Higley, Stephen Richard. *Privilege, Power, and Place: The Geography of the American Upper Class.* Lanham, MD: Rowman and Littlefield Publishers, Inc., 1995.

Hitchcock, Ethan Allan. *Fifty Years in Camp and Field, Diary of Maj. Gen. Ethan Allan Hitchcock, USA.* New York: G. P. Putnam's Sons, 1909.

Hoke, Jacob. *The Great Invasion, Or General Lee in Pennsylvania.* Dayton: W. J. Shuey, 1887.

Hoppin, William Warner. *The Peace Conference of 1861 At Washington: A paper read before the Rhode Island Historical Society and the New Haven Historical Society, 1889–1890.* Providence, Rhode Island: Standard Printing Company, 1891.

Howe, Julia Ward. *Reminiscences, 1819–1899.* New York: Houghton Mifflin Co., 1899.

Howells, William Dean. "A Confession of St. Augustine," *Harper's Magazine* (April and May, 1917).

Humphreys, Andrew A. *From Gettysburg to the Rapidan: The Army of the Potomac, July 1863 to April 1864.* New York: Charles Scribner's and Sons, 1883.

Huntington, Tom. *Searching for George Gordon Meade: the Forgotten Victor of Gettysburg.*

Hutton, Andrew Paul. *Phil Sheridan and His Army.* Lincoln and London: University of Nebraska Press, 1985.

Hyde, Bill. (editor) *The Union Generals Speak: The Meade Hearings on the Battle of Gettysburg.* Baton Rouge: Louisiana State University Press, 2003.

Irving, Theodore. *More Than Conqueror; or Memorials of Col J. Howard Kitching.* New York, publisher unknown, 1873.

James, Edward, Janet Wilson James and Paul Boyer (editors). *Notable American Women 1607–1950: A Biographical Dictionary.* Three volumes. Cambridge: Harvard University Press. 1971.

Johannsen, Robert W. *Stephen A. Douglas.* New York and London: Oxford University Press, 1973.

Johnson, Allen. (Editor) *Dictionary of American Biography.* New York: Charles Scribner's & Sons,1964.

Jordan, David M. *Happiness Is Not My Companion: The Life of General G. K. Warren.* Bloomington: Indiana University Press, 2001.

Judge, Joseph. *Season of Fire: The Confederate Strike On Washington.* Berryville, Virginia, blank press, 1994.

Kauffman, Michael W. *American Brutus—John Wilkes Booth and the Lincoln Conspiracies.* New York: Random House, 2004.

Kautz, Lawrence G. *August Valentine Kautz, USA: Biography of a Civil War General.* Jefferson, North Carolina and London: McFarland & Co., Inc. Publishers, 2008.

Kautz, August V. "From Missouri to Oregon in 1860," *The Pacific Northwest Quarterly*, Vol 37. Edited by Martin F. Schmitt. CAPITOL: The University of Washington Press. (July 1946).

Keckley, Elizabeth. *Behind the Scenes, Or, Thirty Years a Slave, and Four Years in the White House.* New York: G. W. Carleton & Co., 1868.

Kennedy, Elijah R. *The Contest For California In 1861: How Colonel E. D. Baker Saved The Pacific States To The Union.* Boston and New York: Houghton Mifflin Company, 1912.

King, Willard L. *Lincoln's Manager: David Davis.* Chicago: University of Chicago Press, 1974.

Knetsch, Joe. "The Business System of Henry Flagler," *El Escribano: The St. Augustine Journal of History.* St. Augustine Historical Society. Vol. 40. (2003).

Kundahl, George G. Editor. *The Bravest of the Brave: The Correspondence of Stephen Dodson Ramseur.* Chapel Hill: The University of North Carolina Press.

Lachman, Charles. *The Last Lincolns: the Ride and Fall of a Great American Family.* New York: Union Square Press, 2008.

Larsen, Lawrence H. and Cottrell, Barbara J. *Steamboats West—The 1859 American Fur Company* Expedition. Norman: University of Oklahoma Press, 2010.

Lavaas, Jay and Nye, Wilbur S. "The Campaign That History Forgot," *Civil War Times Illustrated*, Vol. VIII, (November 1969).

Lee, Elizabeth Blair. *Wartime Washington: The Civil War Letters of Elizabeth Blair Lee.* (Virginia J. Laas, editor). Urbana: University of Illinois Press, 1999.

Lee, Henry. *Lee's Guide To Saratoga: the Queen of the Spas.* New York: Unknown publisher, 1886.

Leech, Margaret. *Reveille In Washington: 1860–1865.* New York: Harper & Brothers, 1941.

Leonard, John William. *Woman's Who's Who of America, A Biographical Dictionary of Contemporary Women.* (Vol. 1) n.d., n.p.

Leonard, John. *The Book of Chicagoans: A Biographical Dictionary of Leading Men of the City of Chicago.* Chicago: A. N. Marquis Publisher, 1905.

Longacre, Edward G. *The Man Behind the Guns: A Biography of General Henry Jackson Hunt, Chief of Artillery, Army of the Potomac.* Cambridge, MA:

DaCapo Press, 2003.

———. *A Soldier to the Last: Maj. Gen. Joseph Wheeler in Blue and Gray*. Washington: Potomac Books. 2007.

Malone, Dumas. (Editor). *Dictionary of American Biography (DAB)*. Vol VIII, pg. 245, 1932.

Marschner, Janice. *Oregon 1859: A Snapshot In Time*. London & Portland: Timber Press, Inc, 2008.

Martin, Sidney Walter. *Florida's Flager*. Athens: The University of Georgia Press, 1949.

Marvel, William. "Thorn in the Flesh," *Civil War Times Illustrated*, Vol. XLI, No. 3, June 2002.

Mason, Edward G. (Editor) *Early Chicago and Illinois: Chicago Historical Collections* (Vol. IV). Chicago: Fergus Printing Co., 1890.

McAfee, Robert B. *The Life and Times of Robert B. McAfee and His Family and Connections*. (Part 8), 1845.

Mabel McIlvaine. *Reminiscences of Early Chicago*. Chicago: Lakeside Press. 1912.

McLean, James. *California Sabers: The Second Massachusetts Cavalry in the Civil War*. Bloomington and Indianapolis: Indiana University Press, 2000.

Michie, Peter S. *General McClellan*. New York and London: blank press, 1915.

Miller, J. Michael. *The North Anna Campaign: Even To Hell Itself, May 21–26, 1864*. Lynchburg: E. Howard, Inc. Publishers, 1989.

———. "Strike Them A Blow: Lee and Grant at the North Anna River," *Blue & Gray Magazine*, Vol. X, Issue 4, 1993.

Miller, Richard Lawrence. *Lincoln and His World: The Early Years, Birth to Illinois Legislature*. (Vol. 1).

Moore, Frank. (Editor) *Rebellion Record: A Diary of American Events, With Documents, narratives, Illustrative Incidents, Poetry, Etc. (Vol. 3)* New York: G. P. Putnam Publishers, 1864.

Nawrocki, Robert. "Fine Dining in St. Augustine," *El Escribano: The St. Augustine Journal of History*. St. Augustine Historical Society. Vol. 49. (2012).

Nichols, Edward J. *Toward Gettysburg: A Biography of General John F. Reynolds*. Pennsylvania State University Press, 1958.

Nicholson, John P. Editor/Compiler. *Pennsylvania at Gettysburg: Ceremonies at the Dedication of the Monuments.* Pennsylvania Gettysburg Battlefield Commission. Harrisburg: Wm. Stanley Ray State Printer, 1914.

Nolan, David J. "Tovar 'Cannonball' House," *Florida Master Site File.* Site 8 (SJ2518), Illinois State Archives, Tallahassee, 1988.

Nolan, David J., Fitzpatrick, Jean E., and Barrett, Ken. *The Houses of St. Augustine.* Sarasota: Pineapple Press, 1995.

Nolan, David J. "St. Augustine's ties to Lincoln are strong," *St. Augustine.com.* St. Augustine (Feb. 15, 2009).

O'Brien, Geoffrey. *The Fall of the House of Walworth, A Tale of Madness and Murder in Gilded Age America.* New York: Henry Holt & Company, 2010.

——. "A Gilded Age Murder," *New York Archives Magazine.* Winter, Vol. 11, No. 3, 2013.

O'Donnell, Terrence. *An Arrow In The Earth: General Joel Palmer And The Indians of Oregon.* Portland: Oregon Historical Society Press, 1991.

O'Kane, Thomas. *The Walworth Parricide.* Philadelphia: Old Franklin Publishing House, 1873.

Owensby, Betty J. *Alias Paine: Lewis Thornton Powell, the Mystery Man of the Lincoln Conspiracy.* McFarland & Company Publishers: Jefferson, NC, 2005.

Palmer, John M. (Editor) *The Bench and Bar of Illinois* (2 vols) Chicago: Lewis Publishing Co., 1899.

Pappas, George S. *To The Point: The United States Military Academy, 1802–1902.* London and Westport, Connecticut: Praeger Publisher, 1993.

Parker, John H. *The Gatlings at Santiago.* Teddington, England: The Echo Library, 2006.

Patchan, Scott C. *Second Manassas: Longstreet's Attack and the Struggle for Chinn Ridge.* Washington, D.C.: Potomac Books, 2011.

Patterson, Gerald A. *From Blue to Gray: The Life of Confederate General Cadmus W. Wilcox.* Harrisburg, PA: Stackpole Books, 2001.

Peterson, Charles J. *The Military Heroes of the War of 1812 with a Narrative of the War.* Philadelphia: J. B. Smith Publishers, 1858.

Pfanz, Harry W. *Gettysburg: The Second Day.* Chapel Hill and London: The University of North Carolina Press, 1987.

Pinsker, Matthew. *Lincoln's Sanctuary, Abraham Lincoln and the Soldiers' Home.* Oxford and New York: Oxford University Press, 2003.

Pohanka, Brian C. "Destruction of the Fifth New York Zouaves," *Civil War*

Magazine, September 2002.

Poleo, Barbara. "James Edmundson Ingraham: Florida, Flagler, and St. Augustine," *El Escribano: The St. Augustine Journal of History*. St. Augustine Historical Society. Vol. 40. (2003).

Pond, George E. "The Shenandoah Valley in 1864," *The Army in the Civil War.* (Vol. XI), New York: Charles Scribner's Sons, 1885.

Powell, William. *History of the Fifth Army Corps.* New York: blank publishers, 1896.

Pratt, Henry E. "Illinois As Lincoln Knew It: A Boston Reporter's Record of a Trip in 1847," Reprinted from *Papers in the Illinois History and Transactions for the Year 1937,* for Members of the Abraham Lincoln Association. Springfield, 1938.

Pryor, Elizabeth Brown. *Reading the Man: A Portrait of Robert E. Lee Through His Private Letters.* New York: Viking Press, 2007.

Pullen, John. *The Twentieth Maine: A Volunteer Regiment in the Civil War.* Philadelphia: Lippincott Press, 1957.

Randall, Ruth Painter. *Mary Lincoln, Biography of a Marriage.* Boston: Blank publishers, 1953.

Ramage, James A. *Gray Ghost: The Life of Col. John Singleton Mosby.* Lexington, University of Kentucky Press, 1999.

Reid, Whitelaw. *Ohio In The War: Her Statesmen, Generals, and Soldiers.* (2 Vols., orig. 1898).

Reilly, Tom. *War with Mexico! America's Reporters Cover the Battlefield.* Edited by Manley Witten. Lawrence: University of Kansas Press, 2010.

Redd, Robert. *St. Augustine and the Civil War.* Charleston: The History Press, 2014.

Remini, Robert V. *Henry Clay: Statesman for the Union.* New York & London: W.W. Norton & Company, 1991.

Rhea, Gordon C. *The Battles for Spotsylvania Court House and The Road to Yellow Tavern, May 7–12, 1864.* New York and Baton Rouge: Louisiana University Press, 1997.

——. *Cold Harbor: Grant and Lee, May 26–June 3, 1864.* Baton Rouge: Louisiana State University Press, 2002.

——. "Butchery at Bethesda Church," *America's Civil War Magazine.* (January 2002).

Robbins, S. S. *A Happy Winter in Florida.* Publisher unknown, 1888.

Robertson, James I. *General A. P. Hill: The Story of a Confederate Warrior.*

Robinson, Blackwell P. (Editor) *The North Carolina Guide: Federal Writers' Project.* Chapel Hill: University of North Carolina Press, 1955.

Ropes, John Codman. *The Army Under Pope.* New York: Charles Scribner's & Sons, 1885.

Ross, Ishbel. *The President's Wife: Mary Todd Lincoln.* New York: New York: Putnam & Sons Publishers, 1973.

———. *Silhouette in Diamonds, Life of Mrs. Potter Palmer of Chicago.* New York: blank publishers, 1998.

Sanders, Robert Stuart. (Editor) "Colonel John Hardin and His Letters To His Wife—1792," The Filson Club Historical Quarterly. Vol. 39, January 1965.

Sanger, Donald Bridgman, and Hay, Thomas Robson. *James Longstreet: Part 1. Soldier Part 2. Politician, Officeholder, and Writer.* Baton Rouge: Louisiana State University Press, 1952.

Schaff, Morris. *The Spirit of Old West Point.* New York: Houghton, Mifflin & Co., 1907.

Schairer, Jack E. *Lee's Bold Plan for Point Lookout: The Rescue of Confederate Prisoners That Never Happened.* Jefferson, North Carolina and London: McFarland & Co. Publishers, 2008.

Scott, Robert Garth. *Into The Wilderness with The Army of the Potomac.* Bloomington: Indiana University Press, 1985.

Sears, Stephen W. *George B. McClellan: The Young Napoleon.* New York: Ticknor and Fields Publisher, 1988.

———. *To the Gates of Richmond, the Peninsula Campaign.* New York: Houghton Mifflin, 1992.

Seward, Frederick. *Reminiscences of a War-Time Statesman and Diplomat.* New York: George P. Putnam and Sons, 1916.

Sharf, Frederick A. "St. Augustine: City of Artists, 1883–1895," *Antiques Magazine,* Vol. XC, (August 1966).

Shaw, Archer H. Editor. *The Lincoln Encyclopedia, The Spoken and Written Words of Abraham Lincoln.* New York: MacMillon Publishers, 1950.

Sherry, Jefrey F. "The Terrible Impetuosity: The Pennsylvania Reserves at Gettysburg," *Gettysburg Magazine.* Issue 16. (January 1997).

Simon, John. (Editor) *The Papers of Ulysses S. Grant.* Vol. 2 (June 1, 1864 thru August 15, 1864) Carbondale: Southern Illinois University Press. 1984.

Smith, Laura Chase. *The Life of Philander Chase: First Bishop of Ohio and Illinois, Founder of Kenyon and Jubilee Colleges.* New York: E.P. Dutton & Company, 1903.

Smith, Nicholas. *Stories of Great National Songs.* Milwaukee: The Young Churchman Co., 1899.

Sparks, David S. Editor. *Inside Mr. Lincoln's Army: The Diary of Marsena Rudolph Patrick, Provost Marshal General, Army of the Potomac.* New York and London: Thomas Yoseloff Publisher, 1964.

Stackpole, Edward. "The Day The Rebels Could Have Marched into the White House," *Civil War Times Illustrated.* No. 10. (February–March 1961).

Stinson, Byron. "The Invalid Corps," *Civil War Times Illustrated.* Vol. X. No. 2. (May 1971)

Stone, William L. *Reminiscences of Saratoga and Ballston.* New York: Virtue and Yorston Publishers, 1875.

Strong, George Crocket. *Cadet Life at West Point, With a Descriptive Sketch of West Point by Benson J. Lossing.* Boston: T. O. H. Publishers, 1862.

Strong, George Templeton. *The Diary of George Templeton Strong—the Post War Years, 1865–1875.* Edited by Allan Nevins and Milton H. Thomas. New York: The MacMillan Company Publishers, 1952.

Swinton, William. *Campaigns of the Army of the Potomac.* New York: blank publishers, 1866.

Sword, Wiley. *President Washington's Indian War: the Struggle for the Old Northwest, 1790–1795.* Norman: University of Oklahoma Press, 1985.

Swinton, William. *Campaigns of the Army of the Potomac.* New York: Charles Scribner's and Sons, 1882.

Sylvester, Nathaniel Bartlett. *History of Saratoga County, New York.* Philadelphia: Everts and Ensign Publishers, 1878.

Sypher, J. R. *History of the Pennsylvania Reserve Corps.* Lancaster: blank publisher, 1865.

Taaffe, Stephen R. *Commanding The Army of the Potomac.* Lawrence: University Press of Kansas, 2006.

Taft, Robert. *Artists and Illustrators of the Old West (1850–1900).* Princeton: Princeton University Press, 1953.

Tagg, Larry. *The Generals of Gettysburg—The Leaders of America's Greatest Battle.* Campbell, CA: Savas Publishing Co., 1998.

Taylor, John. *The Report of the Committee on the Services of the Pennsylvania Reserves at Gettysburg.* Philadelphia: Pamphlet, 1889.

Tebbel, John. *The Marshall Fields.* New York: E. P. Dulton & Co., Inc., 1947.

Thomson, O. R., Rauch, Howard and William H. *History of the Bucktails: Kane Rifle Regiment of the Pennsylvania Reserve Corps.* Philadelphia: blank publishers, 1906.

Thwaites, Reuben Gold. *Daniel Boone.* New York and London: D. Appleton and Co., 1913.

Tidwell, William A. and James O. Hall. *Come Retribution: The Confederate Secret Service and The Assassination of Lincoln.* Jackson and London: University of Mississippi, 1988.

Tighe, Adrian G. *The Bristoe Campaign: General Lee's Last Strategic Offensive With The Army of Northern Virginia:* Xlibris Corp. Publishers, 2010.

Trudeau, Noah Andre. *Bloody Roads South: The Wilderness to Cold Harbor, May–June, 1864.* Boston: Little Brown & Co., 1989.

Turner, Frederick Jackson. *The Significance of the Frontier in American History.* New York, Ontario, London: Penguin Books Publishers, 2008 reprint of 1894 original edition.

Turner, Justin & Turner, Linda L. (Editors). *Mary Todd Lincoln: Her Life & Letters.* New York: Fromm International Publishers, 1987.

Twain, Mark and Charles Dudley Warner. *The Gilded Age.* New York: American Publishing Company, 1873. (Penguin 2001 edition).

United States Government Printing Office. *Slave Narratives: A Folk History of Slavery (1936–1938).* Federal Writers' Project, Works Progress Administration (WPA), 1940.

United States War Department. *War of the Rebellion: A Compilation of the Official Records of the Union and Confederate Armies.* Washington: Government Printing Office, 1880–1901.

Wadsworth, Richard. *Incident at San Augustine Springs: A Hearing for Major Isaac Lynde.* Las Cruces, NM: Yucca Tree Press, 2002.

Wagner, Richard. *For Honor, Flag, and Family: Civil War Major General Samuel W. Crawford, 1827–1892.* Shippenburg, PA.: White Mane Books, 2005.

Wainwright, Charles S. (Nevins, Allan, editor) *Diary of Battle: The Personal Journals of Colonel Charles S. Wainwright, 1861–1865.* New York: Harcourt, Brace & World, Inc., 1962.

Walworth, Clarence. *The Walworths of America, A Genealogy.* Albany, Weed-

Parsons Printing Co., 1897.

Walworth, Ellen Hardin. *Battles of Saratoga, 1777: The Saratoga Monument Association, 1856–1891*. Albany: Joel Munsell's Sons, Publishers, 1891.

———. "The Ancestry of Mrs. Ellen Hardin Walworth," *Daughters of the American Revolution Magazine*. Vol 3, May 25, 1893.

Walworth, Ellen "Nelly." *Life Sketches of Father Walworth*. New York, 1897.

Walworth, Mansfield. "Col. John Hardin," *The Historical Magazine . . . of America*. Vol. 2 (Second Series), No. 4, April, 1869.

———. "The Death of Colonel John J. Hardin," *The Historical Magazine. . . . of America*. Vol. 6 (Second Series), No. 5, November, 1869.

Warner, Ezra J. *Generals In Blue: Lives of the Union Commanders*. Baton Rouge and London: Louisiana State University Press, 1964.

Watkins, Albert. "The Oregon Recruit Expedition," *Collections of the Nebraska State Historical Society*. Lincoln: The Nebraska State Historical Society (Vol. XVII), 1913.

Welcher, Frank J. *The Union Army: 1861–1865: Organization and Operations*. (Vol. VI). Bloomington and Indianapolis: Indiana University Press of Indiana, 1989–1992.

Welles, Gideon. *Diary of Gideon Welles, Secretary of the Navy Under Lincoln and Johnson*. Introduction by John T. Morse, Jr. Boston and New York: Houghton-Miflin Co., 1911.

Welsh, Jack D. *Medical Histories of Union Generals*. Kent, Ohio: Kent State University Press, 1995.

Wert, Jefrey D. *The Sword of Lincoln—The Army of the Potomac*. New York, London, Toronto and Sydney: Simon & Schuster, 2005.

———. "Rappahannock Station," *Civil War Times Illustrated*. Vol. XV. (December 1976).

———. *General James Longstreet: The Confederacy's Most Controversial Soldier, A Biography*. New York: Simon & Schuster Publishers, 1993.

Whitehorn, Joseph W. A. *Self-Guided Tour: the Battle of Second Manassas: Center For Military History*. Washington: U.S. Government Printing Office, 1990.

Whitman, Karen. "Re-evaluating John Brown's Raid at Harper's Ferry," *West Virginia History*. Vol. 34, Number 1. Published by West Virginia Archives and History. (October 1972).

Wilson, Douglas L. *Honor's Voice—The Transformation of Abraham Lincoln*. New York: Alfred A. Knopf Publishers, 1998.

Wilson, James Grant. & Fiske, John. (Editors) *Appleton's Cyclopaedea*. NY: D. Appleton & Co., 1888.

Williams, Thomas E. "At All Times Ready, The Marines At Harper's Ferry and the John Brown Raid: October, 1859," *Leatherneck Magazine*. (September 2009).

Woodward, Evan M. *Our Campaigns: The Second Regiment, Pennsylvania Reserve Volunteers*. Philadelphia: blank publishers, 1865.

Woodhead, Lindy. *Shopping, Seduction & Mr. Selfridge*. New York: Random House. 2007.

Wright, Mike. *What They Didn't Teach You About the Civil War*. New York: A Presidio Press Book published by Random House. 1996.

Wulfeck, Dorothy Ford. Editor. *Hardin and Harding {families} of Virginia and Kentucky*. Naugatuck, Conn.: Published by author, n.d.

MAGAZINES AND PERIODICALS

American History Magazine, Antiques Magazine, Blue & Gray Magazine, Civil War Times, Collections of the Nebraska State Historical Society, Frank Leslie's Illustrated Magazine, Gettysburg Compiler, Gettysburg Magazine, Harper's Weekly, Journal of the Illinois State Historical Society, Journal of Military History, Leatherneck Magazine, New York Archives Magazine, Oregon Historical Quarterly, Pacific Northwest Quarterly, United States Service Magazine, and West Virginia History Magazine.

ARCHIVAL SOURCES:

(Letters, Diaries, Photographs and Articles)
Chicago Historical Society Museum, Chicago, Illinois; Library of Congress, Washington, D.C.; Jacksonville Historical Society, Jacksonville, Illinois; Abraham Lincoln Presidential Library & Museum, Illinois Historical Society, Springfield, Illinois; U.S. Army Historical Center, Carlyle, Pennsylvania; Walworth Museum, Saratoga Spring, New York; St. Augustine Historical Society Research Library, St. Augustine, Florida.

NEWSPAPERS

St. Augustine Record and St. Augustine Tattler, St. Augustine, Florida; the Times-Union, Jacksonville, Florida; New York Times, New York Sun, Chicago Tribune and Chicago Inter-Ocean Springfield Register, Springfield, Illinois; and Jacksonville (FL) Times-Union, Reading (PA) Eagle; Frank Leslie's Illustrated Magazine, Philadelphia Daily Evening Bulletin, National Tribune, Washington Evening Star.

INDEX

ACKNOWLEDGEMENTS

This history could not have become a reality without the unstinting support of many individuals who have aided me so generously along the winding road to publication. My debt to each is great indeed. My gratitude goes to the following: Mr. Steven Smith, Editorial Director, Ms. Libby Braden, Production Editor and Ms. Tara Lichterman, Publicity Director, of Casemate Publishers; Ms. Agnes Hamberger, Curator, Saratoga History Museum, Saratoga Springs, NY; Dr. Joseph Knetsch, a graduate Florida State University and recently retired staff historian for the Florida Department of Environmental Protection, Tallahassee; Mr. Thomas Day, volunteer archivist and recently-elected President of the Board of Trustees, St. Augustine Historical Society; Ms. Betty Owensby, Civil War author and scholar, Washington, DC; Dr. Amy S. Greenberg, historian and author, Princeton University; Mr. Ron Tendick, three-time mayor of Jacksonville, IL and local historian; Mr. Charles Tingley, Senior Research Librarian and Mr. Robert Nawrocki, Chief Librarian, both of the St. Augustine Historical Society Research Library, St. Augustine, FL; Mr. David Nolan of St. Augustine, author, local historian and historic preservation activist; Mr. Jaimie Parillo, Director of the Saratoga History Museum, Saratoga Springs, New York; the late William McLaughin of Chicago (1929–2012), nephew by marriage to General Martin D. Hardin; Dr. Linda Pulliam and Deborah McKeel of the State Library of Florida in Tallahassee; Renaine Julian, Data Research Librarian, Florida State University, Tallahassee; the staff of the Abraham Lincoln Presidential Library and Museum, Springfield, Il.; and Mr. John E. Elliot of San Antonio, TX, author and independent historical researcher focusing on the Lincoln Conspirators; and Mr. August Marchetti of Mechanicsburg, Pa. and Mr. Justin Sanders of Astoria, New York, co-founders of the Pennsylvania Volunteer Reserve Corps Historical Society Website. Mr. Allan Aimone, a research librarian and historian at the United States Military Academy at West Point Library, was also very helpful. I am also indebted to my cousins Rick and Cathy (Cahill) Rosen of Chicago for their kindness and hospitality in allowing me to stay at their home when I was examining the Hardin Family Papers at the Chicago History Museum. I also wish to thank my wife of 30 years, Judy L. Huffstodt, for her continued love, patience and support.